STAVISKY

Paul F. Jankowski

STAV

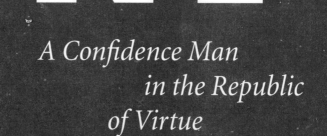

SKY

A Confidence Man
in the Republic
of Virtue

Cornell University Press : Ithaca and London

"Cette vilaine affaire Stavisky" © Librairie Arthème Fayard, 2000
English edition copyright © 2002 by Paul F. Jankowski

First published 2002 by Cornell University Press
Printed in the United States of America

LIBRARY OF CONGRESS CATALOGING-IN-PUBLICATION DATA
Jankowski, Paul 1950–
    Stavisky : a confidence man in the republic of virtue / Paul F.
Jankowski.
      p. cm.
    Includes bibliographical references and index.
    ISBN 0-8014-3959-0 (cloth : alk. paper)
    1. Stavisky, Serge Alexandre, 1886–1934. 2. Swindlers and
swindling—France—Biography. 3. Swindlers and
swindling—France—History—20th century. 4. Stavisky, Serge Alexandre,
1886–1934—Trials, litigation, etc. 5. Political
corruption—France—History—20th century. 6. France—Politics and
government—1914–1940. I. Title.
    HV6692.S73 J36 2002
    364.16'3'092-dc21
                                2001006098

Cloth printing   10 9 8 7 6 5 4 3 2 1

CONTENTS

PREFACE

"Dead scandals," according to Byron, "form good subjects for dissection." Sarcasm to the satirist, gospel to the historian: dead scandals do form good subjects for dissection, and none more so than those that rocked France from the 1880s to the 1930s, punctuating with spectacle and tumult the implantation of a liberal Republic after a century of failed experiments.

Each presented the citizens of the new Republic with a recurrent sequence of violation, revelation, and indignation. Cause or effect of instability, precursor or obstacle to change? And why the persistent suspicion that the Republic's servants only exploited its values, why the hunt for hypocrites? No scandal, in fact, ever concluded neatly; each seemed to invite the next; and the paroxysm that shook the Republic most violently was also its last, the Stavisky affair of 1934.

What exactly was it? A swindler charmed and spent his way to the heights of the Republic, before coming to a mysterious end on Mont Blanc. No single act, real or imagined, provided the plot of another Dreyfus affair; few guilty secrets rivaled the revelations of the Panama Canal scandal; yet the indignation, as mighty as any set off by the two earlier scandals, marked the Stavisky affair as the gravest threat yet to this Republic.

It was the work of incendiaries, most historians assumed later, quite soundly: demagogues, most on the far right, made much of Stavisky's apparent exploits, seizing on them to channel the decade's gathering discontents and turn a fait divers into a scandal.[1] A bonanza for antisemites, others recalled, just as plausibly: for those who cared about such matters, and in the 1930s some did, the swindler's Jewish origins provided a target as well as a vindication.[2] The Stavisky affair was willed, the poisoned gift of rabble-rousers and scandalmongers.

There, at the familiar story of partisan manipulation, the historians stopped. Of the swindler's milieu, of his friends and accomplices and temporary conquests, they took little notice. Yet so wide was his reach, so dogged his pursuit of influence, that his brief passing might reveal at a remove of sixty-five years the inner workings of the Republic's high society, the habits of its deputies, civil servants, lawyers, journalists, and liberal professionals, if only their traces can be recovered. And they can be: in the archives.

No scandal ever provoked a more exhaustive investigation, whatever the charges of cover-up and mystification, and no investigation ever yielded more police reports, expert testimony, supplemental investigations, depositions and transcripts of court hearings, and much more besides. Some, like the leisurely proceedings of the parliamentary commission of inquiry, or the trial hearings of late 1935 and early 1936, have always been open, though rarely opened. Others, notably the police and judicial archives, including the voluminous records of all the pretrial investigations, were closed until they were opened for me, to my great good fortune. Out of such sources slowly emerge, as though drawn in invisible ink, the people of scandal, the portrait of a moment.

An obscure gallery of faces, long eclipsed by the rogue's éclat, awaited me. In the dormant dossiers of the prefecture of police and the Sûreté Générale I found the true physiognomy of the affair, preserved in the precise language of the French police. Brief lives, briefly sketched—here was the record of all who came Stavisky's way and lived to regret it, victims of their weaknesses more than his charms. I entered the world he had exposed to me: was it some nether region of the Republic, where private interests prevailed over public, and hypocrisy over transparency?

No—but nor was it a sunlit province of selflessness. Even more than the police, the magistrates and the courts left behind teeming chronicles of influence and careerism, in cartons and bundles dwarfing any judicial archive I had ever seen. Massively, the archives chronicled the most ordinary of confusions. Deputies doubled as lawyers, generals and prefects as company directors, journalists as publicists, in a seemingly endless demonstration that the Republic's forest of symbols was no more sacred than the interlopers who shamelessly insinuated themselves.

Yet the offenses, once I had sorted them out, seemed oddly banal, risible perhaps to today's specialists in outright corruption. They scarcely deserved the hysteria they set off, all the jeremiads in the press and the Chamber that transfixed the historians of a later day. How could so gray a landscape invite so vivid a storm?

Every scandal reveals an imaginary dimension, a mental as well as a practical state of affairs that invites the spellbound bystander to sort out fact from fancy and offense from blame. If all was not well, the fault must lie within the Republic—"a regime perennially searching for its identity."[3] Lawyers, journalists, and opposition deputies decried the very police, magistrates, and regulators who, by the end, had discovered all about Stavisky and had put a stop to his crimes. He had prospered for too long, cried the critics, and for a moment their show of impatience appeared to threaten the regime itself.

As though to absolve themselves of any wrongdoing, private interests, like Furies, pursued the errant officeholders. Society turned on the state, blind to its own complicities. The truth deranged; and, in this most political of cultures, private citizens easily conceived of vice among the exemplars of virtue, the public servants. Republican ideals were at odds with republican practices, nowhere more so than in the highly symbolic realm of justice, and from the tenacity of the collective ideal sprang scrutiny, indignation, and an urgent wish to set matters right.

How, then, was I to render this on the printed page? Display the rogue only through the eyes of those who crossed his path, and their reactions to him only through their own words and deeds; tell their tale more than his, as the involuntary revelation of an ethos and its ailments. Show rather than judge, describe rather than explain, convey living detail rather than desiccated abstraction. Let the creation speak for itself, so that the author is implicitly everywhere and explicitly nowhere. These were my precepts; let the reader judge whether I was wise to adopt them.

I would like to thank all those whose support allowed me to write this book.

I am grateful to the Centre National de la Recherche Scientifique in Paris and the Camargo Foundation in Cassis for their hospitality, and to Brandeis University for leave and financial support through its Mazer and Bernstein funds.

My thanks are also extended to present or former colleagues at Brandeis for their help and advice: to Rudy Binion, for his characteristically thoughtful reading of an early draft; to Alice Kelikian, without whom Arlette would have appeared in these pages in a moleskin coat and with uncut hair; to Bernard Wasserstein; and to Judy Brown and Dona Delorenzo, for help with word processing and much more.

In France I must thank Ran Halévi of Fayard and my friends Philippe Grand and Brigitte Lainé, *conservateurs en chef* at the Archives de Paris, for their expertise and the generosity with which they shared it. Many other centers of research—notably the archives of the prefecture of police in Paris, the library of the National Assembly, the departmental archives of the Côte d'Or in Dijon, the archives of the Ministry of Justice and of the Interior—opened their doors and their holdings to me, and for this I am most grateful.

I am, in general, indebted to the Archives de France overall for the access they consistently allowed me to extensive series of closed documents.

Finally, I wish to express my gratitude to John Ackerman, the director of Cornell University Press, for all of his support and invaluable guidance.

NOTE *on Translation*

The following terms and titles have been left in the original for lack of any satisfactory English equivalent:

Cour de Cassation Highest court of judicial review

Conseil d'Etat Highest civil service tribunal

Crédits municipaux Municipal pawnshops and lending institutions

Fait divers Noteworthy crime, in the eyes of the press

Gendarmes, gardes mobiles National police under the Ministry of Defense, operating outside Paris and the Department of the Seine

Maître Title given to lawyers and notaries

Police Judiciaire Criminal investigation police, auxiliaries of the prosecutor's office

Sûreté Générale or *Sûreté Nationale* Police under the Ministry of the Interior, operating outside Paris and the Department of the Seine

Tribunal civil de première instance Civil tribunal of first instance

The following terms have been translated into English:

Assistance publique Public welfare

Avocat général Advocate general

Caisse des dépôts et consignations State deposit bank

Chambre des mises en accusation Chamber of Indictments

Chancellerie Chancellery (Ministry of Justice)

Code d'instruction criminelle Code of criminal investigation

Commissaire Superintendent (of police)

Commissaire divisionnaire Divisional superintendent (of police)

Contrôleur général des recherches judiciaires Supervisor of judicial investigations (at the Sûreté Générale)

Cour d'appel Court of appeal

Cour d'assises Criminal court

Inspection Générale du Crédit General inspection of credit

Inspecteur des finances Treasury inspector

Juge d'instruction Investigating magistrate

Mont-de-piété Pawnshop

Parquet Public prosecutor's office

Plaidoirie Summation (in court)

Prefecture de police Prefecture of police (Paris)

Préfet de police Prefect of police (Paris)

Premier président Presiding judge

Président du conseil Prime minister

Procureur Général Prosecutor general

Procureur de la République Public prosecutor

Receveur des finances District treasury receiver

Rente Government annuity

Substitut Assistant prosecutor

Trésorier-Payeur Général Paymaster general

Tribunal correctionnel Correctional court

NOTE *on the French Criminal Procedure between the Wars*

Differences between the French and Anglo-American judicial systems were apparent at the very outset of the criminal procedure. The police, a private party, or the judiciary itself could initiate proceedings against a suspect, but no grand jury met to consider whether to bring charges. Instead a *juge d'instruction,* or investigating magistrate, set out to look into the matter and determine whether prosecution was in order.

During the course of his investigation, the investigating magistrate would often call in the suspect for interrogation. He might well ask the *Police judiciaire* of the Paris prefecture or the police inspectors of the *Sûreté générale,* which operated outside the capital, to investigate as well. He might also call on expert professionals, such as accountants, notaries, or physicians. At least in theory, the process remained secret and *sub judice.* Upon receipt of their findings—which might take months—the investigating magistrate would recommend to the *procureur de la république* (public prosecutor) or more rarely to the *procureur général* (prosecutor general) whether to bring charges or drop the case. If the prosecutor's office agreed that criminal prosecution was in order, a *chambre des mises en accusation* (chamber of indictments), usually consisting of three judges, met to consider the matter. Neither the suspect nor the plaintiff, if there was one, came before the chamber, which voted secretly on whether to prosecute or not.

If the litigation went forward, the accused stood trial either in the *tribunal correctionnel* (correctional court) or in the *cour d'assises* (criminal court), translated throughout this work as "criminal court." The jurisdiction depended upon the nature of the offense. In its various chambers the correctional court—one for each of the ninety departments of France—tried *délits,* or infractions of the law carrying a sentence of imprisonment from six days to five years; some were also punishable by fines. Typical *délits* included theft, swindling, embezzling, and manslaughter, among many others. The criminal court—one as well for each of the ninety departments—tried *crimes,* graver felonies carrying longer sentences of prison, or forced labor, or even death. Typical crimes included forgery, armed robbery, or premeditated murder. (A third set of courts, the police courts, heard *contraventions* or cases of the most minor infractions, free of the elaborate pretrial procedures of the other two.)

Three judges—a president and two assessors—normally sat on the correctional court, in the absence of any jury. The assize court was also composed of a president and two assessors, but it was the only court in France that functioned with a jury. The discretionary powers of a French president exceeded those of an American or a British judge, for he could order as many measures as he deemed useful to the discovery of the truth. He usually interrogated the accused at length, accounting in part for the "inquisitorial" aspect of French justice beside its more "accusatorial" Anglo-American counterpart. Depending on the importance or sensitivity of the case, the general prosecutor, public prosecutor, or one of their assistants, known as *substituts,* brought the government's case, while lawyers from the bar or *barreau* defended the accused.

Appeals against a correctional court verdict went to the *cour d'appel* (court of appeal), which reviewed both the evidence and the procedure—both the facts and the law—and normally heard the defendant. By contrast, all appeals against an assize court verdict went to the criminal division of the *cour de cassation,* where the fifteen judges or *conseillers* ruled not on the merits of the case but solely on the legal procedures followed in the trial (*vice de forme*). By the gravity of the charges it heard, the theatrics its jury elicited, and the near finality its verdict enjoyed, the criminal court was the most dramatic jurisdiction in the land and easily attracted the most spectators.

STAVISKY

Pourquoi l'U.N.C. manifeste Mard...

POSITI...
AU M...
RO...

A SHADOW IN THE COURTROOM

On the day the trial opened, on Monday 4 November 1935, the police set up barricades in the Palace of Justice. Rain blew off Place Dauphine, beat onto the steps, and drove about a hundred members of the public up through the colossal western portico into the *cour d'assises,* the criminal courtroom. The police had expected a larger turnout.

The western facade stood at the prow of the country's historic ship of state, the Ile de la Cité. When it went up in 1868, at the end of the Second Empire, it added a troubling, hybrid figurehead to the island. Napoleonic eagles clasped the cornice; swords of retribution crossed the Doric friezes just below; columns stretched down and set off arched bays that let in the light and opened justice to the City. Around the entrance, severity challenged compassion in allegorical bas-reliefs. Prudence held a looking glass, Truth a blazing torch, Punishment a headsman's sword; tutelary Protection guarded a child, Force dressed in lion skins, and Justice was equity, holding scales and a jury's voting urn. The facade held forth in the rhetoric of its century, and recalled by its strange éclat some Ptolemaic, Hathor-headed sandstone colonnade on the Upper Nile.[1]

The visitors filed in through the narrow entrance, darkened now with the passage of time but opening onto a wide vestibule as light as day. There they joined a small flow of others, novices or palace habitués who had traveled down the galleries, restrained by barriers, watched over by police, making their way to the spectacle upstairs. The vestibule, flanked by effigies of kingly lawgivers, converged onto a portal where steps started for the criminal court and law gave way to equity. Law stood in a niche with her code. But above her sat Justice with her scales, symbol of evidence weighed, of the jury, the public in the courtroom. How unwillingly this old country of Roman law had first allowed the Anglo-Saxon intrusion—but by now the graft had taken, the Republic had matured, and criminal justice presented itself as the vote of a dozen citizens.

Indifferent, like their fellows in the audience, to the higher abstractions of the law, jurors in the past thirty years had pronounced their intimate convictions about Thérèse Humbert, who had swindled millions from bankers and dined with presidents and kings, about Henriette Caillaux, who had murdered the editor of *Le Figaro,* about Raoul Villain, who had assassinated Jean Jaurès, and about countless others. They had listened to arguments before the bar and cast their ballots into an urn, the emblem of curial democracy that crowned equity at the stairs and stood over the citizens as they came up.

How many of them stopped to notice the twin heads of Nemesis sculpted onto the court's bronze doors, warning them against the sin of hubris, or re-

Spectacle: A crowd at the Palace of Justice, 4 November 1935, for the trial of the late
swindler's accomplices. (Photo courtesy of Bibliothèque Nationale de France.)

flected on their own place here, in the most public of all jurisdictions? A
woman in a green corsage came first and rested her elbows on the balustrade.
The others stood in half-light at the back between the bronze doors and the
first witnesses' benches and looked onto the luminous courtroom. The walls
were bright oak and the ceiling splendid, emblazoned with spirals and golden
rosettes and with a radiant incarnation of Justice at its center. Suffused with

the light of positivism, the court seemed to celebrate the Republic and edify the citizenry gathered at the back. God had long since left the room. Marianne had replaced the crucifix above the judges' dais and gazed forth with a vaguely Masonic star on her forehead. Caesarism had vanished too, its talismanic insignia effaced by the irreverent democrats. Public opinion now governed the court, one of its judges had humbly said, and the scales of equity, embossed on the paneling behind him, swayed again over the vestiges of his once-inquisitorial powers.

Off to the public's left, beneath windows that opened generously onto the court, ran the jurors' benches. Today they held a butcher, a wine merchant, a novelty salesman, a tailor, two pharmacists, a retired officer, a postal employee, a carpenter, a cashier, a businessman, and an old sculptor in a Greek skullcap, who looked out alertly through his glasses and began to sketch. They sat in semiobscurity, but the midday light fell obliquely through the glass above them onto the empty dock, "infamy's rectangle," across the room. The defendants had still not appeared on the little stage, crowded by now with the ghosts of their notorious forebears. The dais stood vacant too, awaiting the judges. No one expected them until sometime around one.[2]

All this was routine enough, but the floor was not. There, in the *barreau,* the public beheld pandemonium. Someone had thoughtfully removed the translucent exhibit table to make more room, but fifty black-robed lawyers still circled like giant bats with nowhere to alight. Sixty reporters climbed in and out of the press box next to the jurors and sketch artists from the newspapers sat on folding chairs nearby. More chairs exchanged hands or vaulted overhead to land in tangled heaps on the central floor. The struggle for seating engulfed the *barreau,* once a space of solitary pleading, now pullulating with cliques and anxious antagonists. The atmosphere recalled the revolutionary Convention, heavy with the threat of scandal. Magnesium from the photographers' bulbs flashed, and three floor lamps glowed uselessly. The palace's doctor looked at the thermometer and sent out word to turn down the heat. The room was torrid.

The public waited; some approached the edge of the turmoil and took up positions on the witnesses' benches, empty for the moment like the dock and the dais, each expecting its distinguished guests. What a list of witnesses—three prime ministers, two ministers, deputies, directors of the national and Paris police, inspectors, magistrates, journalists, the Republic's famous—called to the bar to testify but also to justify, defendants in all but name. A whispered rumor had it that they might not come. The nameless experts might, the jewelers and accountants and handwriting analysts whose Jesuitical subtleties damned or absolved, but the celebrities would stay away.

And what had happened to their depositions, taken down during the past year and a half, signed and guarded as evidence for the occasion? More Monday rumor had it that the key to the safe holding them and countless other documents had disappeared. Towering in a corner behind the dais and dwarfing two Republican guards, the light gray safe, big as a bank vault, housed stacks of summonses, police reports, depositions, transcripts, worthless old bonds, jewels real and fake, and much more, nicely catalogued and indexed, and known by now as "the case with thirty thousand documents." The guards stood sentry around the clock, but still the rumor spread. For a moment all hung on an absent key. Then the clerk came along and pulled it out and swung open the door to reveal the evidence; suddenly, a motley crew of twenty defendants, united only by their friendship with a late famous swindler, walked in and entered the dock.

First came the free, accused but still in limbo, spared for the moment the affront of captors, truncheons, and manacles. A newspaper editor in his mid-fifties led the way and sat down, smiling pleasantly, in front of the dock. A mulatto from Martinique followed jauntily, in a three-piece suit and a bow tie, and after him a lean-faced man, frankly furious. Both edited scurrilous weekly papers, vied for the attention and respect of elected officialdom, and lived by gossip, scandal, and blackmail. Did these journalists of the Third Republic report the news or make it? Had they kept faith with this most liberal of regimes or succumbed to its temptations? Their colleagues, packed into the press box across the floor, looked at them curiously, as though at some distorted reflection or dark shadow of themselves.

By the 1930s such professionals of the pen had done much to discredit the press in the eyes of its readers. Memories of Panama were dim, but repeated revelations kept alive the conviction that the freedom of the press disguised its financial servitude. In 1923 *L'Humanité* scored a propaganda coup by listing all the newspapers that before the war had accepted Russian money to promote Russian loans. That year *Le Quotidien* appeared, proclaiming an exemplary independence as well as a purifying mission. Four years later, much of its editorial staff resigned amid a scandal that exposed its pretensions and delivered what remained of it into the hands of Hennessy, the cognac magnate. The breath of scandal even touched *Le Temps,* when in 1931 the discreet industrial presence of the Comité des Forges behind the august daily came to light. But the little rags, unlike the great dailies, had no reputation to uphold, no pretenses to maintain.[3]

Some disgraced lawyers climbed into the dock, stripped of their black robes like unfrocked priests. Their confrères still swirled about the courtroom floor, their calling as well as their clients on trial. Did these lawyers of the Republic uphold or exploit its liberal laws? One of the accused was stocky and imposing and wore a long pointed beard and steel-rimmed glasses; another seemed gray and diminished; a third, normally confident, even garrulous, seemed preoccupied; anguish visibly gripped a fourth, a Radical deputy from Paris as well as a lawyer, whose very presence fed an angry suspicion that something was rotten in the *République des avocats,* that its elites had somehow violated the public trust.

Gambetta, herald of the new age, had welcomed them in a famous speech in Grenoble in 1872, soon after the western wing went up and the criminal court opened its doors. He had hailed the lawyers, doctors, accountants, notaries, and hard-working professionals of the "new social strata," whose accession to public office would consecrate progress and an open Republic. Then they were newcomers, now they walked the corridors of power. In its statuary, emblems, and icons, in its torches and shining crowns, their Republic represented transparency, the light of science and knowledge, and the promise to expose in its bright courtroom the darkest of deceptions. But once in a while—today—the open society itself suddenly seemed to deceive and dissemble. Its light blinded rather than illuminated, and a good many citizens came to suspect that the press, justice, commerce, finance, and elected officialdom conspired to serve only themselves beneath a feigned homage to the general interest. The dock was filling up.

Guards and their captives took the upper rows, while other freed defendants sat together below. Another newspaper editor, red-faced, robust, and vigorous beyond his sixty-three years and usually quick to mock and deride, today motioned pleasantly to his lawyers on the floor. Unbroken by twenty-two months in La Santé prison, he was confidently calling in patrons, protégés, and cronies collected backstairs in the Radical Party and from its press over the past four decades, forty of them, to come and vouch for his probity and irreproachable character. Next sat a guard and after him a frightened insurance executive with curled mustache and a gray beard, which he stroked anxiously. Beside the energetic journalist he looked consumed and emaciated. The two conversed in low voices across the guard between them.

More than the others, he represented "the fat cats." Probably as old as the Revolution, the multicolored myth of the small against the mighty could assume in these depressed times an anticapitalist, or antisemitic, or antiestablishment hue. Right and left exploited it; from their ideological poles Barrès and Zola had promoted it with equal zeal; so, closer to the center, had Alain. Among the people, naive, virtuous, and vulnerable, moved the parasites, sometimes visibly, sometimes not. Only recently, Edouard Daladier had infused a Radical Party congress with the fabulous myth of the two hundred families, now energetically disseminated by the Communists and Socialists as well. The frightened executive in the dock might not sit on the board of the Banque de France, but he provided a proxy for those who did; and he was said to live handsomely.[4]

Beyond him sat a likable, smiling young man, said to be some sort of office employee, and beyond him one more ruined Radical, the deputy from Bayonne, recycled from the bar like his Parisian colleague still at liberty in the front row below. He had not exhausted his reserves of grandiloquence or crabbed self-righteousness, but disgrace had marked him with a mournful, desolate aspect. His cheeks were sunken and his hands shook. He had long been lame in one leg, but now his weight tilted badly onto the cane he had once twirled confidently in the air. Naturally, he and his fellow-suffering deputy below cried persecution and posed as surrogate targets for the Chamber of Deputies or the Parliament itself, personifications of besieged republican liberties.

Founded as a via media after a rapid exhaustion of monarchical and presidential alternatives, the Third Republic had from the start the task of reconciling a parliamentary process relying on compromise with a popular legitimacy all too often excluding it. The Republic's first prime minister, tolerated by Parliament, was execrated by voters. The Chamber acquired, here and there, a reputation for easy virtue in a Republic identified with the genuine article. Latent from the start, antiparliamentary sentiment awoke whenever scandal sounded or the waltz of ministries picked up speed. It was a republican subculture, a sport indulged in by the novelists Mirbeau and Huysmans, the playwright Henry Bataille, and the rising lawyer Vincent de Moro-Giafferi, whose Bonapartist and presidential passions at the beginning of the century led him to denounce *le Wilsonisme* and its traffic in decorations as corruption, *le Panamisme* and its bilking of small investors as theft, and *le Dreyfusisme* as treason. Republicans themselves denounced the institution. The popular monthly *Lectures pour Tous,* staunch friend of the Republic, upheld the parliamentary principle but deplored its betrayal in practice. The magazine might ridicule a deputy one month and applaud the Republic the next. Wanting the great causes that it had once made its own—democracy, education, patriotism, victory—and beset by the devils of economics and diplomacy, the Parliament now lay exposed to its perennial scapegoating tormentors.[5]

The only woman on trial came in hat and scarf, dressed in black, tall and silent—Arlette, widow of the swindler, whose name the other defendants knew too well. Glamour girl of the capital, model at Coco Chanel, Riviera queen and living testimony to the consolations of style, she seemed, oddly, to resent her exposure today. She took off her jacket and sat pensively with her chin on her hands. Then, with her lawyer Moro-Giafferi, she retreated under the photographers' salvos and took cover in the narrow passage that led from the dais to a doorway and judges' chambers beyond. Above the doorway two recumbent lions supported another head of Nemesis, but Arlette had placed her fate in capable hands. Like the other lawyers, Moro-Giafferi thought to save the client by attacking the court. She was the most famous defendant, he the most famous lawyer. The reporters eyed them closely.

An accountant with fine white whiskers took his place in the top row, and a former general with a red-dyed Hitler mustache and a dandy's bow tie sat down after him. He was sixty-nine years old and resembled a ballroom dancer more than a career officer. Some of the defendants were aging; most had practiced solid trades and professions. Another bespectacled accountant, looking bewildered and senescent, then a jeweler with pendulous jowls and a bankrupt theater producer, filed in and took their places. All had overstepped the normal limits of greed —that much lithe Arlette shared with the most ungainly of the accused—and none had stayed out of harm's way. An old actor, who leaned, like the deputy from Bayonne, on a walking stick, had tasted the vanities of stage and screen as well, had made a profession of pretense. Everyone had grasped the possibilities of subterfuge but not its dangers. Even a timid and conscientious bank clerk in their midst had crossed the frontier between service and complicity. He sat below and blinked into the glare.

Twenty were in the dock: but where were the swindler's other friends? Where was Niemen the Polish boxer? Or Dorn y de Alsua, the debonair Ecuadorian diplomat who looked as though he had walked off the set of a musical comedy? Or Rita Georg, the Viennese dancer who, in fact, had walked off the set of a musical comedy, the bankrupt producer's *Katinka* at the Empire on Avenue de Wagram? Where, the defense lawyers demanded, were the negligent magistrates and the political accomplices?

Six magistrates came in at one fifteen and took up their places on the dais. Charles Barnaud, the presiding judge, sat in the middle, flanked by two assistant judges on his left and by the public prosecutor and two assistant prosecutors on his right.

"Odd, Maître, how you like to complicate matters," he said sharply to Moro-Giafferi, who was still trying to solve the seating problem.

"No, your honor, you're reversing our roles," came the insolent reply.

Barnaud had large glasses and a gray mustache. Like the others on the dais, he wore a red robe bordered with white ermine. The colors had a history. The magistrates of the Parlements had worn them under the ancien régime in this same palace, over a black cassock or simar and under a coat of royal purple. The kingly vestment declared that the sovereign had delegated the powers of justice and could take them back — as it had vainly tried to do in the decades of prerevolutionary troubles. Now the new sovereign assembled at the back of the room, its representatives sat on the jurors' benches to Barnaud's right, and Paris had not seen a king since Louis-Philippe hastily left town in 1848. The magistrates looked quaint in their robes. Still, a justice system could antagonize its sovereign as mightily in the Republic as under the absolute monarchy, and deputies with popular mandates could interfere with it as brazenly as a monarch anointed with holy oil.

Nobody cared much for magistrates. "You can imagine I'm not paid to love them," Voltaire declared at the conclusion of one of his many outbursts. Ever since Rabelais created Grippeminaud, "archduke of the gentlemen of the long robe," the country's authors had savaged them. Racine had Dandin in *Les plaideurs*. Balzac had fifty-eight of them in *The Human Comedy,* all but one the objects of his scorn.[6] The ill fame of the magistrate was natural enough, like the scurrility of the attacks on him. More surprising was the enduring indeterminacy of justice's place in the distribution of power. The liberal Republic was turning sixty-five and still its jurists could not agree. Was justice independent, or an arm of a popularly elected government? And did the minister, responsible to the Chamber of Deputies, bend justice to the will of the nation or shelter it from the passions of the hour? Barnaud chided Moro-Giafferi for his exertions on the floor, but he knew that soon they would be arguing over more than the guilt or innocence of Arlette and the others in the dock.

Their exchange, civil enough for an opening skirmish, presaged acrimony in the weeks ahead. In 1913 Moro-Giafferi had found fame in this room when, with passionate conviction, he had defended Dieudonné, the anarchist of the Bonnot band. Later, in 1922, he had fought in Versailles as ably, if not as sincerely, for Henri Désiré Landru, the latter-day Bluebeard. He knew how to find a path to the jurors' hearts and minds, how to plant doubts or draw a sympathetic tear. His courtroom theatrics offset the icy interrogations of judge and prosecutor, and Barnaud wisely thought to mollify him whenever possible. Moro-Giafferi wanted more chairs for the lawyers and he wanted them beside the accused.

"I am asking you, your honor," he went on as he stood at the bar, "to kindly attend to the seating of the accused."

"And I would like only to know whether their counsel would sit down," retorted Barnaud, but he suspended proceedings for ten minutes while attendants brought in more chairs. Arlette left her place again and silently slipped into the crowd on the courtroom floor.

"Things are starting well," said Moro-Giafferi.

When Barnaud returned with the others, the monotony began. First he verified the defendants' identities and swore in the jurors. Then a clerk and his assistant took turns reading an indictment, each relieving the other as they ran out of breath, filling two hours and covering 1200 pages and 1956 counts. That was the legal affair, and one of the jurors fell asleep halfway through. Then the clerk recited the list of witnesses, all 235 of them. That was the political affair, and people sat up. A hundred of the witnesses, Barnaud explained, would not hear of wasting November in a chilly corridor awaiting their turn to testify. They would come later, they had told him. The hyperbolic mind-set of the courtroom floor construed later as never. The reporters passed the word, the lawyers protested, and the public watched.

"If the noise and babble continue," Barnaud exclaimed above them, "I will have the courtroom emptied. This din is indecent!"

Outside, darkness was falling. At five o'clock Barnaud suspended the session, adding that every day proceedings would begin at one and end at five. And the following afternoon, Tuesday, he turned toward the jury and began. "Gentlemen of the jury," he said in his mellow voice, "as you already understand, the shadow of a dead man looms over this trial: Stavisky, Sacha, also known as Serge Alexandre, born on 20 November 1886 in Slobodka, Russia. It is essential, Gentlemen of the jury, that you understand just exactly who he was . . ."

A QUESTION OF CONFIDENCE

One hasn't the heart to play, in a world where everyone cheats. — André Gide, *Journal,* 21 November 1923

Arlette had married Stavisky years earlier, just after he came out of prison. He left La Santé in December 1927, and a month later they went together to the town hall of the eighth arrondissement, near Place Saint-Augustin. Their physician, Dr. Vachet, and Stavisky's friend and associate Henri Hayotte went along as witnesses, and Maître Robineau, the notary on Boulevard de Clichy who prepared the papers for their businesses, drew up the marriage contract.[1]

The Ladies' Man

Arlette was twenty-four, classically tall, conveying just a soupçon of aloofness or disdain. Departures, ruptures, and infidelities punctuated her past like some intermittent curse, invisible behind the cool countenance of her evident breeding. Her mother had affairs, and, when her father died soon after the armistice of 1918, divorce between the two had long been pending. He came from a family of pharmacists in Blois and owned a decorating business on Boulevard Haussmann, in the heart of the commercial district. Arlette was never poor and, like other girls of her background, spent most of the war studying Latin and modern languages at the Cours Dupanloup, named for the great nineteenth-century bishop of Orléans and aptly established since its beginnings on Rue de l'Assomption. She showed some promise there, even though her mother took no interest in her studies. Afterward, in 1920, she moved in with an Argentine who called himself a sculptor and lived nearby in the same affluent sixteenth arrondissement. Their marriage was announced but called off, he went away, and Arlette gave birth to a son, whom she sent off to a distant godmother and rarely saw again. A few years later, her mother ran off with an American dancer and disappeared from her life altogether.[2]

At about that time, at a dinner party, Arlette met Sacha Stavisky. It was early 1925, and she was a model at Coco Chanel. He was of medium build, dark and charming, and shared her sybaritic appetite for luxury and display. He lived, like her and Chanel, in the smarter part of the eighth arrondissement, and said he worked at some sort of import-export bank. Arlette, unschooled in postwar finance, delighted in his largesse whatever its source, and by Pentecost she had left Chanel's employ a woman of some leisure. Sacha cut a figure of uncertain but conspicuous means—too well dressed, a green Georges Trat and a blue Rolland-Pillain parked in the same garage, vacations in hotels on Channel beaches. He had curious friends. Once, at a hotel on the coast, Arlette met a Polish boxer who trained there and called Stavisky "Monsieur Sacha."[3]

Did she know about her predecessors? In fact, Stavisky was thirty-nine and a ladies' man. In recent hectic years he had spent his nights with Mlle Devillier, or the actress Suzanne Le Bret nearby, or with another actress, Jeanne Bloch, née Dreyfus, also known as Jeanne d'Arcy, who by now hated him.[4]

Jeanne would drag him out of the Café Napolitain and the customers there would watch the two, a short round woman and a trim, dapper man, quarrel up and down Boulevard des Capucines. She was a droll rich demimondaine, eight years his senior. For twenty years she had sung in *café-concerts* and Montmartre music halls, in comedies including *Ki-Ki-Ri-Ki* and *Le roi Maboul,* and had amused the crowds with predictable puns about her legendary stoutness—*Le Tas, c'est moi, allez-graisse,*[5] and countless others. Jeanne Bloch became a household name in bars, gaming rooms, and the Palace of Justice. Her depravity, or so the police thought, encompassed harlotry, morphine, and a lesbian singer called "Chouchou." For Stavisky, she was at first all sacrifice and devotion. She met him in April 1917, when the army had released him and he wanted money to buy a nightclub—a Russian bar and pocket theater called the Cadet-Roussel. He promised marriage, she promised the money.[6]

The mercurial fortunes of show business captivated him, and he had already shown his face in other theaters. He had even tried acting in *café-concerts,* without much success. Once in 1909 the Palais Royal theater gave him the best seats in the house when he presented a publisher's card that he had not stolen, only forged. Later that year, readers of the classified pages in *Le Matin* and *Le Petit Parisien* saw that the Folies-Marigny, the little white theater that stood on the Champs-Elysées amid flora and greenery and that put on farces and musical tableaux, was advertising paid positions. It asked for usherettes, flower girls, a secretary, a tobacconist, program vendors, and the usual multitude of mostly female hirelings and concessionaires who crowded about the stage. Stavisky and his grandfather had somehow rented the place, a summer theater, late in autumn, without any capital or expertise but with enough forethought to ask their new employees for customary if oversized deposits. Two weeks later the theater folded. It reopened, and back came Mistinguett, the Marigny Girls, and vaudeville singers in plaid suits. But Stavisky had vanished, along with the deposits.[7]

From Jeanne Bloch, in 1917, he took some four hundred thousand francs and launched the Cadet-Roussel with the songwriter Maxime Guitton. They put on sketches and attractions alternately, in that terrible year, jingoistic and farcical or burlesque, musical numbers that Guitton, d'Astorg, Serge, and others had composed—"The Good Patriot," "Conjugal Confrontation," "The Soldier on Leave," "Herminie Isn't to Blame." Rue Caumartin resounded at the time with nightspots and cabarets. At number 11 was another dance club, the Becasse, and at 25, the Cagibi, which put on Jean d'Armoy's *The Huns,* songs from Massenet's *Werther,* ancient dances, and Kip-Kap's ragtime band. And at 17 was the Cadet-Roussel, soon the terra incognita of an already nocturnal street. Late at night, after the songs and the skits, neighbors heard altercations loud enough to raise the dead. The police began to watch the place. Talk began of narcotics changing hands at the bar, of Guitton holding onto the riches of a jailed journalist, one Jacques Landau of the defeatist *Bonnet Rouge,* of Stavisky and Guitton and la Jeanne all falling out over money. Stavisky kept his partner but not his mistress at bay, for she finally hired a lawyer, took him to court, and had him sentenced to prison—not for the first time.[8]

First there was the jeweled ring. "Be quick and come back for lunch," she told him one day in June 1917, and gave him fifteen thousand francs to redeem a ring she had pledged. He left, and returned with neither ring nor money. He had lost his billfold, he claimed, and prevailed on a switchboard operator from the Cadet-Roussel to confirm his story. A tearful Jeanne made an appearance amid the mahogany furniture and green walls of an office at the Police Judiciare on Quai des Orfèvres. Tragicomedy followed on the stage of justice, full of bitter recriminations and sweet reconciliations and sudden improvisations by Jeanne and Sacha that strained the magistrates' credulity. Four years later, she relented, and he produced a magical receipt from her for the long-lost fifteen thousand francs. "Very suspicious," thought the magistrates, but they dropped the charges against Stavisky and the switchboard operator at the Cadet-Roussel, who had dignified his treachery. Stavisky appeared to like such allies.[9]

After the ring came the Peugeot Torpedo. The couple walked into the Auto-Stand on Rue Pergolèse in October 1917 and left ten thousand of Jeanne's francs and some promissory notes for the car, a nice open cabriolet. Later Stavisky came back, drove out in the Torpedo, and, once away, sold it. Jeanne, a participant herself, Stavisky's sidekick as well as his mistress, nevertheless reproached him for his piracies. The two eventually made their peace with the Auto-Stand but, with her, his credit was fading fast.[10]

Next came the Schwartz check. M. Schwartz was Jeanne Bloch's dressmaker, and when Stavisky's check to him bounced, it set off a grotesque melodrama of feigned self-sacrifice. Stavisky and his mistress half-confessed to the offense, sanctimoniously, as though to save each other, but he in particular struck the prosecutor as a charlatan of the golden rule, and the two soon ended their charade by paying off M. Schwartz. Justice signed off, Jeanne Bloch ordered more clothes from her mollified dressmaker, and Stavisky returned to the Cadet-Roussel.[11]

Then came the Cadet-Roussel itself. In time la Jeanne came to her senses and insisted that, like the Peugeot, the little nightclub at number 17 belonged to her and not to him. In 1918 it brought him 165,000 francs, in 1919 120,000, and in 1920 she angrily laid claim to the income. She hired a self-styled lawyer, yet another predator of the demimonde, a swindler and charmer who came from Russia and oddly resembled Stavisky himself. He had even lived a few doors down from the Cadet-Roussel until his landlord evicted him. Jeanne Bloch did not greatly benefit from his counsel. She produced a promissory note for 300,000 francs from Stavisky; he produced renunciations from her—extorted, she said, but the handwriting experts could not say for sure. In the end, she won some legal injunctions against him, but the days of the Cadet-Roussel were numbered. Soon it changed hands, reappeared in 1922 as the Sans Souci, and Stavisky, la Jeanne, and her errant lawyer went their separate ways.[12]

By then the aging comic had sold her apartments and furniture and was wandering sadly between hotels and furnished rooms. For a while she lived with her mother. Stavisky had ruined her, in full sight of café customers and the little crowd at the Cadet-Roussel. They deplored his cruelties but thought her simpleminded, and so she was. How artless she looked—but did she differ so much from the others whose hopes he had manipulated? From the usurious widow who had lent him money back in 1914 in return for his worthless stock certificates? Or from the young woman who met him in the Café Cardinal in 1922, sold him a yellow Citroën and lent him fifteen thousand francs, which he did not repay? They too had allowed him to exploit their cupidity as well as their affections—more sinned against than sinning, but not much more.[13]

From Arlette, however, Sacha took nothing. He spent lavishly on her and she returned his tributes with her constancy. A surprising fidelity assured their union, untroubled by his ways or the implacable conceits of family, country, and religion. She was a bourgeoise whose family came from the Loir-et-Cher and counted Joseph Paul-Boncour, a lawyer, deputy, and former minister, among its friends. He was a Jewish immigrant whose family had come to France only in 1889 from the Ukraine, land of pogroms. His parents, Emmanuel and Dunia, became French citizens in 1900, when he was fourteen, established his nationality along with their own, and sent him to absorb the country's culture and the Republic's values at one of its most prestigious high schools, the Lycée Condorcet. Yet when Arlette met him twenty-five years later he still spoke with a slight accent, Slavic or Eastern European Jewish, and with an alien, exotic suaveness that added spice to his charm. Emmanuel Stavisky, a dentist and, since 1920, a widower, took kindly to Arlette. Early in 1926 he welcomed her to their apartment on Rue de la Renaissance, a good address in the eighth arrondissement, with five comfortable rooms on an upper floor costing five hundred francs a month. He had lived there since 1898, so well lately that the police came to believe that the son's takings swelled the father's earnings. He practiced there as well, but no dentist's income could support so ample an establishment. Arlette did not worry. She moved in for a while early in 1926 and contemplated marriage to Sacha. But the police claimed him first. They took him to La Santé prison, and she had to promise Emmanuel that she would stand by his son in his hour of need.[14]

The Parvenu

Henri Hayotte, bosom companion and witness at their marriage at town hall, had met Stavisky around the time Arlette did, early in 1925. He was twenty-one and needed money. In the feverish ninth arrondissement, among the bankers and brokers, he found Sacha Stavisky, who rented offices in his own name for about 650 francs a month, in a handsome stone building at 64, Rue Taitbout.[15]

The offices stood only ten minutes from the late Cadet-Roussel, and in the heartland of finance, as in that of night life, Stavisky's conduct looked equivocal. Investors asked about him at Bradstreet France, an agency that since 1920 had informed bankers, businessmen, and anyone who cared enough to pay, about the solvency of clients, suppliers, and competitors. It spoke of Stavisky with nervous, uneasy caveats. "His means, like his transactions," it concluded, "are difficult to assess. . . . It would be prudent to ask him for guarantees for any unsecured transactions." But Stavisky was in good company, minutes away from adventurers more renowned than he. Rochette around the corner, and Oustric and Marthe Hanau nearby, gambled on the postwar inflation and contrived new ploys to separate citizens from their savings. Next to the Banque Oustric or Hanau's *Gazette du Franc,* which led investors astray with plausible promises of riches now and more to come, Stavisky had nothing, ostensibly, to offer. Humbly he started up Le P'tit Pot, a consommé company without, as yet, employees or consommé, and when Hayotte appeared in the doorway Stavisky liked him and made him a director.[16]

They were unlikely partners. Hayotte, an impulsive, stupid man, strutted and chattered and made up in motion what he lacked in thought; Stavisky, in conversation, worked his fingers, thumbs to his vest, or freed his hands to gesture with precision and control. Hayotte's handwriting was clumsy and bloated, Stavisky's delicate and sly. But their appetites united them. They liked easy money, and when they conversed in the vile, coarse dialect of the underworld, Stavisky displayed a virtuosity that shocked the unsuspecting. They became fast friends, in and out of the offices on Rue Taitbout. Hayotte added a lesser Arlette whom everyone called Ginette, once an extra at a theater next door to the Cadet-Roussel and now a model nearby. The foursome spent the summer of 1925 at Houlgate on the Channel. Later, a hired hand said that Hayotte and Stavisky seemed to be pulling the same purse strings.[17]

Le P'tit Pot never brought in any money. Publicity posters touted the meat-based bouillon, like Liebig or Viandox only better, and the company's two directors claimed that a factory was producing four hundred liters of it a month, but no consommé ever found its way to storeroom shelves. Once a salesman in Le Mans, calling himself Count Mikorski, extolled its virtues to such an extent that a wholesaler there traveled to Paris and Rue Taitbout to learn more. Stavisky and Hayotte offered him a contract to sell it to the grocers of the

Sarthe at a competitive price, but some months later the police put them both in prison, Count Mikorski went on his way, and Le P'tit Pot's brief commercial life came to an end.[18]

■

As legitimate a venture as any Hayotte ever joined, Le P'tit Pot provided a cover for deals with fraudsters far more practiced and adept than he. They gravitated to the neighborhood, and when they ran into Stavisky partnerships quickly flowered and wilted, like that with Sylvain Zweifel and his wayward Romanian compatriots.

Zweifel was an accountant from Bucharest who had found gainful employment there as a German counterespionage agent during the war. He turned in, among others, his own first cousin, but summoned few loyalties himself; he fared badly at the hands of the Germans and even worse at the hands of his countrymen. Zweifel returned to the more calculable pleasures of accountancy and its sibling, fraud, which soon drove him into exile under a cloud of scandal. In Paris, on Boulevard des Italiens, he ran into his childhood friend Smilovici, a deserter from the Romanian army and a casual associate of two bankers who had set up shop on Rue Taitbout. Zweifel agreed to meet them.

Introductions took place in a brasserie. Zweifel found Stavisky charming and affable, and they all went over to the offices of Le P'tit Pot. There Zweifel beheld the unbridled bedlam of speculation, paper credit, and shoestring margins—a telephone on every table, mountains of paper bearing on seventy-odd different short-term securities, employees everywhere, including a secretary called Arlette Simon: the ninth arrondissement in miniature, more than a notional consommé called for. Could Zweifel put the accounts in order, Stavisky asked. People on all sides were demanding money back from him. Zweifel agreed but soon gave up trying to make sense of Stavisky's recondite operations, the screens and assumed names and accounts shifting needlessly from one bank to another. Stavisky found other work for him, at a little villa he had rented south of the city in Brunoy, out toward Corbeil.[19]

There Zweifel and his wife—an unemployed French governess he had met in a hotel bar in Bucharest—found a concealed hive of industry. They found the deserter Smilovici, an actress called Nénette already known to the *police des moeurs* (vice squad), a photolithography specialist, and other artisans from uncertain trades. They also found some lithographic stones, ink, zinc for photogravure, acids, and a camera, all the matériel they needed to forge bank checks, stock certificates, and bonds of one kind or another. Stavisky had promised Zweifel one hundred francs a day and 6 percent of any paper issued by the suburban mint. But none was ever issued. In a fit of sartorial jealousy over Nénette's taupe coat, Madame Zweifel ran to the police. The others hastily destroyed their equipment. They scattered broken stones and debris in the garden and in the Bois de Boulogne, and Hayotte drove away with the rest of it. So ended the Brunoy operation. Zweifel vanished from Stavisky's life, but not for long.[20]

Zweifel had exposed himself dangerously while Stavisky, well hidden, had stayed back. Fraud, even the fraud of strangers, attracted Stavisky as a drug attracts its secret user, and Zweifel was not the first naïf to support his habit. With imagination but restraint, Stavisky engaged the inventors, forgers, and check launderers who passed his way, preferring the conception to the execution and the wings to the limelight. He could transform a check with a master's hand, but in time his skills grew more cerebral than manual.

Years before, he and a partner had promoted a device they called a "Matryscope," guaranteed to detect pregnancy within twenty-four hours. More recently, he had masterminded and directed a coup at Zelli's Dancing, around the corner from Arlette's old Cours Dupanloup. He had sent another Romanian, Popovici, there, looking like a world traveler of consequence. The danseuse who drank champagne with him thought him "a real son of privilege." Later he presented an impressive fifty-dollar bill in payment for his evening and asked elegantly for a check by way of change, protection, as he explained, against his drunkenly dissipating any more cash. Stavisky had provided the currency and the suit of clothes; Stavisky expertly converted Zelli's check for six hundred francs into a new one for forty-eight thousand two hundred; Stavisky waited outside the American Express office while the plucky Popovici went in and cashed their creation. Afterward they went their separate ways, Popovici to Italy, he back to the transient operators of the neighboring arrondissement.

The ninth arrondissement crawled with other Popovicis, check forgers, fences, and securities thieves who briefly joined forces with Stavisky, often to suffer alone when their fleeting combinations came undone. Another Romanian forged checks for him and was arrested in the offices of the Banque Ottomane; another acquaintance from the Cadet-Roussel passed on stolen stock certificates for him and was arrested in Belgium. Popovici too was arrested when he returned from Italy. Somehow, Stavisky took precarious cover, just out of reach, a survivor for the time being.[21]

How could he keep the other side from tearing his veil of secrecy? A corporate smokescreen denser than Le P'tit Pot might deflect unwelcome inquiries, avert mishaps like Brunoy or the downfall of the occasional colleague, and allow hoaxes less crude than the fabrication of bonds or the laundering of checks. Stavisky had not yet arrived; he still lacked the imposing friend and the sheltering screen. But the open society of fraudsters held few class barriers, only degrees of talent, and doors opened for him when he rang. In 1923 a partner from the streets found him a friend in a boardroom.

Poulner was a minor swindler and forger, the frail, curly-haired son of a tailor in Montmartre. He had a nervous tic, spoke with a stammer, and called himself a salesman for Le P'tit Pot. But like his colleague Popovici, whom he knew well, he distributed more paper than soup. Gambling clubs, tired of his bouncing checks, were complaining about him, and the police duly ordered

15

him not to set foot in them anymore. Poulner had walked into the Cadet-Roussel shortly after it opened in 1917, and soon he and Stavisky began haunting the outer galleries of the stock exchange, the same nightclubs, and the gambling rooms of Cercle Haussmann. Then he disappeared for a while.

In about 1923 he reappeared and introduced Stavisky to his cousin Himmelfarb, also known as Himmel or André, young and crooked like himself, but less limited in his imagination and more ambitious in his enterprise. Poulner engaged the passing fool, Himmelfarb whole corporations and their stockholders. When he met Stavisky he had just laid to rest his short-lived Corporation Cinématographique Franco-Américaine, known among his confederates as the Trust du Cinéma, and was fighting lawsuits from angry investors. Hayotte, driven by his enthusiasm, had coincidentally blundered into the affair and so already knew Poulner's venturesome cousin. When Stavisky came along, Himmelfarb immediately brought him into an elaborate *carambouillage*, a commercial credit swindle.[22]

Corporate deception, Himmelfarb knew, required the appearance of solidity and the spell cast by establishment names. When he set up the Compagnie Générale d'Importation et d'Exportation, he persuaded a senior civil servant, the former subprefect Schroeder, to act as chairman and, as befitted a legal company, to register and notarize the founding statute shares. Trust, unimpeachable appearance, and the residual capital of an ailing company it had gallantly rescued allowed the Compagnie Générale to start buying jewels, perfumes, champagnes, and silks on credit even before it opened its doors. By the time it closed them a year later it had bought and resold 2.3 million francs' worth of goods, but in the Compagnie Générale little besides the merchandise was genuine. The original shareholders were impostors, the bank receipts forgeries, the account books cooked. Even some of the customers were fictitious. The purchasing agent who bought a coachload of champagne from them was none other than Himmelfarb's cousin and Stavisky's old friend, Poulner. The bills went unpaid, the suppliers complained, the Compagnie Générale went into liquidation. But even the liquidator turned out to be one of Himmelfarb's men, paid to stall and prevaricate. About seven hundred thousand francs' worth of goods disappeared from the accounting altogether: briefly left as security for cash loans, they were then sold off below market value like the rest. That was Stavisky's doing.[23]

In the spring of 1925 Himmelfarb was raising some new scaffolding on the ruins of the old and issuing fifty thousand shares in yet another projected company, a "Société de Commerces et d'Industries Réunis." But by then he and Stavisky had parted ways. For a while they had collaborated in the artifices that could turn credit, accounting, and surface respectability into theft, but Stavisky's gaze now wandered more to the frontiers of influence he had glimpsed. New entries opened prospects more grand than the marginal, treacherous terrain he had once walked with the likes of Jeanne Bloch and Popovici; better a retired subprefect than a wayward accountant, a Schroeder than a Zweifel. Stavisky still kept lowly company. But he had begun to ascend;

he now craved entries and introductions more than fast money. A bellhop from Fouquet's who knew him from a modest *café-tabac* off the Champs-Elysées now also spotted him taking an aperitif once in a while at the fashionable establishment on the Champs-Elysées, where menus bore no prices and customers came in evening dress. By the time Arlette met Stavisky in the hectic year of 1925 he had just penetrated the outer circle of the smart set, the postwar parvenus glinting with brilliantined hair, powdered eyes, and the garish look of new wealth.[24]

Countless others before him had brought a comedian's mask to their rise from trickster to tycoon. Street swindlers no less than corporate conjurers exacted from their victims the same willing acts of faith and suspension of disbelief as did actors from their audiences. They began the same way, wearing some disguise or peddling some small-time inventions or illusions. When Stavisky acquired such arts, the arcane lexicon of swindling already had a term for every act and a name for every actor. The law called him an *escroc*, a swindler; the criminal milieu called him a *drogueur*. The language of the same milieu christened *fusilleurs,* who built credit among suppliers and disappeared with their goods, *philiberts,* who did the same with bankers and their loans, and *charrieurs,* who lived off the trust of tourists. When, in 1906, a false Russian countess bought necklaces on credit and took them to pawnbrokers, *Gil Blas* seized on the parallel with Marie Antoinette's diamonds, the centerpiece of the famous hoax of the 1780s, and told its readers of "the affair of the countess's necklace." But the trade knew it merely as a swindle *à la Robert Macaire,* after the confidence trickster in the satirical Restoration play *L'Auberge des Adrets.* All of them exploited the trust of others in some way, and, long before Stavisky was even born, Balzac's common sharpers stalked the pages of *César Birotteau, Eugénie Grandet, Lost Illusions,* and the big new world of credit opened in the 1820s and reflected everywhere in *The Human Comedy.*[25]

When Stavisky was pushing the Matryscope for pregnant women during the war, the rising banker Marthe Hanau was promoting marvels for men at the front, including a portable hot plate called "the soldier's chafing dish" and its companion, "the soldier's tube," a zinc vial supposed to hold some sort of coffee-and-rum concoction. Now, in 1925, as Stavisky moved on from Himmelfarb, Hanau was setting up a mysterious real estate company with very little capital, a brokerage house and financial publicity service that drew lawsuits as well as investors. Rochette their senior was back, unable to sit out the open postwar season. Like Stavisky, he had tried his hand at acting early in life. He had played three roles in a revue in Melun in 1897, the "Méli-Mélo Melunnais," before he launched the Mines de la Nerva, Mines and Banking, the Buissons Hella, and all the other early stock swindles that had brought him scandal and ruin during the waning years of the Belle Epoque. His methods differed more in degree than in kind from the ventures of his Balzacian predecessors, built on quicksand, chimeras, and pretenses, but when Stavisky came along a new era had begun, composed of currency ills, structural crisis, and the illusion of a boom.[26]

The financial disorder of the 1920s encouraged and abetted the descendants of

Balzac's Roguins and Nucingens. They too started out with little more than their wits to live by. With the postwar inflation undermining the prestige of government annuities and national defense bonds, the new operators had new drawing cards. Like revolutions in Balzac's day, war had subverted the rules of the game and filled the scene with some raffish new players — the financial swindlers of the mid-1920s. Now the Oustrics, Hanaus, and others who never made the headlines, could exploit the swelling sums in circulation, the screens and curtains of the joint stock corporation, and the hopes and fears of a nation of legendary small savers.[27]

Himmelfarb found Stavisky searching for the connections that might join his talent to the opportunities of the day. In 1916, Stavisky had sold the Italian government munitions he had never paid for, but the stunt fell short of systematic war profiteering, and in any case the war was over. Now he tried his hand at the postwar stock exchange; Zweifel had rubbed his eyes at the swirls and baroque spectacle of the office on Rue Taitbout. But compared to Marthe Hanau, the audacious banker exactly his age who had already disguised herself as the defender of the franc and had launched newspapers and press agencies to promote her cause, Stavisky ran a bucket shop. Not until Pierre Vachet appeared on the scene did he start to move up.

Dr. Vachet, witness alongside Hayotte to Stavisky's marriage to Arlette, was a man of science and a man of the world. Psychologist, physician, relentless status seeker, he liked to have a following of friends and devotees, and extended his professional life well beyond his consulting room. He taught at the Ecole Libre de Psychologie, gave free psychotherapy sessions on Sundays, and knew prefects, deputies, and at least some of the notables holding the keys to the realm of influence and prestige still closed to Stavisky. Hayotte introduced them, and Dr. Vachet, family friend as well as physician, began treating Arlette and the Staviskys, father and son; through him, Stavisky one day came upon the wide new world of radio.[28]

Dr. Vachet's avocations included a medical program called "Stay Healthy" on the new "Journal Parlé" — talking news — at the Eiffel Tower radio station. In 1923 the journalist Maurice Privat had insisted that talking news would come to the airwaves today and to the movie screens tomorrow. To prove it, Privat leased the concession for the Eiffel Tower station from the government. Radio was new, its organization unsettled. For the time being, the army owned and ran the Eiffel Tower station, one of only a few in the country, but sometimes the Post and Telegraph Ministry, the PTT, used it, and when Privat came along they leased it to him for one hundred francs an hour. The studio began broadcasting in November 1925 and soon the "Journal Parlé," daily from six to seven in the evening, had perhaps a million listeners. But Privat needed money, fifty thousand francs a year, more than the benevolent Amis de la Tour could give, so he took in advertising. This, as Privat knew, the government had prohibited. But sometimes, in the exploratory regulation of the untried medium, the spirit allowed what the letter forbade, and into the breach stepped Stavisky. One Sunday evening early in 1926, after his "Stay Healthy" show, Dr. Vachet put in a word to Privat for the P'tit Pot and vouched for the nutritional and dietetic merits of a consommé he could not possibly have tasted. I know the two in charge, he told Privat, why not let them sponsor the "Journal Parlé?" And Privat asked his publicity agent Brouilhet to call on them in their offices at 64, Rue Taitbout.[29]

Charles Brouilhet was an old friend of Privat's from the newsrooms of the capital. A few years earlier he had called himself a business employee, but no business employed him, and a journalist, but no paper claimed him; he had performed magic and card tricks in the cafés of the capital before the war, and had taken up Communism after it, writing an occasional article for *L'Humanité* and calling routinely for revolution. Now Brouilhet was a habitué of Privat's studio in the Eiffel Tower. He announced the sports news on Sunday, composed broadcasts, looked for sponsors, and gainfully worked the serried intersections joining journalism to publicity. He had already seen newspaper advertisements for le P'tit Pot and was happy to offer its vigorous director an advertising contract that would bring him, the agent, a commission of 30 percent. Soon the airwaves carried spoken word of the new consommé and an offer of free samples; when inquiries began inundating the Eiffel Tower and his office, Stavisky expressed a keen interest in a monopoly on the "Journal Parlé" advertising, all of it.[30]

This Privat was delighted to grant. But why did the new sponsors decline for the time being to broadcast any more advertisements? It seemed bizarrely unselfish. Stavisky had dark film star eyes and dazzled Privat with penetrating glances and untiring alertness. He conveyed, moreover, the confidence of a man of plenty. Next to him, Hayotte made an execrable impression—blustering, ill-mannered, hatted in company. For a while the improbable couple came nightly and joined the busy little studio's habitual crowd of musicians, broadcasters, and famous guests of the hour—the trial lawyer, the author, the nightclub singer. Listeners from the public came too, curious to see what so far they had only heard. Sometimes Privat noticed a striking woman—Arlette—with Stavisky.

Why did they not wish to use any of the airtime they were buying at such expense? Stavisky explained that he planned advertising for a Chartreuse-like liqueur called "la Jurançonne" and a building project in Marseilles, Les Nouveaux Terrains. The first catered to the palate, the second to the postwar search for housing. In the meantime he wished to deny the air to any other advertisers. This seemed sound enough to Privat, and in March 1926 he signed over exclusive commercial advertising rights to Stavisky and Hayotte for the coming year at one thousand francs a day.[31]

No Nouveaux Terrains buildings ever went up and no Jurançonne ever went down during Stavisky's brief stewardship, and in the end the Eiffel Tower never beamed a word of praise for either. Hard times soon put an end to each, to Le P'tit Pot, and to much else besides. But for a moment Stavisky had unlocked a wide door, and who can say how he might have exploited the reach of the "Journal Parlé" microphones or of its stars? Several times, Stavisky brought in a banker who reassured Privat; and Privat in turn impressed him. Later, Stavisky's checks went bad, his overdrafts swelled, and his obliging banker resigned in disgrace. But for a moment Stavisky had exploited the cachet that financiers and journalists carried in each other's eyes; he had played his first tentative hand in the manipulative, illusive game of public relations. Brouilhet, the agent and self-proclaimed journalist, had left Privat's employ to join Stavisky's at 150 francs a day and to buy publicity for Stavisky instead of selling it for Privat. With him came the prospect of studied new appearances, infinitely more refined than the crude disguises of Stavisky's receding past, carried to an unlimited audience by airwaves, space advertising, and the financial pages of the country's extended press.[32]

One day Brouilhet noticed Stavisky in the studio shaking hands with Jean Galmot, a journalist, aviator, bankrupt rum tycoon, and former deputy from Guyana. Ruined once already by politics and the breath of scandal, Galmot was resurfacing in the borderlands of money and the press, his path predestined to cross Stavisky's.[33]

He was a gaunt, slightly bent man in his mid-forties who spoke without passion and dressed without style. He looked chronically unwell. Twenty years earlier, Galmot, as a Dreyfusard journalist at *Le Petit Niçois,* had made a name for himself with some dubious scoops toward the end of the Affair. Then he made his fortune in the jungles of Guyana from tulipwood, attar of roses, sugarcane, balata rubber, and gold; and from the sweat of the convicts there, the successors of Alfred Dreyfus. He made millions more at the end of the war, out of wheat from Argentina and sugar from the Antilles, and from rum—the rum that finally undid him when, as deputy from Guyana, he defended himself successfully in the Chamber in 1921 against accusations of speculation and profiteering but unsuccessfully in the courts in 1922 and 1923 against the more precise charge of swindling. Galmot brought aviation to Guyana and linked Cayenne by air to Saint-Laurent-du-Maroni, wrote endlessly of the distant colony's riches in the metropolitan press, even bought a radio station for the cause; he acted as Guyana's spokesman and never ceased his campaign, but in truth he was a posturer and an adventurer, a latter-day corsair.[34]

Released from prison, at odds with the tax collectors and heavily in debt, defeated in the elections of 1924, Jean Galmot was putting the pieces of his overbold life back together when he met Sacha Stavisky. Like everyone else in the political ring, he had a hand in a paper, an ideologically capricious scandal sheet called *Aux Ecoutes*—"Listening In"—that mixed gossip columns with financial rumors and blackmail. And, like everyone else, he still needed money. One day early in 1926 Zweifel met him in the office. "Monsieur Galmot, former deputy," Stavisky said to him, and uttered a few words aside to Galmot, who soon left the room. Stavisky explained nonchalantly to Zweifel that the former king of rum owed him some seven hundred thousand francs, borrowed to support an election campaign in Guyana. In return, Galmot had floated mirages of Guyanan gold before Stavisky's eyes and the tantalizing prospect of an agent in the Chamber of Deputies.[35]

"Everything can be bought," the saying went, and once in a while everything was sold. From time to time, a deputy had to explain himself. Such corruption was rare, though many did not think so, and isolated revelations could breed generalized cynicism. Still, elections cost money, so that sums donated, presses paid, and meeting halls hired could pave the way to a deputy's heart. Whoever controlled the press might hope to control the deputy. And whoever controlled the deputy carried a laissez-passer to rarefied zones of influence. Stavisky, employer of Brouilhet, moneylender to Galmot, and sponsor of the "Journal Parlé," now finally drew his first breaths of the intoxicating air. But he did not enjoy it for long; his new entourage cast him back to his old environment below, to the streets, the courts, and the prisons.[36]

The Accused

Stavisky had already appeared in the courts of the Palace of Justice and had occupied the cells of Fresnes prison, but more often than not he had artfully sidestepped the law.

Twice he slipped. Once in 1915 the courts sentenced him to six months in prison for swindling an avaricious old woman out of some twenty-five thousand francs. He lodged appeals and hastily abandoned residences, eluding his persecutors for more than two years. Finally they took him to Fresnes in November 1918, but three months later a general war-related amnesty freed him. In 1924 Popovici, back from Italy, turned him in for stage-managing the caper at Zelli's Dancing and the ensuing check forgery, but two weeks later he walked out on probation and soon extricated himself from the business altogether, while a beggared Popovici was locked away for eighteen months.[37]

Usually Stavisky spun matters out and appeased his victims with reparations measured out in driblets. Weary, mindless, or blinded by the sand he habitually threw in their eyes, the fools would drop their suits and just as quickly his payments to them would cease. After the Folies Marigny operation in 1909, Stavisky bought off some of the theater's plaintiffs and was still appealing a conviction for swindling the others when war broke out. La Jeanne gave up trying to recover her ring; Zelli withdrew his action against Stavisky, and Popovici languished in prison. Some never pursued him at all. Dupes rarely craved the attention that legal battles invited.[38]

The victims might relent, but would the authorities? Now and again the police found Stavisky more useful at large than behind bars; now and again during his days at the Cadet-Roussel he turned informer. "Stavisky, [Inspector] Leroy's informer," he was obscurely called for a while at the Sûreté Générale. In return, the police might protect him and so produce a precarious equilibrium. During the investigation of Zelli's complaint against Stavisky and Popovici at the prefecture of police, the falsified check mysteriously disappeared. Two years later, in 1925, securities stolen from a steamer lying at anchor in Marseilles after a South American run turned up in Belgium, and one Inspector Bayard at the Sûreté Générale covered Stavisky with unseemly haste. Bayard had about twenty informers, most of them former convicts or escapees from the law, birds of passage in Montmartre, the Porte Saint-Martin or the Porte Saint-Denis in Paris, or brothel owners in the provinces. Stavisky and Bayard, Stavisky and Leroy—such passing accommodations, jealously private, owed much to chance, and sometimes the reciprocal exploitation went badly awry. The police, fair-weather friends at best, could turn on their informer whenever he threatened even minor embarrassment, and if Stavisky could use them one day, they could spring traps on him the next.[39]

He had, in addition, the legal professionals, the notaries and lawyers, to retain and the overburdened magistrates to keep at bay.

Maître Robineau, the notary who drew up his marriage contract in 1928, helped him to keep up appearances and a semblance of legality on paper. In 1924 Robineau had helped him set up a short-lived realty company; other notaries, mindful of custom and the growing weight of legal precedent, might have shown him the door. Magistrates and citizens were beginning to hold notaries accountable for some of the ways of their clients, and the civic responsibility of their position now looked like a legal liability. The Revolution had demanded civic virtue of notaries and imposed on them a patriotic obligation to advise far exceeding the passive, almost clerical functions that had sufficed for the ancien régime. When in 1803 the state councillor Réal explained a new law—that of 25 Ventôse year XI—regulating the profession, he placed the notary alongside the judge and the priest and had him minister just as vitally to the happiness and tranquillity of the citizens, as a disinterested counselor lucidly setting out to each the meaning of his commitments.

But the law of 25 Ventôse left notarial liabilities vague, and when Stavisky walked into Robineau's office some 120 years later, jurisprudence, driven by the volume of notarial business, the occasional scandal, and the malevolence of social satirists, was compensating in practice for what legislation lacked in theory. Were notaries legally answerable for the harm they might cause their clients? Yes, answered some courts in the 1840s, as venality and improprieties came to light, and as Balzac culled crooked notaries like Cruchot in *Eugénie Grandet* from his own unhappy memories of clerking for one. Must they refuse their services if their clients persisted in illegal designs, and were they legally responsible to clients' defrauded creditors? Yes, the courts ruled, as the century advanced and more vocational abuses came before them. During the Belle Epoque, notaries allowed a false heiress, Thérèse Humbert, to concoct an American inheritance out of thin air, allowed a mercenary liquidator of the outlawed Catholic Congregations, Duez, to enrich himself indecently, and a crooked banker, Boulaine, to set up his Novo Pavlovka Mining mirage. "This black band of a new kind . . . parvenus millionaires," a critic called them in 1904, and one of the vilest characters in the serialized popular novel *Scandales,*

Misères et Cie of 1896 was the notary, "base, squalid, greasy, and, strangest of all, pretentious." Already at risk if he somehow misled his client, the notary, by the time Robineau was receiving Stavisky, might even have to answer if his client misled him. To overlook the illegalities, the jurists argued, was to betray the public trust. Even if Robineau did not know what Stavisky was up to, he had an obligation to find out. But these were gray areas. The courts often exonerated a notary whose client seemed so practiced and worldly-wise as to need no counsel or admonition. The compliant Robineau might justify in just that way the good offices he provided his elegant new caller. He knew little about him, and, despite the centennial troubles of his liberal profession, might count on the saving infirmity of the law, its ambiguity.[40]

And, their defenders asked, why should notaries be vulnerable and lawyers not? Three years before he retained Robineau, Stavisky acquired the devoted services of Maître Gabriel-Georges Gaulier, a twenty-four-year-old novice lawyer from Brittany who had just been called to the Paris bar. Puny, impressionable, money-hungry, Gaulier had found employment as secretary to the more eminent Maître Lévy-Oulmann. Only in the offices of established lawyers or agencies could a newcomer from the provinces earn money, start a career in the capital, and build a clientele of his own. That was how Gaulier met Stavisky. It was 1917, Stavisky was already at odds with the courts, and Lévy-Oulmann gave the case over to young Gaulier.[41]

Lawyers, like notaries, were not greatly loved, and Maître Henri-Robert, one of the most illustrious barristers of the day, gloomily resigned himself to the ingratitude that repaid his calling. But their order and the carapace of liberalism protected lawyers in a way notaries might have envied. Occasional critics charged that their black robes now symbolized subterfuge rather than sanctity and that they threw themselves indiscriminately at any client who came their way. They answered in the measured tones of public service and human rights. "The lawyer may hesitate before accepting a case, because of the client's character," declared Maître Appleton, another eminent member of the bar. "[But] if it's a criminal matter, he must guard against such a sentiment: every accused has the right to counsel." In any case, added Maître Henri-Robert, lawyers rarely know the full truth about their clients' guilt or innocence, and even more rarely do they try to discover it. So when Gaulier launched his career on Stavisky's behalf he did not unduly interrogate his conscience, especially since more troubling questions about money, honoraria, and the dividing line between lawyer and business agent did not arise, at least not yet.[42]

In the end, Gaulier failed to spare his new client his few months in Fresnes late in 1918. He left Lévy-Oulman's employ, lost sight of Stavisky for a few years, and helped him through the judicial sequelae to Zelli's forged check—through Popovici's denunciation, Zelli's withdrawal, the abortive investigation and the happy ending, the charges dropped and the matter closed. Saved again from the short-lived Brunoy counterfeit operation, Stavisky could dispense with Gaulier's services.[43]

Still, all was not well with Stavisky. The army had released him permanently because of stomach ailments, appendicitis, and enterocolitis. Dr. Vachet and others soon came to suspect that Stavisky suffered from persecution mania, an occasional delusion that his enemies were intent on poisoning him, and later they noticed depression and even thoughts of suicide.[44]

■

Stavisky, as he shook hands with his first corporate operator, his first deputy, and his first media baron, might ambitiously imagine that his troubles were over and his future secure. But his tussles with the law, endemic in his station, went on. How was he to assure his impunity, if not by hiding where the law could not reach him? It might catch Popovici or Zweifel or Poulner, less easily Himmelfarb or Galmot, and still less easily Privat, whose expedients outclassed those of the law of the day. How was he to jettison the first group and insinuate himself into the second? He now appreciated notaries, lawyers, journalists, and doctors, as well as the glow of public office; and suddenly one day,

THE LIBÉRAL PROFESSIONS
Stavisky's Baptism of Fire

A deputy's sash should never appear through a lawyer's robe.—Maître Henri-Robert, *L'avocat*

If the ever-observant Zweifel had not noticed Stavisky one day at the bar of the Helder Grill Room in the Bonbonnière de l'Opéra, the courts might never have opened proceedings at all. Upon such happenstance justice often relied, and Zweifel's chance encounter soon set its wheels in motion.

When the trouble began, Stavisky's skirmishes with the law had for the most part resembled those of the petty thieves of his entourage. He defrauded and then compensated his victims, just enough to dampen their interest in legal action, in a game of limits that courted and then warded off the threat of incarceration. Usually he made off with fractions of the wealth of others, in discrete episodes of converging plots yet diverging profit.

But to stay the courts once they had acted called for a grasp of magistrates' minds and mores, a sense of how they groaned under the press of business, feared the eruption of scandal, and above all respected a lawyer of standing; and such intelligence, even to Stavisky, came only with experience.

Stockbrokers

Stavisky usually appeared in the Helder Grill Room about noon. There, at the bar, a stranger once handed him a bundle of stock certificates. Close by, watchful, Zweifel started: a former accountant, he knew that the zinc countertop, even in a *bar américain,* was no place for a stock transaction, and, as a former Romanian double agent, he did not forget what he had seen.[1]

The stranger, called Loiseau, had already served Stavisky well. In 1923 some eight hundred thousand francs' worth of Argentine securities had disappeared from the steamer *Valdivia,* tied up alongside the docks of Marseilles, and had reappeared on the streets of Paris, to be peddled by the shady broker Loiseau on behalf of a client "presenting all guarantees"—Stavisky.[2]

Away from the Grill Room and its cocktails, another broker, one Léopold-Fernand Pourcelle, was also trafficking in stocks with Stavisky. Like Loiseau, Pourcelle worked for the brokerage house Laforcade and knew Stavisky well. He was a bachelor from Amiens in his mid-forties and had first met Stavisky in 1909 during his brief tenure as director of the Folies-Marigny theater. Now he had a hand in the P'tit Pot venture, saw Stavisky two or three times a week, and often lunched with him. In January 1926 he sold Stavisky half a dozen shares of

Royal Dutch at more than 25 percent below their quoted market price, but never recorded the sale on the books of Laforcade. Felonious from beginning to end, the operation married the crudity of securities theft to the subtlety of occult or parallel bookkeeping and, for anyone given to such improvisations, suggested a fabulous future.[3]

That winter Loiseau and Pourcelle made away with about 3 million francs of Laforcade's stocks and securities. Stavisky disposed of most of them. In February Pourcelle suddenly cut off the flow, but Stavisky did not mind—he said that he had larger fish to fry, Le P'tit Pot, La Jurançonne, the Terrains de Marseille. And by then he also had another broker, this one self-employed, Edouard Labbé.[4]

In August 1923 Labbé, too, had sold some of the errant Mendoza bonds from the *Valdivia*. In November 1925 he first sold Stavisky himself some stocks, and in February he joined the lengthening list of Stavisky's victims. Once again enlisting Zweifel, cast as a rich landowner come to town with plenty to invest, Stavisky played his habitual confidence game. Zweifel impressed Labbé with a few substantial deposits, and soon Stavisky managed to extract from the hapless broker 1.1 million francs' worth of stocks in return for two checks, which the bank later returned. The following month Labbé went along to the Palace of Justice, filed suit against Stavisky for securities fraud and bad checks, and requested that an investigating magistrate open an inquiry forthwith.[5]

A few days later, two other banks followed with similar suits of their own. One complained that a man called "Sacha Stavisky," of obscure origins and multiple but indeterminate occupations, had opened an account in February, won their confidence with a few open and aboveboard stock operations, and then withdrawn over a million francs against some phantom stock certificates. Another denounced bad checks and other capers at its Neuilly branch. Laforcade, whose stocks Loiseau and Pourcelle had purloined for Stavisky, was not far behind. How was Labbé to know that his private litigation would attract the eager curiosity of the mass dailies and, years later, set off a terrible scandal in which he himself would stand before an august Parliamentary Commission of Inquiry?[6]

"The sublime profession of stockbroker," as Proust called it, was one of the most tightly regulated métiers of this permissive Republic. Its ancestors, the go-betweens of medieval trade fairs and the money traders housed over the Seine on the Pont au Change, had provoked royal regulation almost as soon as they began to flourish. Now, protected in status but restricted in scope, the seventy brokers of the exclusive *Compagnie* traded shares inside the visible confines of their protected turf, the *corbeille*, the inner circle of the Paris Bourse, or stock exchange. A decree of 7 October 1890 had added newly coercive legal rigor to the self-imposed standards of the ancient profession—it had imposed financial and educational conditions for the appointment of new brokers, had insisted on both confidentiality and documentation in their dealings with clients, and had forbidden them from investing their own funds. Lawsuits against them were rare, rarer than against their fellows in public trust, the notaries. But clinging to them like votaries to their gods were proxies, half-commission men, clerks and informants, and above all the outside brokers, the *coulissiers* weaving through the columns around the *corbeille,* traders in new, unquoted stocks and shares issued by all manner of enterprises solid or shaky. Few rules of law or habit governed their lot; poorly paid and poorly regulated, no strangers to temptation, the employees, aspirants, and artful underlings like Loiseau and Pourcelle might casually enter into momentary partnerships with adventurers like Stavisky. Against such an affiliation the solid stockbroker Labbé now tried to invoke the laws of the Republic.[7]

Magistrates and Policemen

Whether a private plaintiff or the state itself set the courts in motion, months or even years might elapse before justice was served. The investigating magistrate, the public prosecutor, and the chamber of indictments successively spun matters out, even without the delaying tactics of an able lawyer. And able lawyers abounded. That was one way the Third Republic had come to the defense of the defendant, finally granting him, in 1897, the right, during the pretrial investigation, to a lawyer, to silence, to access to the evidence marshaled against him, and to adequate warnings of impending interrogations before the investigating magistrate. Long before he stepped into the dock of the criminal court, a defendant might hope to entangle the law in its own rules and avail himself of the liberal protections the Republic proffered him, so foreign to the ancien régime and both empires.[8]

Yet an investigating magistrate could, if he chose, hold a suspect in prison throughout the protracted pretrial skirmishes—almost indefinitely. He could send him straight to prison, with or without prior questioning. And Stavisky, to those who knew him, seemed to fear prison above all else.

To Abel Prouharam, the public prosecutor, Labbé was a routine plaintiff and Stavisky a common felon, one more in the unwholesome multitude that flowed through the Palace of Justice and the public prosecutor's office. Ordinary theft, even of stock certificates, did not call for the refined attentions of the financial section, which investigated and indicted shady bankers, illicit speculators, tax evaders, war profiteers, and all the new-fashioned freebooters of postwar commerce and finance. Prouharam therefore passed Labbé's suit on to René Decante, an investigating magistrate in the more mundane fifth section, the jurisdiction of thefts, swindles, confidence tricks, offences that the lawyers knew as common misdemeanors.[9]

Fifty-six years old, practiced and seasoned, Decante looked again at Labbé's story, as it was his duty to do. He raised his eyebrows at the seven-figure sums before him and, from his office on the south side of the Palace of Justice, sent for Superintendent Pachot, just across the way among the Police Judiciaire on Quai des Orfèvres. He wanted to see what Pachot knew about "Stavisky."[10]

Edmond Pachot was the genuine article, a dedicated professional, fifty-six years old like Decante, with twenty-five in the service. Like Stavisky, he was of medium height but bespectacled and bewhiskered and well spoken, yet with a bulldog's bearing, suggesting a formidable mix of intellect and tenacity. He brought to his profession a doctorate in law and a degree in literature, the fruits of studies to which some day he fully intended to return. Meanwhile, he pursued criminals. In 1912, in a carefully prepared operation fed by undercover intelligence from the criminal milieu, he and his men caught forty-two thieves in Montreuil in the space of six weeks. A little later, he began to specialize in financial crime. Over the years he arrested the fraudsters, swindlers, and blackmailers who had sold illegal Portuguese wines and Caribbean rum, had smuggled silver fox, concealed war profits, and engaged in the dark acts of commerce that consumed his time and tried his patience. Such investigations could be frustrating, and sometimes Pachot chafed at how his employer, the Police Judiciaire of the Paris prefecture, restricted him. Unless specially authorized, he confined his range to the capital and the department of the Seine, his mission to the investigation and apprehension of criminals sought by the public prosecutor's office and its magistrates, and his means to whatever the prefecture could give him. It had no independent financial brigade as yet, but one or two inspectors, relying on inside informers who often supplied their damning disclosures freely, discerned some of the obscure trafficking that went on in the shadows of the Bourse and the banks.

Pachot already had Stavisky in his sights. When Decante called him in he told the magistrate what he knew, and also asked an inspector to draw up a written report for them on the man whose name was fast becoming a household word among the Police Judiciaire. Decante listened and decided to summon Stavisky. He would make up his mind when they met whether to arrest and prosecute—would summon a free man and probably send in a captive.[11]

Stavisky had just crossed paths with another investigating magistrate during the Brunoy counterfeiting fiasco in February. On the 23rd of that month, three days after Mme Zweifel ran to the Batignolles police station and told all, the investigating magistrate Grébaud issued arrest warrants for the whole gang at Brunoy, including Hayotte and Stavisky. That day, the police picked up Zweifel and the other scattered accomplices, but looked in vain for Hayotte and Stavisky. They searched their offices on Rue Taitbout, went to the Café Cardinal and the Café de Madrid on the boulevard nearby, thought to call on cafés frequented by Romanians, all to no avail. Someone had tipped Stavisky off.

Ten days after issuing his warrants, Grébaud withdrew them, and just as suddenly Stavisky and Hayotte, as well informed as ever, turned up in town again. They reappeared on the *grands boulevards* and in the usual cafés. Stavisky and Arlette moved into a hotel near the Saint-Lazare station, and from there Stavisky went several times a day to the offices of La Jurançonne next to the Café Cardinal. He was back in business, and life returned to normal for a few weeks.[12]

Why had Grébaut withdrawn the warrants? Tipped off by Mme Zweifel, the police had found the remains of the Brunoy counterfeiting operation, the zinc plate on Avenue du Bois de Boulogne, the lithographic stones and smashed matériel in the villa, more than enough, they thought, to arrest and prosecute. And Mme Zweifel had designated Stavisky as leader and prime mover. Why should the magistrates relent now, with the culprit himself at hand?

Not enough evidence, Grébaud decided. With twenty-seven years as a magistrate behind him, the last four of them in Paris, he now handled some five hundred cases a year, especially frauds and swindles. This one did not look as though it would ever hold up in court. The only evidence was some wrecked equipment, no counterfeit paper—hardly enough, Grébaud thought, to convince a jury in the criminal court that any of the seven were guilty of forging public bonds. And attempted forgery was not punishable under the penal code. Prosecution would be difficult. A few weeks later Grébaud asked for a dismissal.[13]

This surprised and irritated the police inspectors, more eager than the magistrates to "snag," as they said, their man.[14] But the judicial retreat was routine enough. To prosecute or not to prosecute—the question arose daily, its resolution in the Republic made more difficult than ever by the newly assured status of the defendant, the jury, and the evidence itself. At times even the prospect of a partisan or excited citizenry gave the prosecutors pause: sometimes they feared scandal more than they coveted a conviction, and dropped the case.

Some twenty years before Grébaud withdrew his warrants for Stavisky, during the passions aroused by the anticlerical prime minister Combes—"the little Father" to the satirists—the chancellery flinched, now and again, at bringing recalcitrant or seditious priests before juries in devout corners of the land. Why pour oil onto the fires, and suffer some triumphant, resounding acquittal? But sometimes such forbearance rebounded against its practitioners, and the other side castigated the magistrates for their timorousness. Even when no passionate convictions came at once into play, a failure to prosecute, even a delay, could later recoil violently on the Palace of Justice. Scandals often began that way. In 1901 a banker called Boulaine launched a new sugarcane extract on the market, a sweetener called "l'Edulcorant." Like Stavisky's P'tit Pot, it turned out to be fanciful. A few lawsuits followed; Boulaine paid off the baying, panic-prone investors; the prosecutors dropped the case and the affair soon blew over. But in the press and the Chamber rumor had it that Boulaine had friends in the ministry, and for a moment a trivial legal delay provided the transgression on high that no accusation of arbitrary justice, no scandal, could live without.[15]

But early in April 1926 Stavisky was, as yet, no Boulaine. At first an assistant prosecutor in the public prosecutor's office, preoccupied that day with three other cases, misidentified him as a restaurateur on Rue Taitbout.[16] Grébaud called off the police, and the assistant prosecutor dropped the charges. Nothing yet suggested to them the breath of scandal that would one day again touch the Palace of Justice.

And neither knew that in the same palace, from Grébaud's very floor, a search was on for the same man. Labbé, the aggrieved stockbroker, had brought his suit on 29 March, and on 1 April Grébaud's colleague Decante, after conferring with Superintendent Pachot, had sent for Stavisky. The two investigations, one of the Brunoy counterfeiter and the other of the Paris stock swindler, had crossed in the night.

Sometimes the prosecutors in the Paris public prosecutor's office handed down five or six complaints against the same person to five or six different investigating magistrates. No system of canals there stemmed or controlled the flow of assignments coursing through the palace toward the investigating magistrates, who might learn only by hearsay or professional chatter that several among them were going after the same man. Then they would combine their dossiers and concert their efforts. But Grébaud never learned that Decante was looking into a different suit against the same man, and so never reconsidered leaving him at large. Nor did the public prosecutor's office itself. Stavisky slipped through their fingers — not, this time, through any skill of his own. But the more he observed the many moving parts of the Republic's tired legal machinery, the more he might learn to stall it.

For now, he still had to face the magistrate Decante and fend off the stockbroker Labbé. Zweifel, his accomplice, had not helped matters when the police arrested him after his wife had revealed the goings-on at Brunoy. They were still holding him on other charges when Decante summoned Stavisky. Zweifel told them all he knew of the Labbé operation as well—how he had assumed a false name and deposited large sums from Stavisky and even taken a furnished room to receive correspondence, all to build up Labbé's confidence, the better to defraud him. Later he told them about the Laforcade stock certificates he had watched migrate to Stavisky's busy hands in the bar of the Helder Grill Room. The evidence was beginning to accumulate.[17]

On the afternoon of 1 April 1926 Stavisky, at Decante's invitation, appeared at the door of his office in the Palace of Justice. With him was Maître Gaulier, his obliging little lawyer and confidant of nine years' standing. They sat and answered the magistrate's questions for hours on end. Night was falling when Superintendent Pachot came down the hall to help move matters along. The magistrate and the superintendent retired into a small room at the back to talk matters over, and there Decante decided to place Stavisky under arrest. But a minute later the suspect had disappeared. Pachot's demeanor, a sign from the watchful Gaulier, an ominous word overheard in the back room — some portent had unnerved Stavisky and awakened his dread of prison. He fled the palace in his black overcoat, a medium-sized man with chestnut brown hair, fine features, and a dark complexion, and vanished into the late winter evening.[18]

After that, he left traces of himself, no more. Decante issued a warrant for his arrest, Pachot sent out physical descriptions, and the Sûreté Générale closed the frontiers to him. But he always kept a step ahead of his pursuers, again informed, it seemed, by someone who knew as much as they did.

The concierge at La Jurançonne on Boulevard des Italiens claimed not to know of him. The room was still in Stavisky's name at the hotel beyond the Saint-Lazare station, where he and Arlette had stayed when he resurfaced after the Brunoy scare. Mail for him still came there, addressed to another lodger. Occasionally his father went to pay the bill. In Normandy, he was once seen driving the blue Rolland-Pillain with Hayotte, Arlette, and another woman. At Easter he was seen briefly in Montigny-sur-Loing in Seine-et-Marne, where a widowed aunt lived. But he did not stay there long. Before his flight he had rented an apartment in the seventeenth arrondissement, where a woman calling herself Madeleine Lemercier had ordered some restoration work. The police watched the place, and so, to their surprise, did two private detectives hired by a bank suing Stavisky. They had to ask the concierge who their unexpected coworkers were. But neither Stavisky nor the woman Lemercier reappeared.

Arlette could have told them where he was. Logically enough, they began following her. With her height and her full blond hair, the former model was distinctive enough. Besides, she was six and a half months pregnant. Her coat was crimson, with taupe collar and cuffs, or violet with an otter stole around the neck, and sometimes she crowned her head with a small beige chapeau cloche. They saw her at the fur department in the Bon Marché, where she consigned a coat of Hudson otter worth 7,500 francs and reclaimed a scarf of silver fox for 3,800. Stavisky's mistress and Stavisky's money, they assumed—and the furriers at the counter told them that the woman they knew as the elusive Madeleine Lemercier of the empty apartment was in reality Arlette Simon.[19]

Often Jean Galmot, the former deputy from Guyana up to his usual intrigues, could have told them where he was as well. Stavisky had entrusted handsome sums to him, at least six hundred thousand francs left over from the thefts and frauds that had now put him to flight. They continued to make plans, and the vista of Guyanese gold that Galmot still floated before Stavisky's eyes took on a timeliness all its own.[20]

Often Hayotte could have also told them where he was, because the two were keeping in touch. He found Stavisky in a terrible state, close to collapse, haunted by the prospect of prison: his father depended on him, the fugitive said, and would never survive it. He was going to disappear for a while. And, in the meantime, would Hayotte find Gaulier and ask him to do whatever he could to settle out of court with Labbé and the other plaintiffs? See what they would agree to? Afterward the two conferred through intermediaries or in person, outside and sometimes even inside Paris, at unaccustomed haunts like Georgette's *bar américain* on Rue Pasquier, to find their way out of the predicament and try their hand at the only game left to them, the game of influence.[21]

Lawyers

The game of influence, they knew by now, consisted of finding and retaining a new lawyer imposing enough to sway the other side—"a grand lawyer," Stavisky insisted. Gaulier did not take offense. Labbé and the other plaintiffs had retained their own notables of the bar, and Gaulier felt too young, too lowly, to cross swords or even skirmish with them. He therefore went to see Maître Marcel Caen, who for almost twenty years had worked for one of the most influential lawyers in town, Senator René Renoult.[22]

Renoult was a dignitary in the Palace of Justice, a public figure now aging along with the Third Republic itself. Perhaps the blood memory of the regime's troubled infancy ran in his veins. His father had fought for the Republic during the Second Empire, his brother took up the cause in time, and so did he, when he was barely twenty-one years old. It was 1888 and the fragile republican consensus was still young, threatened by the fall of President Grévy and by the handsome and seditious General Boulanger. The country, as one of its leaders said, could hear the hoofbeats, even if it could not yet discern horse and rider, and René Renoult, novice lawyer, republican, anti-Boulangist, declared his colors and began his political career.

His patrons came from the left. One, Charles Floquet, was another old republican of empire vintage, who had risen with Gambetta, founded a Radical group, the *radicaux de gauche,* championed the Chamber against the Senate and the executive, and dueled that year with Boulanger; old Radicals still hailed Floquet as a man who had remained faithful to the political ideals of his embattled youth. Another, Paul Doumer, already a Radical deputy, was an outspoken supporter of impeaching General Boulanger. With them Renoult founded the new Radical Party and introduced into the Republic's politics the weighty and often misquoted slogan, "No enemies on the left!"

Now, in the late winter of 1926, the Radicals embodied the republican consensus, Senate and all, peopled the Establishment, and had ever so many enemies on the left. They were the party of government, close to the middle way. Floquet had disappeared long ago, hastened on his way by the Panama Canal scandal, but Paul Doumer, en route to the presidency of the Republic and the Elysée Palace, occupied the Ministry of Finance on Rue de Rivoli; and René Renoult, Garde des Sceaux, now nearing sixty, ran the Ministry of Justice from its elegant seat next to the Ritz on Place Vendôme.[23]

Four times a deputy, twice minister of justice, once vice president of the Chamber and ever since 1914 senator from the Var, Renoult had continued his rise in Clemenceau's long shadow before and during the war. In 1920 he had abandoned the "artisan of victory," conspiring along with his fellow Radicals to deny him the presidency. "Some favors are so great that only ingratitude can repay them," Talleyrand had said, and Renoult's desertion of his political benefactor betrayed an unsteady sense of professional honor, which Stavisky's emissaries would test once again.[24]

When they came to him, he had already left Place Vendôme two months earlier, in March, during yet another cabinet shake-up. He was practicing law again. First Gaulier approached Maître Caen, who was to Renoult what Gaulier had been to Lévy-Oulmann back in 1917 when he met Stavisky—an occasional colleague and helper, more nearly a minion. Stavisky had fled Decante's office,

Gaulier explained, but moneys might be found to pay off the plaintiffs if they were interested. Perhaps Caen could get Renoult to approach their distinguished lawyers, too illustrious for Gaulier to reach.[25]

A few days later, Caen ran into the investigating magistrate Decante in one of the many corridors of the palace. Would he consider lifting the warrant for the fugitive Stavisky's arrest if they could reach a satisfactory arrangement with the plaintiffs, he asked. No, replied Decante, he would not.[26]

Thus they had to bring Renoult in, as Gaulier had asked. In his apartment on Rue de la Boetie, the senator began receiving the varied participants, including Hayotte, who left an envelope on the desk for him containing fifty one-thousand-franc bills.[27]

Were they hiring the lawyer, the former minister of justice, or the sitting senator? The law forbade deputies and senators from practicing many professions, but not that of law itself. Acts of 1875, already, and of 1887 forbade them from holding most paid civil service positions, and in time special acts excluded them as well from the railroads, the postal service, the Banque de France, and other operations in which the state had a say or more than a say; but no act excluded them from the bar. Lawyers became statesmen; Berryer and Dufaure, fifty years before the Third Republic, and Gambetta at its start, had practiced their oratorical skills in courtroom and assembly alike. How many ministers, how many paragons of the Republic of lawyers had defended criminals in flourishing practices outside the Chamber or Senate walls — Jules Favre, Jules Grévy, Waldeck-Rousseau, Raymond Poincaré. Renoult had distinguished company.

But should a man who had left Place Vendôme less than three months earlier be pocketing the fat honorarium of a fugitive from justice? Waldeck-Rousseau had taken one hundred thousand francs to defend an industrial magnate, Max Lebaudy, and that was before the inflation. As far as Renoult was concerned, lawyers established their own fees and his fifty thousand francs was a reasonable price to ask of a client being pressed for 7 million. He had nothing to hide. In 1926 he earned one hundred and seventy thousand francs in fees and he duly entered Stavisky's fifty thousand into his accounts, reported them to the authorities, and paid taxes on them in 1927. He lived alone, modestly, and who could pretend to regulate the honoraria his clients saw fit to pay him?[28]

Only—and here the profession's canons began to darken, its practices to vacillate—Gaulier, Hayotte, and Stavisky were not paying a lawyer to plead. They were paying an incumbent senator and former minister of justice to prevail on plaintiffs and magistrates to lift the arrest warrant, end the litigation, and somehow settle the debt. At least Waldeck-Rousseau and all the others had stood and argued before the bar, clients at their side. However palpable the litigants' grievance, however obvious the defendant's strategy, Renoult was trafficking in the intangible and the indistinct. He was selling his influence, for money of doubtful provenance.

Influence peddlers—whom Italian jurists were already calling *venditori di fumo,* merchants of smoke—saw their acts appear in the pages of the penal code in 1889, just as Renoult was beginning his career. The year before, in the absence of any article in the code defining the sale of influence, the court of appeal had upheld the conviction of a retired senator and general. He had started a dealership in official decorations, and promised, so said the courts, what he could not deliver. That was a swindle. But then the same court overturned an identical conviction, that of Deputy Daniel Wilson, son-in-law of the former president, who had likewise traded on his status to expedite the delivery of Legion of Honor ribbons. He had not made any firm promises, the court concluded, and had offered a real service, the product of a real influence. There had been no swindle, nor even any corruption, since article 177 of the code defined this as "the act of a public official who peddles his authority to perform or not perform a duty of his function," and did not treat "influence" as an attribute of office, elective or appointed. The ruling provoked much comment, even rekindled the scandal, one of the Third Republic's earliest, and urgently moved the Chamber and Senate to sharpen an unduly indulgent law. Now a clause had been added to article 177 to punish elected officials for trafficking in their influence, making it a felony for them to sell it and a misdemeanor for others to buy it. Still the law was fuzzy, the infraction difficult to spot, its traces obscure. Conviction required a double psychological proof, of the agent's desire and of the official's willingness to exchange cash for the occult powers of influence. If a professional service also governed the exchange, the demonstration was almost impossible. By 1926 the Republic still had few precedents to go by, none involving the crime concealed behind the service, and nothing yet barred an elected representative from practicing law during or after his tenure in office. It was no crime to be a former minister of justice or a sitting senator, and René Renoult agreed without much hesitation to approach the lawyers who so cowed young Gaulier, the lawyers of the stockbrokers and bankers intent on setting the justice system on Sacha Stavisky.[29]

Every Saturday morning, solicitors, lawyers, expert witnesses, arbitrators from the commerce tribunal, all the familiar belligerents of the moment would meet for an hour and a half in the palace and talk freely among themselves. That was often how they reached out-of-court settlements, and that was how Renoult tried to reach an agreement with Stavisky's persecutors. He would encounter his colleagues in the vast lobby and sound them out, and on 11 June he felt confident enough to invite Labbé's distinguished counsel to a meeting in his office. Gaulier came as well. They sat in Renoult's office and listened to him set forth the offer from his invisible client.[30]

Hayotte had conveyed it because Hayotte, without going into unnecessary details, had explained to Renoult that he was in touch with the fugitive, who acknowledged 3 million of the 7 million francs the plaintiffs were claiming, and proposed to pay it off at the rate of twenty-five thousand francs a month. He insisted that, in return, they allow the courts to lift the warrant for his arrest.[31]

Labbé found the proposal preposterous. His lawyers rejected the offer. The negotiations dragged on. One day in the palace Gaulier entered the wide Galerie Marchande from the main lobby and ran into the lawyers for the other side. He thought, wrongly, that they had reached some sort of agreement. So did Renoult, who now donned his lawyer's robe and went along with two assistants, also in robes, to the office of the public prosecutor, Abel Prouharam. Renoult told him that he was close to a settlement and asked the prosecutor to lift the warrant for Stavisky's arrest.[32]

The request was unusual but not illegal. Prouharam had never heard one quite like it throughout his long and brilliant career in the provinces and the palace. Now his friend and sometime superior, the former minister of justice, was making it, draped though he was in the black robes of his profession. Article 94 of the code of criminal investigation allowed an investigating magistrate to revoke an arrest warrant with the public prosecutor's authorization, and a few precedents established some jurisprudence, but Renoult's proposal seemed oddly in Stavisky's interest. Labbé, the principal plaintiff, had certainly never authorized it. Prouharam, slightly shaken, said he would look into the matter. It was three o'clock on Saturday afternoon.[33]

In his antechamber he encountered Albert Cauwès, who had headed the financial section of the public prosecutor's office for the past four years. Cauwès knew Renoult by sight and had seen him and his two assistants enter and leave Prouharam's office. And he knew Prouharam well enough to find him unnerved and preoccupied.[34]

Would he object to lifting the arrest warrant? Prouharam asked him. Never in his twenty-eight years in the profession had Cauwès heard such a proposal, not even during his missions on the mined terrain where politics and the law met—as parliamentary attaché when the Senate, transformed for the occasions into the High Court of Justice, had tried Senators Malvy and Caillaux for sharing wartime intelligence with the enemy. Cauwès was known in the palace for his puritanical rigidity. But Decante, still pursuing the man who had fled his office weeks earlier, felt the same way, even though in 1924 Renoult himself had appointed him to his present post. To Prouharam, he and Cauwès vigorously protested that lifting the warrant was unthinkable.[35]

"No, I cannot," Decante told him. Cauwès went further. Whatever the pressure put on him, he said, he would refuse. He would rather leave the financial section and move elsewhere. "It's annoying, it's annoying," the prosecutor Prouharam complained, "he's M. René Renoult, it's annoying." But he did not insist. He shook hands warmly with each and they left.[36]

Renoult did not insist either. The plaintiffs now told him that Stavisky's proposals did not interest them. He withdrew from the scene, his role played out, and kept Hayotte's fifty thousand francs. But he and others had left behind an aura of complicity. He had used his influence to protect a fugitive. And Gaulier, through Hayotte, continued to represent the fugitive.[37] Lawyers for private plaintiffs had toyed with the idea of subverting the public action against a compulsive, predatory, and insatiable swindler, and even the public prosecutor had not rejected the idea out of hand. Was this how the Republic's laws and liberties were meant to operate? And if ever the newspapers developed an interest in the affair, what might they make of it?

Cauwès, for one, had had enough. He went up to Decante's office and found him depressed and overworked. "This business is driving me into a brick wall," Decante had already told Superintendent Pachot, "demands of all kinds come up in my office, they importune me, they exasperate me." The two talked matters over. A few days later, Decante came down to his office and said that he feared more pressure from Renoult. Cauwès called Superintendent Pachot into the office and told him it was time to put an end to it all. "For you and for me," he added, "the situation could become unbearable." Find Stavisky, he urged.[38]

Journalists

Pachot, meanwhile, had not been idle, but matters had suddenly become ungovernable. He was convinced that someone within the prefecture of police was helping Stavisky elude his grasp, and he finally tried to get at the fugitive through his father. Earlier in that month of June he went to the apartment on Rue de la Renaissance and interrogated the aging dentist. Pachot had heard from his inspectors that Emmanuel Stavisky appeared to be living off the fruits of Sacha's swindles and that the father must know the whereabouts of the son. Decante decided to indict him for complicity and summoned him to appear in the palace on 5 June, a Saturday.[39]

On Friday morning the police found Emmanuel Stavisky's body by the hedge along the railroad tracks in Seine-et-Marne, near the house of his sister Esther. They identified him by his voter's card. He was well dressed, had his hat and glasses on, and still held a pocket revolver in his right hand. He had shot himself in the mouth. Unmanned by adversity, by his fright, and by his son's misadventures, Emmanuel Stavisky had outstripped Sacha's own flight from Decante and the palace, and had elevated with one shot the legal squabble of 1926 into a fait divers, a crime in the news, and even a miniature scandal.[40]

They moved the body to the family apartment on Rue de la Renaissance. There the police set up a discreet surveillance, thinking the son might put in an appearance. He did not. On Sunday a funeral procession took Emmanuel Stavisky across Paris to section 94 of the Père Lachaise cemetery and buried him in the small family crypt where his wife Dunia had lain for six years. Again the police watched and again the son failed to appear.[41]

But the reporters came. The suicide made the front pages of most of the mass dailies that week, and through them the son, now the object of newly unwanted attentions, also appeared on the national stage. Stories both accurate and imagined appeared about him during the next few days. He had been seen at the funeral but had escaped before the police could catch him, said *Le Journal* and *Le Petit Parisien*. No, only a rumor, he had not been seen at the funeral, said *Le Matin*. He was pulling off a new swindle every week, they announced, he always stayed one step ahead of the police in pursuit of him, had made an incredible escape from the palace. They told their readers of the Zelli's caper with Popovici in 1923. "Stavisky Don Juan," *Paris-Soir* baldly claimed, had always managed to slip from the hands of the magistrates and walk away with an acquittal. *La Liberté* spoke of an "affair," revealed by the "deplorable but sensational development" of the father's suicide. Then the story faded, a fait divers starved of *faits*. Some of the newsmen had heard of Sacha Stavisky and traded stories among themselves; one of them, an editor from the *Progrès de Lyon*, had even warned his friend Privat at the Eiffel Tower radio station about the new sponsor of "Journal Parlé." "He's a scoundrel," he had said. But they knew nothing of Renoult's efforts on Stavisky's behalf in the palace. And where was the villain? They could not keep asking the question day after day. Until the police found him the story would have to wait.[42]

Besides, other faits divers that month filled their columns. To prosper, to survive even, a mass daily now had to transform some incident obscure enough for competitors to miss into a drama original enough for them to follow. "True, this approach to faits divers," wrote one of its practitioners in 1920, "opens a paper to the charge of scandalmongering. . . . It's a way of misleading the public. But what can we do about it?" Ideas, doctrine, polemic, the historic arms of the press since Théophraste's *Gazette* in the seventeenth century, were giving way to information, and information, the conventional wisdom held, was "basically the revelation of fact, the rendition of spectacle." The freedom of the mass dailies had coincidentally withered their intellectual content, and there was no telling where the process might end now that new photographic technologies were just beginning to let readers see more and read less.[43]

Romanesque reporting, the search for scandal and the true-to-life novel, had already dominated some of the circulation struggles among the mass dailies of the Belle Epoque. During the Steinheil affair of 1908, when a former mistress of the late president Faure was accused of murdering her mother and husband in a house on Rue de Vaugirard, an editor from *Le Journal* stayed up nightly in a brasserie. At dawn he would buy the morning papers, measure their coverage of the affair with a long seamstress's tape, and exclaim that *Le Matin* had fifteen centimeters less than they or *Le Petit Journal* twenty-eight centimeters more. During the same affair, newspapers vied for the discordant confessions and revelations by the accused, who was finally acquitted a year later. Two journalists from *L'Echo de Paris* received one confession, *Le Matin* a second, *Paris-Journal* a third, and most of the others solved the crime just as privately, confidently, and triumphantly. Modern journalism, explained *Le Matin*, searched above all for the truth, and often, alas, had to resign itself to reaching it while the wheels of republican justice were hardly yet in motion.[44]

The reporter-policeman, product of the frequent marriages of convenience between two professions with much to offer each other, now appeared on the scene. Each informed for the other: the policeman on criminals, the reporter on politicians. One withheld the precious confidences, even hoarded them, the other lived by publicizing them. A Paris prefect of police was one of the best-informed persons in town, a practiced reporter one of the best detectives. Madame Steinheil herself hired a reporter from *Paris-Journal* to investigate her young butler, and *Le Matin* once confronted her with another suspect in its own editorial offices. A few purists on the far left or right—in La *Guerre Sociale* and *L'Humanité*, in *Les Nouvelles* and *L'Autorité*—condemned "the Sherlock Holmes of the mass press of scandal" and journalism's incursion into criminology. But they were fringe voices, unengaged, a trifle holier-than-thou. The press was becoming an industry, and such practices sold copies.[45]

The war and its aftermath only accelerated the process. The cost of newsprint, the devaluation of the currency, the size of the printing runs that Marinoni's new rotary press both allowed and required all imposed iron economies of scale. The papers had to maintain circulation or shut down. By the time the dailies discovered Stavisky, in June of 1926, six of them in Paris could command between five hundred thousand and 1.5 million readers each. Their readerships fluctuated in a precarious equilibrium, the fait divers more salable and the reporter-policeman more brazen than ever.[46]

On 6 June, the day after Emmanuel Stavisky shot himself in Montigny-sur-Loing, a taxi pulled up there at the Hôtel de la Gare. A couple went in, identified themselves as friends of the son, and began asking questions of the owner's wife. She sent them to the mayor, who sent them away. At the tobacconist's next door the stranger identified himself as a correspondent for *Excelsior* and pulled out a press card to prove it. Back at the town hall they finally agreed to tell him what they knew of the incident, and he produced another card, this one in the name of Police Inspector Bayard of the Sûreté Générale, the same Bayard who had known and probably used Stavisky before his flight from the palace in April.[47]

What was he playing at now? He had first intruded as a reporter and then fallen back on his true professional identity. The first perhaps he found more congenial, but it profited *Excelsior* little, for the next morning the shiny daily, photograph of Stavisky and all, revealed nothing that *Le Journal* had not shared with its readers the night before.

Inconsequential as an investigative journalist, Bayard had no luck as a detective either, and Stavisky remained at large. But not for much longer. As an inspector of the Sûreté Générale, with a writ running beyond Paris and its prefecture of police, Bayard was the man who arrested Stavisky when, the following month, they finally found him.

On the evening of Monday, 26 July, Edmond Pachot, the superintendent pursuing Stavisky, and Jean Galmot, the adventurer from the tropics who had befriended him, met in the cellar of the Brasserie Zimmer, amid the Alsatian fittings. The policeman already knew the former deputy; he had arrested him five years earlier during the calamitous rum affair; now he listened to him talk of Stavisky and Arlette.[48]

Galmot had left them the day before in their improvised hideaway outside Paris, a six-room house with a garden in Marly-le-Roi, a camouflage of suburban complacency. There the fugitive was keeping himself, receiving friends and associates, and issuing directives now marked by desperation. Arlette was about to give birth. But Stavisky was planning to go abroad for a while, and talked about it with Galmot until late Sunday night.[49]

Monday night, Stavisky thought, they were to cross the Swiss border. He would disappear, most likely into Galmot's Guyanese stronghold, until matters calmed down at home and he could pay everyone off. Meanwhile Galmot would continue to look after the war chest, or what was left of it, perhaps six hundred thousand francs.[50]

Instead, in Zimmer's beery cellar, Galmot turned him in to Pachot. Stavisky was in a house in Marly-le-Roi, he revealed, hosting a farewell dinner for himself in white tie and tails. His guests included Hayotte and his mistress, Ginette, and another woman, along with a Polish boxer and a hotel keeper from Le Tréport and their mistresses, and, of course, Arlette. A car was waiting to take some of them to Switzerland, and, if Pachot and his inspectors did not get there by midnight, they would probably lose their man along with the whole seraglio. Why, Pachot asked, are you telling me all this? To protect Arlette from Stavisky, Galmot replied—disingenuously, since his Judas kiss at Marly had neatly put away a burdensome associate, accommodated the powerful Paris police and left him holding the vestiges of Stavisky's ill-gotten gains.[51]

At eight thirty that night, as Stavisky was expecting Galmot, Pachot and his inspectors arrived instead. The prefecture had given him two of the finest cars, and the Sûreté Générale two inspectors; Marly-le-Roi lay outside the jurisdiction of the Paris police and neither Pachot nor the men he brought with him from the prefecture had any authority to make arrests there. The two from the Sûreté already knew Stavisky, had even used him as an informant once or twice—so fickle were the loyalties of Leroy and the ubiquitous Bayard. Obligingly, Germaine, the Polish boxer's mistress, opened the garden gate.

A festive dinner scene greeted them, revelry one minute and panic the next. They took an indignant Hayotte away, and pregnant Arlette, and Stavisky as well when Bayard finally found him cowering in a water closet. The others they released.

Pachot suspected that Arlette knew all there was to know about Stavisky and his ways. But her pregnancy was advanced, her obstetrician arrived, and Pachot agreed to send her under guard the next day to a clinic not far from her old school on Rue de l'Assomption. There, the next day, she gave birth to a son. If the child were to be stillborn, Stavisky had announced ten days earlier, he would kill himself.[52]

■

"The undiscoverable one is rediscovered," announced *Paris-Soir* the next afternoon, and attributed 10 million francs in swindles to him. "Sacha Stavisky, the swindler who stole 6.5 million francs, is finally arrested," *Le Matin* reported more soberly the following morning. The fait divers was back on the front pages. "Russian, effeminate, lascivious," *Le Petit Parisien* specified, "seducer, deceiver, insinuating himself everywhere . . ." None of his women, it added, had ever brought suit against him, not even the one from whom he had extorted forty thousand francs. And he had been naturalized only in 1923. *Le Journal* went further. "Don Juan or Rasputin?" it asked, and evoked just as breathlessly the ghost of Arsène Lupin, the gentleman thief outwitting the police whenever they drew near, and defying, like so many other heroes and villains of popular fiction at the turn of the century, the laws of nature and of men.[53]

"Criminal romanticism," soon to return to the new escapist novels, already pervaded the faits divers columns of the daily newspapers. Aveline, Simenon, MacOrlan, authors of mystery novels, soon began weaving crime, psychology, and fatality into widely read narratives of deviance. The Stavisky serial, in the summer of 1926, briefly transfigured the man, turned Pachot's and Decante's banal crook into the metro rider's master of deception and seduction. Reporters now pried into his love life. *Le Journal* gave its readers "The Love Story of Stavisky"—the conquest of innocent Arlette, once showered with pearls, now left only with a newborn son and the wreckage of her illusions. In the early days of August photographers caught her waiting outside Decante's office in the Palace of Justice. Stavisky was inside; she sat on a bench and waited to show him their son, Claude. Sudden magnesium flashes bleached her black dress and captured good bathos for the dailies, mixing glamour, temptation, and downfall.[54]

Then a shadow of scandal passed lightly over the serialized novel. *L'Intransigeant* reported a swindler in the Eiffel Tower radio station. Stavisky had run the "Journal Parlé," controlled its broadcasts to the unsuspecting listeners. A crook at the helm of a government-owned station? M. Privat, the concessionaire at the Eiffel Tower who had taken up Stavisky's proposals, thought he detected the hidden hand of his competition, of the privately owned Radio-Paris and its friends in the press. But he had to leave in disgrace, the victim, like so many others, of his own cupidity and of Stavisky's poisonous friendship. Jeanne Bloch had fared no differently in private. But Privat was almost a public figure, and a fait divers in the public sphere could easily take the name of scandal.[55]

A little later, *Aux Ecoutes* found out about Renoult's maneuvers at the palace. It was a weekly scandal sheet, made up of gossip, financial rumor, innuendo, and half-truths. No consistent political line distinguished its flimsy pages, on sale to the highest bidder, but its tone remained fractious, often latently hostile to whatever government happened to be in office. The founder and editor, Paul Lévy, wrote most of the copy himself in an office on Rue Volney with a staff of five employees. He was fifty years old, a thin-faced bachelor, and lived in a furnished room behind the Gare Saint-Lazare. Once, twenty years earlier, he had worked at the Ministry of Justice, armed with a law degree. He used to arrive early, rifle through the legal briefs and dossiers, and sell their secrets to the plaintiffs and defendants who hovered about the ministry and Place Vendôme. He tried his hand at finance, at the stock exchange, and soon left, trailing charges of embezzlement and swindle behind him. Later, *Paris-Midi* threw him out for selling off its scoops and stories before it could publish them, and *L'Oeuvre, La France, L'Intransigeant,* and *On-dit* in turn harbored him before he launched his own brainchild, *Aux Ecoutes,* in the spring of 1918.[56]

He took money from the Ukrainian legation to run an anti-Bolshevik account of the civil war. Just as quickly, he backed down under the Foreign Ministry's entreaty or encouragement. Lévy craved such attention, even courted opprobrium and rebuke; once he gave to the editor of *L'Eclair* a general's secret report on German rearmament, hoping to invite the kind of prosecution that could only boost his circulation. He campaigned against the doubtful, the controversial, and the vulnerable—against Ernest Judet the suspected spy and André Breton the surrealist poet, against Catholic charities and against banks run by his Jewish coreligionists who were too thick with foreign financiers. *Aux Ecoutes* was as jejune as its editor, as matter-of-fact in its venality. Little set it apart from all the other scabrous rags that had drifted about the stock exchange and the ministries, like *Paris-Bourse* or *La Guerre Financière et Politique* before the war, or *La Rumeur, Le Petit Bleu,* or *Bourse et Finance* since. But *Aux Ecoutes* enjoyed a certain vogue. It was infinitely shabbier than a mass daily, and its revelations and low-budget meanness could still bemuse readers, perhaps several thousand of them. Bunau-Varilla had taken thousands from the financier Raffalovich and the Russians to promote their bonds in his paper, *Le Matin,* before the war; he had pursued targets from the king of the Belgians to absinthe makers in campaigns that had brought him readers as well as money. What was the difference, except of degree?[57]

Now, in the late summer and early autumn of 1926, Lévy looked into the Stavisky story. He gave his readers a few vignettes from Stavisky's past. A dark theme emerged: the idleness of the justice system, powerless to quarantine the swindler or otherwise separate him from his victims, especially poor Jeanne Bloch. Then Lévy learned that Stavisky had retained one former minister, René Renoult, and that Arlette's uncle, the pharmacist in Blois, had retained another, his old friend Joseph Paul-Boncour, a socialist deputy from the Tarn. The two of them, *Aux Ecoutes* duly reported in October, were trying to quash the affair and smother the legal proceedings. "Everything about this affair is strange," it concluded, and fell silent. Stavisky disappeared from its pages.[58]

By then everyone else had dropped the story as well, but *Aux Ecoutes* alone had pushed it to the frontier of scandal. Who had helped Lévy? And why had he drawn back?

Behind most scandal sheets and rumor organs hid some patron or moving spirit. That autumn Superintendent Pachot himself investigated three typeset apparitions—*Bourse et Finance, Le Moniteur Financier,* and *Le Journal des*

Rentiers, which all touted, with impressive consistency, the offerings of the crooked old financier Henri Rochette, still busy in his office on Rue Saint-Lazare. Lévy did not act alone either. Behind *Aux Ecoutes,* providing money, support, and even premises, lurked Stavisky's nemesis, Jean Galmot.[59]

He had helped Lévy launch the scandal sheet in 1918 and had given him his apartment on Rue Volney. Thus Lévy waged a few campaigns for the adventurer, the first in 1919 against a former employer, now turned competitor and foe, the Chiris perfume company. Chiris on its side pilloried Galmot just as violently through generous subsidies to a mirror publication, *Les Potins de Paris.* Now Galmot did not want any trouble from the vengeful Stavisky camp, and Lévy obligingly published an exposé that camp would have rather avoided. Galmot had reason to threaten Stavisky and his friends, however subtly, and Lévy was playing his game. *Aux Ecoutes* became a weapon, the first wielded in that manner against the hapless swindler, but not the last.[60]

If Stavisky were ever to return to the fray and avert a comparable calamity, he would have to learn to play this game called freedom of the press. He would have to learn as well to exploit the recurrent torpor of the justice system, to play on its weaknesses and subtle servility, and to command for such strategies the friendship of the famous.

A senator who defended him, a deputy who informed on him; a magistrate who ignored him, another who pursued him; a broadcaster who promoted him, an editor who exposed him—with their Janus-like countenance of promise and threat, the elites of liberal society both beckoned and betrayed, welcomed and ostracized. And although Stavisky did not know it, the pattern of his adventures with them in this year of 1926 presented the premonitory but imperfect quality of a rehearsal.

Physicians

Now he languished in cell number 25 at La Santé prison. Five cells down, in number 30, across the way and around an oblique bend, resided his old associate Henri Poulner. Poulner had moved into his dank new abode ten months earlier. He was awaiting trial for forging national defense bonds, living in limbo, captive yet innocent. Stavisky now joined him. The investigating magistrate Decante could keep him there as long as he wished—an eternity even, for all the haste that he and the experts were showing. A court-appointed accountant was looking for all the errant stock certificates, going through Labbé's and Laforcade's records, trying to trace the hidden pathways of peculation. He had found some of Laforcade's certificates in the villa in Marly-le-Roi. But to find and attribute all the others took time. Meanwhile Stavisky waited in La Santé.[61]

He had made a new friend inside, a prison guard called "Victor Boitel." Alcoholic and corrupt, Boitel lived nearby and haunted a kind of halfway house for former inmates. Poulner and Stavisky, like everyone else, knew him as "Nectar," because he chattered oddly and compulsively about the virtues of nectar during meals in La Santé. Most likely he meant a terrestrial rather than a celestial beverage. He quickly reached a lucrative modus vivendi with the two new arrivals. He had easily learned to visit cells 25 and 30 unseen by his more upright colleagues, and now began to transmit a rich and altogether illegal correspondence between their occupants. Barred from communicating with each other, Stavisky and Poulner could still address letters to their lawyers, which the officials in the prison registry had the right to open. By common consent Nectar diverted each inmate's letters to the other until, for this extracurricular avocation, the administration fired him. He found work as a security guard at the Citroën works, but soon disappeared into the ranks of the unemployed.[62]

Stavisky was urging his lawyers to get him out. Marcel Caen, Renoult's junior associate, began to rouse himself again, now that his august senior colleague had washed his hands of the business, but Poulner, through Nectar the drunken go-between, advised Stavisky to get rid of him, to stop paying him. One of his letters went astray—Nectar's gaffe—and reached its titular addressee, Caen, who read its derogatory contents with mounting rage. But he was not accomplishing much anyway. Tireless Gaulier redoubled his efforts, and Arlette kept asking Galmot to pay up, fifty thousand francs at least, enough perhaps for Stavisky to post bond. Meanwhile M. Israël, the court-appointed expert, continued his exploration of Stavisky's finances with maddening deliberation. Months went by. In November the criminal court convicted Poulner of trying to use forged national defense bonds and sentenced him to eight years of hard labor. An old friend of Arlette's, who had found her the job at Coco Chanel's, came and warned her against Stavisky. He was unfaithful, she said. Arlette paid no attention.[63]

In 1927 Stavisky began to turn green. Caen noticed it when he called on him in La Santé. He was badly depressed and complained of stomach ailments. In July the prison doctor sent him to Fresnes, where the medical surveillance was less amateurish, and where in August the magistrate Decante sent a court physician, Dr. Paul, to examine the ailing prisoner.

Dr. Paul found him suffering from intestinal problems, but in no imminent danger. He thought an operation in order, but Stavisky refused. Back to La Santé he went, where in October Dr. Paul examined him again. He was wasting away, so feverish, emaciated, and weak that the guards had to carry him around on a chair. Dr. Paul concluded that his circulatory and abdominal troubles were so severe that he ought to be sent to a hospital or released conditionally to seek treatment on his own. He even diagnosed some kind of abdominal tumor. The next month the La Santé physician announced that they could no longer care for Stavisky and that he ought to be released, as Dr. Paul had proposed. "He's worsening daily," he told Decante.[64]

The plaintiffs—Labbé and company—objected vigorously, and the Chamber of Indictments, which had jurisdiction, saw the matter their way. There could be no question of releasing the man. But in November the investigating magistrate Decante assented. Stavisky might die tomorrow, he thought, even as the master accountant Israël pursued his interminable investigations. Once again the plaintiffs protested. But, at length, the Chamber of Indictments assented as well, provided that Stavisky post bail of fifty thousand francs. Arlette, Gaulier, and a few remaining friends managed to scrape the sum together, and on 28 December 1927, a spectral Stavisky left La Santé prison—sick, penniless, the law and its trials still chasing him, but once again master of his movements.[65]

So, in the end, after the financiers, the lawyers, the magistrates, and the journalists, another liberal profession just as celebrated by its friendly Republic, the doctors, had entered Stavisky's world, this time to rescue him. Had it acted honorably? He took poorly to internment, his terrors were perhaps self-fulfilling, and the doctors only recorded what their examinations revealed. Stavisky was a sick man. But once outside he seemed to mend quickly. Still he came to the doctors to help fight his battles with the law, in sickness as in health, in good times as in bad. Along with the others, they had their cupidity, and who better than he to exploit it? Out of the crucible of scandal, suicide, incarceration, and sickness he now emerged, phoenix-like, bearing new plans, new strategies, and even a new name.

THE FALSENESS OF NAMES

A great banker? He's the greatest of all! Artist, sage, judge, journalist? You are nothing. Banker, you are all!—Summation of Maître Campinchi for André Benoist in trial of Oustric and Benoist, criminal court of the Seine, 29 May 1931, in *Le Parisien,* 30 May 1933

The investigating magistrate Decante naturally asked the police to keep an eye on Stavisky, find out what he was doing and what had happened to his old ventures, especially Le P'tit Pot. What sort of life was he leading?

Stavisky kept regular hours, an inspector from the Sûreté duly noted. Daily he left the flat on Rue de la Renaissance at about ten o'clock in the morning, came home for lunch, left again at two thirty and returned at about seven. He rarely went out after dinner. No surgery seemed to have disrupted his schedule, and he crossed the street with the brisk step of a man untroubled by sickness, fear, or irresolution.[1]

He did not return to his old office on Rue Taitbout. And Le P'tit Pot, gastronomic fiction of the airwaves, was history. During Stavisky's stay in La Santé the imaginary consommé had finally expired. Early in 1927 only a secretary occasionally appeared on Rue Taitbout; in May a M. Delcambre, one of Stavisky's creditors, took the place over, and once in July he turned up to pay the rent for the ghostly premises; but by now, early in 1928, the office was closed and M. Delcambre, like Le P'tit Pot, was gone.[2]

Once, in the street, Stavisky ran into another former creditor. With an accomplice from a bank now closed, he had feloniously sold off about a million francs' worth of the man's stocks back in 1925. He now promised to repay the sum, but asked his former victim to stop calling him Stavisky. His name was Alexandre, he said, Serge Alexandre, and he showed him a rail pass, first class, in that name.[3]

And Arlette? She and Stavisky were married now, and lived with their infant son, Claude, on Rue de la Renaissance. The law had shown indulgence, as it sometimes did to glamorous women whose only crime, their lawyers would argue, was their pick of husbands. When they took her to the Molière clinic that day after Stavisky's arrest, the inspectors had even gone through her bags. But the public prosecutor's office had soon dropped the proceedings against her. Now she extracted from Stavisky a promise to behave himself and stay out of trouble.[4]

He still called on his old tailor, but only as M. Alexandre, and suits now came labeled for "Alex."[5]

In a café on Place Saint-Augustin he ran into Inspector Bayard of the Sûreté Générale, the same fair-weather friend who had arrested him in the house in

Marly-le-Roi eighteen months before. Bayard asked him if he would help him, provide him with information now and again, and Stavisky agreed enthusiastically. But he wanted to be called "Alexandre."[6]

He went back to Ciro's, a fine restaurant near the Opera. "Bonjour, M. Sacha," said the chasseur who took his coat. "You are mistaken," Stavisky answered. "If you know a M. Sacha, it is not I. My name is M. Alexandre."[7]

He had jettisoned his patronymic more to erase his past than to disguise his origins. No one now forcing open the doors of high finance could afford to observe the higher call of ancestry. Worse than foreign, his name was disreputable; not long before, it had darkened for a day or two the front pages of national newspapers; how now could its owner expect to command the reputation that brought trust, and the trust that brought lenders?

In finance confidence was all, and it often took its cue from the Republic. Confidence went to the appraisers and accountants who manned the Republic's lending institutions, the retired generals and ambassadors who dignified by their participation a private call for the public's money, and to the deputies and senators who with a word or a nod could bestow respectability on even the most doubtful entrepreneurs. Upon such beacons of reliability the new M. Alexandre now fixed his gaze.

False Gems, False Bonds

But he had first to raise some money, some venture capital, and he turned to the jewels of his predilection, however unpracticed his touch and amateurish his judgment.

One day before his fall he had noticed a plaque on the door of the building at 64, Rue Taitbout: "Henri Cohen, jeweler." Later he passed a plucky fellow on the stairs. "You are M. Cohen? Would you do me the pleasure of coming up to see me this afternoon around four o'clock? I might have some small purchases to make from you."

Henri Cohen was about forty. Some thought his dark looks and meridional insolence typical of his native Morocco. He had grown up in Fez in the Mellah, the city's Jewish quarter, where for centuries his coreligionists had cut and mounted jewels, sometimes massive, for sultans, pashas, and merchants of note. Now he lived on Rue Taitbout. He had moved into the building with his wife in 1921, after living in furnished hotel rooms for two years, victim like so many others of the postwar housing crisis. They lived in a little apartment on the third floor, just below Stavisky's expansive operations. Down the street, in a tumbledown building with leprous walls, surrounded by moneylenders, he carried on a small commerce on the side, a trading post in assorted articles of minor value—pottery, glassware, chocolates, and imitation pearls.

But in Stavisky's building he traded in gems. Sometimes, when appraising and negotiating, he threw objectivity to the winds. In fact, once or twice he had already run afoul of the law. In 1924 a court had convicted him of swindling and sentenced him to four months in prison, a sentence that was suspended. Now he came punctually to Stavisky's offices on the floor above him.

Stavisky took five or six thousand francs' worth of jewels from him that afternoon. He bought the expensive ones without a second thought, seeming to warm to their value, yet quibbled endlessly over the lesser stones—unperturbed by a price in four figures, distrustful of one in three. Cohen found it strange. They began to meet regularly.

One day in 1926 Stavisky disappeared. Cohen had no idea what had happened to him until a few months later when he read variations on the truth in the daily newspapers. Early in 1928 Stavisky reappeared, on one of his now rare visits to Rue Taitbout. He was planning to start a jewelry business, he told Cohen; did he have any advice? You will need money, Cohen suggested, to pay cash, if you want discounts from sellers. "Money I'll have," Stavisky announced, "I'll soon have lots of money, I'll have a rich backer."[8]

And that was the start of the Etablissements Alex. M. Alexandre planned to buy diamonds on the open market, set them smartly in the stylish mounts of the day, and resell them in boutiques in the spas, resorts, and coastal playgrounds of the bejeweled rich.

Nothing intrinsically fraudulent distinguished the conception or the enterprise, not even the imitation emeralds it soon began peddling, for everyone wore those and thought nothing of it. But very quickly the Etablissements Alex became a riverhead, the source of a flow of cash that coursed and swelled through a public savings institution and into the hands of M. Alexandre and his cronies, leaving alluvial deposits along the way. The scheme was simple, diabolical, and wholly subversive of one of the Republic's most hallowed lending institutions, its pawn offices, known as *crédits municipaux.*

Hayotte, Stavisky's eager partner, had unwittingly planted the idea in his mind. Money was short and one day in February 1928, soon after his friend's release from La Santé, he went to Orléans to pawn some silver at the local crédit municipal. He came away with a loan of 314,000 francs, an encounter with the crédit's treasurer, and a mental grasp of how the institution—half-bank, half-pawnshop—worked. It had its treasurer, Hayotte told Stavisky, and an appraiser to estimate the cash loan the pawned articles might command, as well as a comptroller and some *commissionnaires*—approved agents here and there who brought in the borrowers, engaged their valuables at the crédit in their own name, and kept a register of their own clients. This intrigued Stavisky. He thought it might be an idea for Hayotte or someone they knew to become a *commissionaire.* "And it will be fine." he added. "If I can, I'll find customers for you." That was where the Etablissements Alex came in. They would engage the jewels, real or fake, make sure somehow of the appraiser's goodwill, and turn the crédit municipal into their own personal cash cow.[9]

The crédits municipaux, all thirty-four of them in France and Algeria, lent about 100 million francs a year to the indigent, the straitened, or the embarrassed, who came in with their gages. They were bankers to the poor, descendants of the charitable pawnshops that had opened their doors in 1777 and that Sébastien Mercier had written about in his *Tableau de Paris*. In Paris alone, fifteen kilometers of "streets," walled by lockers, safes, and vats from floor to ceiling, traversed the pawnshop on Rue des Blancs-Manteaux. Before the war about 350,000 watches—one for every eight Parisians—found their way there each year, along with 60,000 wedding rings, 160,000 sets of sheets, 2,500 umbrellas, and bridal dresses and even an occasional gem from someone very rich, fallen for the moment on hard times.

No calculation of profit or gain, no usurious stratagem governed the dimly paternalistic body, only a tutelary concern for the deserving poor. They took whatever the appraisers would give them for their objects, and could redeem them at any time during the next year by repaying the loan and a small amount of interest. Or they could renew the engagement in the thirteenth month, for a fee; or finally, they could resign themselves to watching their keepsakes and heirlooms disappear forever at public auction. Whatever profit accrued to the pawnshops went to operating expenses or toward public welfare. They could also issue short-term bonds as needed to support their operations, but never, of course, in amounts exceeding the gages and deposits they currently held. The pawnshops, one popular weekly declared, provided a great public service.[10]

That much had not changed by Stavisky's day, but the forward march of liberal legislation and the financial individualism of the 1920s were imperceptibly transforming the character of the pawnshops. From beacons of republican philanthropy they were becoming instruments of commercial gain. Now most took private depositors, issued more bonds, and subtly changed their names to *caisses de crédits municipaux*—municipal pawnshops and lending institutions. And now the Ministry of Commerce, not the public welfare office, regulated them. A few worried that they had strayed from their original mission. The Finance Ministry even said so in internal memoranda. But none was yet known to have broken any law, attracted undue attention, or defrauded its clients and depositors, until Stavisky and his friends drove to Orléans.[11]

Stavisky asked Cohen to recommend an expert, someone who could buy and appraise jewels for the Etablissements Alex, and Cohen suggested his own father, Samuel. Stavisky began spending days, sometimes evenings, at their apartment on Boulevard Malesherbes, just off Place Saint-Augustin. That square had become the hub of his universe—there he had married Arlette, there he met Inspector Bayard from time to time, and there he sat up with the Cohens, father, mother, and son, and caressed and manipulated what precious stones they passed him. The building was Second Empire, its entrance massive and marbled, exuding an air of sober achievement. But Samuel Cohen's handsome apartment was all he had left, all that his checkered and rocky career had yielded him. Years earlier he had left the jewelry business to set up a cookie factory in Enghien, and had gone bankrupt. Now creditors pursued him, including two angry banks, one nearby in Saint-Denis, the other even closer on Boulevard Haussmann. Stavisky had no money either. Nor did Hayotte—even the car he drove, an American Erskinne, belonged to one of his mistresses. They were starting with nothing other than the remnants of Cohen's ties to other jewelers, upright or not. His apartment became the corporate seat of the Etablissements Alex, and soon enough their little operation began to grow.[12]

When Hayotte went to Orléans to engage his silver at the crédit municipal he met the director and treasurer, Fernand Desbrosses. They began to talk. Desbrosses was a wily old accountant, almost sixty years old, short and bent, a native of the town, who had worked in its banks since he was sixteen. He looked out distantly through glasses set heavily on his aging, clean-shaven face. By now, after six years running the crédit municipal, he had prospered moderately and enjoyed the respectable standing of a minor notable, a son of the Orléanais. He lent Hayotte the 314,000 francs. Soon their horizons expanded. Hayotte proposed that the crédit municipal widen its operations, appoint some agents and correspondents here and there, and work with the Etablissements Alex to bring in customers and their jewels. Later he brought Stavisky along. Desbrosses pointed out that the crédit municipal might not have the money on hand for the kinds of loans they seemed to envisage. "But that's of no concern to me," Stavisky answered, "you can give me cashier's bonds."[13]

And shortly after that, in mid-May 1928, Hayotte brought in one Henri de Saunois-Chevert to see Desbrosses. He was from Lorraine, and Hayotte presented him as the new president of the Etablissements Alex.

Stavisky had already met him at Garnier's restaurant, next to the Gare Saint-Lazare. De Chevert, as he was called, had fallen on hard times too, but still had some valuable connections, still dressed nattily, wore a monocle, and spoke winningly, glibly, and abundantly. During the war, twice wounded, he became an agent for military intelligence and retained from those years a few friends in the police, along with a penchant for the double life and its concomitant peculiarity, treachery. De Chevert prospered for a while in the volatile postwar real estate market, then lost it all in an art gallery. He started falling in with the unlicensed brokers of Stavisky's natural habitat. The two would have met sooner or later, but Hayotte forced the pace by bringing them together at Garnier's.[14]

It was December 1927, and Stavisky, just out of prison, was not yet calling himself "Serge Alexandre." He had assumed the nominal identity of Nectar, his drunken jailer at La Santé, and tried calling himself "Victor Boitel." That did not last long. Stavisky had debts and was on the verge of selling the furniture, the ornaments, and the unused dental equipment from his late father's apartment on Rue de la Renaissance. But he had plans. He wanted de Chevert to become the president of their new jewelry operation and simultaneously an agent of the crédit municipal in Orléans. I know nothing about the jewelry business, de Chevert objected. Not to worry, Stavisky and Hayotte told him, they would handle everything.[15] And they did: in the spring Hayotte drove him to Orléans in his mistress's Erskinne, took him to lunch with the directors of the crédit municipal at the Auberge de la Montespan, and set him up as *commissionaire*. Stavisky's name—by now Alexandre—appeared nowhere.[16]

That summer the younger Cohen, Henri, opened a small boutique under the ensign of ALEX in Le Touquet on the Channel, with jewels somehow scavenged by his father. So did Hayotte in Biarritz, in an old furrier's boutique around the corner from the casino and the Bay of Biscay. One more trader, one more jeweler by the sea—but at Le Touquet a neon-lit sign in the window proclaimed that ALEX engaged jewels at the crédit municipal of Orléans, and a door off the entrance hall opened directly onto a side boutique and the crédit's foppish agent, Henri de Saunois-Chevert.

Through de Chevert, the gentlemen of ALEX merely lent themselves the crédit's money. De Chevert kept up pretenses, but soon needed no customers at all. The crédit's board of directors did not need to see any, or any jewels, or their confectioners, or any appraisals. The board, as long as it still had confidence in its treasurer Desbrosses and its new business agent, de Chevert, only needed to see the accounts. Since Desbrosses took charge of those, the board might not ask any questions at all. And how many would think to question the probity or sureness of the Republic's pawnshops? In the end, once again, it all came down to a question of confidence.[17]

The little band now followed an ascending line of trickery, their meaningless jewelry business left far below.

As Desbrosses had told Stavisky when they met, the crédit municipal of Orléans did not operate on a bottomless treasury. For most of its twenty-five-year history it had handed trifling sums, perhaps forty thousand francs a year since he had taken over, to hapless citizens parting with sewing machines and first communion rings. How was it now to issue millions monthly to distant, unseen owners of diamonds and emeralds?[18]

Bonds, Stavisky answered again, bonds that the Etablissements Alex would discount to any bank or insurance company willing to take them and pay out cash in return.

One day in December 1928 Stavisky told Hayotte that he wanted 3 million francs from Orléans for a stock of emeralds. As always, he was pressed for time. Samuel Cohen had just bought the emeralds from Alfred Chiche, a leading supplier of imitation jewelry on Rue de Provence. Hayotte picked up the phone and called the appraiser in Orléans.[19]

Emile Farault, the appraiser, was a large, jowled, self-satisfied man who had spent most of his fifty-four years slowly amassing money. His face was sanguine, his short beard pointed, and his glasses heavy and imposing like those of Desbrosses. He said little and sometimes had trouble hearing. He came from a rich and reputable family in Vendôme. But since leaving the Collège de Chateaudun at the age of seventeen he had worked for his living, in a notary's office in Bonneval, in an auction house in Paris, and finally as the auctioneer in Orléans. He owned the house itself and lived modestly in an apartment over the auction block. Whenever a death in town left an estate to be settled, or a nearby landowner sold off the objets in the château, Farault was at hand. And ever since the crédit municipal opened its doors in 1903 he had appraised the assorted incoming gages before they went down to its vaults, taking, like Desbrosses, his commission of 0.05 percent along the way. By now he had squirreled away millions. But no suspicion or ill will came his way. The Orléanais thought him an honorable man, and when Hayotte called about his emeralds, Farault expressed some reservations. He said they should talk the matter over.[20]

Stavisky wanted Farault to accept a box, which they would seal in his presence—no stone-by-stone appraisals. "That seems awkward to me," Hayotte told him, "it's something I wouldn't ask of Farault." But an old friend of Stavisky's, Georges Hattot, happened to be around that day. Why could he not go along as the representative of the jewels' owner? "Fine," Stavisky said, "we'll tell Farault he's representing a Colombian owner"—loan seekers usually preferred anonymity, he explained.[21]

Hattot, as it happened, was an unemployed actor. He came from nearby, from the Faubourg Saint-Denis, where he had grown up in the 1880s. At twelve he left school and went to work in the butter and eggs stalls in Les Halles, and later, at eighteen or so, he drifted onto the stages of the Bouffes du Nord, the Théâtre Moncey, and the Théâtre Libre. Then he found his way into the first film studios of the Lumière brothers. Cinema was in its infancy and Hattot helped it grow. He made sets for the Lumière & Normandie company, built studios in Montreuil and Les Lilas, worked for Pathé, went back to acting at the Hippodrome, tried his own film business, and went bankrupt. The police thought of him as someone who would do anything for money, as an occasional swindler and fence. He was a great potbellied man, with an ample clean-shaven face and a voice that carried as an actor's should.

At the end of the war, still living on Rue du Faubourg Saint-Denis, Hattot wandered into the Cadet-Roussel and met Stavisky. The two struck up a desultory friendship and started running into each other here and there in Paris every six months or so. By 1928 Hattot was fifty-two and out of work, and Stavisky was calling himself "Alexandre." He had gallicized his name, he explained: "Sacha" in Russian was "Alexandre" in French. Stavisky also redeemed for Hattot and his wife some of their belongings from the Paris pawnshop and reengaged them in Orléans for a larger loan. Such acts from the heart drew and held Hattot as they had Hayotte, Poulner, and all who entered the magnetic field of Stavisky's charm. Now Hattot thought to repay the favor and oblige his friend.[22]

They all drove to Orléans. Stavisky, Hayotte, and Hattot sat with Farault in his appraisal office and Desbrosses the treasurer came too. Mixed in with Chiche's fake emeralds were some genuine stones, two mounted on rings and two set in earrings. These they gave Farault to appraise, and when he handed them back, he loosely agreed to estimate the value of the lot at ninety-seven carats and to let Hattot close up the box with a seal bearing his own initials for his rich Colombian employer. He and Stavisky had bought the seal at a stationery shop. They left with bonds from the crédit municipal for 3 million francs.[23]

It was all highly irregular—the presence of the borrower in the appraiser's office, the loose appraisal, the owner's seal on the box. But if Farault suspected dirty dealing he chose not to ask. He did not fully understand and could always claim that he had been had. He and Desbrosses pocketed their commissions, and Stavisky took the bonds to the Banque Jordan and the Banque Spéciale de Crédit, which discounted them and gave him the cash.[24]

Soon a rivulet of emeralds flowed alongside the Loire into Orléans. Chiche the jeweler gave them to Samuel Cohen, Cohen gave them to Stavisky, Stavisky gave them to Hattot, Hattot gave them to Farault, and Farault gave them to the lowly guard or warehouse boy to take down to the vaults. Most were entered in de Chevert's name, on behalf of the Etablissements Alex. De Chevert had become an automaton, signing away stones he rarely saw. But once, through an open door on Rue Saint-Georges, he was startled to see a heap of them sitting innocently on top of a table. Was it safe, he asked, to leave such precious gems alone? Samuel Cohen laughed. "Whoever steals them," he said, "won't make much."[25]

They were green and rectangular and came in all sizes. In February and again in April the band came back with more of them, about forty in all, supposed to weigh over five hundred carats. Hattot played his part, now representing the rich Colombian, now the Negus of Ethiopia, the distant land of ancient emeralds. He began to accept fees for his services—five, seven, twenty-five thousand francs, the last sum already higher than the annual salary of most civil servants. To those in the know it represented danger money. "For one hundred thousand francs I wouldn't do what Hattot did," Samuel Cohen said.[26]

In Orléans, Farault's commissions began to climb, but soon he grew nervous. He displayed an odd sense of urgency, a sudden need to cover himself. Have the stones appraised separately, he told Stavisky, we need some certified estimates to accompany my own.[27]

In May, therefore, Stavisky and Hayotte borrowed genuine jewels, had them appraised reputably, returned them, and arrived in Orléans with certificates in hand, affixed to the wrong jewels—a new lot of gleaming impostors. It was good enough for Farault. And for Desbrosses too, since they left with a loan of 8 million francs.[28]

In June they returned, bearing ninety-six emeralds. Most jewelers would have taken four or five hours to appraise so rich a harvest of gems, but Farault spent just sixty minutes. He took each stone and removed its red tissue wrapping, held it with pincers, examined it briefly through his jeweler's lens, weighed it, and inscribed its value on a small certificate of appraisal. Desbrosses transcribed his estimate onto the register, and Stavisky, Hayotte, and Hattot left with bonds from the crédit municipal for 10.4 million francs.[29]

By then they had engaged 155 emeralds and borrowed 25,714,000 francs against them. The world had never seen a collection like theirs. One day Samuel Cohen opened the deepest jewelry box in the world and showed a friend of his, a jeweler, its mine of iridescent green. "Look at that. . . . What do you think?" he asked him. His friend laughed. "Really, M. Cohen, if these emeralds were real, the fortune of a Rothschild wouldn't suffice." Everyone in the trade and some outside it knew that emeralds that year were rarer than ever. The Colombian government had suspended their mining operation after a succession of accidents; its concessionaire in Paris had never boasted more than three on hand at a time. Dealers in Paris, London, Berlin, Vienna, and New York—all the major trading centers—prized them singly and sought them where they could. The 155 emeralds sitting in the vault in Orléans, all thirteen hundred carats, could not belong to the Ethiopian Negus either, since their blatantly modern cut was plain to the rankest of amateurs. Had they been genuine, they would have fetched at least 80 million francs on world markets. As fakes, they were hardly worth the gasoline for the trips to Orléans. It was the most brazen of swindles, even if no one had yet been defrauded. The younger Cohen, Henri, began to fret. "It was folly," he complained, "to have engaged so many emeralds. There's no such quantity on the market."[30]

Undaunted, Stavisky went on selling the bonds to banks, to La Zurich, the Union Banque, the Crédit Lyonnais, and to insurance companies, to Le Soleil and La Confiance; when they matured he sometimes redeemed them with the proceeds of new operations, but more often he renewed them. Once he even took some of them to the Banque Française d'Outremer to reassure the director. He brought Hattot along, this time as an eventual buyer. "Aren't they beautiful?" Stavisky exclaimed as the director looked on. And Hattot warmly agreed.[31]

When time finally came to redeem the bonds—what then? Their holders could not renew them indefinitely and the emeralds in Orléans could not stay there forever—especially if anyone ever came to suspect that they were fakes and asked for another appraisal. In time the squeeze might tighten and drive Stavisky to ever more dangerous expedients, including outright forgery.

Did he know it? The arts of deception can beguile their own practitioners. A watchful operator at first, Thérèse Humbert, false heiress of the Belle Epoque, soon blinded herself to the dangers of her act and to the advancing day when her bankers would have to open the safe in her town house and find in it no Crawford inheritance at all. When the authorities confiscated and sold her belongings, she could not contain herself. "What an outrage," she said, "to have sold for nothing my possessions and my paintings!" A swindler postulated that some player would always join the diversion, always buy into the mirage, but the intricacies of the illusions soon entangled their creator as well. Like the blackmailer certain of his own redemptive mission, the swindler mistook plunder for property and vice for virtue. Exposure and downfall provoked the most self-righteous indignation. "My jewels are my personal property," Marthe Hanau insisted when the police came for her in the offices of the *Gazette du Franc* on Rue de Provence. They asked, among other questions, where she kept all the jewelry that had clanked about her the night before and that she had bought with her readers' investments. "I have no reason to tell you where they are," she added, with all the pharisaism and demented self-pity of one who by now identified her own good with the good of all. That was in December 1928, just as Stavisky, a few minutes away, was setting his eyes on kingdoms of indecent riches and boldly beginning to explore them. But he kept his wits about him and traveled, more often than not, in the shadow of his fellows. An acquired vigilance qualified his bonhomie, and Stavisky, smiling, genial, and winning, still seemed to those around him an instinctively wary man.[32]

Humbert and Hanau, like Rochette, Oustric, and Stavisky himself until he went to Orléans, had swindled persons, exploited private credulities and vanities. But Serge Alexandre now fancied institutions, faceless and impersonal, and risked public rather than private vengeance. If a consecrated custodian, a mayor, prefect, treasury inspector, banking dignitary, or police investigator should suddenly have it in mind to poke around the crédit municipal and open its books and its vaults, then officialdom might shine its unwelcome torch on the Etablissements Alex and their obscure creator. Behind the bondholder loomed the regulator, and keeping him at bay called for new riches to repay the old; and new riches called for new friends.

A False Company

Unlike the crédits municipaux, which enjoyed the blessings and boasted the guarantees of the state, private financial institutions spoke for themselves. But their operations were limitless, and less likely besides to attract the inquiring eye of public officials.

In April 1929 Alexandre and friends moved into splendid new offices in the heart of the ninth arrondissement — two floors, complete with boardroom, in a handsome town house standing behind ornate grilled gates at 28, Place Saint-Georges. They set up the Etablissements Alex on the third floor of the building, and on the second, with a room for secretaries, a kitchen, and a suite of offices for themselves, they quickly launched a brand new venture, the Compagnie Foncière et d'Entreprises Générales de Travaux Publics, or real estate and public works company.[33]

The idea for it came from a financial artist who brought to the table the baroque name of "Aramis Lherbier de Lestandière," a long history of bankruptcies, foreclosures, and evictions, and a bank of his own creation on Rue Vignon, the Banque Centrale Métropolitaine. Lherbier had already found some takers for the Orléans bonds, and now that the debt was climbing, he suggested a way to pay it off. Launch a new company, he told Stavisky, and issue more bonds.[34]

A land development company, a construction outfit that would bid on public contracts — something like that, and the task of defining it fell to a new employee of the Etablissements Alex, one Edouard de Cazenave. "Cook something up," Stavisky told him, draw up a charter, some shareholders' forms, minutes and proceedings, all the paperwork to make real a corporate fiction. Cazenave was an accountant, a modest, depressive young man of twenty-six without many means, intellectual or financial. At the time, he lived behind the Gare du Nord, but would soon divorce his wife and move back to live with his widowed mother. He marveled at so few jewels bringing in so many bonds and so much money. But M. Alexandre was paying him two thousand francs a month, and, asked in March to help set up the new company, the infinitely docile Cazenave drew up some papers and went with his new employer to Lherbier's bank on Rue Vignon.[35] Stavisky gave Lherbier 625,000 francs, or a quarter of the founding capital, as the law required. The banker gave him a receipt but made it out to Cazenave, whom Stavisky now asked to act as founder and principal shareholder of the Compagnie Foncière. A little later Cazenave learned that Serge Alexandre was Sacha Stavisky and that he had skirmished with the courts. But he thought the charges had been dropped. They issued five thousand founders' shares at five thousand francs each, and Cazenave bought four thousand eight hundred and forty of them, in his name, with cash from Stavisky. Then the apprentice quietly retroceded the shares to the sorcerer. Now, on paper, the lowly accountant was a director and principal shareholder of a land development and public works corporation. The money for all the shares had come from Orléans bonds.[36]

They called on Maître Robineau, the faithful notary on Boulevard de Clichy, and Cazenave gave him Lherbier's receipt and the statutes he had drawn up. The next day Stavisky quietly recovered the founding capital from Lherbier, who cooked the books and later burned them when his bank failed. But by then the Foncière was on its way.[37]

For appearance' sake they added other directors and shareholders. Stavisky's newfound riches had magically opened doors. He began to people his little boardroom on Place Saint-Georges with worthies of the Republic whose carriage proclaimed their rank, who doffed top hats, displayed rosettes on their lapels, and lent by their presence dignity and solidity to even the most airy of enterprises.

A member of the august Council of State, a treasury inspector, a mayor, an administrator of the regions liberated by the war, all retired; two old friends of Pierre Laval, then a senator, soon to be a minister again, and one former member of his cabinet; a government auditor—Cazenave was in good company. Later Stavisky added, for good measure, an elegant former Ecuadorian diplomat called Dorn y de Alsua, who dressed well and had signed the Treaty of Versailles on behalf of his distant country.

To enterprises like theirs, relying on names and appearances to make their way into the public eye, status signified survival. Marthe Hanau and Albert Oustric had each built their banks on the vanities of dignitaries, she by publishing interviews with statesmen as though they backed her ventures, undertaken solely in the public interest, he by co-opting a deputy, an ambassador, and a former minister. The game of appearances undermined industrial as well as political democracy, and gave rise to some curious inversions, in which the faces of the players superseded the rules of their game. René Renoult's robe became a means to subvert rather than uphold the law, the Foncière's board of directors an instrument to bypass rather than practice open competition; symbols became subterfuges, and the illusions of customers, the substance of the commerce.

The Foncière's new dignitaries all came to the inaugural meeting and paid in cash or by personal check for twenty-five shares each, enough to add a directorship to an already substantial curriculum vitae. How could so penniless a bookkeeper take so commanding a position among them, how could Cazenave dwarf such dignitaries? M. Alexandre represented the company, they understood vaguely, but Cazenave was its official spokesman, and when the new directors considered the reassuring imprimatur of each other's presence they kept still and observed the better part of valor.[38]

Friends, phone calls, and word of mouth had typically brought them here. A rumor had reached the ears of a retired general in their midst, Albert Bardi de Fourtou, a few weeks earlier. Alexandre paid him a visit on Boulevard Malesherbes where he lived, not five minutes from the Cohens' apartment, birthplace of the Etablissements Alex. The energetic financier pressed his plans on the aging general. But who will make up the board, the general asked, with whom will I sit, and he listened to Alexandre and liked what he heard: "Those are very good names," he said. The next day his good friend René Dardennes, one of Pierre Laval's intimates on the new company's board, sounded the same theme. "Come in with us," he urged, "you see people you'll be joining." But Bardi de Fourtou needed no urging. The Compagnie Foncière promptly added him to its distinguished directors.

Half-general, half-dandy, tall and well groomed, he carried his sixty-three years well and lived with a thirty-year-old mistress. The family was distinguished—the father a minister several times over, the son all Saint-Cyr and cavalry, a credit to his rank during the war. But recently, his general's stars had lost some of their luster. Abruptly and noiselessly, under pressure from his superiors, he had left the army after displaying unseemly, unmilitary greed. After the armistice he presided over the allied control commission in Bulgaria, a hybrid affair that mixed economic, political, and military responsibilities and invited a casual impropriety or two through its broadness as well as through its dominion. Bardi de Fourtou duly sold the captured matériel of the defeated army and placed the proceeds in a blocked French government account. But he seemed to confound the public treasury with his own, since the interest accruing from the government account somehow found its way into his. This the army's investigators soon noticed. They took a dim view of the general and his ways, but Marshal Foch considered his rank and record of service and settled for a reprimand. Bardi de Fourtou repaid the interest and quickly turned his attention to civilian life.[39]

No one dealing with the new Compagnie Foncière needed to know it, but the director's virtues never approached those of the general. For six years Bardi de Fourtou had sat on one company board after another, leaving each, more often than not, under some kind of cloud. No conviction yet dishonored his name, but once, to defend himself, he had had to employ Camille Chautemps, lawyer, sometime Radical minister, and brother of Pierre, who had once defended Hayotte's own father against multiple charges of swindling. Bardi de Fourtou brought name and rank but no expertise to the enterprises he joined; most of these financed construction or land development, and he climbed on board uninitiated in the recondite ways of capital formation and credit and bond issuance by which they kept afloat. Many of his codirectors knew no more than he did. Colleagues for a day, they trusted in each other's good names and agreed to the projects that more seasoned hands placed before them. Stavisky made Bardi de Fourtou the president of the Etablissments Alex and soon asked him to start handling the Orléans bonds.[40]

Louis Hudelo, the chairman of the board of the new company, knew nothing about finance either. No matter: he was well connected. He had just retired from the Ministry of the Interior after a distinguished career that had included a stint in 1917 as prefect of the Paris police. Delavenne, a friend of his on the city council and chairman of its public works committee, had called him in and told him about the new company. It's a public works company, he told him, you're still in good health and need something to do, join. Delavenne then introduced him to two contractors already committed to the Foncière and the city of Paris. For some 60 million francs they were to build the *îlot* number 24, a block of buildings rising on the city's edge by Boulevard Lannes, where the government had razed the fortifications built during the July Monarchy. One of the two contractors was also talking about developing something far off in Perpignan for the Foncière, but that was none of Delavenne's business. Paris was his construction site, and for now he seemed keenly concerned to confine the work to his friends. Hudelo joined the board of the Foncière.

One of the contractors had told him that some sort of jewelers' consortium, represented by a M. Alexandre, was financing the company. Hudelo already knew most of the other directors. Like them he received a stipend, supposed to represent a percentage of the profits, of three thousand francs a month, more even than his prefectoral retirement income of twenty-five hundred. But unlike them he was also drawing forty thousand francs a year as comptroller of the public housing office, an odd semiofficial position that made him an appointee but not a payee of the government, gave him a say in municipal construction, and closed the circle with the contractors, *îlot* 24, and city councillor Delavenne.[41]

So cozy an arrangement might one day have profited its makers and raised some eyebrows, had the Foncière ever built anything. But neither in Paris nor in Perpignan nor anywhere else did the new company raise any edifices or even sink any foundations. The vacant lot in Perpignan was worth 2 million francs at most, that in Paris not much more. Instead, the company issued bonds, and who could say where the proceeds went? As it happened, the gentlemen of Place Saint-Georges had abdicated their powers to the Foncière's energetic and persuasive founder, Serge Alexandre.[42]

Almost at once, in April 1929, they issued two hundred thousand bonds of five hundred francs each at 7 percent a year over fifty-five years, from 1940 on. In October they issued two hundred thousand more. And in November, to support the expanding operations, they issued fifteen thousand new shares, all purchased, once again, by Stavisky's compliant stand-in, Edouard de Cazenave.[43]

Some of the Foncière's directors had blessed such operations before. Charles Wurtz, the councillor of state on the Foncière's board, and Dorn y de Alsua, the Ecuadorian diplomat, also sat together on the board of a rail firm offering one hundred and twenty thousand bonds of five hundred francs each, under the sharp criticism of observers who did not widely share the company's view of its own financial health. Wurtz also sat on the board of an electric heating company then floating its third bond issue, forty thousand bonds at five hundred francs each, even after a disastrous year in which it had made almost no profit at all. Such extravagant proposals, out of all proportion to the corporate borrower's capacity to repay, were neither illegal nor unusual. In liberal eyes, the rational market best spotted irrational actors, imposing only transparency on all, so that anyone could compare a company's capital to its borrowings and pronounce the directors reckless or unwise. Knowingly releasing false information to attract investors or lenders was swindle, according to the law of 1867, and publishing inaccurate information even unknowingly was itself a minor infraction, defined in a law of 1907. But since then, the courts had allowed a measure of exaggeration in financial advertising. And no law defined financial folly. Most bond issues, unless mortgaged by property, were not guaranteed in any way. Their soundness was a matter of judgment.[44]

But the law did condemn the contrived acquisition of initial shares, so that the Foncière was illegal even before it began to publicize itself. This it now undertook to do, with self-promotion both brazen and cunning. "As of now," its prospectus declared, "signed contracts bring the company control and financing of major projects." The contract for Perpignan was signed but unpromising, the contract for the îlot 24 in Paris promising but unsigned. To guarantee the repayment of the first 10 million francs' worth of bonds, the company claimed, it had purchased and deposited at the state deposit bank various government annuities. The idea was unimpeachable, the guarantee illusory. The company passed over the volume of annuities. It had bought only 41,280 francs' worth, which would indeed, at 4 percent a year, precisely cover the first 10-million-franc bond issue—but only after fifty-five years, in 1984![45]

Announcements appeared in the *Bulletin des Annonces Légales Obligatoires,* the weekly that informed investors every Monday, matter-of-factly, of the latest offerings; brochures went out to bankers and brokers; advertisements ran in major dailies and financial weeklies. Samuel Jean Henri Astruc, a local publicity agent, had arranged it. Born and twice married in the ninth arrondissement, Astruc still lived there; he was one of its creatures, as much as Stavisky or Hayotte. He was by now a rich man, one of the largest distributors of financial publicity in the capital. That year, 1929, he sold more than 13 million francs of advertising, and 1.7 million of that was for the Foncière. Astruc found the directors reputable and M. Alexandre beguiling. He took their advertising copy and bought space for it in the newspapers, in *Le Temps* for twenty thousand francs, *Le Matin* for fifty, in *L'Information* for seventy-five, and in *L'Agence Economique et Financière* for a hundred.[46]

Most of these needed the money. So did the Agence Havas, the news and publicity agency that handled, thanks to a near monopoly, the arrangements with the major dailies; it lost 2 million francs that year. The press did not need to worry much about misleading or fraudulent content. The courts would not invoke the law of 1867 and its successors against them, or against intermediaries like Astruc, unless secret and collusive arrangements with the advertisers came to light. *L'Agence Economique et Financière* and *L'Information,* which now published the Foncière's sanguine communiqués, had each faced aggrieved investors whose appetites their advertising pages had once aroused, and each time the courts had dismissed the complaints. The life of the press could not hang on the good faith of the sponsors. Astruc knew this.[47]

He knew also that he had spent the Foncière's 1.7 million francs defensively as well as aggressively, on silence as well as space, to keep busybodies at bay and goodwill from turning sour. "Few journalists are unaware that in general a banker prefers silence to praise," Emmanuel Berl wrote that year. "In some papers, praise is the first indication of imminent blackmail. Here, truly, the saying 'silence is golden' means what it says." Years earlier Stavisky, during his dismal spring and summer of 1926, before the gates of La Santé prison swung shut on him and his story, had suffered the unwanted attentions of the press. No editors now openly threatened him with such intrusiveness. But it was best to propitiate these restless scavengers, to give before they took. Astruc's contract with the Foncière even said so, obliquely. In return for his fees, it said, "M. Jean Astruc undertakes . . . to attend to the goodwill or neutrality of the financial press." Neutrality, here, was benevolent.[48]

He paid financial weeklies such as *L'Information* sums out of all proportion to their circulation, in tribute to their discretionary power of harassment, exposure, and defamation. Their allegiance was for sale, and when financial scandal broke they obeyed rather than opined. This was a matter of record. In 1921, when the Banque Industrielle de Chine could no longer keep its follies and excesses secret, its friend and backer Horace Finaly of the Banque de Paris et des Pays-Bas came to its support. He orchestrated a press campaign on its behalf; he mobilized great mass dailies such as *Le Petit Journal* and small financial weeklies such as *L'Information,* and demonstrated with impressive ease the loyalty of his press. Such power began with the purse. The Foncière, not yet in a comparable predicament, needed no comparable savior, but Astruc had already bought the beginnings of influence for Stavisky, protection as well as promotion.[49]

In slender gazettes named *Pour et Contre, Commentaires,* the *Tribune de Paris,* and like-minded gossip sheets that cost nothing to write and almost nothing to publish, Astruc bought editorial silence, sometimes even without any concomitant advertising. He gave them eight, ten, twenty thousand francs each, just to avoid any trouble. They were blackmailers, a deviant breed of the journalistic species, living off the fears of their victims more than the curiosity of their readers. For two years the first among them, Georges Anquetil of *La Rumeur,* had indulged Marthe Hanau and her bank in his "Rubrique de la Bourse" column, so long as she bought half-pages of advertising or sent him payments of seventy-five thousand francs through their obliging intermediary, the banker Mimoun Amar. But now, in 1929, the two had fallen out. "My pen is at your disposal," Anquetil had proposed to her, and asked for one hundred and eighty thousand francs. She refused, and he began his campaign against her. "*La Rumeur* is a great lady," Anquetil told an official at the Banque du Nord. "Better to be our friend than our enemy." Stavisky and Astruc did not want any campaigns, by Anquetil and his kind or anyone else. They valued such friendship enough to pay for it. The Foncière launched its bonds.[50]

The directors, esteemed former servants of the public interest; the 7 percent interest, which was more than any national defense or other government bond brought; the construction contracts; the seemingly solid guarantee, backed by state annuities—what more could an investor ask?

A railway man in Périgueux and his wife sent for the Foncière's prospectus and studied it closely. Bardi de Fourtou, scion of a prestigious Périgourdin family, was on the board. The couple had fifteen hundred francs to invest and sent them by postal check to Place Saint-Georges. Three bonds came back, and the company began paying, every April and October, semiannual interest on each, seventeen francs and fifty centimes. A tailor in Lille saw the Foncière's advertisements in the *Echo du Nord*. Louis Hudelo, former prefect of Nord, was on the board—he bought twenty bonds. A state policeman in Louvres, Seine-et-Oise, saw advertisements and even some posters, and spent all his savings, sixty-five hundred francs in national defense bonds, on the new offering. It paid more interest, and General de Fourtou was in the company. The guarantee, the 4 percent 1918 obligations inscribed on the Great Register of Public Debt, reassured everyone, including the bankers handling the issue and the roving canvassers calling on savers and investors in towns and villages far from Place Saint-Georges. "A unique opportunity," the Banque Française in Dijon wrote to the mayor of Lux, Côte-d'Or, "an investment bringing you maximum security"; and the mayor sold all his shares in an enterprise of Albert Oustric, then under indictment and a cloud of scandal, and bought Stavisky's instead.[51]

In Paris callers to Place Saint-Georges paid their money or gave their coupons to a cashier downstairs and waited while a garçon was dispatched into the recesses of the building. The garçon went to a well-removed office at the end of the second floor, occupied by a self-effacing little man aptly named Henri Depardon. He was head of certificates and dividends, and gave out bonds in return for money, and interest in return for coupons. Depardon had worked in banks since he was fourteen, first in his native Lyons and then on the right bank of the Seine, and, now in his late thirties, was as fearful of reprimands and as anxious to please as ever. At the Union Française de Banque on Avenue de l'Opéra, he once so ingratiated himself with a man calling himself "Victor Boitel" that he heard from him when a new bank, the Société Foncière, opened its doors. "I'm not called Boitel anymore here, my name is Alexandre," Stavisky told him in a cathedral of an office. "As you'll see everyone calls me that." Depardon went to work at three thousand francs a month in the second-floor office, where the bondholders never came. He handed bonds or interest payments to the errand boy to take back to them below, and they went out past the gate and onto the square and Rue Notre-Dame-de-Lorette.[52]

A traveling salesman in Tunisia bought thirty of the bonds, a customs inspector in Saïgon forty. In Saint-Etienne, a customer came into a bank and showed the manager the Foncière's advertisement in *Le Mémorial de la Loire*. The banker sent for fifty copies of the new company's prospectus, and his customers began taking them away. They came back and bought two hundred and thirty-nine of the bonds. In the Somme alone the Foncière sold several million francs' worth. In Brest one hundred and five subscribers spent almost a million francs on them; some took just one bond, one took eighty-five. By the end of October the Foncière had placed 20 million francs of bonds in the market. It was a success.[53]

Aramis Lherbier de Lestandière the banker, Cazenave the accountant, Robineau the notary, Depardon the minor employee, the company's lawyers and all its directors, and the nation's press had also served Stavisky well, at the most propitious of moments. The bond market, just now, was taking off. It had stagnated or declined for most of the decade, shunned by investors steadily losing confidence in the value of their national currency. During and just after the war they accepted inflation as the cost of patriotism. But they shied away from fixed-interest bonds of all sorts, governmental or private, when peacetime prices continued to rise, the return to gold inexorably to recede, and the franc helplessly to suffer the assaults and depredations of the exchange markets—would it follow the crown and the mark? Now that Poincaré had stabilized the franc, investors were withdrawing funds from abroad, and interest rates, they thought, seemed bound to decline in the coming years. Bonds therefore regained their confidence. They had taken a mere 3 billion francs' worth in 1925; they took 13 billion francs' worth this year—1929, the year of the Foncière, Place Saint-Georges, and Stavisky's dizzying ascent to affluence.[54]

False Friendships

Along the way M. Alexandre collected friends, who brought more trust, which in turn brought more friends, with gathering speed and a hint of forward flight.

The Orléans connection brought him another senator, not nearly as grand as Renoult but far more desperate. For Auguste Puis, an Independent Radical from the Tarn-et-Garonne, the wolf was at the door, his creditors were closing in, and Alexandre was at hand.

His career in politics had been mostly quiet—once, in one of Briand's governments, he had served as undersecretary of agriculture, but now his voice, when he used it, died amid the bravura of the parliamentary stage. Puis, who was in his late fifties, parted his hair in the middle and waxed his mustache. He lived modestly, had no secretary, no car, and never traveled abroad. But he led another life, uncertain and disastrous. Most of the companies and banks he had founded or presided over now lay idle or bankrupt, victims of his optimism. One of his establishments had nothing left in its treasury, two others had ceased to exist, and a fourth, set up to sell anything to the USSR, including

61

defense fortifications, seemed at a standstill. He was not meant for business. Soon his problems drove him into the outstretched arms of moneylenders.[55]

"What headaches in my mail," he wrote to a friend on returning from a trip one day. "What threats of imminent seizure in the letters awaiting me." A dressmaker on Avenue de Suffren found lenders for him, whom he repaid slowly and painfully. In time he began paying in the one currency remaining him, his influence. He repaid one of his creditors with a job as cashier at the offtrack betting office, another with a contract for art in the metro. He also engaged family jewels at Sutton's, the London dealer, and when he heard of the Etablissements Alex he listened with interest.[56]

He learned of them from one of the self-styled lawyer-consultants, neither lawyers nor consultants but hirelings, intermediaries between straitened borrowers and bloated lenders. Jean Potier, a Marseillais of about fifty, lived with a prostitute just off Avenue de Clichy, frequented gambling clubs, wrote bad checks, and had, when he talked to Puis in 1929, no bank account at all. Through his dubious offices Puis pledged some family belongings—a Louis XIV tapestry, a traveler's *trousse*, assorted trinkets—against a loan from the crédit municipal of Orléans. As Potier was leaving, one M. Alexandre approached. He had noticed, this Alexandre said, the identity of the borrower, and would very much like to meet him.[57]

The senator and the financier duly met. Alexandre expressed his delight, and how happy he was to have been of service; Puis found him charming, every bit a man of the world, well connected and well presented. When time came to renew Puis's valuables, Alexandre quietly saw to the interest payments. Puis came to regard him as something of a friend, and began calling several times at Place Saint-Georges, where his unfashionably high wing collar bobbed incongruously among the flow of other visitors.[58]

And through the Société Foncière Stavisky met another member of Parliament, Edmond Boyer from Maine-et-Loire, no lawyer like Renoult or debtor like Puis, but a rich businessman. He was a republican archetype, a provincial success story, self-made yet inglorious. Now an imposing man with a graying goatee, he had found work in Angers in 1900 as a gardener, at the age of eighteen, and had married his employer's daughter a few years later. With the attendant dowry he had started his own landscaping business, prospered, moved on to public works, and taken on four thousand workers by the outbreak of the war. After the armistice he entered politics. He first joined the *républicains de gauche,* moderates who exalted laissez-faire, owed their election to their status as local or regional notables, and by now differed from the Radicals only in their dissent from the perennial anticlerical cause of secularism. So close was the Radicals' center left to their center right that Boyer, for a while, joined the "social and radical left," itself somewhere adrift in the Chamber's amorphous middle. The voters of Angers sent him to the Chamber in 1924 and again in 1928, but Boyer's destiny shrank there, and when Alexandre entered his life he had some worries at home. Intermittent run-ins with the taxmen threatened the land and buildings he owned all around Angers, most of which were heavily mortgaged besides. Perhaps M. Alexandre could help?[59]

Stavisky was trying to interest the deputy in a company the Foncière had just acquired, the Société d'Installations Mécaniques et Agricoles, or SIMA. The company had started out a few years earlier on Boulevard Montparnasse, hoping to sell agricultural equipment, but when Stavisky and the Foncière chanced upon it, the enterprise, though not yet wholly illusory, was manufacturing more stock certificates than farm machines. SIMA had become a house of speculation and casuistry: its image was its substance. Its advertising contract with Astruc's agency on Rue de la Bourse alone came to several hundred thousand francs, an expenditure so wildly incommensurate with sales as to alarm anyone who cared to ask. But no one did. The gentlemen from Place Saint-Georges had just paid Astruc over a million francs to promote the new Foncière. They did not think to challenge the lesser eccentricities and vanities of the company on Boulevard Montparnasse.[60]

Early in 1930 the Foncière moved its new subsidiary off Boulevard Montparnasse and into new offices at number 1, Rue Volney, by the Opera and the Café de la Paix. Stavisky began shuttling back and forth between there and Place Saint-Georges. He had a plan and, he insisted, an asset—SIMA's miraculous new refrigeration machine called the Phébor, which required no electricity at all. It would generate artificial cold, as they called it, by an odd combination of wooden insulation outside and ammonia gas and other congenial substances inside. It might appeal to farmers in regions without access to electricity, in remote parts of the countryside or in North Africa, if only it would work. This was a matter of conjecture and some contention. Yes, insisted M. Alexandre, but technical experts demurred and pointed out that the design ignored the fundamental laws of physics. The apparatus would never work, they claimed, but M. Alexandre ignored the Cassandras of the trade and went ahead with the Phébor.

Production started up somehow at SIMA's single factory in Tours, behind the train station, conveniently close to Orléans and its crédit municipal; shares were launched, advertising contracts signed, sales agents hired; soon some orders for the new machines arrived. Awhile later the first lawsuits started to come in.[61]

So Deputy Boyer prudently declined M. Alexandre's invitation to join the board of directors of SIMA. The company seemed shaky to him, especially this Phébor machine that Alexandre kept talking about. He declined, citing a possible incompatibility with his parliamentary responsibilities. Nevertheless, his name appeared on SIMA's list of directors, and Boyer, ensconced in his château between Angers and Saumur, still opened its gates to M. Alexandre. Who could tell? Some day they might need each other again.[62]

Besides, Boyer had already served handily: he had introduced Stavisky to his parliamentary colleague and traveling companion, the senator from the Vienne, Victor Boret. Former minister of agriculture in Clemenceau's wartime cabinet, director of a national society for the promotion of agriculture, onetime maker and seller of artificial ice in Saumur, Boret now became the object of Alexandre's assiduous attentions. Like Boyer, he had first prospered at home and had then entered politics, yesterday's customers handily transformed into today's voters, and had never strayed far from the pragmatic center. He was a Radical now and a stable presence on agricultural commissions in Parliament. What would Alexandre not give for Boret's cachet, for his endorsement of the Phébor?

They met at the Palais d'Orsay restaurant. General Bardi de Fourtou, M. Hudelo the former police prefect, and Charles Wurtz all came from the Foncière, along with other nameless nabobs from the business circles of the capital. Alexandre explained that he had capital, that financiers should help agriculture, that he had refrigerators for the butchers and innkeepers of the countryside—new refrigerators that worked without electricity, by "absorption." Boret guardedly expressed his interest; he thought them too heavy for the women who habitually stored perishable food, too thirsty for the water that allowed for the absorption of the ammonia; Alexandre acknowledged that the Phébor was still "mostly theoretical." Later Boret accepted an invitation to the factory in Tours, and there, as lunch was ending, Alexandre insisted that he join SIMA's board of directors. Our machine might not be quite ready yet, he granted, but we have orders for a million of them. Profits of 150 million francs! You've given us valuable advice, he told the senator, we would like to reciprocate by welcoming you to our board of directors.[63]

Boret declined. Like Boyer, he cited his parliamentary duties. He would only consider three great companies, he added rudely as well as inconsistently—the Canal de Suez, the Banque de France, and the Crédit Foncier. "Our company is as good as those," Alexandre insisted. But Boret held back. Neither law nor custom stood in his way; no proscription denied him a seat in the boardroom or the company of its enterprising occupants, only the exercise of official influence on their behalf. But he was not interested. SIMA looked unsound. Still Alexandre and he kept on the most cordial of terms, happily saluting each other in their correspondence: "Mon cher Ministre," "Mon cher ami," deference tempered with a hint of familiarity. Soon Alexandre stopped talking to Boret about agriculture and raised with him instead the infinite possibilities of the crédits municipaux. Rise or fall, the SIMA, like each of Alexandre's ventures, had been a stepping-stone on a road to influence, a road traveling through the Senate in the Luxembourg Palace.[64]

Within a year the SIMA had debts of almost 4 million francs. It had sold fifteen thousand Phébors, enough to provoke a steady stream of complaints, which the company strove meticulously to settle out of court, giving each its due weight and time. Suppliers demanded payment, customers repayment, sales agents their commissions. No lingering sense of decorum or etiquette held back their mounting rage. "It's all your fault, your machines are worthless," a customer shouted at Alexandre over dinner one night in Tours. "They reek, I tell you. You understand?" Indeed, the Phébor's more serious shortcomings included a malodorous insulation of wood and charcoal. The troubles multiplied.[65]

Still names, titles, and the holders of some small part of the public trust gravitated toward the doubtful machine and its untiring promoter, Serge Alexandre. He entertained them, courted them, and, when he could, hired them.[66]

One day Diagne, deputy from Senegal, came to lunch. General Bardi de Fourtou and Prefect Hudelo had invited him. They introduced him to M. Alexandre, and soon at table he was hearing all about the miraculous Phébor. It held out the promise of refrigeration, Alexandre explained, for the parched villages of Africa, and he offered Diagne the concession for the continent in return for a modest financial arrangement. And a deposit, he added. Diagne thought the machine of some possible use in tropical hospitals, and promised to study the matter. Later he learned that Alexandre was a felon called "Stavisky," and he spoke angrily and indignantly about it to the general and the former prefect who had inveigled him into coming. The Phébor never did arrive to cool the huts or the hospitals of France's African colonies, and a little later old Diagne died, his integrity intact.[67]

Emile Blanchard, by contrast, threw caution to the wind. He was a highly placed civil servant, the director of the agricultural services for Seine-et-Oise. But he also served as a technical consultant for SIMA, frivolously ignoring a circular of the year before from his minister, and indeed all the government, that prohibited civil servants from participating in private commercial enterprises. Blanchard did not readily grasp the idea that appointed and elected officials followed different codes of service, that the Republic held its functionaries to a standard it deemed impractical or even degrading for the elected representatives of the people. A deputy might practice law, gainfully pursue a career outside the chamber of the Palais Bourbon, even sit on the board of a company; but not a functionary. Blanchard was to reserve his agricultural expertise for the public sphere. But when the Foncière took over SIMA, Blanchard went to lunch with Alexandre and his friends. Soon he sat on SIMA's new board, owned some Foncière shares he had never bought, and received monthly stipends of fifteen hundred francs he had never requested. To his surprise and delight, he had become a director without spending a penny, and M. Alexandre welcomed him into his growing family. "Life will be beautiful as long as there are simpletons on earth," Stavisky remarked one day, and Blanchard was one of them, a naïf, a fool who had not yet committed the last of his follies.[68]

Each new ally might lie dormant for a while, gratefully savoring Alexandre's kindness before opening some hitherto closed door in return. Once, long after Alexandre had helped him in Orléans, Senator Puis arranged for him to meet the undersecretary of state for the merchant marine. The two went along to Place de la Concorde, and Alexandre explained the virtues of the Phébor machine, the ideal means for shipboard refrigeration. Every merchant vessel should have one, he said. But the undersecretary was not interested.[69]

Even the little man who sat humbly at the entrance to SIMA on Rue Volney represented a potential entrée to another guarded world, and reflected as well the catholicity of Alexandre's growing attachments. Emile Digoin demonstrated the workings of the Phébor machine to visitors still curious enough to call, ran errands for M. Alexandre, cashed checks, and did just about anything else that was asked of him. He still sported a rich mustache of the kind rarely seen since before the war, yet looked wan, twisted, and feeble. Various illnesses, including a nervous breakdown, had left him with a bad memory and defective hearing; he spoke inarticulately and laughed idiotically. Sitting in the doorway he seemed a poor advertisement for the troubled enterprise. But to M. Alexandre, his new employer, Digoin represented a peerless asset. He had just retired from the Police Judiciaire.[70]

An automobile dealer had introduced the two of them several years earlier, before Stavisky's *annus horribilis* in 1926. Digoin was an inspector at the Police Judiciaire, already thinking of retirement. He had grown up in poverty on Boulevard de la Villette in the 1870s and 1880s, had left school at thirteen, worked, spent fifteen years in the colonial infantry and the foreign legion. He had served in Cochin China and Tonkin and had gone along on the military expedition to Guangzhouwan in 1898, but when he returned to Paris, the best that civilian life briefly offered him was a job at a fishmonger's on Avenue Victor Hugo. So, in 1909, when Clemenceau ran Interior and was called the *premier flic de France,* the country's top cop, when his prefect of police Lépine was chasing anarchists and his constables and inspectors had not yet discovered the automobile, Emile Digoin joined the police.[71]

He had somehow passed the entrance exam, a competition that asked more of him than his formal education alone could provide, but amounted to a school diploma and an entry-level position. At 36, Quai des Orfèvres, the Police Judiciaire had almost eight hundred inspectors, and the newcomers among them, who now included Digoin, spent their early days and years there, at its vital administrative humdrum. They kept records, maintained files, searched for documents and official acts, followed up on fines, warrants, and summonses. Some moved up and joined the professional bloodhounds of the prestige brigades, the special, street, or mixed brigades. But not Emile Digoin. He started in a service routinely regulating furnished rooms, and moved on to one keeping records, where he and about a hundred other inspectors guarded 1.8 million files and 400,000 photographs, a living, organic archive of crime that was famous among all the police of Europe. There Digoin stayed.[72]

Along the way he had some trouble, since his professional ethics were not above suspicion. Superiors gravely suspected him of violations, of sharing, most improperly, the contents of files with their own criminal subjects. One such was Stavisky. Twice, during Digoin's early acquaintance with him, damning documents disappeared from his file. The check from Zelli's Dancing, so profitably transformed by him in 1923, left the desk of Superintendent Faralicq never to reappear, and the investigating magistrate Grébaud's arrest warrant in February 1926 vanished along with Stavisky's identity record. Such acts of evidentiary piracy, Digoin's superiors reasoned, pointed to some intelligence of their inland sea, and each time they suspected Digoin. Once they suspended him. But they could prove nothing. And Digoin pursued his friendship with Stavisky, who sent for him after emerging from La Santé prison in 1928.[73]

On Place Saint-Georges Digoin found jewels, tables, and dealers everywhere, a rich hive of activity, and a splendid office in which M. Alexandre, as he now called himself, received him. He had rid himself of his commercial foes, Alexandre boasted to his awed visitor, the ones who had plotted his arrest. Would Digoin like to take over his jewelry outlet at Le Touquet for a summer? He need not do much, just take care of the place and hold onto the keys to the safe. Digoin took leave of Quai des Orfèvres for August and September 1929, went to Le Touquet Paris-Plage, and ran the Etablissements Alex on Rue Saint-Jean. He collected twenty-five hundred francs for each month, no less than the Police Judiciaire would have paid him, and when he left the old place for good the following March he went back to M. Alexandre, who offered him the same salary at SIMA on Rue Volney. Now he sat in the entrance there, a *flic en bourgeois,* a cop in civilian clothing, selling revolutionary refrigerators.[74]

Thus did hollow enterprises draw in confidence-building politicians and functionaries, middling yet substantial figures, endowed by the Republic with status, though rarely with riches. On them Monsieur Alexandre lavished a charm calibrated to their pretensions, and repeated small but telling gestures, including the use of his car—now complete with its symbol of success, a chauffeur in livery.

The chauffeur, a Russian in his early thirties, had appeared one day to Hayotte and Alexandre in their office on Rue Volney. As an officer, he had driven armored cars in the czar's army during the war, and had been wounded and decorated five times; as a White, he had joined Wrangel's army at the end of the war and fought the Reds under General Koutiepoff; as an émigré, his family one more casualty of the new order, he had shared with others like himself the bread of exile in Gallipoli, Constantinople, Belgrade—where he had taken a degree in literature at the university—and finally Paris. There for a while he trained apprentice chauffeurs and tended to the Bugatti of the comte d'Harcourt, an amateur racer, soon killed in a crash in Morocco. Eugène Bortchy-Melnikoff was a survivor, and something of a snob as well. He found Hayotte rakish, and M. Alexandre so carefully constructed as to resemble some dummy from a tailor's window. *Nouveaux riches,* he concluded, as they haggled over salary and M. Alexandre demanded manners and a distinguished bearing. That day, behind the wheel of a blue and yellow Buick, Bortchy-Melnikoff drove M. Alexandre and Hayotte to Orléans and back. The next day found M. Hudelo of the Foncière in the back seat. He's a former prefect of police, Monsieur Alexandre told him, treat him with great respect.[75]

After that, Eugène always heard about the rank and standing of his passengers, the colleagues, guests, and friends of Serge Alexandre. In time, faces in the newspapers at corner kiosks also began appearing in profile in the rear windows of Bortchy's Buick, the fleet home of notables, and he recognized them with a start.[76]

Quickly he came to recognize his new employer's acts and affectations. Once, on the way to Deputy Boyer's château, Eugène listened curiously as M. Alexandre in the back seat lapsed with Hayotte into the unbridled vernacular of the streets. But once past the gate and on the château grounds, Stavisky effortlessly assumed the grace, measure, and dignity of the surroundings, and when Boyer emerged to meet him he walked grandly and solemnly up the steps with him.[77]

Bortchy-Melnikoff noticed as well how proud Alexandre was of a find, a brain wave, an inspector Digoin at the door of the office! "You see, Eugène," he said one day, "I only hire the best sorts."[78]

"As happens to idols, the image of a god is adored in his place," wrote an observer of the financial market in 1929. "Stocks and shares . . . have created a kind of confusion between property and paper title. And paper title has become too often a chip tossed onto a number."[79] Like his various bond offerings, M. Alexandre was all image and no substance, a maker of trust, but also sometimes of amends, a comfort and a promise to everyone who came his way. All sorts came and went through the door, poised grandees and slinking outcasts, Jewish diamond dealers and the most Christian of buyers. But M. Alexandre greeted all his callers with a winning tone and manner, attentive and appreciative, and unfailingly conveyed an impression that is the high ambition of good manners—a sense that he was taking great pleasure in their company.[80]

JUSTICE IN THE LAND OF FINANCE

De minimis non curat praetor. [A judge does not bother with trifles.]

"What an idiot he was, Oustric, to get caught," Bortchy-Melnikoff overheard Stavisky saying grandly. "I have two hundred million francs in debts and I live in the utmost tranquillity."[1]

Albert Oustric was Stavisky's age, had launched a bank that was all sail and no anchor, and enjoyed the company of friends in high places. The bank, which he named after himself, stood not ten minutes away from Place Saint-Georges and the Compagnie Foncière. When it introduced some Italian shares onto the market, a minister of justice, a deputy, a senator, and an ambassador all contrived to help. Once out of office the minister, Raoul Péret, proffered Oustric his legal services; René Renoult had done no less for Sacha Stavisky. Oustric's bank finally went under in October 1930, amid a storm of indictments and a scandal that soon sank André Tardieu's government as well. Oustric duly left his bank for La Santé prison. Later, the authorities released him on medical grounds, and he returned penniless to the reopened bank as a lowly employee at three thousand francs a month.[2]

"The big question," Stavisky went on as Bortchy-Melnikoff listened, "is to know how to arrange things. There's always some way to reach an understanding, with everyone!"[3]

And so there was, as long as he could penetrate the regulatory and judicial bastions of the state with charm, flattery, or the most convincing intercessor of all, an emissary from Parliament.

The Third Republic tolerated such incursions into its administrative apparatus. After 1815 the authoritarian machine bequeathed to the country by Napoleon already had to contend with an impertinent rival, Parliament. Deputies asked prefects to win elections, magistrates to drop prosecutions, ministers to appoint or promote protégés. During the July Monarchy, budget debates in the Chamber and scandals in the press exposed the administration's once-mysterious ways, even as its members came to sit among the deputies and respect their local concerns. A kind of modus vivendi between functionaries and elected officials developed by 1848, corrupt enough to weaken but open enough to embarrass a once-proud administration. The sweetness of administrative revenge under the Second Empire only raised the specter of Caesarism once again, and once they had laid it to rest the founders of the Third Republic set about peopling the old machine with officials of staunchly republican and secular loyalties.

But, after that, they declined to curb its prerogatives much further. Like their predecessors, they needed the administration themselves; no longer threatened, they came to prize and exploit the power they had once feared. Two legitimacies thus cohered, as in a marriage of convenience—that of the administration, founded by the constitution of 1799, and that of the Chamber, consecrated by the laws of 1875. Subtle compromises alternated with enduring suspicions; the appointed official resented the incompetence of the elected official, who in turn resented the unaccountability of the other, and usually accommodations took the form of courtesies from the former, benign neglect from the latter. Intrusions by deputies were frequent, investigations rare, and in this regime of universal ideals and particular accommodations the administration maintained its standing even while sacrificing its autonomy. Here lay an opportunity for a Serge Alexandre.[4]

By the 1930s, the administration, its mission but not its morale intact, was showing signs of stress. Career civil servants, underpaid, locked into positions that rarely led to promotion, and then only after long years of frustration, threatened, especially after 1932, by government cutbacks, lost heart. Even within their ministries they contended with mounting numbers of temporary newcomers, the auxiliaries and proletarians of the civil service. Such insults to a confirmed esprit de corps might finally leave a susceptible junior official, a *rédacteur,* or assistant bureau chief, vulnerable to subtle temptations that suggested nothing improper and only the best of intentions; and here too lay an opportunity for Serge Alexandre.[5]

The Timidity of Justice

He was still under indictment for the swindles that had landed him in La Santé in 1926. A court-appointed accountant had been sifting through the recovered stock certificates, bad checks, bank records, police files, and recondite documentation needed to reconstruct the obscure episode, and was signing his report, all several hundred pages of it, just as its principal protagonist recovered his freedom. A banker called Dreyfus was suing Stavisky in yet another pending action; it too was taking time; so it was not until July, two years after Stavisky's arrest at the dinner party in Marly-le-Roi, that the courts accused him formally of swindle, complicity in theft and receipt of stolen goods, and the issuance of bad checks.

Stavisky urgently sought to stall the suits. The loyal and self-effacing little Gaulier, who had acquired the services of Renoult the year before, now brought in André Hesse, like himself a lawyer, and like Renoult a former minister.[6]

Maître Hesse had run Public Works for several months in 1925, and during a short-lived government of July 1926 Herriot made him minister of colonies. Deputy from the Charente-Inférieure, chairman or member of legislative commissions on judicial reform, occasional legal counsel to government ministries, Hesse was a member of the parliamentary establishment, a discreet figure close to the summit. His credentials were so conventionally and unimpeachably Radical that militants in the party sometimes questioned his zeal. He had started out, and stayed on, the via media. In Versailles in 1902, during his first political campaign, he put up platitudinous posters calling for "neither left nor right," avoided incendiary topics, and attacked the nationalist anti-semites to his right and the internationalist CGT to his left. Now fifty-four, in 1928 he was as eligible for a ministry as ever. "Life is funny," he told the author Roger Martin du Gard. "The hard part is becoming minister the first time. Afterward, they always come back looking for you again."

As a young lawyer, he had joined the office of the great Maître Henri-Robert, had worked on some celebrated defenses, including that of Thérèse Humbert, the swindler and false heiress of the Belle Epoque, and had entered, by the eve of the war, the company of the dozen or so best-known lawyers holding forth in the Palace of Justice. André Hesse was a success, and when the insignificant figure of Sacha Stavisky crossed his path, he heedlessly added him to his long list of clients.[7]

They had first met in the gloomy visiting rooms of La Santé prison. Later, with Stavisky at liberty, Hesse arranged legal delays that brought liberty for the swindler, fees for the lawyer, and, later on, scandal for the deputy.[8]

Gaulier usually appeared in person to request the postponements of the hearings, but behind him loomed the larger figure of Hesse, "held up," as Stavisky's lesser advocate would explain, "in the Chamber of Deputies." Either the plaintiffs thought Stavisky might settle out of court, or the lawyers could not all assemble on the same day, or the court had the wrong addresses; but deliberately and wittingly, Hesse also set the medical profession, the judicial bureaucracy, and his own parliamentary cachet to work for his artful and elusive client.[9]

In March 1928 Dr. Vachet came to the help of his old patient and friend Sacha Stavisky. On Sundays the doctor still did his medical hour for "Journal Parlé" at the Eiffel Tower radio station. He also spent Sundays enthusiastically promoting psychotherapy in free public sessions. Stavisky, the genial doctor declared in writing, was suffering from an intestinal tumor and needed rest. He later certified that Stavisky was "afflicted by general paralysis," and that he "displayed speech difficulties, both muscular and mental." The magistrates could have observed that the free man knew few of the captive's torments, which seemed to leave him at the prison gates.[10] The creator of the Etablissements Alex and the Compagnie Foncière displayed perpetual motion more nearly than "general paralysis," and whatever intestinal growth the doctors had detected in the prisoner soon disappeared in the financier. But a hint of madness went a long way, especially when another court-appointed physician called for a neuropsychiatric examination. The men of the law yielded to the men of science. They began moving back the hearings. Slowly and inexorably, Dreyfus's and Labbé's suits approached the statutory three-year limit on the trial of correctional offences, and the extinction of the public action against Sacha Stavisky.[11]

Besides, they were overwhelmed. Squeezed into the southeastern corner of the palace, below an old turret and behind a sober facade that vaguely resembled a provincial town hall, even the chambers looked poorly adapted to the press of modern litigation. Every year the Paris prosecutor's office flooded the correctional courts with fifty thousand cases it wished to prosecute. The chambers daily found themselves trying to judge forty of these and sometimes more, in addition to twenty-five or thirty prima facie cases that the police brought in from the streets. With no jury to sway, and only three judges close by, defense lawyers avoided oratorical seduction, appropriate to the criminal court, but otiose here. And the magistrates of the correctional court judged more swiftly and convicted more often than the jurors of the criminal court. Still they could not keep up. One of the chambers, the tenth, devoted every Saturday to wine and aperitif fraudsters alone, and became known as the "Halle aux Vins," or wine market.[12] Another, the dark and drab thirteenth, tried to cope with the most substantial swindlers of the day. But it could not quickly bring Stavisky face to face with his several persecutors. The trial might last two or three days and would pit prolix lawyers against one another; some of them thoughtfully warned the court that their summations would be long. The mass of petty crime stymied the litigants and reprieved Stavisky, even promised that, when the day of the trial came, the court would once again agree to the postponements that the accused would not fail to request through his lawyers.[13]

One of those lawyers sat in the Palais Bourbon when not pleading in the Palace of Justice. André Hesse enjoyed influence, and sometimes spoke as though he controlled the courts. In its halls one day, on the eve of a scheduled hearing, he ran into the court-appointed accountant whose findings might damn his client. Don't even bother to show up tomorrow, Hesse told him. The court will put off the hearing.

And it did: swayed by the prestige of a parliamentary lawyer and the medical professionals he invoked, the court gave in, already weakened by the onus of current business. Influence had worked nicely.[14]

Tenacious as ever, Superintendent Pachot of the Police Judiciaire had not forgotten about Stavisky, but he had reached a dead end. The prosecutor's office investigation was over, a bureaucratic stalemate had set in, and a policeman like him, the auxiliary of justice, could only passively await another chance—a mistake by his man, a new crime, even a new investigation of an old one. Pachot summoned him and warned him not to return to his old ways, but Stavisky only shrugged his shoulders and smiled ironically. Pachot renewed his earlier opposition to letting this man travel abroad, but Stavisky went to the prefecture of police in the autumn of 1928 and recovered his passport anyway. The pattern set in, and the frustrated superintendent turned to other matters.[15]

Besides, Stavisky had a friend elsewhere in the police, Inspector Bayard at the Sûreté Générale. The pact they had reached was working nicely to his advantage. The informer fed the inspector morsels about the forgers, swindlers, illegal aliens, and drug addicts he frequented in their distinctive milieus, and received in return the protections that his own trade urgently required. Quickly Stavisky came to rely on them, and when they failed he reacted with hurt and indignation.

In November 1928 Stavisky, owner of a new passport, drove to Italy. On the way back French police detained him for several hours at the border, near Menton. The next day Inspector Bayard read all about his ordeal in a vexed and lofty letter: "Any recurrence of this incident would be unacceptable and, unwilling to face such vexations again, I would be grateful if you would kindly take all measures called for by this situation."[16]

Bayard obediently provided a letter of safe-conduct to charm, like an amulet, the life and travels of its holder.

"I authorize," he wrote on the letterhead of the Sûreté Générale, "Stavisky, Alexandre Sacha, born 20 November 1886 in Slobodka (Russia), director of corporations, residing at 5, Rue de la Renaissance in Paris (eighth arrondissement), a correspondent in my division, to invoke my recommendation, if need be to my colleagues."[17]

He looked after his protégé, shielding him when he could from the intrusions of officialdom. Once he even kept the Belgian police at bay. They wanted his man Stavisky, who had in his possession stock certificates stolen in Brussels. But Bayard knew nothing of the matter, he told his Brussels colleagues, and he so obstructed their pursuit that the stolen securities floated out into the great financial estuary of Paris.[18]

Stavisky also had Digoin, formerly of the prefecture, sitting in the window of the SIMA office. He and Bayard at the Sûreté complemented each other, even as Stavisky learned to play on the rivalries between the two services. In the train stations of the capital, agents of the Sûreté policed the outside, constables of the prefecture the inside; at the Elysée, the prefecture controlled the police, the Sûreté the official drivers; surely Stavisky could exploit such confusions? They were born of a spirit of administrative decentralization, liberal in its conception, and of the gulf between Paris and the rest of the country, and they now allowed the mouse to manipulate the cat. Stavisky could dispense with the influence he had brought to bear against the courts, and display the effortless assurance that came with a growing sense of the administration and its inner weaknesses. He was at last learning the ways of impunity.[19]

In the summer of 1929 Stavisky and Arlette moved to La Celle-Saint-Cloud, to a nice villa called La Forêt, which they rented from Gustave Téry, former editor of *L'Oeuvre,* for about twenty thousand francs a year. They were moving up in the world. They had an excellent cook and two maids, and a nurse for their son, Claude, and Eugène Bortchy-Melnikoff, the chauffeur, who drove Stavisky every morning to Place Saint-Georges in the blue and yellow Buick.

Stavisky and Arlette each had sumptuous wardrobes; they cultivated appearances with almost religious fervor, and heads began to turn when they appeared together in town. Stavisky tired quickly of his dress. Sometimes Bortchy-Melnikoff would park outside a tailor's on the Champs-Elysées and wait behind the wheel while his employer went in. Stavisky would enter in a gray suit and emerge in a brown one. Arlette, Mme Alexandre, spared neither money nor driver, and from La Celle-Saint-Cloud her White Russian chauffeur would drive her to a dressmaker, a furrier, a hatter, to Chanel and Jean Patou, and to Lanvin on Rue du Faubourg Saint-Honoré where, in two days in October 1931, she spent eighty-five hundred francs. Bortchy-Melnikoff piled hatboxes into the car, replaced missing stones for her bracelets at jewelers, stopped at the shops of seamstresses, boot makers, and florists. Stavisky paid. He seemed to crave the expense of it all.

Arlette took on airs, and treated the servants condescendingly. They did not like her; the cook, in particular, resented her incessant demands. But she had manners and style as well as looks, and her husband adored her. She had a second child, a girl called Micheline, and an intimate family began to flourish in the evenings, since Stavisky usually came home and rarely entertained at La Forêt. He doted on his son, Claude, showered him with gifts and toys, and the child clung to him in return as though to a life preserver.[20]

The Obscurity of Regulation

The first person to notice anything odd going on in the town of Orléans was one of its city councillors. They were all reviewing the budget of the crédit municipal for the coming year, 1929, a routine enough exercise until M. Aubin, the assistant mayor for finance, voiced his alarm at its size—18 million francs, versus 5 million for 1928. It supposed, he observed, a dramatic rise in the level of indigence in Orléans.

Aubin told the prefect of the Loiret, M. Génébrier, about the bizarre growth in the operations of the crédit municipal in his town; the assistant fretted over the actions of the treasurer Desbrosses and the dizzying number of bonds he was issuing. A little later, Génébrier received a visit from Stavisky and Desbrosses themselves.

Stavisky was clearly trying to impress the prefect, and he did—unfavorably. He spoke of plans to expand the crédit municipal of Orléans with capital flowing in from branch agencies in Cannes, Biarritz, and Le Touquet. The Ministry of Commerce, he added, was behind the project; he boasted of friends there and at the Ministry of the Interior, but gave no names. Génébrier was skeptical. He decided to phone the ministries and find out for himself.[21]

He asked Interior if it knew who this man Alexandre was, and his inquiry disappeared into the depths of the Sûreté Générale. No answer came back. He asked Commerce if it knew that the crédit municipal had issued many bonds and was planning to issue more, which it hardly seemed to need, and a functionary there expressed surprise at his intrusion. Crédits municipaux, he objected, were local organizations, outside the central government's domain. I am responsible, the prefect retorted, for communal as well as departmental administration—we are the guardians of the communes. The exchange ended there, sharply, inconclusively.[22]

The conscientious Génébrier had wandered into an administrative no-man's-land, an obscure zone that ministries, municipalities, and prefectures could squabble over and claim or disregard at will. The statutes and decrees that had defined and redefined the old pawnshops had also enveloped their liberal descendants, the commercial crédits municipaux, in an opaque regulatory muddle. The matter carried no great sense of urgency, placed few claims on a cabinet's time, because the modest establishments had until now stayed out of trouble and so had given none to public officialdom. If anything went wrong, the administrative ambiguities might exonerate the administrators, but they might also damn the system.

Who in Paris had jurisdiction over the crédits municipaux of the provinces, Commerce or Finance? A crédit municipal was a public institution, accountable to the government. Each year it sent its estimate of revenues and expenses for the coming year, its annual budget, to the district treasury receiver and to the paymaster general, agents on the scene of the Ministry of Finance. But oversight of their day-to-day administration had wandered like a bureaucratic nomad from the Ministry of the Interior to Hygiene and Public Assistance, to Labor, and finally, in 1926, to the General Inspection of Credit at the Ministry of Commerce. The migration seemed finally to settle their new entrepreneurial identity. But their place among the dispersed ministries of the capital still floated back and forth across the Seine, between Finance in the New Louvre on Rue de Rivoli and Commerce in the old Hôtel d'Argenson on Rue de Grenelle.[23]

The presence on the provincial scene of a prefect, and through him of the Ministry of the Interior, added to the uncertainty. The prefect's role left room for interpretation. He too oversaw the budget of the crédit municipal; he appointed its officers, or at any rate approved the nominations it proposed; he could inquire, advise, or reprimand. Such prerogatives conferred on him a measure of independence, but what, then, of the ministers and their ministries? Some insisted that the prefect drew his authority from them and might not act independently of them. A few maximized his discretionary powers. Others assimilated his role to that of the appellate Cour de Cassation in the administration of justice—he had a right, they felt, to administrative review over the form but not the substance of official deliberations. In a Republic built around a representative assembly and the powers it delegated, the prefect still raised the specter of Bonapartism, even in the untroubled setting of a provincial crédit municipal.[24]

Local politics and the chronic electoralism of the day added their distinctive note to the preoccupations of appointed officials. The town council also had to approve the budget of the crédit municipal, and town councils, since the war, had come to crave whatever revenues their constituents could generate. In 1926 the government had taken a few steps to decentralize the country's administration, even as it transferred responsibility for the crédits municipaux from Labor to Commerce. Combined with the inflation and rising social expenditures of the postwar era, the measure placed obligations on town councils that some were hard pressed to meet. The councillors of Orléans welcomed the growing contributions from the crédit municipal in its old warehouse by the docks; its rising profits had helped pay for the hospital, the boys' orphanage, and the charity bureau. They did not know much else about it, and approved its budget for 1929 in spite of Prefect Génébrier's irksome questions.[25]

Génébrier, meanwhile, had asked the crédit municipal itself for some explanation. But he did not torment it much longer. The Ministry of the Interior moved him from the Loiret to the Loire, and in February 1929 he left Orléans for Saint-Etienne. Before he left, he drew his successor's attention to the swollen budget and ambitious bond flotations of the crédit municipal. Castanet, the new prefect, began to watch the place.[26]

In time he too heard from Stavisky.

Word came in the form of a pressing letter signed by Auguste Puis, the straitened senator from the Tarn-et-Garonne whose tapestries, furniture, and bibelots Stavisky had generously helped engage in Orléans. The senator and the prefect had known each other for seven or eight years, since Castanet's earlier tours of duty in the Haute-Garonne and the Lot. Now Stavisky asked Puis to put in a word for him with the prefect in Orléans. Tell him, he instructed the senator, that the Ministry of Commerce is behind the crédit municipal and that important friends of Puis had interests there at stake. Puis's letter to Castanet followed. It did not shine for its originality. He insisted that the city council grant the crédit municipal its budget, said that the Ministry of Commerce had given its approval, and that time was of the essence. "But act on your own to speed things up," he added. "I've told you how many close friends of mine are involved, and that all is entirely normal." Castanet ignored the letter. His misgivings persisted. But he fell ill and died soon afterward. A new prefect, Jozon, arrived to take his place.[27]

Now the mayor of Orléans began to worry. Eugène-Maxime Turbat, aging, silvery, and dressed in a wing collar, sensed dangers, real though inexact. He feared some sort of crash, but dreaded public repercussions as well, and so never asked the local police to investigate the strange happenings at the crédit municipal. He preferred to unload his worries on the prefect. If the crédit municipal was a charitable institution, he had insisted to Castanet, it should confine its loans to the poor; if a commercial enterprise, as the Ministry of Commerce seemed to think, why should the city council become involved when the day-to-day operation was beyond its control? Prudently, the city council cut back the crédit municipal's budget for 1930, from 23 million to 12 million francs.[28]

Turbat too heard from M. Alexandre. This time, Stavisky resorted to the good offices of Edmond Boyer, the rich deputy from Angers who had received him in his château and was dealing with SIMA and the Compagnie Foncière. Boyer and Turbat knew each other well. The deputy had started out as a horticulturist in Angers, the mayor was still a horticulturist in Orléans, and a prewar collegiality between them had given way to a postwar personal friendship. Boyer had moved on to Public Works and the Chamber of Deputies, but when Turbat came to Paris he sometimes called on his friend Boyer at the Hôtel du Palais d'Orsay, where he habitually stayed, and they might lunch with other horticulturists who had come to the capital to defend and promote their trade. Naturally Turbat saw nothing unusual, one day early in 1930, when Boyer asked him to dine with two friends of his, MM. Hayotte and Alexandre.[29]

For most of the dinner Alexandre vaguely offered loans and public projects to the city of Orléans. He gave Turbat his card, and when the conversation turned to gardens, flowers, and landscaping, he asked the mayor-cum-horticulturist to send him his catalog. He had extensive properties, he explained, and might want to order some fifty thousand francs' worth of flowers. Then, as dinner ended and Boyer left to catch his train for Angers and his voters, M. Alexandre raised the subject of the crédit municipal of Orléans. Our good friend Desbrosses is the director, he said, the municipality is giving him trouble, and we would welcome your kind assistance.[30]

Turbat the mayor prudently held back; M. Alexandre struck him as extravagant. But Turbat the entrepreneur sent him his catalog the next day. He also made inquiries about him. The horticulturists' legal association replied that the man had a good reputation, but that he seemed not to direct the company he had founded on Place Saint-Georges, and that if he ordered fifty thousand francs' worth of flowers it might be wise to demand some guarantees before shipping them.[31]

Stavisky never did order the flowers, but he and Hayotte turned up in Turbat's office fifteen days later. This time Hayotte talked. He had already made his views known through Desbrosses, and now he came back to his blunt, crude arguments. The city had blundered, it should allow the crédit municipal to become a commercial establishment and to open branch offices elsewhere in the country. The loans-for-jewels business would go to London, leave the country; but the wary old mayor maintained that the crédit municipal was first and last a charitable institution. Finally Alexandre, silent till now, spoke up. You understand nothing about business, he told Turbat, you are badly mistaken in your judgments. Our operations, he added, will go abroad. And the couple from Place Saint-Georges, blustering Hayotte and studied Stavisky, left Orléans once again.[32]

From such local suspicions an unhappy moral emerged. A prefect might back down or disappear, but a mayor required an incentive. Surely somewhere they might find a suitably eager one. Before long, however, an octopus-like regulatory animal began to stir in the capital as well.

They had not been idle there either. Paris, like Orléans, was home to officials whose professional curiosity Stavisky and friends sought to transform into personal support.

Late the year before they had acquired a friend at the Ministry of Commerce, in the very office supposed to oversee the crédits municipaux. Farault, the helpful appraiser at the crédit municipal, asked a relative of his at the ministry to bring a colleague from the Inspection of Credit to lunch. M. Constantin was a capable but disgruntled functionary, passed over for promotion often enough to entertain compensatory attentions from outside the walls of his confinement. He had placed first in the civil service entrance examination of 1920, and now candidates who had finished well behind him were assistant directors and directors in their ministries while he marked time in his, still a mere *rédacteur*, not even an assistant bureau chief. He looked unimposing. Stavisky and friends took him to lunch at Drouant's, famed for its oysters and its wine cellar, and Constantin quickly fell under the spell of his host. Henri de Chevert, dandified president of the Etablissements Alex, impressed him with his monocle, facile speech, and diplomatic past. But M. Alexandre enchanted him. He told Constantin of the Foncière and its directors, its prefect of police and its inspector of finances, and exuded the essence of a Paris unknown and inaccessible to the junior official until now, a glittering cloud land of names and connections. How could Constantin resist his subtle flatteries? Alexandre seemed to ask little of him, only a vague promise of guidance, preferring, so he explained, to operate by the book. They lunched again. What had Constantin to lose?[33]

At work he was party to their cause, and expressed views they could only applaud. He drafted replies for his minister to send to Finance, which had joined the regulatory fray and challenged the notion that crédits municipaux could lend whatever they liked, without limits or controls. This was a dangerous doctrine, Finance warned, undermining the mission of the pawnshops, which were not granted tax-exempt status just to take in jewels and lend millions in return. But for Commerce their freedom to lend was absolute, and jurisprudence as old as the Third Republic tended to support the claim. Constantin helped assemble it. His superior at the Inspection of Credit, Léon Delamarche, agreed, as did Paul Maze, the director of the crédit municipal of Paris and president of the national trade association; and so did M. Alexandre.[34]

Commerce prevailed. In March 1930, the Council of State decreed that the crédit municipal could lend as freely as its incoming gages allowed. But the dispensation was small consolation to Stavisky and friends. The doctrine freeing loan ceilings still left the door open to the zealous regulators who might materialize at any moment: Finance, Commerce, Interior, even Justice and its police, if anyone dared venture where the mayor and the city's elected officials feared to tread—the Hydra-headed threat of an inspection was more than Stavisky could parry.[35]

Paul Maze, the president of the national association of crédits municipaux, also began receiving the uninvited company of M. Alexandre and his entourage. The association had no regulatory powers, but it could reprimand or even expel an errant member, a disgrace that any institution of credit preferred to avoid. Maze was getting wind of unsettling rumors about bonds, jewels, and the persistently gray eminence of the Etablissements Alex; serious crédits municipal did not shower bonds on financial agents to discount in banks. M. Alexandre called on him and insisted contritely that he only wished to operate lawfully. Later Maze suspected that his visitor had come on a reconnaissance mission, a sortie to see what sort of a man he was. Desbrosses, the director-treasurer of the crédit municipal, came several times. He usually boasted of powerful connections. Once he loftily told Maze that the minister of commerce would shortly receive Alexandre and some "parliamentarians." But he did not name them, and the ploy failed.[36]

Maladroitly, out of formation, the public powers advanced on the crédit municipal of Orléans. Their dispersion expressed an ethos, a distrust of concentrations of any kind, seeming to epitomize the virtues as well as the defects of liberal government. Hampered by the competing bureaucracies, the liberal administration had to move slowly in order to move at all. But the very redundancies armed it handily against subversion, since one agent of its power could proceed even if predators had undermined another. In a different day, Stavisky's fortunes in Orléans might have turned on the character, conscience, and attentiveness of the prefect there. To succeed now, a determined intruder would have to reach the source from which the many powers sprang, the elected representatives of the people. And Stavisky could find no senator or deputy, no Renoult, Hesse, Boyer, or Puis in Orléans, save the fanciful parliamentarians of Desbrosses's idle threats.

Thus, in July 1930, Hayotte and Stavisky beat a retreat. The Etablissements Alex suspended their dealings with the crédit municipal of Orléans, piously deploring the obstruction of the city council and the jealousies of the other crédits municipaux.[37]

But, like an ocean liner, regulation could not quickly reverse itself. Rumors flew of extravagant bonds secured by suspicious jewels.[38] Who could pursue, who could sanction? The Ministry of Finance, the prefect said. The prefect, the Ministry of Commerce said. Not I, the mayor said; but finally he asked the prefect to request an inspection from the Ministry of Finance.[39]

Prefect Jozon did, several times; slow as ever, the ministry did not react. In June 1931 Jozon appealed to the minister of the interior, André Tardieu, who also happened to be prime minister. Finally, the next month, a treasury inspector appeared at the door of the crédit municipal in Orléans. His name was M. Ardant, and he began by asking about the jewels in the vaults. He would like to take a look at them, he said.[40]

The specter of an Ardant, Desbrosses's nightmare, had already troubled the aging accountant's recent prosperous years. He had earlier panicked at the prospect of just such an inspection. Several times he had implored Alexandre to redeem the jewels in the vaults, entered into his books in the fabulous amounts for which old Farault had agreed to appraise them. "I am quaking in my shoes," he wrote him during the first of his crises in the summer of 1929, "I fear all that might happen." He wanted him to repay the bondholders, return the bonds, and recover the sealed boxes and their dubious contents—or face their exposure to everyone at a forced auction. "If you don't badger your bank and tell it that you urgently need funds," Desbrosses continued, "we'll be caught, and that means catastrophe."[41]

Once, Alexandre took one of the few real jewels in their possession to London, pawned it at Sutton's, and with the proceeds paid off a bondholder the next day. Soon after that, the Foncière started to yield its riches, and, with the new moneys flowing onto Place Saint-Georges, they paid off maturing Orléans bonds. The jewelry boxes, for now, dwelt in their cool sepulchral home. But another squeeze came in late summer 1930, as bonds were falling due and officialdom gathered its disorderly troops. Stavisky arrived desperate in Desbrosses's office. He threatened to shoot himself, said the fate of the crédit municipal hung in the balance, and begged Desbrosses to take the only step that could save them: to forge bonds outright.[42]

Unlike the earlier bonds, coated in their patina of emerald green, these came out of thin air, unsecured, unrecorded, unseen. On the stubs from the bonds and in his account book, Desbrosses entered the trifling amounts that Stavisky gave him, the characteristically modest offering of some local Orléanais bondholder, usually five hundred francs. He made the bonds out to cash; Alexandre filled out the amounts, usually in the vicinity of a million francs, and took them back to Paris, to the Compagnie Zurich and the Union-Banque. They gave him the cash and kept the worthless paper. Sometimes General Bardi de Fourtou donned his Etablissement Alex hat and took the bonds to the Soleil-Aigle insurance company. There his brother-in-law, the director, obligingly bought them. He made out the checks to the Etablissements Alex. Twenty-three bonds, the early bloom of Stavisky's frauds, brought him 22 million francs in this way over the months and appeared in the books in Desbrosses's hand as a sane and sensible obligation of 13,500 francs. In time, of course, they would have to redeem the bonds with new funds from somewhere. But for now they could use the proceeds to redeem the outstanding obligations in Orléans, disengage their damning trumpery from the vaults of the crédit municipal, and leave for the investigators only the least culpable traces of their presence.[43]

Therefore, when Inspector of Finances Ardant turned up on the steps, he was too late. Some emeralds remained, and he asked to see them. Desbrosses demurred. The owner had sent them from Paris appraised and sealed, he explained. Mayor Turbat, conveniently, was away, but his assistant Aubin told Ardant much the same. So did the prefect. The inspector went back to his ministry, but when he returned the boxes and the last of the emeralds had gone. Cash had taken their place. The mysterious owner had redeemed them and disappeared. Only the bespectacled Desbrosses remained.[44]

It had taken Aubin, Turbat, Génébrier, Castenet, Jozon, Maze, Delamarche, and now Ardant two and a half years to reach a bureaucratic impasse. It provided a sort of solution. The elected officials escaped scandal, the civil servants in the end reined in the crédit municipal, and the members of the national association of crédits municipaux expelled the lost soul from their midst and upheld in that way the honor of their association. But justice eluded them all. Imposing enough to frighten Stavisky off, but too slow to catch him, the lumbering officials had sacrificed the higher interest. Stavisky had slipped away. But only just.

Along the three coasts of France, ushers, chasseurs, and croupiers began to recognize Stavisky and Arlette as, intermittently and then seasonally, they began appearing in renowned casinos, restaurants, and hotels.

At first they returned to the Channel, the old haunt of their courtship. They spent the summer of 1928 at Le Touquet, in a rented villa named "All Right." It was more work than pleasure—Stavisky, Hayotte, and Henri Cohen were there to open the short-lived branch of the Etablissements Alex—but Sacha and Arlette both showed their faces in the local casino. By 1930 they were staying at the Negresco in Nice, and in the following year Stavisky, flinging money around like a newly anointed plutocrat of the waterfront, conquered with Arlette one fashionable resort after another.

Spring found them at the Hotel Plaza in Biarritz. They frequented the Café de Paris and the Bar Basque there, and Stavisky made a name for himself at the Casino Municipal and the Casino Bellevue by the size of the stakes he threw away on the baccarat table. They went to the Hotel Miramar in Cannes, and Bortchy-Melnikoff drove them up and down the Côte d'Azur in a dark green-on-black Marmon 879; and briefly to Deauville, and to the Atlantic Hotel in Saint-Jean-de-Luz for August and September. Stavisky spent 57,500 francs at the hotel, 38,500 of them in its restaurant, and much more than that in the casinos. In the Pergola he met any bet on the table and boasted he would break the bank at the Bellevue in Biarritz. He tried, and lost 2 million francs in two days. Such catastrophes conferred mark and even a little fame, though in time people began to ask where all that money came from.[45]

The Hazards of Prosecution

No secret lasted long at the Paris stock exchange, and before the Compagnie Foncière et d'Entreprises Générales de Travaux Publics was six months old a journalist learned a great deal that its founder saw little need to publicize.

His name was Mennevée, and he edited a small weekly called *Les Informations Politiques et Financières*. He filled its columns with the schemes and rackets he unmasked, and sold it to stock exchange watchers in Paris and the provinces. Some ministers and parliamentarians received free copies in their offices, sometimes even at home when Mennevée felt inclined to clamor for their attention. He knew the stock exchange and its ways, promoted himself vigorously, and presented himself as the avenging angel of the small saver. Most blackmailers wove a comparable cocoon of sanctity about themselves, but Mennevée was more muckraker than blackmailer. He lived more by revealing than by withholding the sins of his victims. Occasionally, like almost everyone else, he traded discretion for financial support, but for the most part he peddled scandal, and none knew better how to find it.[46]

In September 1929 an item in the *Bulletin des Annonces Légales Obligataires* caught Mennevée's watchful eye. A Compagnie Foncière was issuing the first of two hundred thousand bonds of five hundred francs each. But its founding capital amounted to only 2.5 million francs. Had it even been fully paid? To guarantee the bonds, the company announced, it had deposited through appropriate channels some fifty-three thousand two hundred and eighty francs' worth of 1918 state bonds at 4 percent per annum at the state deposit bank. This, thought Mennevée, was no guarantee at all. And the Foncière's bright prospectus seemed mendacious—how in less than six months could so many contracts, "the control and financing of major projects," fall into its hands, especially since the directors included one General Bardi de Fourtou, whose professional past was not above reproach? The Foncière was advertising its bonds in the financial pages of most of the major dailies, and Mennevée now boldly advised his readers to beware. "We can only counsel," he wrote in his first issue of October, "total abstention."[47]

Mennevée's article set off an interministerial altercation that, like the dither over Orléans, gave the Foncière some breathing space. This time the resistance came from the Ministry of Justice and from the very quarter that would have to investigate the Foncière, the financial section of the public prosecutor's office.

Five years in prison might await the bearers of a misleading or hollow corporate promise, as long as they were in demonstrable bad faith, since article 15 of the law of 1867 on public corporations assimilated them to swindlers. Therefore, officials at the Ministry of Finance sat up when they saw the Foncière's publicity and read Mennevée's revelations. The minister, the portly, energetic, and forthright Henri Chéron, quickly brought the matter to the attention of his colleague at the Ministry of Justice, Louis Barthou. He asked for an immediate investigation.[48]

But already the directors of the Compagnie Foncière were taking preemptive action; these directors were former senior civil servants so well connected that they knew of Chéron's note even before the minister of justice received it. One director was well acquainted with Pierre Laval—once deputy, now senator, twice a minister, and a flourishing lawyer as well—and took his colleagues, including Alexandre, to see him. Had the distinction between Parliament and the bar meant so much for René Renoult and André Hesse?[49] And another director, Hudelo, called on another old friend, the director of criminal affairs at the Ministry of Justice, to keep the inquiry discreet; he hinted incidentally at the name of Pierre Laval.[50]

Thus, when Chéron's inquiry about the Compagnie Foncière finally reached the prosecutor's office, the file was wrapped in mystery and taboo. Quickly it became known among the magistrates as "the Hudelo affair," the chairman's name being more consequential than his company's practices. Once again, title and influence blinded the servants of the public interest, and prominence cast its baleful spell over the Palace of Justice.

Discretion, for the head of the public prosecutor's office, was the better part of valor anyway, even without the dissuasive presence of Hudelo, Laval, and the Foncière's dignitaries. Prosecutor-General Donat-Guigue had just lived through the Marthe Hanau uproar. Almost a year earlier, the journalist Anquetil, the Mennevée of the Hanau affair, had attacked the fraudulent banker in the columns of his blackmail sheet *La Rumeur*. The same minister of finance, Henri Chéron, brought her to Donat-Guigue's attention, as rumors spread already in the financial press of the impending judicial action against her bank on Rue de Provence. It was on the verge of collapse, they said. The prosecutor's office investigated, searched the premises of Hanau's *Gazette du Franc*, and quickly arrested her. Clients cried they had lost any dwindling hope of recovering their shares, the Human Rights League denounced the illegal search and seizure, and the press revealed the names of Hanau's finer associates. Donat-Guigue had not heard the last of it, and still reflected with some melancholy on the hazards of opening an inquiry without a plaintiff. "I ask that you kindly examine this affair," he wrote of the Foncière to his public prosecutor, Georges Pressard, "and open a discreet inquiry"; and Pressard sent the instructions on to the head of the office's financial section, Albert Prince. "Very discreet," Prince wrote on the file.[51]

The fate of the Foncière now rested in the hands of a man as different as night and day from Mennevée, the journalist who had so noisily raised his voice against it. Albert Prince was a dignified and cultivated magistrate, withdrawing behind a reserve often mistaken for aloofness. He was an archetypal grand bourgeois, a scion of the Republic's own nobility of the robe, son of a magistrate of the court of appeal of Aix, son-in-law of a prosecutor general in Bourges. Early in his career, after his degree from the Sciences Politiques and his law doctorate in 1909, his superiors noted his eloquence, erudition, and perfect manners. Prince was a man of character, a thrice-decorated infantry officer whose service was cut short when the Germans took him prisoner outside Verdun at the outset of their offensive in February 1916. He spent the rest of the war in the gloom of the Black Forest, at a place called Vöhrenbach, where he studied the language and law of his captors. After the armistice, he returned to his books, his cello, and his ascent through the judiciary of his ambitions. Prince, though married and the father of two, was a solitary man; in the mornings he walked alone to the Palace of Justice from his apartment on Rue de Babylone, sometimes taking a detour through the Luxembourg Gardens. Probity, even moralism, lent a perceptible stiffness to his ways, but he entertained nicely, enjoyed the cinema and the theater, and liked a glass of beer in Montmartre or Montparnasse after a day at the palace. Often, in the early evening, his tall profile appeared among the customers and tables on the terrace of the Café Flore or at Lutétia, where the chasseur venerated his former commanding officer and slipped him, when he could, theater tickets at reduced prices. Prince was a bon vivant, measured but authentic.[52]

In the financial section he was overwhelmed. Assistant prosecutors helped him guide the flow of litigation, but an accusation, suit, or report came first to him and he made the initial, most delicate decision—to investigate a complaint or ignore it. And sometimes he had to make ten such decisions a day; sometimes Pachot alone sent more than ten reports a day from the Police Judiciaire. Each could take months to investigate, and the file could swell into a monster almost half a meter thick. Witnesses were heard, experts appointed, suspects summoned, and before Prince and his colleagues made up their minds, months might elapse and the object of their attention might disappear, the victim of rumor, opprobrium, and shareholder fright. To drop the matter, to caution the company quietly and move on, might serve the public interest best, if the wrong was slight and its correction easy. Did a misleading advertisement justify a capital sentence?

The financial section had emerged from the fifth section, which investigated ordinary theft, in 1912. It consisted at the time of a magistrate and a secretary only, directed to attend to the aggrieved victims of confidence men, fly-by-night bankers, and corporate fraudsters. After the war, flooded with complaints, the section expanded, and now Prince at its head had four assistant prosecutors to help stem, channel, or divert the river of litigation. They were not enough. Nor were the investigating magistrates, on hand to send out the summonses and hear the witnesses if Prince and his colleagues so ordained. The prosecutor's office had thirty-five such magistrates, and as many as fourteen of them were supposed to specialize in financial matters. But still their offices overflowed, the files backing up outside. The bankers and brokers of the roaring twenties, as they exploited the inflation, its attendant disorders, and the plight of those whose fortunes it had eroded or swept away, provoked more complaints than the section and the investigating magistrates could conveniently handle.

Still less could they aspire to a preventive role. To act before the damage was done, before a plaintiff sounded the alarm and set off the ominous prelude to panic—to anticipate and foil lay within the section's powers but beyond its means. Without instruments of detection or intelligence or oversight, it was at the mercy of a jealously independent police or, failing them, a public scandal. But by then the section was too late, a fire brigade arriving on the scene of a smoking ruin. Proposals to reorganize the section and provide it with the means for its mission, to arm it with administrative as well as judicial, regulatory as well as repressive powers, fell on deaf ears. Such talk undermined the very separation of powers that the Republic so ardently preached. "And you are from the land of Montesquieu!" a minister of justice once exclaimed to a boldly reformist deputy. "It's up to the Ministry of Finance to intervene," specified another representative of the people, himself a lawyer. It would not work, and the Chamber of Deputies that allowed its members to don lawyers' robes and wander the halls of the Palace of Justice would not hear of endowing the magistrates there with powers other than penal. This suited financial interests well.[53]

Louis Hudelo had obeyed just such considerations by diverting the file of the Foncière to the financial section and the desk of Albert Prince. Better the discreet judiciary than the embarrassing police, he had argued—disingenuously, since the former prefect of police knew that an inspector could inquire just as discreetly as a magistrate. But, poking around the offices on Place Saint-Georges, an inspector intruded more violently than did a magistrate sitting behind a crowded desk in the Palace of Justice. Hudelo counted more on the fatigue of the prosecutor's office than on its discretion, and trusted as well in the margin of difference afforded him by the least quantifiable of his assets, his name.[54]

"L'affaire Hudelo," Prince called it at once. He took the file to the department office of the section, which adjoined his own, and asked its head, Monsieur Geoffroy, to record the file and give it a number. But he shrouded its contents in secrecy, said nothing of them, answered Geoffroy's questions elliptically. This wounded Geoffroy's professional pride; he found it needlessly untrusting; odd, too, that the file had come into Prince's hands straight from those of the public prosecutor, bypassing his own. "You understand, Hudelo is involved in this business," Prince finally said. "I can't talk to you about it," and Geoffroy entered the file as "16.170L. Ministry of Finance-Hudelo." Thereafter, Prince himself tended the file. He entered in his own hand the documents as they came in or went out, returned the file to his desk drawer, and studiously kept Geoffroy and everyone else out of the picture.[55]

Prince made no secret of his wish to leave the financial section. He looked enviously on the rarefied atmosphere of the court of appeal and the "seated magistracy," where he might sit in sovereign judgment rather than stand in accusation, summon, pursue — and suffer the meddling of men mightier than he. Once he met Geoffroy in a café and complained openly to him. He was tired, he told the head of his department, of all the pressures and intrusions from influential parliamentary lawyers — tired of all the "affairs."[56]

For now, he could only carry out his instructions. Quickly, early in the morning when no one was around, he summoned Hudelo and Monod and heard their dim versions of the Foncière's operation, examined some documents the company had provided about its founding capital, bond guarantees, and construction contracts, and suggested, cogently but a trifle hastily, that prosecution seemed pointless.

He overlooked the incongruous presence of Cazenave, the lowly accountant who appeared to hold most of the founding shares. But no mention of anyone called "Alexandre" hinted at the mischief behind the Foncière's beginnings, and only an accountant, persistent and disposed to doubt, could expose the financial artifices of Stavisky and the banker Aramis to the light of judicial inquiry. Besides, the Ministry of Finance was complaining about the company's bond guarantees and publicity, not about its creation, and those, Prince thought, were innocuous enough. The claims about public contracts exaggerated the truth, he acknowledged, but an accountant could probably verify that the bondholders' moneys had so far gone into real rather than imaginary projects. None had complained. Legal action now might ruin the company. Drop the file, Prince seemed to say.[57]

Back up through Justice went his answer, to his superiors who had rushed the question on down, and who now agreed with him; and back to Minister of Finance Chéron, who did not. He questioned the bond guarantees again.[58]

Punctilious Finance now challenged pragmatic Justice, exalting correctness over forbearance and seeming preemptively to proclaim its own higher virtue. Enough that we find the fault; let the magistrates assume the risks of a sudden legal assault on a star-studded enterprise, and incur the threats and vilification that such actions habitually provoke. But Justice demurred in turn, and once again Albert Prince formulated its reply.

The Foncière had rectified its bond guarantees, he wrote, which was true: one of its lawyers had hastily withdrawn the annuity certificates from the state deposit bank and given them to La Confiance, the same insurance company that had taken some of the bonds from Orléans, as a premium to insure the bonds when they fell due fifty-five years hence. It was another illusory guarantee, but it satisfied the Ministry of Labor, which had a say in the matter, and it satisfied Albert Prince. All seemed resolved, he concluded. Once more his report gathered his superiors' support along the winding path of the prosecutor's office, entered the Ministry of Justice on Place Vendôme, left with its benediction to travel up Rue de Rivoli to the Ministry of Finance, returned riddled with objections, and landed back on Prince's desk in the Palace of Justice. It was March 1930.[59]

Only some newly damning secret could decide the issue. Who could disclose it? Hudelo had kept Pachot and his Police Judiciaire out, Justice and Labor folded their arms, and Finance awaited their action with studied indignation. But the journalist Mennevée, with an author's license, was still pounding the pavement around the stock exchange. He had called on the commerce tribunal and the justice of the peace and had examined the declarations that any new company had to make and that any citizen had a right to examine—including the names and occupations of the shareholders. Mennevée dwelt on the name that Prince had disregarded. Who is this accountant Cazenave, he asked in *Les Informations Politiques et Financières* in December. He is the sole shareholder. Where do his resources come from? And Mennevée pried a little and learned of Cazenave's modest income and rent. He is an intermediary, he announced in his issue of 10 February the following year, under an inviting headline:

THE MYSTERIES
of the
"Compagnie Foncière
et d'Entreprises Générales
de Travaux Publics"

Cazenave could not possibly have bought all those 7.5 million francs of new shares and paid cash, as he was obliged to do, for the first 1.875 million francs. Who was behind him? Must the public wait on scandal to protect its interest?[60]

Two days later, at three thirty in the afternoon, someone from the Compagnie Foncière called Mennevée's office on Boulevard Montmartre. Mennevée was out, and his secretary took the message. The caller said he was from the suburbs and proposed a meeting with Stavisky. He left no name. Mennevée haughtily rejected the advance, but left the door ajar, and declared in his next issue that he preferred signed and official letters to anonymous telephone calls. He was putting on the pressure.[61]

So baneful Mennevée threatened the Foncière while high-principled Prince shielded it. Names and titles emboldened the journalist and daunted the magistrate; one exposed, the other disposed; one tried to polarize, the other to resolve. The Republic unchained its journalists, however indecorous, but still reined in its magistrates, their freedom untroubled in theory but sometimes problematic and contentious in practice. Ministers of justice who publicly upheld the independence of the prosecutor's office privately apprehended, as nervously as their colleagues, the temper of the Chamber and the vagaries of an unknown quantity, public opinion. Prince, in his present post, enjoyed few of Mennevée's freedoms.

"What's happened in the end to the in-depth investigation that officialdom was duty-bound to carry out?" Mennevée asked in his issue of 31 March. "In any event, a clarification is essential and we're surprised it hasn't yet been provided." But a few days earlier, Prince had replied to the latest objection from the Ministry of Finance. Once again he declared the bond guarantees, now at La Confiance, satisfactory. "Under the circumstances," he concluded, "I deem it pointless to examine the details and for that reason I recommended in my report of 31 December that this matter could be considered closed."

His superiors at Justice, of course, approved every word. Albert Prince had given satisfaction.[62]

Stavisky and Hayotte, no strangers to the racetrack, were buying thoroughbred horses. In 1928 Hayotte had bought Cocochéri, Nadirshah, and Lost Friend for about fifty thousand francs in all. Between them they promptly won four consecutive races in Cannes and brought in almost four hundred thousand francs. The following year Cocochéri ran in Belgium. She won two handicaps in Ostende and the Grand Steeplechase in Warengen and another million francs for her proud and happy owners.

Excited, they bought a whole stable, thirty-six yearlings, from Senator Maurice de Rothschild. They paid out 1.5 million francs, housed the horses in stables at Maisons-Laffitte, and hired a trainer to look after them. M. Alexandre preferred to remain in the shadows and did not want the horses to run in his name. Instead, Dorn y de Alsua, the Ecuadorian diplomat, signatory of the Treaty of Versailles and member of the board of directors of the Compagnie Foncière, agreed to act for him and provide for the stable what the accountant Cazenave supplied for the Foncière, a name and a face.

Hayotte lit candles in the church of the Madeleine before races. "It will bring me luck," he said. Dorn handled most of the betting with a bookmaker and sometime furrier, Maurice-Moïse Zekri. When they won, Zekri went with cash in hand to the grilled gates at 28, Place Saint-Georges. When they lost, M. Alexandre gave him a check. Often Bortchy-Melnikoff drove them all to the races and back, to Chantilly nearby and Deauville and Ostende farther away. Afterward he contemplated the ruins in the rear of the car, the empty bottles, cigar butts, betting tickets, papers and hundred-franc notes strewn about like used confetti. "A real dustbin," he reflected.

Maurice de Rothschild's horses turned out to be no good. He had sold them his worst, and the trainer could not even resell them. The accommodations at Maisons-Laffitte began costing more than their disappointing guests were worth, and soon Stavisky and Hayotte had only memories to draw on, of the fine afternoon in 1929 when Cocochéri won the steeplechase in Warengen.[63]

∎

Years earlier, just after he had joined the financial section as an assistant prosecutor, Prince first heard of Sacha Stavisky. It was the spring of 1926, and his friend Albert Cauwès headed the section at the time. He told Prince about the fugitive, and about the efforts on his behalf by a former minister of justice, René Renoult. But Prince had little to do with the case. Soon the police arrested the man, and Cauwès moved on to the court of appeal. Now, in the spring of 1930, Prince headed the section, and he suddenly heard "Stavisky" again, an echo from his first days there.[64]

It first resonated in a new report from the Police Judiciaire. Pachot and his inspectors, unbeknownst to the Ministry of Justice, had reentered the fray, and pronounced the name in a way that Prince and all his superiors found impossible to ignore.

Pachot had finally acquired his own autonomous financial brigade. Driven by the Hanau affair and lesser scandals like it, Prefect of Police Chiappe and his director of the Police Judiciaire, André Benoist, had launched the new brigade at the beginning of 1930. It took its place alongside the other brigades on Quai des Orfèvres, the criminal, the mixed, the street brigades, and the various services that kept the records, hired the personnel, did the accounts, and generally kept "the old house" running. The four inspectors of the new brigade served the Paris prosecutor's office, and acted on paper like all their colleagues, as the auxiliaries of justice. But they also claimed to have a mind all their own and voluntarily, on occasion gratuitously, undertook discreet inquiries at their own initiative, even though their right to detain suspects without a warrant from the prosecutor's office was a matter of some contention. Just such an inquiry now revealed the presence of Stavisky behind the Compagnie Foncière.[65]

Tipsters and confidants, the correspondents of the new brigade's inspectors, roved through the stock exchange and its surrounding province. Former colleagues from Quai des Orfèvres, now retired, had already moved up there; one of them investigated commercial establishments for Albert Oustric's bank on Rue Chauchat, and that March, a month after the creation of the brigade, Emile Digoin left the records service and went to work for Stavisky in the offices of SIMA on Rue Volney. Bankers of standing and renown, sitting behind desks in the Banque Morgan, the Banque de France, the Banque Nationale de Crédit, and the Union Parisienne, paid five, fifty, a hundred thousand francs into the paid services fund of the Police Judiciaire, incited by former police in their employ or moved by a recurrent sense of obligation toward the pursuers of counterfeiters and check forgers. It was a gesture openly recorded, a customary kindness. Bank directors who later ran afoul of the law accommodated police directors with more dubious personal favors. Oustric once met the very man who had set up the new brigade, André Benoist, for lunch in the Café de Paris on Avenue de l'Opéra and afterward bought shares for him so profitably that he chose not to record the transaction. Later, the two stood trial in criminal court, the banker for corrupting, the policeman for being corrupted, but the court acquitted them both. Amerongen and Sacazan, financiers in the vicinity, had done no less for Benoist. The police had friends there among the bankers. And they had sources there among the knowledgeable journalists of Mennevée's breed who knew the stock exchange and traveled the *grands boulevards,* from the Café Cardinal to the Café Napolitain and back, and who divulged, sometimes sparingly, the secrets of their terrain to the inquisitive gentlemen from Quai des Orfèvres.[66]

When seasoned inspector Gripois, newly appointed to the financial brigade, went in, he soon began hearing all about the Compagnie Foncière. He was a veteran of the special brigade and its hunt for thieves and murderers, yet wise to the ways of the stock exchange, and he already knew of Stavisky. In 1926 Gripois had helped track down Stavisky after his flight from the Palace of Justice. Benoist and Pachot now asked him to help set up the financial brigade, to choose the other inspectors, and to launch its first investigations. First he heard rumors in the stock exchange of some sort of company that Stavisky had formed and that seemed headed for a resounding crash. It was, he gathered, an open secret. Find out more, Benoist and Pachot urged him.[67]

Discreetly, Gripois did so. He took no notes, but on 18 March sent Pachot a full account of his findings about the Compagnie Foncière. He repeated what Mennevée had already reported on the front page of *Les Informations Politiques et Financières*—among other anomalies, that a lowly accountant called Cazenave, who earned three thousand francs a month and rented an apartment for three hundred, owned almost all the founding capital. But he revealed too that the company had already taken over an outfit called SIMA, and that behind the grilled gates, corporate facades, and decorated dignitaries was the conniving Sacha Stavisky, whose crimes, customs, and pseudonyms he proceeded to enumerate with impressive precision.[68]

Pachot alerted the prosecutor's office. Stavisky is up to his old tricks, he told Prince at one of their weekly meetings, see how he's using his liberty. He sent him Gripois's report and added his own urgent covering note. Give me the powers I need to put him away, he demanded again. But nothing happened. Gripois's report attracted all the attention of a dead letter.

Prince paid almost no notice to it. As far as he was concerned, the affair was settled and his conclusions stood; Gripois's report added little to his understanding. Nothing it revealed was actionable, he said. Then at least revoke his conditional release, Pachot argued. Too difficult, Prince replied.[69]

Every morning at eleven o'clock Prince met with his immediate superior in the prosecutor's office, the public prosecutor Georges Pressard. He told Pressard that he had received some new information from Pachot about the Hudelo affair, but that it did not change much. Yes, Stavisky was a dangerous man. "But being suspicious and dangerous isn't enough," Prince argued, "you also have to commit an actionable deed."[70]

Pressard was a decent but spineless man, the kind of bureaucrat who kept his door open, tried to satisfy everyone, and regularly gave his automatic assent. Incapable of challenging his own subordinates, let alone parliamentary lawyers or ministers of justice, he lacked the character and the motivation to doubt or question Prince, who made light of Gripois's and Pachot's alarms. Pressard looked birdlike but not quite aquiline, his cheeks hollow and his thinning hair brushed well back. He was sixty-five, nearing the end of his career, and now agreed with Prince, as he inevitably did, about the Foncière file.[71]

Thus Gripois's report died. Finance and Justice continued to skirmish over the Foncière for another year, as ministers came and went, but Gripois's and Pachot's findings never became part of their arguments or enlightened their dialogue. Whenever Pachot went to the prosecutor's office and started talking about Stavisky, he sensed Prince's reticence and his own intrusiveness, officious and unwanted. He felt he was a nuisance to everyone there.[72]

In October 1930 a new minister of finance, the alert and combative Paul Reynaud, objected again to the magistrates' passivity. He had picked up the scent of fraud in the file he had found on his desk. A new minister of justice, Raoul Péret, answered that prosecution would only disgrace the directors, whose good faith, he added, was beyond doubt. Péret knew nothing of the matter; a new director of criminal affairs in the ministry, his old friend and protégé Georges Rateau, had drafted the letter for him. Reynaud protested but washed his hands of the affair. What could he do? The Foncière presented a fine facade, complete with a former prefect of police, and could Finance prove what Justice denied? Later a new minister of labor, Pierre Laval, agreed with the two of them to let the Foncière alone. They met coming out of a cabinet meeting, and, in the space of a minute, Laval indifferently, Reynaud reluctantly, and Péret gladly allowed that the Foncière's misleading announcements were not actionable.

As though prescient of their passivity, Prince had just written another report, which Pressard gamely signed. He had not ruled out a further inquiry, but had reminded Finance again of the risks to the company and to M. Hudelo. The general prosecutor had signed off, as had Rateau at criminal affairs and so the minister. Now two other ministers agreed with him. No one had uttered a word about Inspector Gripois's report.[73]

Two governments fell; new ministers at Labor, Finance, and Justice exchanged more notes about the Foncière; Prince wrote more reports. In March 1931 he wrote his last and his longest, dense with juridical analyses, and suggested in it that Finance listen to Hudelo and the arguments marshaled by his lawyers. Pressard signed again, but this time the report stayed at the Ministry of Justice, and the case against the Foncière fell victim, finally, to bureaucratic strangulation.[74]

Mennevée had fired his last shot in *Les Informations Politiques et Financières* the previous May. Was the famous Stavisky behind the Compagnie Foncière, he had asked on his front page, in boldface, and he cast his crusade in the form of an open letter to Prime Minister André Tardieu and two of his ministers—Paul Reynaud at Finance and Raoul Péret at Justice. Then Mennevée fell strangely silent. He never mentioned the matter again. He complained once of threats, but of course acknowledged no gratifications. Stavisky's name disappeared from his columns, and no one else, after Prince's chat with Pressard in April, mentioned it either.[75]

A businessman from the provinces had bought fifty of the five hundred–franc bonds after reading the Foncière's advertisements in December 1929. He saw Mennevée's articles and, already suspicious, began writing to Place Saint-Georges. Only dilatory replies came back from a General Bardi de Fourtou there. He declined to reimburse Grand for his bonds and reminded him that the company was paying the semiannual interests punctually. That was all he had a right to expect, the general explained. What could the hapless businessman do? On the unofficial market the bonds were now worth three hundred francs at most.[76]

Thus the facade of the Foncière, the titles, proxies, and fictions, the bogus bank accounts and the notarial niceties, had served their maker well. Justice had drawn back, too cognizant of the men of mark and too apprehensive of scandal to strike blindly with its laws. Prince, caught up in the system, hated it. As he was trying to resolve the Foncière imbroglio, Oustric's bank crashed, and he and Pressard answered for their past reluctance to interfere with his operations. The financial section's powers were repressive, not preventive, they argued, and to intervene with almost no plaintiffs, in the absence of "serious presumptions," just when share prices were rising, would have ruined the shareholders. Besides—but this they did not say—Oustric had friends. One of his lawyers had been Raoul Péret, now minister of justice. It was a delicate choice, a matter of judgment. The press and the public had denounced Justice for acting too soon in the collapse of Hanau's bank in 1928, not soon enough in that of the Banque Industrielle de Chine in 1921. Directly or indirectly, fear of the public or its representatives hobbled Justice, and popular sovereignty did not easily suffer the arrogance of an independent magistracy.[77]

In one of the turns of the waltz of the cabinets, Henri Chéron, the minister of finance who had requested an investigation of the Compagnie Foncière in 1929, found himself at the Ministry of Justice at the end of 1930. He moved into his new office on Place Vendôme and on Christmas Eve sent out a circular to general prosecutors all over France. He had noticed, he said, that they hid behind the Ministry of Justice and covered their indictments with its prior approval. Clarifications on points of law or administration were sensible enough, he said. "But I insist, in penal pursuits, and whoever the suspect, that only the heads of the prosecutor's office take the decisions." This would bolster the independence of the magistracy, "the essential guarantee of our public law," he added. Chéron had not drafted the letter. Georges Rateau, director of criminal affairs, had—the same Rateau who had helped Péret, Chéron's predecessor, to persuade the Ministry of Finance to leave the Foncière alone. His letter for the new minister thus floated uncertainly on the thin line between hypocrisy and idealism. But Chéron had asked for the letter, and he signed it and sent it out. There had been others like it before. There would be more later. The independence of justice, far from settled even at this late date, eternally upheld and daily ignored, invited such homilies.[78]

In their various ways, liberal reformers since 1789 had sought to separate law from politics, to render judges and politicians free from mutual interference. Boldly at that time, timidly after 1815, temperately after 1871, new regimes had tried to free magistrates from authoritarian executives and legislators from compliant, politicized judiciaries. Elected judges, tenured judges, open trials, juries, so many experiments in judicial autonomy; parliamentary immunity, the demarcation between penal and political responsibility, so many devices for legislators to parry the threat of judicial retribution. An ardent wish to separate the powers drove such measures, yet circumstances repeatedly conspired to subvert their autonomy. After Thermidor, the constitution of Year III, enshrining the principles of an independent judiciary, could not save the courts from being pressed into service against royalists and especially Jacobins; still less could the constitutions of the years VIII and X. The July Monarchy reaffirmed the distinction between the penal and the political, yet recruited the courts to silence its opponents, restricted eligibility for jury duty, and promoted only the most docile magistrates — fifty-eight of whom, in 1834, sat in the Legislative Assembly. Subtly or not, regimes deviated from the liberal tenets that had inspired them, less anxious in practice than in theory to hold the state and its politics at bay from the courts and from society's other institutions. Justice, first envisaged in 1789 as a brake on executive power, tended all too often to sustain it. Agent or counteragent of power, instrument or constraint?[79]

With the advent of the Third Republic, jurists were as divided as ever on the proper place of justice within the balance of powers. Some saw it as a third power, others as a dependency of the other two. Characteristically, the early Republic advanced liberal principle with one hand while moderating it with the other. Magistrates of the bench were irremovable, but not those of the prosecution; investigating magistrates could arrest and indict, but only as required by the prosecutors, themselves serving under the minister's watchful eye; jurors were free, but ministers could interfere obliquely, restricting eligibility, requiring that they consult with the judges, even removing some crimes — like those of the anarchists — from their purview altogether. "Judicial lackeys," Georges Sorel had called the magistrates of the Dreyfus affair. And to impose new statutes or reform the penal code, the ministers could always resort to the delegates of the sovereign, assembled in the Chamber and the Senate. The magistrates of the Third Republic were independent, but only relatively so.[80]

Often those closest to the summit, yet still rising in their careers, deferred most spontaneously to political power, a species of tact and self-restraint that

Prince and Pressard were now observing in exemplary fashion at the Paris prosecutor's office.

■

Pachot's last chance came in Orléans, when a monocled and debonair de Chevert, former spy and improvised jeweler at Stavisky's side, turned traitor and told an inspector from the new financial brigade all about the goings-on at the crédit municipal.

Old inspector Gripois had brought into the section a capable young police officer, Robert Cousin. Pachot called him "my boy," and when Gripois returned to the special brigade, Cousin inherited the Stavisky file from him. Soon he was learning about Orléans, the Foncière, and almost everything else. In February de Chevert had begun talking to them about his association with M. Alexandre. Stavisky, he felt, had exploited him; he feared prosecution; he became Inspector Cousin's informant.[81]

In finding a discreet informer, Cousin was following standard practice. The inspectors of the Police Judiciaire, no less than the magistrates of the prosecutor's office, feared setting off rumor, panic, or debacle by their sudden appearance at the door of the bank. Bringing the banker to their headquarters on Quai des Orfèvres could be just as dangerous, since word quickly went down the staircase and out into the street, passed on by financial journalists or idly curious observers. The inspectors therefore favored the obscure associate, the faceless employee endowed with knowledge and entrusted with authority but known to few outside the bank. Even so, they tried at times to meet well off the beaten track, even on occasion receiving their informers at home. By such tactful means did Cousin discover much of what de Chevert knew.[82]

At the end of May 1931, just as the prefect of the Loiret was asking Finance to investigate the crédit municipal of Orléans, and two months after Prince had signed his last report on the Compagnie Foncière, Cousin sent Pachot his own report. It took up twenty-one pages, single-spaced. All Pachot knew was already here, along with much that he did not: the crédit municipal of Orléans, he learned, was issuing bonds at will to the jewelers of the Etablissements Alex, which Stavisky then cashed at a discount at Parisian banks. Cousin said nothing of the fake emeralds that supported the airy, immaterial edifice; de Chevert had not yet told him of them. And he knew nothing of the protracted wrangling between Commerce, Finance, the prefect, and the mayor over the same crédit municipal. Still Cousin did report that Orléans seemed to have exhausted its possibilities for Stavisky and his friends, and that they had hatched a plot to take their operations elsewhere, all the way to the capital of Basque country, Bayonne.[83]

Pachot sent Cousin's report to Albert Prince at the financial section. Prince's reply astounded them both: he asked them to verify the identities of Stavisky and Cazenave. That was all. Grudgingly, as though reinventing the wheel, Pachot and Cousin confirmed their identities; but by then it was early July, and Prince had left the palace for summer vacation.[84]

CHAPTER 5

It looked to Pachot like another delaying maneuver by his operational superior at Justice. When, to make matters worse, his administrative superior at the police, Xavier Guichard, objected to his methods, he almost gave up in despair. A year earlier Xavier Guichard had succeeded André Benoist at the head of the Police Judiciaire. Benoist had not much liked Pachot, but had left him alone to operate as he wished for the prosecutor's office. Guichard, who did not much care for Pachot either, was rougher in his ways. The two differed in all but their profession and their age. Each had spent most of his adult life in the police; Guichard was fifty-nine, Pachot sixty-one; but Guichard had none of his energetic subordinate's education, distinction, or acumen. He had grown up poor, reared by his widowed mother, a midwife in Montparnasse, had left school at fifteen, had joined the army at eighteen and the police force at twenty-three. He had displayed courage, selflessness, and energy on the streets. But he knew little of financial matters and had also retained the manners and practices of the barracks, so that he now treated Pachot like the subaltern that, technically, he was. This did not go over well. When Guichard learned of Cousin's report he did not easily understand its importance or the fuss that Pachot was raising about it; he reflected on the haste with which Pachot had sent it to the financial section, and remarked to him that he ought first to have interrogated some of the suspects himself rather than rely so blindly on young Cousin. Pachot reacted angrily.[85]

The incident blew over, but it rankled Pachot and fed his suspicion that occult, powerful interests were working to keep Stavisky out of harm's way. Unable to identify them, yet confident of their action, Pachot dared not take his case over the heads of Albert Prince or Xavier Guichard, to Public Prosecutor Pressard or Police Prefect Chiappe. In 1908 another police prefect, Lépine, had gone to his superior Clemenceau at the Ministry of the Interior, and forty-eight hours later the fraudster Rochette, who oddly prefigured Stavisky, was under arrest. Lépine had arranged to find a suitable plaintiff. But he was a prefect of police, and Pachot was only a superintendent, with the rank, but not even the title, of divisional superintendent. Lépine's action had set off a panic on the stock exchange and a scandal in the press. If he pushed forward any more, Pachot imagined, only his own career would suffer.[86]

He imagined too much. Guichard was no more an instrument of the powers of darkness than Prince. The magistrate, a paragon of caution, had as yet never reproached Pachot for his zeal, and the police director, limited by his respect for the hierarchy, had only questioned his subordinate's haste. With his false collar and white goatee, Guichard looked more antiquated than the other two, more a venerable relic of the Belle Epoque, a captor of anarchists, than a connoisseur of new-fashioned financial crime. Prince had understood the status of the felons better than the gravamen of their felony, and Guichard had understood almost nothing at all, but neither now tried to suppress the report Pachot waved at them. Guichard sent it routinely to Prefect Chiappe, and Prince sent it to the Orléans prosecutor's office; neither served some unseen power, the gray eminence of Pachot's imagining.[87]

94

Yet Pachot had seen through the bureaucratic screen, and could just make out the parliamentary lawyers, eminent directors, and well-oiled influence machinery that ran silently at their command. He knew of them from experience, however his imagination might take flight, and had said so to Chiappe a few years earlier, just after Stavisky left La Santé prison. He himself deserved the rewards as well as the rank of divisional superintendent, he argued then, because, behind the suspects he pursued, he all too often found men of weight and renown — "figures from the world of the press, of Finance, of politics.""Some of these figures," he added, in the sort of envoi that set him apart from colleagues like Xavier Guichard, "excel at the art of lending their influence to the most varied interests; and their preferences do not always go to the best of these." Now he supposed his old bête noire was another of their causes — supposed prematurely, since Stavisky as yet enjoyed no patrons and only deployed concurrent subterfuges, names, and cachets. So far they sufficed. But Pachot, less precise than prescient, did not know that.[88]

Overwhelmed by Oustric and Hanau, Albert Prince's assistant prosecutors at the financial section had ignored the less important Stavisky. But in July, with Prince away on vacation, one of them, André Bruzin, began perusing the secret file with a mounting sense of incredulity. Why all the postponements of Stavisky's hearings in court? he asked. He investigated and learned that the thirteenth correctional chamber had agreed, more or less routinely, to requests from Stavisky's lawyers. Who was de Chevert, and was he a reliable informer? Which banks had cashed the Orléans bonds? How exactly had the Foncière started? Bruzin met with Pachot, whom he knew and liked, sent out instructions for a full judicial inquiry, and awaited the results as Cousin went back to work.[89]

This time the young inspector reported, among other discoveries, that the emeralds supposed to guarantee the Orléans bonds had probably been fake, or so de Chevert now said. But where were they? They had disappeared from the crédit municipal, redeemed, it seemed, by their owner. And Stavisky and his colleagues had spent much of the summer redeeming the Orléans bonds they had discounted at banks. With the bonds and emeralds had gone much of the evidence.[90]

Neither the police nor the magistrates yet knew of the inspection by the Ministry of Finance that had frightened Stavisky away from Orléans. As he was evacuating the place at the end of August, he heard of de Chevert's treachery. Word of the interrogations by Pachot and Cousin had reached him, brought perhaps by the lowly employee Digoin from one of his former colleagues on Quai des Orfèvres, perhaps by his mighty lawyer Hesse from the whisperings of the cavernous lobby of the Palace of Justice. Stavisky, ardent name-dropper, boasted of friends high up in the police force to all who would listen, and some even believed him. "I know hourly of your revelations," he told de Chevert vindictively, "but I can warn you today that you won't succeed. I've fixed the matter of the emeralds and, as for the Orléans bonds, they've been redeemed." He advised de Chevert to disappear, and the two never spoke again.[91]

But in the Palace of Justice Cousin's report was breathing new life into the Foncière-Orléans file. On the evening of 5 October 1931, Bruzin sat studying it in his office. The next day Public Prosecutor Pressard and some of the assistant prosecutors, Bruzin included, were to meet with General Prosecutor Donat-Guigue to review, as they did several times a year, the pressing files of the day. Stavisky's, by now, was one of them. Prince, back from vacation since the end of August, came in and leaned over Bruzin. What are you doing? he asked. Studying the spurious share purchases that may have started the Foncière, Bruzin replied. Prince replied absently that he had paid more attention to the construction contracts. He seemed interested but not unduly concerned.[92]

They all met in Donat-Guigue's office the next day, and spent all but fifteen minutes of the two-hour review talking about the Oustric-Benoist affair. The banker's favors for the former director of the Police Judiciaire had come to light in the press, Chiappe had fired Benoist, and both were facing indictments for corruption. It was a difficult and delicate matter. Finally, Bruzin spoke up about the Stavisky file. Prince asked again about identities; Bruzin, irritated, told him of the Police Judiciaire's confirmation. They talked of the hearings put off by the thirteenth correctional chamber—the action was normal, they agreed—and of the exchanges with Finance. Donat-Guigue thought for a minute and instructed Bruzin to draft a full report—yet another—for the minister of justice. They proposed to investigate the whole matter thoroughly.[93]

By December time was running out. In a few months the statute of limitations would expire and the men of the Foncière would retire in tranquillity.[94] Before the prosecutor's office could indict anyone, the lawyers moved in and extricated Stavisky and his crowd once again. In extremis, they contrived by means of an arcane technicality to transfer the case to another jurisdiction.

A jaunty young lawyer, the surprising discovery of Stavisky's normally blundering and ungifted associate Hayotte, had set the solution in motion. Georges Guiboud-Ribaud, a struggling novice at the bar, had clung to Hayotte much as young Maître Gaulier had to Stavisky—out of need, greed, and, in the end, friendship. But Gaulier was small and withdrawn; Guiboud-Ribaud, clean-shaven, outgoing, and showy in his bow tie and tortoiseshell glasses, more resembled Hayotte, and was his age besides, only twenty-eight. He had helped Hayotte, and Hayotte had helped him. Guiboud-Ribaud had helped get him out of La Santé eight months after the arrests at Marly-le-Roi in 1926, and had helped again to persuade the courts to drop the charges. In return Hayotte brought him into the Etablissements Alex. There Stavisky spoke of great projects, dangled names, money, and the prospect of success before young Guiboud-Ribaud's wide-open eyes. With no property to his name, newly married, tenant of a small apartment on Rue Laugier, the ambitious lawyer thought to hitch his practice to Stavisky's star. He became legal counsel to the Foncière, and even bought a few of its shares.

A climber, socially and professionally, Guiboud-Ribaud collected friends as well as clients. Journalists and politicians had seen his smooth face before. He vacationed with Léon-Antoine Migeon, alias de Chattencourt, filmmaker and editor of a popular scandal sheet called *Le Petit Bleu,* and called regularly on him in his office on Boulevard de la Madeleine. He had tried his hand at politics, and during a passing infatuation with the Soviet experiment had joined Friends of the USSR and Red Aid, and had celebrated the tenth anniversary of the October Revolution in its own land. Guiboud-Ribaud had spoken often at Communist Party meetings, had traveled for the cause to Italy, and had defended imprisoned comrades in court there. All that was behind him. But what by now he had lost in fervor he had gained in sophistication. He had connections. In 1924 some highly disobliging words of his about the anti-Communist author Henri Béraud had provoked a libel suit, and Guiboud-Ribaud had turned for help to Anatole de Monzie, lawyer, deputy, and former and future minister. De Monzie had tried his best to settle out of court with the aggrieved Béraud and had failed, but Guiboud-Ribaud remembered him gratefully. Now, late in 1931, he passed him in a hall of the Palace of Justice and asked if he would receive him and a confrère, Gaulier. It was about a Compagnie Foncière, he said.[95]

They arrived, and de Monzie listened with interest. The names impressed him. Then came Dorn y de Alsua, former diplomat, titular owner of Cocochéri and all her stablemates, and director of the Foncière. He was charming and elegant, and admired de Monzie for the paintings on his walls. He seemed to the parliamentary lawyer anything but a businessman. M. Alexandre followed, and with animation told de Monzie all about the Foncière; finally, another director appeared at the door, Victor Dargent, mayor of Romainville. On his large and crowded business card he advertised himself, among titles and offices and honors, as an alternate justice of the peace in Noisy-le-Sec.

De Monzie sat up at this, because article 479 of the criminal investigation code conferred on chevaliers of the Legion of Honor and justices of the peace the right to trial before the court of appeal instead of the correctional court. It was a jurisdictional privilege, a remnant of justice by caste, out of place in a modern Republic; but it had survived, just as surely as the red and white robes on the magistrates' backs. Guiboud-Ribaud and Gaulier had hoped for a personal approach by de Monzie, some new move in the ongoing game of influence, like those of René Renoult and André Hesse; but this was simpler.[96]

The palace yielded: it could challenge the foreigner Dorn's claim to the privilege, but not the Frenchman Dargent's; and if Dargent belonged before the court of appeal, so did every director of the Foncière. They could not each answer for the same company in different jurisdictions. The financial section relinquished control, the case adopted the more stately pace of the court of appeal, and Stavisky and his friends sat back once again to observe the soothing spectacle of the administration of justice.[97]

Old Pachot was nearing retirement, and gave up. Young Guiboud-Ribaud savored his triumph. He was serving Stavisky well.

■

By then the judges of the thirteenth correctional chamber had put off hearing Labbé's and Laforcade's suit against Stavisky thirteen times. Once they sent the summons to Rue Saint-Georges instead of Place Saint-Georges. Again they committed the same physician to examine the defendant; again he suggested a psychiatric exam, and even though Stavisky never called on a psychiatrist he extracted two more months from the court. Twice summer vacations interrupted the short, crowded cycle of the judicial year. Weeks, months went by while new judges acquainted themselves with the case, lawyers coordinated busy schedules, and plaintiffs showed themselves willing—even Labbé and Laforcade put off hearings when Stavisky, in sporadic paroxysms of generosity, began to pay them off. The judges bowed to their wishes, seeming to ignore for the occasion the vital dominion of public action over private. Little in the law compelled so dilatory a magistracy to quicken its pace and hasten the day of judgment. The delays, in theory, could stretch on forever.[98]

"It's a joke," Assistant Prosecutor Fillaire of the thirteenth correctional chamber said to Bruzin. The postponements were routine, he explained, each stopped the clock on the statute of limitations, and sooner or later Stavisky would come to trial. Bruzin was reassured.[99]

Again a parliamentary lawyer stepped in to stave off another plaintiff. André Hesse donned his black robe, just like his parliamentary colleague René Renoult five years before, and went to see the public prosecutor, Georges Pressard, in his office in the Palace of Justice. Hesse railed at the docile prosecutor, complained about an investigating magistrate called Glard who was investigating the suit, and left. Pressard sent for Glard.

"Be careful," he advised the indignant investigating magistrate, who hoped for a seat on the bench. "It's in your interests not to have any problems."

"Kept from the court of appeal because I've done my duty! It's too much!"

"Be careful," the irresolute prosecutor said again. "Be careful."

But Pressard did not stand in the way of Glard's promotion. The summer recess intervened, and in October the investigating magistrate became a judge in the court of appeal. He relinquished the case that had driven Hesse into the prosecutor's office.[100]

Soon Prince too rid himself of the troublesome file and moved on to the higher court. That autumn he had seemed to Pachot slightly defensive about Orléans and the Foncière. "Why do you keep on so much about this pawnshop? It's been repaid," Prince said, once again raising dark suppositions of corruption in Pachot's mind. "So this man's on the take as well," the superintendent reflected to himself back in his own office. Later he suspected mere amour propre, a reluctance by Prince to recant his earlier caution. But at the end of October Prince left the prosecutor's office for the seat on the court of appeal that he had so openly craved. Kindly Pressard had supported him, even accelerated his promotion, and Prince reacted as though delivered from evil.

"How happy we are to be judges now. I myself was disgusted, disgusted! by the parliamentary interference and its consequences," he said to the investigating magistrate Glard, as he too exchanged his old black robe for a new red one. Stavisky receded from the life of Albert Prince, but not forever.[101]

　　　■

Regulatory redundancies, reflecting a suspicion of the concentration of power, hobbled a Republic imagined to be indivisible, and allowed Stavisky a moment of impunity in Orléans. But just as often the Republic's representatives, functionaries, and moneyed worthies, united by the lingua franca of influence, ignored the various demarcations of status, and quietly exchanged or surrendered their appointed roles. Such confusions on occasion paralyzed justice, as susceptible as anyone to the charm of fame and fortune, lulled it into moderating a natural curiosity, and revealed to Stavisky the secret to protracted immunity.

Sometimes he crossed paths with his addled foes on neutral ground, now confronting their solemnity with an impish insouciance. At a hairdresser's on Avenue Georges-V, he fraternized, quite without design, with Théodore-Paul Lescouvé, presiding judge of the Cour de Cassation and one of the highest magistrates in the land. The hairdresser's establishment was a charming incongruity, a quaint relic of the Belle Epoque, like the old farmhouse that stood off the traffic circle nearby, complete with courtyard and well. In one window a lady of wax showed off the establishment's permanent wave, and in the other powders, cosmetics, and vials of scent proclaimed the owner's devotion to the vanity of his customers.

His wife sat at the cash register, between the women's salon on the right and the men's on the left, where four predictable chairs sat in a row in front of their basins, bounded by a linen cupboard at the far end. Behind the third of these stood the hairdresser himself, who had reserved the place for his customers of mark.

Lescouvé sat there often; so did Stavisky. Sometimes their visits coincided, and one waited while the other took his turn in the chair. They never spoke to each other, never exchanged flickering glances of recognition. Lescouvé had a drooping mustache and wore a wing collar. He arrived quietly and carried himself gravely but urbanely. Usually, he asked only for a cut, sometimes for a *friction,* a scalp massage, as well, and he left without much fuss. Stavisky came in with brio; he was natty and dashing, offered jokes and smiles all round and a compliment for the lady of the establishment at her register. In the chair he accepted every treatment known to the trade, every act the coiffeur could perform; the aging barber singed, shampooed, dried, perfumed, waved, and doused with lotion the hair of his enchanting customer, and when Stavisky left he stopped at the florist across the street, as though to commemorate in merriment his latest encounter with the ponderous Lescouvé.[102]

A BANK FOR BAYONNE

The local deputy terrifies the national prefect. We asked for statesmen; we received creatures of the constituency. —Alain, *Propos,* 1 September 1934

His Majesty the Deputy

For many years, Joseph Garat had yearned for a crédit municipal in his native town of Bayonne. He was its mayor as well as the Radical deputy from the Basses-Pyrénées, and saw no reason why the Côte d'Azur should have three crédits municipaux and the Côte d'Argent none. The Atlantic too boasted casinos, gaming establishments, and chic hotels, and drew seasonal hordes willing to exchange their jewelry for some cash on hand; but it had not a single crédit municipal to save them from the clutches of private usurers and to bring in some local tax revenue besides. Garat's little Basque town, with its half-timbered red and green houses and August corridas, stood inland from the ocean, well out of the way, and seemed an improbable spot for a new commercial lending institution. But Mayor Garat never thought so, and was delighted to meet a financier called Serge Alexander who appeared, most cordially, to regard Bayonne's remoteness and tranquillity as irresistible incentives to invest money there.

Edmond Boyer, the deputy from Angers who had supped with Stavisky but had stopped short of selling his soul to him, had introduced him to Garat in Biarritz in 1930, and Garat at once fell under the spell of his parliamentary colleague's rich friend.[1]

At the time, Garat had occupied the town hall, quaintly placed at the junction of the Adour and the Nive rivers, for all but six of the previous twenty-two years. The voters had sent him to the Palais Bourbon just as faithfully since 1910, but Joseph Garat rarely stood up to speak there and always thought of himself as a mayor first and a deputy second. Even some of his enemies acknowledged that on occasion he had served the town and its thirty thousand citizens well, that a hospital here and a charity there owed their presence in Bayonne to his untiring efforts. There at least he made the most of the powers that the Chamber bestowed upon him. Like many elected officials, he needed funds for local projects, including his own reelection, and was naturally amenable to friendly proposals that came his way. The mayor sought to add the prefect's good will to the banker's, and to profit from a rare show of trilateral harmony among representatives of the people, of the state, and of money. In such ways Joseph Garat, notable, delegate, and lawmaker, assured for a while longer his hold on power.

But he was not a likable man. Morose, authoritarian, and unyielding, he sometimes erupted in violent outbursts, which some attributed to an iron will, others more discerningly to weakness. They heard bluff in his vehemence, a sad attempt to cow his company or sway his voters. And, limping, large, and ungainly, clad in ready-to-wear suits from the Samaritaine department store in Paris, he conveyed sadness, his political ambition unleavened by grace, polish, or any visible cultivation of pleasure.[2]

He was born in Bayonne in 1872, the youngest of nine children, to a father who had made a small fortune in the United States and so provided for his son's education and entry into the legal profession. But Joseph Garat never flourished as a lawyer, and practiced only when out of office. His partners found him artless with clients, quick-tempered with themselves, and concerned above all else with multiplying connections and accumulating the distinctions that would advance his career in politics. Such single-mindedness left him at times indifferent to the source of his revenues and even more incurious about the integrity of his friends.[3]

When in Paris, he stayed with his wife, son, and young Basque maid in an apartment on Rue Lalo in the costly sixteenth arrondissement. But they furnished it simply, entertained only family members there, and kept no car. In the capital Garat traveled by metro, second class, his wife sometimes by taxi. Nothing in their life in Paris hinted at indecent expenditures or hidden outlays, but in Bayonne Garat was always short of money. He owned property in the area—some land nearby at Hendaye-Plage and farther away at Libourne, and a lot in Bayonne on which, when he met M. Alexandre, he was building a villa, "Loustilholès." Garat was neither greedy nor especially venal, but his holdings drained his means, and together with the costs of power were slowly but inexorably driving him into debt. From a banker on Boulevard Voltaire, delighted to be of service to a parliamentary client, he borrowed twenty thousand francs, invoking the cost of elections in Bayonne. From his sister, who preferred the reassurance of gold ingots in hand to the notional contents of a remote bank account, he accepted donations and subventions, including most of what he needed for "La Loustilholès." From a widow who owned a nursing home in Cambo-les-Bains, who spoke Basque and no French, and who disdained both the Legion of Honor and the official status he pressed on her, he accepted a gift of fifty thousand francs in return for a promise to leave her alone. Once before, the law had objected to his ways, when hectoliters of illegal wine that customs officials had impounded at the border somehow found their way into his cellar. He escaped prosecution. Garat was careless about such matters.[4]

So much inadvertence accompanying so much need might tempt even the most timid of opportunists, and associates of doubtful repute recurrently attached themselves to Garat's progress in politics. The mayor who returned from the Army of the Orient's campaign in Salonika with a Croix de Guerre on his chest also appointed to his local wartime charities a woman whom police soon arrested as a swindler and a German agent. Garat was too greedy for power to wonder about virtue, and his want of discernment left him vulnerable to reproach and even to scandal.[5]

He had seen Serge Alexandre in Biarritz before, in the casino, along the beach, on the jetty, and when Boyer introduced them formally Garat found the man preternaturally compelling. His utterances and arguments were music to Garat's ears—you need a crédit municipal, M. Alexandre told him, to build your reputation, to finance charities and public works; the crédit municipal had worked wonders in Orléans, but in the end no one there had understood him; he expected more, he added astutely, from the quick, subtle minds of the Gascons. And with rich Spaniards fleeing the troubles across the border, there would be no shortage of jewels and valuables to stock the crédit's vaults and guarantee its loans—and he himself was a jeweler of rich and varied means.[6]

A few months earlier, Garat had thought of setting up a crédit municipal there, in Biarritz rather than Bayonne. Despotically, speaking as the deputy from the constituency, he demanded it of the mayor, who rejected the idea. Garat raised his voice, bragged of his years in office, threw one of his fits; but a year later he returned and just as typically seemed to have forgotten their altercation. All he proposed this time was an agent in Biarritz for the crédit municipal of Bayonne, which had opened its doors and was, he announced, already doing a thriving business.[7]

The Heart of Fraud

In September 1930, after the summer recess and his seminal encounter with Stavisky, Garat proposed to the city council of Bayonne that it create a crédit municipal. It would operate under the same nineteenth-century statutes as all the others, issue bonds at 5 percent interest to raise cash for the loans it would make at 7 percent, and use the difference to cover its operating expenses and contribute to the general good of the town. This appealed to the assembled councillors, who twice voiced their enthusiasm with their votes.[8]

They did not bother to tell M. Mireur, the local prefect. He sat quietly in Pau, an irrelevance. Garat had mentioned the matter to him, but only informally, and had instead reserved his most assiduous attentions for the Ministry of Commerce in Paris. The minister, new in office, besieged by other parliamentary callers, unacquainted with the rules and regulations of the crédits municipaux, had sent him to see Delamarche—the inspector general of credit, who had vaguely looked into the goings-on in Orléans, believed in the commercial destiny of the old pawnshops, and now urged the prefect of the Basses-Pyrénées to clear the way for a new one in Bayonne. The compliant Mireur hastily inquired, approved, and transmitted; the Council of State and the minister in Paris then also ratified, in their own ponderous way, the wishes of the distant city council. Garat could not have been happier. The administration had served nicely.[9]

The cloud of ambiguity that had floated over Orléans now drifted over Bayonne, even before the crédit municipal opened its doors. The ministry in Paris, the prefecture in Pau, and the city council in Bayonne had each blessed the new establishment. But who among them had consecrated it, and who might excommunicate it? Prefect Mireur had no exact comprehension of his powers and responsibilities. Like Genébrier and Castanet in Orléans, he operated among powers that might claim authority one day only to disclaim it the next. And Mireur was not disposed to obstruct. Why should he? The mayor of the town, the deputy from the department, the surrogate for the popular sovereign, stood behind the project. The fiction that made the servants of the executive branch, from minister to messenger, responsible to Parliament also rendered the prefect alert to the will and wants of the omnipresent local politician. Once again, as in the halls and galleries of the Palace of Justice, elective authority weighed heavily on appointed officials and naturally exploited its precedence in a representative democracy. As a deputy, Garat was worth his weight in gold to Stavisky.[10]

Two city councillors, two directors of local charities, and two Bayonne merchants made up the board of directors, presided over by Joseph Garat himself. In February he called them together to hear his proposals for the financing, staffing, and running of the new crédit municipal. He had already raised the founding capital, he explained to them, two hundred thousand francs to allow their establishment to open. Why point out that all of it had come from a Parisian financier called M. Alexandre? A stranger present at the start might alarm or offend the Bayonne notables, drawn by the prospect of a local crédit municipal. But two hundred thousand would not be enough, and so he requested authority to issue an initial 5 million francs' worth of bonds. He already had an investor in Paris, he added. As for the posts they had to fill, he mentioned some names, naturally unknown to them, including Emile Digoin, a retired inspector from the Sûreté Générale, Samuel Cohen, an experienced jeweler, and Fernand Desbrosses, a treasurer from the crédit municipal of Orléans. Such was Garat's authority, and such the new directors' enthusiasm, that they all ratified his wishes, and Garat's own secretary from the town hall, whom he had brought along for the occasion, drew up the minutes of the inaugural meeting of the crédit municipal of Bayonne.[11]

Stavisky brought his experienced hands down to Bayonne. Old inspector Digoin moved into a nice villa called "Mirasol," and began for the moment to take in the gages of borrowers and to hand them their loans. Samuel Cohen, the aging Moroccan jeweler who had helped launch the Etablissements Alex, and whom Alexandre called his "ace in the hole," came too. He could still barely read and write French, but that did not matter: he could dictate his appraisals to Digoin or to the guardian of the valuables.[12] Stavisky summoned Desbrosses, as the accountant of the hour whose skills, acquired in Orléans, would clear the ground and lay the foundations in Bayonne. Desbrosses bought furniture, advised the new board of directors on practical matters such as the installation of lockers and storerooms, and quietly issued the crédit's first bonds.

Prefect Mireur routinely approved their appointments. But he balked at Desbrosses. Not in the least suspicious of Garat or his project, he nevertheless entertained serious misgivings about his chosen treasurer's recent past in Orléans. Garat angrily defended his nominee. He had never asked about Desbrosses, never requested even a perfunctory background check on him, yet he railed at Mireur, he found the allegations incredible, unfounded. Garat knew almost nothing of finance or banking. He asked few questions, heard what he wished to hear, and rode roughshod over his opposition when he could not brush it aside. He had reacted to Mireur as he had to the mayor of Biarritz a year earlier, truculently and highhandedly, but also naively. No apprehension of Trojan horses, of financiers bearing gifts, sharpened his witless political ambition, and a few days later he returned to tell Mireur just as innocently that he would withdraw Desbrosses's name and place in nomination instead that of another accountant, one Gustave Tissier.

M. Alexandre had arranged it. "I have someone in hand," he had said, and brought down the new man to Bayonne to present to the perennially compliant board of directors.[13]

Beside his gaunt and decrepit predecessor Desbrosses, he looked a solid man, well built, with white *moustaches gauloises,* a florid complexion, and large round glasses. Tissier was fifty. He spoke a Parisian French with some working-class intonations, acquired perhaps from his father, who had delivered wine for a living in Bercy, or from the warehouses there where he himself worked after leaving the school on Rue de Charenton at the age of twelve. At first he was a simple clerk, then a full-fledged accountant; much later, after the war, he took up selling cars and then radio sets. Badly shell-shocked at the front, rehoused by the government after German bombs destroyed his modest Paris apartment, he had long since resumed his laborious prewar life when he met M. Alexandre.[14]

Tissier was an ambitious and hard-working man, respectful of his superiors yet mindful above all of his own interests. Advancement, for him, proceeded at the cost of submission; his loyalty was self-interested, based on a tangible return, self-promoting rather than self-sacrificial. By the time he met Alexandre he was tired of Paris and wanted to start a new life somewhere in the provinces, and when the affable financier proposed one to him he seized the chance.[15]

The two had first become aware of each other at Le Touquet in the summer of 1929, when Tissier began frequenting the Etablissements Alex there. A year later a friend pointed to SIMA on Boulevard Montparnasse and announced its imminent takeover by one M. Alexandre of the Société Foncière, on Place Saint-Georges. Tissier remembered the jeweler and now resolved to meet the banker. By such accidents did Stavisky's acolytes enter his charmed circle; Tissier went to call on him, and from then on grew daily more dependent on his largesse, more instrumental in his stratagems.

Might there be a job for him in the provinces? he asked Alexandre when they met. Yes; and soon Tissier was traveling around France trying to mollify the aggrieved buyers of SIMA's Phébor refrigerator. He liked M. Alexandre, was touched by his kindness and reassured by his entourage, and his new employer in turn told him how much he liked his work and promised not to forget him. True to his word, he called Tissier to his office in April 1931. "Would you like to go to Bayonne for a few months?" he asked him, and Tissier agreed happily, regretting only the brevity of his sojourn there. But Alexandre's protégé voiced doubts about his own competency in matters of crédit municipal finance. "Don't worry about it!" Garat exclaimed in the town hall in Bayonne when, on the Saturday before Easter, Alexandre brought in Tissier. "Desbrosses will give you the necessary information." And, over lunch at the Grand Hôtel and then in more private meetings, the old treasurer from Orléans imparted to the new one in Bayonne the esoteric secrets of his trade. He showed Tissier models of bonds, examples of registers, and some highly eccentric techniques of record keeping in a crédit municipal.

Tissier moved into a house in town with his mistress. They lived frugally and privately. A housekeeper came daily for three francs an hour, but hardly anyone else came, and they never went to cafés or cinemas or theaters. On the weekends they went to Spain in his Ford, across the border to San Sebastián and sometimes farther, to Barcelona and Madrid. She ran the house and went to the market and complained sometimes about money and prices, chafed at how she could not spend on her toilette what the *Bayonnaises* could on theirs, but Stavisky's chauffeur, Bortchy-Melnikoff, noticed that Tissier was beginning to dress quite smartly, much more smartly than before he went to work in the crédit municipal of Bayonne.[16]

The month Spain lost its king, April 1931, Bayonne gained its crédit municipal. Revolution in Madrid had come just in time for Stavisky and his hirelings, and had made plausible their fable—of jewels from Alfonso XIII and the royal family, from Countess San Carlo, from rich Antonio Valenti of Barcelona, and from frightened Spaniards reported crossing the border to seek safe haven for themselves or their valuables. Rumors of plunder and flight justified by their proximity the little town's new crédit municipal, launched with a budget that would have been extravagant even in a teeming metropolis.[17]

Forty-two million francs that year, the sum they expected to borrow with bonds, would go out again for loans on valuables placed in pledge, and for operating expenses, Alexandre had explained. That was the budget for 1931, and Garat duly submitted it to the new board of directors. Nobody asked any questions; nobody opposed it. Nor did Prefect Mireur, who bowed once again to Deputy Garat. Nor, finally, did the district treasury receiver, who bowed to the prefect. Yet all was not well with this inaugural budget. Its authors invoked rich but unnamed Spanish émigrés whose distressed presence no one observed or thought to verify, and they inflated sums wildly. At first the budget had foreseen lending just over 20 million francs to cover a corresponding 20 million in bonds. Now a codicil to it limited each loan to six months, incidentally violating their founding statutes, and the budget slyly doubled the loan limit to allow for the twelve months of the year. By such sleight of hand they turned a budget of 20 million into one of 40 million and an instrument of openness into one of dissimulation. Who would question bonds in circulation that fell within officially approved limits? Several months later, a supplementary forecast repeated the maneuver, and in time the budgets became hermetically sealed fantasies of revenues, expenses, and rates of interest.[18]

The crédit municipal occupied a large white building on Rue Thiers, not far from Garat's town hall, and presented a pleasant facade to the passersby. Wide windows beckoned, square on the ground floor and arched on the second, and the floors above were ringed with balconies and intricately latticed iron balusters that recalled architectural ornamentations well to the south.[19]

Digoin settled into his villa Mirasol a few minutes away, and gamely began doing as he was told. At first Hattot, the congenial actor who had lent his good offices in Orléans, came down bearing bagfuls of jewels. They belonged, he said, to assorted Hispanic owners. It was the old charade rescripted for a sunnier setting; their nominal jewelry came neither from royal coffers in Madrid nor from émigrés escaping from the new Republic south of the Pyrenees, but from the safes of the crédit municipal of Orléans. Samuel Cohen appraised them, Digoin entered them, and Hattot signed the register. Stavisky and Hayotte came too, but soon they all disappeared. After that, Tissier, the new treasurer, took over. He gave Digoin the goods, duly appraised, and told him what to do. Digoin never saw any clients, genuine or spurious, again.[20]

Soon he began carrying bonds to M. Alexandre, who took them away to Paris. By May, almost 8 million francs' worth had already passed through their hands, a flow sanctioned by their self-fulfilling budgetary prophecy. A more vigilant treasury receiver, routinely examining the bonds and the accounting that came with them, might have closed the shutters on the bank on Rue Thiers soon after it opened them. Why, he might have asked on behalf of officialdom and the public interest, had the first bonds been drawn up by a treasurer, Desbrosses, whose nomination had never been approved, and the next ones by an interim treasurer, likewise unapproved? Only then did Tissier take over. Why were the bonds drawn up before the prefect approved their issue, why the unseemly haste? What, for that matter, had happened to the proceeds from the bonds, since Tissier recorded their entries only belatedly, when he formally assumed office in May. But it looked careless rather than criminal, and very quickly Tissier took matters in hand. He signed the bonds, kept the records and the accounting, and on paper carefully balanced sums lent against sums borrowed.[21]

One day Piet, the comptroller whom Garat had named to countersign the bonds as regulations required, came in to see Tissier. They had just met. Piet was unable to come in every day, and Tissier asked him as a matter of convenience to countersign, in advance, a stack of thirty or four blank bonds. "To meet customers' needs," he explained.[22]

Lucien Piet was a *Bayonnais* born and bred, an accountant in his late fifties who had worked for a wine wholesaler, the Bristol Hotel, and the commerce tribunal. Now, as director of the charity bureau, he sat on the board of directors of the crédit municipal. He had known Garat since childhood. They had sat on the same benches in primary school and at the Collège Saint-Louis-de-Gonzagues. Their paths had diverged; Garat had risen, Piet had not. Yet the tie still bound, still drew him into the crédit municipal and then into Tissier's occasional service, without pay, when Garat so asked. You will work at his direction, Garat said, ignoring the arrangement's bizarre anomalies. To act as comptroller even while sitting on the board of directors, to obey the treasurer whose acts and signatures he was supposed to endorse or invalidate — Piet the accountant might reasonably hesitate, but Piet the friend of Garat entered willingly. In his incuriosity about rules and procedures he surpassed the treasury receiver, the prefect, and Garat himself. He asked no questions. Besides, he trusted Tissier as he did Garat; the new director seemed to him a likable and conscientious professional. Tissier even pulled out a regulation declaring that "the comptroller is under the direct orders of the treasurer." Piet signed all the blank bonds that Tissier placed before him. Later he came back and signed more.[23]

Tissier took the bonds and put them aside. He had a second supply, and these he made out for plausible amounts, for a hundred, perhaps a thousand francs, to plausible takers or simply to "cash." He signed them, forged Piet's countersignature, and recorded the modest amounts on the stubs in the bond book and on the separate, mandatory counterfoils. Regulation, the law, and its authors had left little to chance. When the bonds fell due Tissier repaid and neatly filed them away, as probity and efficiency demanded; why would any inspector stop to question them? The duplicate bonds signed by Piet, their numbers corresponding to their modest brethren and to the equally modest stubs and counterfoils, he made out for a million and more, sometimes much more, whatever M. Alexandre had asked for, and mailed them to 28, Place Saint-Georges in Paris.[24]

Two bonds for each operation, for each stub and counterfoil, one masking the other; one for officialdom, one for M. Alexandre; one that went nowhere, one, countersigned by Piet, that joined the mass of paper circulating among the financial institutions of the land. Tissier had worked it all out with Desbrosses, who had already created a few such instruments for Alexandre, in extremis, in Orléans. Garat had told Tissier to stay away from the board of directors, to listen to Alexandre and do as he was told — because Alexandre was the financier of the affair. In any event, he added, the utmost discretion was in order. Tissier loyally obeyed. From above, from his town hall, Garat watched the crédit municipal take shape. He was happy to help when he could. When the matter of the extra book of bonds arose, he helpfully suggested that they take their business to the press most friendly to him, that of the regional paper *Le Journal du Sud-Ouest,* and print them there. But he kept his distance and did not burden the board of directors with unnecessary details about daily operations or the distant doings of their unseen Parisian backer, Serge Alexandre.[25]

The Uses of Insurers

Serge Alexandre went to 26–28, Rue Drouot, ten minutes away from Place Saint-Georges, to the headquarters of La Confiance, the insurance group that had already helped discount the Orléans bonds and launch the Compagnie Foncière. It was March 1931, several days before Desbrosses began drawing up the first Bayonne bonds and several weeks before Tissier began issuing his own paper and keeping his own intricate books. To one of the directors at La Confiance, Guébin, M. Alexandre warmly recommended the forthcoming bonds of the crédit municipal of Bayonne. He was its financial backer as well as its agent, he explained, providing funds for the venture as well as raising them.[26]

Dignified, portly, his beard and mustache well trimmed, Paul Guébin looked prosperous, as bourgeois as his profession. He had joined La Confiance as a young man at the beginning of the century and, now in his early fifties, had risen to its uppermost echelons. He earned about 150,000 francs a year, lived with his second wife and their three children in a sumptuous apartment house on Place Malesherbes, and kept a powerful Peugeot in his name, a Renault in his company's, and a chauffeur to drive them. His family spent winters in Cannes, and some weekends he joined them, because he was also a family man; but he also went to the casino in the evenings. Some thought he lived beyond his means. On Sundays, in season, the concierge of the building on Place Malesherbes watched him leave for the races at Auteuil, Chantilly, or Longchamps, in morning coat, light gloves, and pearl gray top hat, a pair of binoculars slung around his neck.[27]

He already knew M. Alexandre. The two had met late in 1929, when La Confiance had agreed to underwrite the eventual reimbursement of the bonds issued by the new Compagnie Foncière, trying to pacify troublesome government ministries. Texier, their common lawyer, had put Alexandre in touch with him, just as he had put Alexandre in touch with Edmond Boyer, the deputy; a lawyer's most precious potential blossomed outside the law. Guébin and Alexandre began to lunch together, and in time they crossed paths in Cannes as well. La Confiance also took some 10 million francs of bonds from the crédit municipal of Orléans. Guébin did not ask why M. Alexandre began redeeming the last of them so hastily. All he knew, as Alexandre now returned to propose the new bonds from Bayonne, was that La Confiance had recovered its capital with handsome interest as well.[28]

Insurance companies felt squeezed. Returns were uncertain, interest rates variable, policyholders demanding. To bring them 4.25 percent and themselves a modest profit as well, companies such as La Confiance urgently needed the security of a 5 percent return on their capital. In 1926, during the inflationary crisis of the franc, the directors of La Confiance had set up a new subsidiary to help its pinched member companies invest their funds. They placed Guébin at its head, and told him to invest their capital in land, property, stocks, and shares. The task was not always easy, especially not by 1931, when the world economic crisis finally reached France. Guébin's hands were not always free. Sometimes the government applied pressure. Government bonds were falling in value, it would say, buy some to drive them up. They might bring only 4 percent. But La Confiance would agree, overhearing ominous talk now and again in the halls of the Chamber of Deputies, of nationalization or a state monopoly. Here came M. Alexandre proposing a fixed rate, not of 5 but of 6 percent—since he offered a special discount to Guébin, which brought the return up a point. And crédits municipaux, Guébin and his superiors believed, enjoyed the government's blessing. A decree of 1916 had added their bonds to a list of approved holdings for insurance companies, to the state annuities and railway, treasury, and Crédit Foncier bonds already allowed by a decree of 1906. You do not really need to look into them, the government seemed to say, they are sound holdings; but did it therefore guarantee them? Would it protect an insurance company holding false or invalid bonds, and indemnify the indemnifier? Neither Guébin nor his superiors knew, and not only because they did not ask: nobody else knew either. It was too gray an area. The question was unsettled and supposed a public lending institution so subverted as to swindle rather than protect the citizens, so contrived as to employ the state in its own felonious stratagems. Guébin and his superiors lightheartedly bestowed on the Republic the status of guarantor, as unimpeachable a fiduciary as the borrower behind the annuities and treasury bonds they held. They agreed to take M. Alexandre's bonds.[29]

Why a new crédit municipal in a town the size of Bayonne should display so Gargantuan an appetite for funds, why the proceeds from its bonds should pass directly into the hands of a Parisian financier, why that agent should offer such generous terms and commissions—Guébin's not to reason why. But, prudently, he wrote to Bayonne asking for confirmation, as though to cover himself against conjectural busybodies or intruders.

From Garat he asked, as a formality, for samples of the bonds and of the signatures they would bear. A few days later, they came in the mail with Garat's compliments, but when Guebin compared them to the bonds Alexandre pressed on him he thought he noticed a discrepancy between the signatures of the comptroller, M. Piet. Did he catch a whiff of forgery? Garat phoned. "You can negotiate the bonds," he told Guébin, and he followed up his call with a letter on Chamber of Deputies letterhead. "There may be differences of pen or ink," he wrote, "but truly it's the signature of M. Piet, I can assure you."

From Tissier, a little later, Guébin asked for independent confirmation that he was to hand the cash over to Alexandre. Yes, Tissier replied.[30]

Thus Serge Alexandre began appearing intermittently in the halls of La Confiance. Once, M. Isabelle, president of the Confiance group, saw him waiting outside Guébin's office, and invited him into his own. Why did he have a monopoly over the Bayonne bonds, he asked him. Each crédit municipal had an agent with exclusive rights, Alexandre replied, and he himself had put up the initial capital for Bayonne's. But he could not move to Bayonne, and besides, he was a friend of the mayor there and did not wish to attract too much attention. Indulgent M. Isabelle found this bizarre, perverse explanation convincing enough. He continued to pass Monsieur Alexandre in the corridors of his company, and the board of directors of the group grew accustomed to the continuing presence of Bayonne bonds in their portfolio of investments.[31]

Presently Guébin began finding other corporate takers. He became Alexandre's emissary, the agent's agent. Toward the end of May a stockbroker he knew, M. Dubois, came in and proposed some 5 percent railroad bonds. But Bayonne bonds bring 6 percent, Guébin replied, and the insurer selflessly suggested to Dubois that he find more takers and help himself to his own commission. So successful was Dubois that Guébin decided to start marketing the bonds himself and to oust the good M. Dubois.

His visits to confrères in the insurance companies of the ninth arrondissement surprised them. None among them had taken it upon himself to promote others' offerings so vigorously. Why was Guébin doing so? But they reasoned as he had reasoned, and stifled their sense of wonder.

One of them, the director of l'Urbaine, heard first from Dubois and his own agents, then from Guébin and La Confiance. Interest rates were falling; where could l'Urbaine find a decent return on the company's money? These Bayonne bonds were backed in some way by the state, they would bring in a steady 6 percent, they did not vary—and that, as far as the director of l'Urbaine was concerned, was primordial. In June he took five Bayonne bonds of a million francs each from Guébin, the first of a series that might have been infinite had he not, some two and a half years later, accidentally made a nasty and altogether unwelcome discovery.

Another insurer, L'Avenir Familiale, received a visit from Serge Alexandre himself. Who is this man, the director asked his fellow insurer Guébin in writing, and how can he talk of 4 million francs a month in bond issues from so modest an establishment as the crédit municipal of Bayonne? Guébin wrote back. He sidestepped the questions about Alexandre but sung the praises of Bayonne. He exalted the crédit municipal, vouched for its security. The director of L'Avenir Familiale took 4 million francs of bonds. He was reassured by the 10 million that Guébin held, and impressed by Garat, and a year later he took 8 million more.

That summer and autumn La Paix took 2 million, the Compagnie d'Assurances Générales sur la Vie 1 million, La Paternel-Vie 1.5 million; Lloyd de France, the Banque Française, La Populaire, le Nord, and the Epargne Méridionale followed suit, and Guébin always delivered the bonds at once, drawing on the supply he now kept at La Confiance. In offices, on the phone, to any and all he touted their value and their solidity. He submerged his listeners in documents, the crédit municipal's statutes, the mayoral decree, a letter from Garat declaring that the town and the state regulated the establishment, the budget, duly approved, all the official decrees about pawnshops since 1906, and much more besides; he repeated all that Alexandre had told him, spoke unflaggingly of Spanish refugees and Parisian jewelers, with passion and conviction. He became a virtuoso of the bond market, Alexandre's most eloquent proxy in the capital.

Elsewhere, the enthusiasts materialized as though by magic. Maître Robineau,

Stavisky's faithful notary, helped place the bonds, turning his office on Boulevard de Clichy into a rendezvous point for buyers and sellers. Around Orléans notaries, brokers and clerks began hearing of the new crédit municipal. Desbrosses spread the word, and Garat himself wrote from Bayonne to announce the bonds, their "absolutely safe character," and their high rate of tax-exempt return. Some had placed bonds for the crédit municipal of Orléans and now explained to their clients that Orléans was closing down. But they had even better bonds, they trumpeted, the bonds from Bayonne. A notary in Bellegarde-du-Loiret placed 2.5 million francs' worth of the bonds this way, many of them made out in modest amounts to unsuspecting widows. He himself bought a few, as though to demonstrate his good faith. Another, in Barneville, had no trouble persuading his clients to part with their defense bonds and acquire instead the new and lucrative Bayonne obligations. He invoked Garat and his compelling arguments.[32]

By the end of the year they had all placed eighty-seven bonds and taken in 63.5 million francs for M. Alexandre. Orléans receded, a modest prelude to the achievement of Bayonne. Cash commissions changed hands smoothly and all expressed their satisfaction. When La Confiance bought a bond from Bayonne for a million francs, Guébin would give M. Alexandre the amount in cash, less the interest on the bond, less an additional commission of 0.55 percent, which he himself took. A year or perhaps two later, Bayonne would redeem the bonds and repay La Confiance a million francs. But by then Guébin had already pocketed his prize. The company took commissions when it found other corporate clients for Bayonne, and paid them their commissions as well. All expressed satisfaction. And the young cashier at La Confiance watched Guébin and Alexandre move heaps of thousand-franc banknotes around the company's conference table, and watched too the dark financier leave the building with a packet of them under his arm, wrapped in a newspaper, and disappear into the midsummer bustle of Rue Drouot.[33]

The Support of a Ministry

Born of self-interest closely attended by self-delusion, the episode took on the character of a confined, miniature mania. The insurers, displaying a credulity bordering on complicity, bought up the Bayonne bonds as fast as Stavisky instructed Tissier to issue them. Untroubled by the ethereal enterprise, and even less curious about its unusual Parisian promoter, they looked approvingly on the improbably rich returns and placed their trust in ambiguous official endorsements. Such contagions had recurred at almost regular intervals in the financial history of the kingdom and of the Republic. Effrontery and audacity elevated the forged bonds of swindle above the merely hazardous offerings of reckless finance, but each found infatuated takers notable for their amnesia or voluntary blindness. In 1719, investors flocked to the old Exchange on Rue Quincampoix to buy shares in John Law's Compagnie d'Occident, only to discover soon enough that it had neither gold nor land in Louisiana to back its notes. Passersby bought into the Compagnie Universelle du Canal Interocéanique in the 1880s, after reading posters outside the new Exchange about Panama; sanguine subscribers to Marthe Hanau's *Gazette du Franc* parted with savings in her bank on Rue de Provence in the 1920s. The insurers of Rue Drouot, fewer, richer, and quieter than their exuberant forbears, still succumbed to their variety of folly.[34]

So, in their own way, did the custodians of the public interest, the regulators in the Republic's Ministry of Commerce.

"There are nice things to see in Bayonne," Garat told Léon Delamarche at the General Inspection of Credit in the Ministry of Commerce. "There's a Basque restaurant and a beautiful museum." But Delamarche did not go. Instead, he sent his subordinate Constantin, who, resentful, long-suffering, overdue for promotion, suddenly found himself named assistant head in charge of crédits municipaux. Truly, his magical new friend M. Alexandre could work wonders. Since their lunch at Drouant at the end of 1929, the two had continued to meet intermittently, and now, in May 1931, Alexandre fulfilled through his artistry the spellbound civil servant's rising hopes of deliverance.[35]

Months earlier, Alexandre had sent Garat to meet Constantin in the ministry. They were planning to open a crédit municipal in Bayonne, Garat explained, and he asked the embittered official for advice and information. Constantin happily obliged. Alexandre's powerful associate impressed him. There had been some problems in Orléans, Constantin acknowledged, but nothing serious. Without a second thought, he vouched for Desbrosses. Later he asked Garat for help at Commerce, a word in the minister's ear, a recommendation for promotion. Now Garat obliged in return. He had friends in the ministry—the minister himself, for one, who was a fellow deputy, and his second in command, the undersecretary of state, whose own subordinates included Delamarche and, echelons below, Constantin himself. Such men held his future in their hands. Early in May Garat began insisting to them with unusual urgency that Delamarche needed a roving inspector in his service, someone to visit and inspect crédits municipaux, and that Constantin was the right man for the job.[36]

His was not the only voice from the Chamber of Deputies suddenly speaking up for Constantin. "Ah! If you would like M. Proust to recommend you," Alexandre had genially proposed in that bountiful month of May 1931. He had just met the Radical deputy from Tours at a lunch at Viel on Place de la Madeleine. Guiboud-Ribaud, the Foncière's jaunty and upward-bound young lawyer, had arranged it; he had known Proust for years, ever since his own days as an occasional contributor to the dubious weekly rag *Le Petit Bleu*. Then he had sought him out in the Chamber of Deputies; now he enticed him into Viel's to meet the financier Serge Alexandre. Like Stavisky's other lawyer Texier, Guiboud-Ribaud began to promote rather than defend his rich client, preferring lucre to law and restaurants to courtrooms. The Phébor refrigerator, he told the deputy, is what M. Alexandre wishes to launch in the colonies, and Proust, happily, liked to busy himself with the colonies. He traveled to them, wrote articles for the newspapers about them; he had published one book called *Visions d'Afrique,* another called *Les Iles Canaries;* he represented the Sudan and Upper Volta on the High Colonial Council and sat on the Chamber's Algerian committee. At lunch he and Alexandre talked about the Republic's distant possessions, about the forthcoming Colonial Exposition, about the Phébor, and toward the end of their meal Alexandre asked him to put in a word with the minister of commerce for one of his friends, one M. Constantin. He deserves a promotion, Alexandre told him, to the post of inspector of crédits municipaux.[37]

Proust himself was a man of the law. He came from a family of small farmers in the Loir-et-Cher and had risen through school in Vendôme, university in Tours and the Sciences Politiques in Paris to a modest post in the provincial magistracy. Along the way, he had also acquired a degree in medicine, as though to reinforce his already archetypal credentials for Radical politics, which he then entered. Since 1908 he had been mayor of Neuillé-Pont-Pierre, since 1919 a deputy from Tours, along with the local Radical notable Camille Chautemps, whose rising star he alertly followed. Unlike Stavisky's other acquaintances in the Palais Bourbon and the Luxembourg, unlike Boyer or Puis, he haunted the Chamber and its varied dependencies, devoting himself to matters colonial, commercial, and above all judicial. He rose to speak often, served his party well, and soon found himself chairing its powerful fund-raising Mascuraud committee. He was a modest man with a dark, clipped mustache. Like Garat he wore a Croix de Guerre on his chest for valor at the front.[38]

"My dear friend," Stavisky began calling him at once, and they agreed to lunch again. A few weeks later they dined at Guiboud-Ribaud's luxurious apartment off Avenue du Bois with a dozen others in dinner jackets. Proust sent Stavisky and Arlette tickets to a gala at the Théâtre de Madagascar in Vincennes, regretting that he could not come himself. He agreed to recommend Constantin.[39]

Recommendations were the oil of the administrative machine. Magistrates like Prince, police inspectors like Stavisky's Digoin, and senior civil servants like Delamarche had at one time or another allowed a deputy or senator or minister briefly to better their lot, to favor their careers with an opportune word or whisper, or a note handwritten on parliamentary letterhead. Neither Garat nor Proust, benevolently donating to the cause of Constantin's future, exceeded or abused their power of patronage, which came ready-made with their seat in the legislative assembly. Such were the unseen prerogatives of representation, confirming its sovereignty and hindering, discreetly, the very separation of powers that the liberal Republic proclaimed. Now and again a canting deputy worried aloud about recommendations, called for their abolition, but no sense of indignation, alarm, or urgency compelled the listeners. The matter died. But Garat also happened to preside over a crédit municipal, which his new protégé would be asked to inspect. Buoyed by his new enterprise, eager to benefit his townspeople and his electors, indifferent to the niceties of convention and to the absurdity of the regulated choosing the regulator, Garat forged ahead. Regulatory capture, the seizure of the administrative fortress, seemed to him an indispensable defense, a vital protection, for the bonds of Bayonne as they issued forth into the land. The rest did not matter.

At the end of May the minister of commerce informed Proust that he was appointing Constantin to the inspectorate of crédits municipaux. "I am happy," he added, "to have been able in this way to demonstrate to M. Constantin your generous interest in him." He wrote likewise to Garat, and obligingly acceded as well to his wish that Constantin be sent at once to inspect the new crédit municipal in the deputy's own fief of Bayonne.[40]

Thus Constantin took the overnight train to Bayonne. He went to Tissier's office in the crédit municipal and examined the books—of pledges made, of cash received, of bonds issued. Afterward the crédit municipal put on a huge outdoor banquet and Constantin, the guest of honor, sat at Garat's table along with the subprefect and the treasury receiver. He rose to speak of progress. For two centuries, he said, the pawnshops had lent to the poor. Now they were as good as banks, supporting small businesses, industry, and local life, and this he welcomed. Quite appropriately, their guidance and supervision now came from the Ministry of Commerce, he added. Local papers reported the gala occasion and the speech. His hour in the sun over, the feted functionary returned to Paris and to his office at the ministry in the handsome old Hôtel d'Argenson. He reported that the books in Bayonne seemed fine, the accounting honest, and the treasurer there, Tissier, well up to the job.[41]

How grateful Constantin was, how awed by the powers and connections of his new friend—and he began appearing at the offices on Place Saint-Georges once every two weeks or so. Usually Alexandre, Hayotte, and he went to lunch at Cyro on Rue Daunou or at Delmonico's or the Café de Paris on Avenue de l'Opéra, and afterward Bortchy-Melnikoff drove Constantin back across the Seine to the ministry, where he resumed his day, his work, and his flattering new functions.[42]

Stavisky liked the stories of Edgar Wallace because of the criminals, he told Garat. "I confess I'm never on the side of the police. They bore me." They were sitting in the back of the Buick and Eugène Bortchy-Melnikoff as usual was at the wheel. The two had dined well and even Garat was making conversation. "Those they chase lead much more interesting, risky, full lives," Stavisky went on. "How much more varied, more amusing, are the lives of the guilty!"

"What are you getting at? A defense of crime?" Garat asked.[43]

Garat did not know M. Alexandre very well. Earlier, one morning at the end of 1931, rumors from Orléans had reached his ears in Bayonne. He had just arrived by overnight train from Paris and had come straight from the station to his office in the town hall. A police commissioner with dark eyebrows and a luxuriant mustache came in. Superintendent Gibert was Garat's man, one of his many protégés. A police commissioner from Orléans, he told the mayor, had just warned him about an "Alexandre alias Staviski."

It was Superintendent Fressard, who had investigated the crédit municipal of Orléans in November and found its bonds paid off and nothing left of the dubious emeralds that had backed them. He had heard talk as well of dark goings-on in Bayonne. Nothing actionable in Orléans, he had told the Sûreté in Paris, but he would inform his counterpart in Bayonne anyway. On his way to Spain now, he stopped in Bayonne and called Superintendent Gibert from the Café Farnier opposite the town hall. Bowler hat, wing collar, clipped mustache, and round spectacles—Fressard looked like a relic of the Belle Epoque, another detective from the pages of Arsène Lupin. Are you on good terms with the mayor here? he asked when Gibert arrived in the café. Then do him a favor and tell him that he's been seen too often in Paris with one Stavisky, also known as Serge Alexandre, who may have swindled in Orléans and may swindle again at the crédit municipal in Bayonne. I will send you reports on him when I get back to Orléans, Fressard promised, and went on his way across the border.[44]

"Stavisky? Don't know him," Garat said. Gibert had crossed the street and gone up to see him in the town hall—so easy was access to his patron. "What does he look like? You—do you know him?"

"It's the first time I've heard mention of him," Gibert replied. Then deferentially, reverently: "In any case, Monsieur le Maire, I will allow myself, if you'll let me, to present you with supplementary details when I have them."

"Understood, my good man."[45]

A few weeks later, Gibert returned with some disorderly carbon-copied pages—the Cousin report, the Paris inspector's investigation of the year before, which now lay idle in Paris. Fressard, true to his word, had sent it on from Orléans, along with his own skeptical report of the previous autumn, and Gibert, true to his, now came to share it. He waited patiently for the busy mayor among the secretaries outside his office. Presently Garat emerged and quickly read over the pages that Gibert handed him. "I don't know this individual," he said. "I don't know what it's all about."[46]

Garat's incuriosity bordered on mendacity. He knew little because there was little he wished to know. Willingly he allowed obscurity to envelop the past of M. Alexandre; he shut out the unwelcome rumors, cultivated the art of deafness. Thus he settled the atmosphere. Gibert did not bother to inform the subprefect or the public prosecutor about the matter. Garat, after all, was his mayor, and in any event might comfortably argue that Fressard had found nothing actionable in Orléans. In Bayonne as in Paris, the heavy hand of elective office had quashed the nascent, fragile stirrings of justice.[47]

Now, sitting in the back of the car as Bortchy-Melnikoff drove them through the night, Garat listened on.

"The only way to succeed is to frequent large numbers of people and prevail on them to do what one wants," his friend Alexandre said excitedly to him. "You have to use them, bring them to yield their utmost, by pleasing them, doing favors for them."

115

A note of megalomania sounded. "Some work, others reap the harvest," he observed. "Take deputies in France, for example. They imagine their profession is ideal. Most of the time, they're idiots." He added hastily that he was not speaking of Garat. "Several of them I hold in the hollow of my hand, like this." And, he exclaimed, "We are kings of the world!"

But Garat had fallen asleep.

"Go on, go on, Eugène," Stavisky called to his driver. "Faster, faster!"[48]

EVEN

FREEDOMS OF THE PRESS

The press then was the true Parliament of the country . . . it wasn't the mass circulation press that had the most influence. I saw ministers waiting not only on L'Oeuvre, *but also on* La Volonté *and the highly private* Ere Nouvelle. —Henri Jeanson, *70 Ans d'adolescence*

A hint of menace, conveyed politely enough in an "echo," a rumor in the news, appeared in September 1931 in the weekly gossip sheet *D'Artagnan*. A "M. Alexandre alias Staviski," it reported, was betting huge sums at the baccarat table in the casino in Saint-Jean-de-Luz. He appeared to be colluding in some obscure way with two of the casino's directors, the "echo" declared, before falling silent.[1]

This was mostly true, as the employees and the players of the Pergola Casino might confirm. The barman there often saw him, usually on weekends, in the baccarat room—saw him register as "Stavisky," the name emblazoned on his old gambling permit, but answer to "M. Alexandre" or even just "Alexandre." *D'Artagnan* had innocently mistaken the mask for the man, the stage name for the patronymic. In the baccarat room the footman watched M. Alexandre smile at everyone and converse affably with the other players. Sometimes he dined with Arlette at the Pergola's restaurant. Garat even appeared once in a while, though he did not gamble and entered the baccarat room only to reclaim his wife, who did. Once he and Alexandre withdrew in conclave, away from the table, and talked earnestly for twenty minutes. And, for a while, as *D'Artagnan* chose to reveal, M. Alexandre did conspire with two of the Pergola's own directors to finance bets that would drive away Croesus himself and break the casino's bank. They were bookmakers from Paris, members of the inner circle at Frolic's club on Rue de Grammont, and were contemplating with Alexandre a scheme just as underhanded, just as redolent of chicanery and double-dealing, at the casino in Vichy. But their league soon dissolved. Nothing came of it. *D'Artagnan* dropped the story.[2]

Then, the following March, it picked up the gambler's scent again, this time at the casino in Cannes. It reported the "scandal" of a high stakes, rigged game of baccarat involving a crooked croupier, a police inspector, and his mysterious friend, all three seen together in a nightclub and in a deluxe wagon-lit on their way to Paris. "Everyone talked about the suspicious character," *D'Artagnan* informed its readers, "but few knew him by name." It now revealed his identity: "Stavisky Sacha, also known as Alexandre, of Russian origin, notorious swindler, who was in the news in 1926 and who was arrested while partying with his accomplices in a villa in a Paris suburb." "The Russian," added the knowing journal, "has not yet answered to justice for his last swindle!"[3]

Pécune, the editor, knew all from a fellow journalist, the parliamentary correspondent of the right-wing daily *Le Quotidien,* who in turn was indebted for the information to one of his regular police informants. For obscure, perhaps vindictive, reasons, a source inside the Sûreté Générale had wished to embarrass a colleague or two. The incident suited *D'Artagnan* better than *Le Quotidien,* and Pécune made it the first installment of an entertaining serial, since the story, to his delight, died hard. Once again the pas de deux between the police and the press, joining and separating as easily as practiced partners, blocked Stavisky's way. In 1926, craving obscurity, he had suffered discovery by the one and endured exposure by the other. Now, flaunting his riches among the raffish habitués of coastal casinos, he suddenly attracted their pincer-like attentions again, and this time exposure in the press assumed the unwelcome and unmistakable form of blackmail.[4]

"First the indecency, then the blackmail" — to withhold malice for money was, in the eyes of article 400, subsection 2, to commit the misdemeanor of extortion. More precisely, profit from oral or written threats of revelations true or false could send the recipient before the correctional court and subsequently to jail for as many as four years.

But it rarely did. The victims, the prey, rarely cried blackmail and set justice in motion. Even when innocent of the blackmailer's vile insinuations, they feared the publicity of a court case — especially the financiers, bankers, or industrialists who relied now more than ever on image, reputation, and trust to attract and retain shareholders. In 1930 Marthe Hanau brought the best-known blackmailer of the day, Georges Anquetil, editor of *La Rumeur,* to court and won, but by then she and her extravagant operations were in such trouble that more exposure scarcely mattered. Besides, her suit helped deflect attention from the judicial actions pending against her. We are all powerless against the blackmailers, Superintendent Pachot, persecutor of Stavisky, told her when she first complained to him about Anquetil. Unless you bring suit, there is nothing we can do. And she did bring suit; but most did not. "Whether it's *La Rumeur,* whether it's *Le Journal,*" one of Anquetil's accomplices declared frankly at the trial, "whenever an important paper attacks high finance, it wins." Better to settle before the damage was done.[5]

Usually the victim's payment took the form of an advertising contract. Such devices rendered conviction in court all the more difficult. Who could prove, in the absence of a letter or a witness, that a large fee paid to an obscure weekly just for publicizing a stockholders' meeting or a bond issue had been extorted under threat? When the Foncière launched its bonds, the publicity agent Astruc paid out handsome sums for modest advertisements in papers large and small. No prior threats or explicit warnings had reached him or Stavisky from any of the editorial offices on the *grands boulevards* or the ninth arrondissement. Practices were unstated, accommodations tacit. Now Pécune was attacking Stavisky in *D'Artagnan,* and only a naïf could miss the implicit invitation to settle. Still a charge of blackmail would not stand up in court: Pécune had never explicitly threatened the subject of his gossip column. He could invoke the liberal law of 1881, the freedom of the press, and a higher calling to chastise in his columns those whom the law reprieved in its courts.[6]

The sycophants of ancient Greece, where public prosecutors were all but unknown, used to pursue their fellow citizens with seemingly civic-minded accusations, the better to enrich themselves. They were the first blackmailers, trading silence for their victims' drachmas, exploiting the fear of public opinion and of the dicastery's jury. Whence the fright of notables, Plutarch's trembling rich. Reputation lay at the heart of the matter, the image of a name, and that much never changed.[7]

" 'But blackmail means your purse or your life?' 'Better yet,' replied Lousteau, 'it means your purse or your honor.' "

Balzac, in *Illusions Perdues,* wrongly thought blackmail a recent invention of the English press. It was much older than that, as old as taboos, public opinion, and the circulation of news and money. After Balzac, the authors of all sorts, highbrow and lowbrow, who exploited the theme often left out the press. Lafitte's blackmailer in his popular novel of 1896, *Scandal, Misery & Co.,* was a crooked notary; Emile Fabre's, in his play of 1905 *Gilded Stomachs,* was a director of a colonial railroad company, eager for the support of vulnerable deputies; Jules Romains's, in *Men of Good Will* some twenty-five years later, was an oil magnate at odds with a hostile deputy. In a world in which conventions lasted while customs changed, even an avant-garde play like Ibsen's *A Doll's House* at the Théâtre Libre could turn on private blackmail and still largely omit the more public variety, that of the fourth estate.[8]

Yet the press, as Balzac sensed, magnified the striking power of blackmail many times over. As its power grew, some editors themselves came to practice the ancient art. And when, at about the same time, speculation, trust, and acts of faith came to drive commerce and industry, the targets as well as the weapons of modern blackmail were at hand.

Blackmail, by Stavisky's day, was a by-product of credit. To borrow money and attract capital, persuade investors of the worth of an enterprise they would never inspect, represent an act of faith as an act of reason, to command confidence—such exigencies visited on banks and businesses the avid, menacing attentions of "a press of a rather special sort." They enjoyed an information technology that the Greek sycophants had never dreamed of, financial bulletins and news clipping services to monitor the rumors, and telephones, telegraphs, and private agencies to speed them on their way. But like the sycophants they posed as the guardians of public morality, and accepted the tribute of their victims as virtue's modest reward. "The blackmailer," as one of Anquetil's confrères brazenly claimed, "was created to keep bankers honest."[9]

It was the reductio ad absurdum of a system that left the press with too much power and too little money. Indirectly, less brazenly, most of the great dailies practiced it too. *Le Journal* as well as *La Rumeur* took money from Marthe Hanau, *Le Matin* from the Russian bond promoter Raffalovitch. Financial columns were subsidized by financiers, political columns by politicians. The government's secret funds were a secret to no one, as ministers themselves acknowledged, only the amounts that passed from attaché or chief of staff to editor's emissary. This was not blackmail, but the line between paying the papers involuntarily for silence and habitually for support was clear only in the penal code. The press was venal.[10]

"Blackmail!" exclaimed Eugène Merle, the most literate and the most gifted in the profession. "If you own a mass circulation daily, you're taken for an honest man . . . but if all you have is a small, limited circulation paper, you're taken for a scoundrel. . . . Blackmail, like probity, is a function of the rotary press!"[11]

The press had too little control over its resources, and too much over its subjects, one of which now became "Stavisky dit Alexandre."

The Perils of a Casino

"I'm going to earn my salary," M. Alexandre would say, and would casually toss plaques worth hundreds of thousands onto the green baize of the *tout va* table. "Diagonally," he would tell the croupier. He played hellishly, with abandon, and even his blundering friend Hayotte complained about the spectacle. Such antics, coming from so self-effacing an entrepreneur, seemed suicidal, at least invited gossip, and print gossip, costly to suppress, could quickly sink any enterprise afloat on public trust.[12]

He sat at the baccarat table in the casino in Cannes at aperitif time on a Sunday in January 1932. With him, around the table, sat six other players. This evening they included a known Chilean cardsharper, an uncertain construction contractor, and a Greek-born professional gambler who had worked for French intelligence during the war in his native land and later prospered in the casinos of his adoptive one. At about one in the morning, long after the players had gone home, the Greek went over to a police superintendent who sat alone at a small table at the back of the room. The cards used earlier, he announced, had been marked; the game had been rigged; and Alexandre had walked away from the table with 270,000 francs.[13]

The superintendent, called Montabré, came from the Sûreté Générale in Paris. For seven years he had traveled the casinos, racetracks, and gambling dens of the country. He knew many of the faces. He knew Stavisky's from the Pergola Casino in Saint-Jean-de-Luz the previous September. On a visit there, curious about this Serge Alexandre on every gambler's tongue, he had sent for him and challenged his gambling permit. Ever since an episode of bad checks in 1925 Alexandre had been on a blacklist, forbidden entry to all but a few gaming rooms. But now he produced the laissez-passer from the Sûreté Générale, Inspector Bayard's blessing, bestowed on him when he emerged from the walls of La Santé prison in 1928. Forty-eight hours later, Montabré received a telegram from the Sûreté in Paris instructing him to leave Stavisky alias Alexandre alone.

Over the years Montabré had grown cynical. The gambling section, he thought, had lost its prewar sense of mission, had, since the armistice, slid slowly into a quagmire of indifference and collusion. At racetracks, rich book-makers would roam freely, while in cafés poor ones taking bets of twenty-five centimes would face prosecution. In casinos nabobs at play would return night after night, their movements protected by mysterious orders to Montabré from his superiors at the Sûreté. Move away from their table, he would hear, pay no attention to them. Quickly he accepted the imperium of the casino owners, hesitating to take action without a nod, to investigate without a re-quest. Once the director of the casino in Nice complained to the Sûreté about the five police inspectors snooping around the gaming rooms. Too many, he said. The next day three of the five on duty were reassigned. Once again, like Garat imposing Constantin as inspector of crédits municipaux, the regulated controlled the regulators, and commerce quietly intimidated and suborned the servants of the public interest. Montabré trembled most before M. André, owner of casinos in Deauville, Contrexeville, La Baule, and elsewhere, includ-ing Cannes, where a cheating scandal now threatened to erupt. André now told the superintendent that if he brought in the Cannes public prosecutor's office and opened judicial proceedings, he would close down the casino. Montabré moved cautiously.[14]

At first he reacted skeptically to the sudden denunciation in Cannes. He waited a week, until the Sûreté Générale sent word, to inform the prosecutor's office in Grasse. The cards had been marked, that much was evident. He sus-pected the Chilean, the contractor, the casino's director of games, the other players, the Greek himself, everyone and no one. But this Stavisky had connec-tions; he had flaunted them at Saint-Jean-de-Luz. Besides, Stavisky was not known as a gambling fraudster, the Sûreté said. Montabré gave him a wide berth. Next weekend Stavisky was back. As he left the baccarat table and cashed in his plaques, he suggested pleasantly to Montabré that they dine to-gether. Yes, the superintendent replied, mindlessly; but not here at the casino. With Arlette they went instead to the Taverne Provençale across the street. Montabré's doubts multiplied. The two met once more, as they boarded the blue train for Paris at the Cannes station. But Stavisky climbed into one sleep-ing car, Montabré another. They never met again.[15]

When *D'Artagnan* picked up the story in March, the prosecutor's office in Grasse had already dropped the case. They had detained the Chilean on other charges, but the incident in the Cannes casino was too murky, the evidence too mangled, for public action. Now Pécune's garbled tale—the casino resonating with cries of "stop thief!" a croupier arrested, a superintendent applauded and then accused, seen hobnobbing with the Russian in nightclubs and night trains—gave the affair a new lease on life and poisoned the lives of Montabré and Stavisky all over again.[16]

They somehow appeased Pécune. Three issues later the editor called off his campaign. The incident was closed, he announced; their informant had been intoxicated by the atmosphere in Cannes, the enigmatic kingpin was not foreign and had never been sentenced to five years; the guilty had not been found, but their suspicions came to rest on the Greek—the weekly had received "communications," *D'Artagnan* explained.

As far as Montabré and Stavisky were concerned, however, the damage had been done. The Sûreté acted against both of them. It threatened to haul Montabré up before a disciplinary board. Then his brother, a journalist, intervened and the Sûreté instead transferred him out of the balmy watches of the gambling section and into the mobile brigade in Bourges, back to chasing wanted criminals close to the country's heart. Stavisky found his gambling privileges revoked once again. Montabré left in semidisgrace for the famous cathedral town, and Stavisky set about reinstating himself in his beloved casinos. He was learning. He turned to the press for help.[17]

The Kindness of a Managing Editor

He turned to the short round man with the pointed gray beard and the rose-red face who stood behind him at the baccarat table in the Cannes casino. Albert Dubarry, editor of the Radical daily *La Volonté*, an occasional gambler himself, friend of the casino's owner M. André, was watching the game. Who is the dark, elegant man, smiling, playing for such large stakes, he asked. "M. Alexandre," replied the superintendent of gaming. A few minutes later, during a pause in the game, M. Alexandre came up and introduced himself. He had overheard. He knew Dubarry by sight and by name, he said, and added warmly that they had many mutual friends. They conversed. A few days later Dubarry encountered the charming kingpin of the baccarat table again. No, he could not dine there that night. But he accepted M. Alexandre's quick invitation to lunch in Paris, and one day the following week Bortchy-Melnikoff pulled up outside the offices of *La Volonté* next to the Théâtre de la Michodière. A few minutes later, his corpulent passenger sat lunching with Alexandre at a favored table in the Café de Paris nearby, on the corner of Rue Louis-le-Grand and Avenue de l'Opéra.[18]

La Volonté was more widely read than *D'Artagnan,* and Dubarry more avidly courted than Pécune. He knew almost everyone, especially in the Radical Party: he opened doors for his friends there, closed them to his enemies, called on deputies and ministers at will; energetic and conniving, Dubarry had clawed his way to influence and now displayed some of its godlike conceits. But he needed money. He had needed money all his life.

He was a Gascon, born of a long line in a small town in the Gers where his father taught school. At the dawn of the Radical Republic such solid provincial credentials, crowned by law studies in the capital in the 1890s, entitled their bearer to a career in politics, but Dubarry quickly demonstrated such a precocious propensity for scandal of all sorts that he never held national elective office. He chose instead to live off those who did. He became a journalist.

As a law student, he lived by sponging, swindling, and wheedling, and left debts and unpaid hotel bills wherever his travels took him. Once he laid hands on the funds of a student organization and spent them on his mistress, who stole the show in the scabrous and risqué Bal des Quatz'arts in the streets of the Latin Quarter, and whom prudish senator Béranger, president of the League against License in the Street, decided to prosecute. Dubarry also lived by writing. Vaguely subversive papers on the left, *La Petite République* and *La Bataille,* took his political copy; self-consciously avant-garde periodicals, the *Revue Blanche* and *Gil Blas,* his music and drama criticism. He even wrote a play, "Stéphane's Jewel," which the Théâtre de Cluny put on fifty times and which brought him only a pittance, the theater's profits that he somehow contrived to appropriate. Drama, journalism, and dissipation distinguished his early manhood; words, like petty larcenies, were his expedients, the indispensable instruments of his self-indulgences. He worked on the *Journal de la Corse* in Ajaccio, the *Phare du Littoral* in Nice, *Le Radical de l'Allier* in Moulins; he ran, disastrously, the Théâtre Dejaret and the Bouffes Parisiennes; he squandered his meager earnings and led a debauched and debt-ridden life. Finally, in 1902, Dubarry decided to seek his fortune in the colonies.[19]

In Somalia and Dahomey, in Guadeloupe, Guyana, and La Réunion, in the French colonial administrations of the last years of peace, Dubarry tried his hand as a civil servant. Nasty rumors dogged his progress—that he had made off with overcoats in the Gare Saint-Lazare, had stolen ten thousand francs from a young woman on board ship, had embezzled or otherwise diverted official moneys. By 1912 ministerial inspections were recording Dubarry's wholesale, indiscriminate appetite for goods properly falling under public control. He took crates of textiles from Guyana, superior livestock from Dahomey, stamps from Somalia. There the governor general complained of his coarse and insolent manner. They sent him back to France.[20]

Too myopic for active service, Dubarry had a good war. The Ministry of War unwisely sent him on a mission to Argentina and Uruguay to buy woolens and linens for the armies at the front, and abruptly recalled him when alarming reports began to come in of his behavior there. Through an associate he tried to recruit consular employees, spoke of huge contracts, requested kickbacks, threatened blackmail. So ended his years of public service. He returned to the fold of the Radical Party and its newspapers, and never left.[21]

With flattery and threat, reward and retaliation, Dubarry joined together an empire of connections. Deftly he wielded his editorial powers. Newsprint won him more friends than readers. In the beginning there was Joseph Caillaux, the finance minister whose cause he espoused in the short-lived *La Journée Républicaine* in the elections of 1914. That opened to him the lesser Radical princedoms of Camille Chautemps and Edouard Herriot, and in time Dubarry extended his dominion to the farthest frontiers of Radicalism. The next year he founded a Radical weekly called the *Carnet de la Semaine,* signing himself "Jacques et Jean" at the foot of a gossipy political column and winning more esteem in the august Republican Party of friends and rivals. The year after that he launched *La Rampe,* a theater review, and through the actresses and extras of the stage who quickly came his way, he learned of the countless politicians whom they had befriended in the only way possible. So it went—the ardent, mercurial penman flashing his sinister talent for seduction and intimidation in ephemeral weeklies and ceaselessly reconfigured dailies. *Le Pays* came next, then the *Journal du Peuple,* and finally the postwar torrent of uncensored, unbridled opinion sheets.[22]

He won enemies as well as friends. He was always close to Caillaux and his circle and accordingly hostile to Clemenceau and his. Cautiously in *Le Pays* during the war, boldly in *L'Ere Nouvelle* after it, Dubarry adopted Caillaux's more pacific Radicalism, his language of compromise and negotiation. This drew fire and hatred from the right. *Action Française* accused him of treason. Clemenceau had him interrogated. Berthelot at the Foreign Ministry revealed his shady past in the colonial civil service, and Dubarry retaliated with violent attacks in *Le Carnet de la Semaine.* His life was never quiet.[23]

Blackmailers circled round, familiar creatures of the journalistic landscape. Georges Anquetil of the *Guignol Enchaîné* blackmailed him with the sordid secrets of his student days. But Dubarry had similar professionals in his employ. The author of the racing column in the *Carnet de la Semaine,* who signed only as "Yanot," routinely libeled the varied contenders of the racetrack—owners, trainers, jockeys—until they purchased his silence. For a while he employed as editorial writer in *L'Ere Nouvelle* Anquetil's own accomplice, the "Red Devil" of the *Guignol Enchaîné,* who habitually importuned the valued owners of gambling dens and brothels, among others; such were the weapons of a mercenary war, defensive as well as offensive.[24]

By the time Dubarry took over *La Volonté* in 1925, he had prospered. The student who had lived in furnished rooms, the colonial official driven by poverty to pawnshops before the war, now occupied a house, owned a château in Normandy and a villa on the Côte d'Azur, and gave sumptuous dinner parties. He had mistresses; one wrote a fashion column in the *Carnet de la Semaine,* another, a Polish Jewess, danced in nightclubs in Nice. Dubarry became a man-about-town.[25]

But his income was insecure. Where did the money come from? From advertisers and readers, most obviously; but also from businessmen, from foreign embassies, from the special funds of government ministries. In 1917 U.S. industrialists, hoping for postwar reconstruction contracts, poured 12 million francs into *Le Pays;* in 1926 the ministries of the Interior and Foreign Affairs discreetly contributed half a million to Dubarry's newspapers; Romanian diplomats paid him to promote a bond issue, German financiers to campaign for Franco-German reconciliation. Dubarry befriended the Soviet Commercial Delegation and was seen emerging from their embassy one day in 1926, just when the ambassador was rumored to be seeking friends in the French press. Such support came like manna from heaven, and through the "Red Devil," Dubarry violently attacked a plan of Poincaré's to prosecute papers subsidized by foreign powers. Like other editors, he took a dim view of such infringements on his freedoms. He had to take his money wherever he could find it.[26]

La Volonté was a substantial morning paper, its revenues as precarious as its competitors. Dubarry was squabbling with the Havas wire service over *La Volonté*'s account, several months past due, when he met Stavisky early in 1932. All autumn the newspaper had not paid the agency for its information service, which daily supplied it with dispatches and releases until one o'clock in the morning. "I could never imagine that you could write to me in the terms you used," he had indignantly written Havas during a similar impasse in 1928. Now he handed the negotiations over to an employee. Dubarry needed money.[27]

Sooner or later, he would have met Stavisky even if their predilection for gambling had not brought them together at the baccarat table in Cannes that January. They had mutual friends, M. Alexandre had said as he introduced himself; and indeed they had. Dubarry's rakish associate in Argentina in 1914 was a young lawyer called Adrien Cerf, later the bookkeeper and gambling club manager who tried to break the bank with Stavisky at Saint-Jean-de-Luz. His collaborators on *La Journée Républicaine* included the Radical dignitary René Renoult, who later tried to have the charges dropped against Sacha Stavisky. Landau, one of the wartime journalists in German pay who moved in Dubarry's circle, also frequented the Cadet-Roussel in Stavisky's day there. Later, as the editor of the *Agence Technique de la Presse,* he continued to watch the flourishing financier. One day, he or someone else would have introduced Stavisky to the editor of *La Volonté*.[28]

Dubarry sat at lunch now in the Café de Paris, rotund and florid, his host trim and dark. Stavisky's usual table overlooked Rue Louis-le-Grand; in season, when the restaurant was open, he often came twice a week. He seemed, to Dubarry, to know everyone there, to attract greetings and signs of recognition from most tables in the room. This impressed Dubarry. And Stavisky spoke of grand capital projects, of some vague and vast investment in Hungary—several hundred million francs!—backed by powerful insurance companies and a bank all to himself. Once again megalomania sounded, a delusional din. M. Alexandre added that he would require, in due course, a press campaign. He and Dubarry began to see each other.[29]

One morning he called on Dubarry in *La Volonté*'s offices on Rue de la Michodière. It was on the third floor, looking out onto the narrow, busy street. Alexandre was furious. The Sûreté Générale had suspended his gambling privileges, barred him from the country's casinos. They suspected him of cheating at baccarat in Cannes—a man of his connections, a businessman of his weight? It was unthinkable. Would Dubarry go and sort the matter out with his friends at the Ministry of the Interior?[30]

The first official Dubarry called on was M. Jullien, the director of the Sûreté Générale, who received him in his office on Rue des Saussaies.

The director, an official of prefectoral rank, served at the whim of the minister of the interior. He was the confidant, the eyes and ears, who stayed in charge on

Rue des Saussaies only as long as did his patron on Place Beauvau; when the minister went so might he. It was a political appointment, as fleeting as any in the waltzing cabinets of the Third Republic. Such precarious tenure would have discouraged bold innovations or stands of principle, even if the director had had the means to make one. He did not. Two hundred and nine underpaid employees, most of them in Paris, some scattered around the country, made up his ragtag army, ill-equipped to resist even gentle pressures from such well-armed public figures as the minister or the influential editor of *La Volonté*, Albert Dubarry.[31]

Still Director Jullien tried. He demanded that Inspector Bayard reclaim and tear up the laissez-passer he had given Stavisky in 1928, ordered Superintendent Montabré to Bourges, and banned Stavisky from the casinos in France. Now Jullien demurred when Dubarry came along and demanded that he rescind the measure of exclusion. You have nothing against him, Dubarry protested, only some youthful excesses—for his new friend M. Alexandre had confessed to those. Dubarry went off to see the minister, Albert Mahieu, in his office on Place Beauvau.[32]

They already knew each other. Mahieu was one of many on Dubarry's rounds, and his ministry regularly gratified *La Volonté*, like so many other dailies, with thoughtful contributions from its secret funds. After this latest rendezvous, Dubarry's demands reached the director of the Sûreté Générale from the lips of his own superior. The minister parroted the editor. He told Jullien that there was no proof in the matter against Alexandre, only presumptions. All the other suspects that night in Cannes, the players and the casino employees, had now been reinstated; why not Alexandre?[33]

Mahieu had never heard of Alexandre before. Nor had Jullien. When the Sûreté director saw the article in *D'Artagnan* he asked his assistant directors what it was all about and who this "Staviski alias Alexandre" was. They replied that he had run afoul of the law before, had been banned from casinos, later allowed to reenter some of them; he ought to be banned anew, they added. When their director came back with the minister's sudden wish that the ban be lifted, they dissented. So did Jullien, but he chose not to make an issue of it. "It's a measure of goodwill," he told the minister. "If you wish to take it, take it." And he drew up the order; but to cover himself he asked Mahieu, as his minister, to sign it. Then he put it in his desk drawer to gather dust for a while. Stavisky remained persona non grata in the casinos of the coasts. Like his new friend Dubarry, he grew impatient, restive.[34]

In June, after the elections, the government fell and Mahieu left the Ministry of the Interior. He had spent just four and a half months there. Jullien left with him. When the jubilant Radicals moved back in and the new minister, Camille Chautemps, took over his favorite ministry, the Interior, Jullien went along to pay his respects. He learned then that his brief tenure at the Sûreté was over. Chautemps was bringing in Thomé, the director of the Banque de l'Indochine, to succeed him; Jullien might take Thomé's place at the bank if he wished. The two exchanged offices, and Jullien, as he took his leave, told his successor of the

Stavisky dossier that lay passively in the drawer. Thomé opened it up. Then Dubarry called on him.[35]

Two years earlier, in Thomé's first brief stint as director of the Sûreté Générale, a dossier with Stavisky's name on it had crossed his desk. At the time, he had routinely approved a partial restoration of the subject's gambling rights. But he had paid no attention. And now he had forgotten about it. He was fifty-six and dimly distinguished, with bushy mustache, hair parted down the middle, rimless glasses riding on a pince-nez—an elegance only just passé, recalling yesterday's horse and carriage. Loyally, without brilliance or éclat, Thomé had risen through the civil service, primarily in the provinces. Now he settled in behind his new desk to contend with the fifteen hundred notes, reports, letters, and documents of all kinds that besieged him every day. Stavisky's was one of them.

Yes, of course, it's a matter of honoring my predecessor's decision, Chautemps observed when Thomé came along and told him of Dubarry's insistent visit. He had never heard of Stavisky. But he too was on Dubarry's long list of friends. And Thomé complied, overriding objections from within the Sûreté. He ordered Stavisky reinstated, and that summer M. Alexandre's dark, smiling countenance reappeared among croupiers, kingpins, and baccarat tables on glittering nocturnal waterfronts.[36]

No one had said anything about the gambler's parallel life, about the dark rumors emanating from the Foncière in Paris or the crédit municipal in Orléans or the new bank in Bayonne. Cousin's and Pachot's investigations had remained a dead letter, the prefecture of police jealously guarding its secrets, withholding them from their rival brethren of the Sûreté Générale. Relations between Quai des Orfèvres and Rue des Saussaies were execrable. Each had its territory—one in Paris and the Seine, the other everywhere else. But criminals tactlessly wandered across the boundaries between them and forced a sullen cooperation, poisoned by bureaucratic malevolence. The ill will had lasted at least since the Second Empire, when a brief experiment in administrative absurdity had placed the national Sûreté under the Parisian prefecture. Soon afterward, as the mass press brought anarchists, murderers, and a steady diet of newsworthy crime to the attention of every voter, and as the army slowly shed its repressive domestic mission, the deputies came to sense the urgency of unifying and controlling the Republic's police. But in Stavisky's day the cause of reform still languished. Deputies needed, sometimes feared, both the Sûreté and the prefecture, hoping perhaps to manipulate them more easily; some of them, like Garat, craved as well a docile municipal police among the voters at home. The control of financial crime, especially, bordered on anarchy. At the Police Judiciaire in the prefecture, crusty old Xavier Guichard never bothered to send Cousin's reports on Stavisky over to the Sûreté. Nothing obliged him. Besides, he found them rather arcane. At the Sûreté no one thought to ask him for them, to sound out Quai des Orfèvres about a man who had frequented the clubs of the capital as well as the casinos of the provinces. He remained an unsavory but slight figure, a file in the stacks that stretched to the ceilings, down dark, fusty halls on Rue des Saussaies.[37]

Ducloux, the supervisor of judicial investigation, had once held the Cousin report in his hands. He was one of the two assistant directors of the Sûreté, and oversaw its twelve regional brigades of inspectors around the country. He was the nerve center, the recipient and sender of countless coded messages. When, at the end of 1931, Superintendent Fressard in Orléans investigated the strange happenings at the crédit municipal for the Paris public prosecutor's office, he sent a copy of his findings to Ducloux. To it he attached Cousin's report, in which the able inspector from Paris aired the new rumors about Bayonne and the old ones about Orléans. But Ducloux did nothing. It was up to the courts, he reasoned. Let Fressard inform his counterpart in Bayonne. He had found nothing actionable anyway. Besides, the Sûreté Générale was stretched to the limit—thirty usable inspectors for the whole country, he complained, versus more than seven hundred at the prefecture for Paris alone. Ducloux put the report away, and neither Jullien nor Thomé nor Mahieu nor Chautemps nor anyone else learned about it until, awhile later, scandal rescued it from oblivion.[38]

Dubarry's enduring presence, the constant amid the flux and the gray eminence behind the rotating princes of the bureaucracy, had carried the day. He was too powerful to provoke, his request too trivial to refuse; and for M. Alexandre he had more requests to make.

He became, informally, a guardian angel of the crédit municipal of Bayonne.

In June, as Dubarry campaigned for Stavisky's reinstatement in the casinos, Garat, deputy and mayor of Bayonne, called on him in his office at *La Volonté*. He brought with him a letter for the governor general of the Banque de France, asking the august establishment to pay out cash advances for bonds from provincial crédits municipaux—in effect, to guarantee them. Would Dubarry add his voice to the request in the form of a covering note? Such was the power of an editor that even a deputy and mayor craved his name and signature over his own. Dubarry agreed, but the governor general would have none of it. Such bonds were not even publicly priced or traded, he replied, they were out of the question. The financier, the deputy, and the journalist took their search for sanctity, for the indispensable blessings of the Republic, elsewhere.[39]

M. Alexandre began appearing several times a week at Dubarry's office on Rue de la Michodière. He phoned him there often. Bortchy-Melnikoff too began stopping regularly at *La Volonté* to pick up its imposing editor; he drove him to appointments, to lunch with Alexandre, to Deauville, to Aristide Briand's funeral—and back, while Dubarry soliloquized at length about the late apostle of peace from the moderate left who called out from his tomb to the citizenry. This mystified his White Russian chauffeur. Bortchy-Melnikoff drove him to the races, because Dubarry loved the turf as much as the tables, like his new friends Stavisky and Hayotte. He owned a few horses, and one evening Stavisky paid an overdue trainer's bill for him before they went to dinner together. Out of reciprocal kindnesses an alliance sprang, and when toward autumn Stavisky expressed a wish to buy *La Volonté* outright, to take over the paper as its absent owner, Dubarry reacted with undisguised warmth.[40]

Dubarry, as usual, needed the money. Now more than ever, as the worldwide economic crisis finally reached France, the sources of revenue for political dailies were drying up. No paper, least of all *La Volonté,* had ever been able to live off subscriptions, sales, and advertising alone; now even these were weakening; new, cheap weeklies and reviews were proliferating, competing for readers and the covert handouts of an increasingly parsimonious government. The old expedients no longer sufficed. Dubarry had tried them all, mixing politics, journalism, and publicity just as indiscriminately but noticeably more vigorously than most of his colleagues and competitors. He had organized a Paris-Berlin auto rally to celebrate the Locarno treaty, had played it up in his columns, had given the reporter an old Peugeot renamed "Locarno" for the occasion, and had taken in handsome advertising contracts from the manufacturers. He had met an unemployed pilot and parachutist over lunch at Drouant, had hired him to write an aviation column on commission, and had begun planning with him a Paris-Saigon air rally, complete with a plane from General Aircraft of London to be called "La Volonté." Then Stavisky proposed taking over the paper and, of course, its publicity arrangements as well.[41]

Dubarry knew by now that the dazzling Serge Alexandre hid the obscure Sacha Stavisky, that ignominy dogged his renown. But precisely why, whence, and whither his riches, precisely what dark secrets lay behind the doors of the crédit municipal in Bayonne or the gates of the Compagnie Foncière in Paris—here Dubarry restrained his journalist's curiosity, observed the same tactful discretion that the board members, deputies, employees, and almost everyone else displayed. He would stay on as director general, that much was understood. He and Stavisky began to discuss terms.

At the same time, Dubarry undertook another mission to another old friend, Minister of Labor Albert Dalimier. Ask him, said Stavisky one morning at *La Volonté,* to allow social insurance funds to invest in crédits municipaux bonds.[42]

The social insurance funds took in, invested, and paid out the sums that workers and their employers set aside for accidents, unemployment, and retirement. As usual, confusion reigned over regulation. Who controlled their financial operations, the state deposit bank, which performed them, or the Ministry of Labor, which approved them? The ministry, Garat and Dubarry assumed with Stavisky; for them, it had the additional merit of accessibility, thanks to Dubarry.[43]

He had known the minister, Dalimier, for over thirty years now. They had met in 1900, when Dubarry worked briefly for Waldeck-Rousseau's ministry and Dalimier was a rising young lawyer. When they met again at the outbreak of war, as Dubarry returned from his colonial adventures, Dalimier was undersecretary of state at the Ministry of Fine Arts. Gradually the two became friends, as journalists and politicians did. Once or twice Dalimier contributed to *L'Ere Nouvelle* and *La Rampe*. Now Dalimier was minister of labor and Dubarry called him *tu*.

In between, Dalimier had defended the swindler Rochette in court, had proffered legal counsel to Stavisky's ephemeral crony André Himmelfarb of the Cinema Trust of 1924, and had made a name for himself as both a civil and a criminal lawyer. He was a child of the Radical Party, Dreyfus generation, a protégé, around the turn of the century, of Waldeck-Rousseau and Emile Combes and of the party's tireless seeker for friends and funds, Papa Mascuraud. A lawyer, a native of the southwest, much in favor of disarmament, the League of Nations, and the progressive income tax, a voluble and eloquent speaker, but a very modest legislator who had, in all his twenty-one years in the Chamber, introduced only three bills—Albert Dalimier was a typical Radical. He was a dapper man with a handlebar mustache who frequented the racetrack and vacationed on the Côte d'Azur. Sometimes he and Stavisky crossed paths there but the two had never met.[44]

He sat in his office in the old archbishop's palace on Rue de Grenelle. In 1906, in the wake of the crisis over the separation of Church and state, the government had confiscated the edifice, so that Dalimier, basking in the afterglow of anticlericalism, now governed the house the Church had once ruled.[45] It was September 1932, and his old friend Dubarry came to call, just steps away from the Ministry of the Interior where, in the spring, the corpulent editor had so urgently demanded and so rapidly obtained Stavisky's reinstatement in the casinos.

Would he, Dubarry asked, agree that social insurance funds be allowed to buy and hold crédits municipaux bonds? He explained that a M. Serge Alexandre wanted to recover part of a large investment in the crédit municipal of Bayonne. Would the minister sign a letter urging the social insurance funds to take Bayonne's bonds? He even produced a draft of the letter.[46]

Dalimier knew little about crédits municipaux. But it was not the first time one of Stavisky's emissaries had approached him about them. In June, days after moving into the ministry, Joseph Garat, fellow Radical, deputy, mayor of Bayonne, and president of its thriving new crédit municipal, had written asking him to remind private insurance companies that they could invest their funds in crédit municipal bonds. Never one for half-measures, Garat had prevailed on Commerce as well to intercede with Dalimier, who soon began open letters from that quarter; one came from Constantin, the new inspector so enamored of Garat, Alexandre, and Bayonne. Thus besieged, Dalimier signed, and on 25 June 1932, the president of the General Board of Insurance Companies received a letter from the minister of labor reminding him of the excellence of crédits municipaux bonds. It was a matter, he wrote, of the public interest—employing the term Rousseau had used as an antonym for private interests. Garat and Alexandre added the letter to their promotional materials for Bayonne.[47]

Delicately a deputy had set the bureaucratic clockwork in motion, and the minister had sung like a cuckoo. Now Stavisky moved to wind it up again. This time he had the social insurance funds rather than the private insurance companies in mind, and sought a ministerial endorsement not of crédits municipaux in general but of Bayonne in particular. And this time he turned not to Deputy Garat but to the journalist Dubarry, who knew Dalimier better.

Thus, in September, Dubarry sat in Dalimier's office, told him about Bayonne, and gave him the draft letter for the social insurance funds. He reminded the minister of Garat's interest. Dalimier said that he would ask the social insurance director in the ministry to look into the matter.[48]

Into the regulatory foliage went Dubarry's draft, to emerge, after several wrong turns, in the actuarial and accounting department of Dalimier's ministry. There two perplexed officials conferred, hesitated, hoped for further instructions; one drafted a reply to Dubarry, explaining that the ministry could not tell social insurance funds where to place their capital; and then the phone rang.[49]

Was the caller from Dalimier's cabinet? So the disembodied voice said. Imperiously, it ordered the stunned official to write as Dubarry had asked, to recommend Bayonne to the social insurance funds. It threatened a visit later in the day. Abruptly the line went dead.

Many years earlier, another phone had rung in another ministry. It was 1907, and Dubarry was under investigation at the Ministry of Colonies for his conduct in Somalia. He had, among other things, borrowed money from an employee and failed to repay it. The phone jangled in the ministry and a voice claiming to be that of Emile Combes, former prime minister, councillor of state, haughtily denounced the investigation of Dubarry, and defended him. Abruptly the line went dead.

The voice, it later transpired, did not belong to Combes. Then to whom?—only to someone well acquainted with Dubarry's problem, and a suspicion of trickery dogged his steps for a while. But nothing could be proved. Telephones were like that. When the official at the Ministry of Labor hung up in 1932, he did not think twice about the caller's identity.[50] He returned to the draft letter to Dubarry and its doctrine of ministerial restraint, and gently sweetened its tone. Then he hesitated; and with the caller's voice ringing in his ear, he concluded warmly: "Given the benefit of the security promised by such investments, I do not doubt that boards of directors—especially those in the Bayonne region—will be sure to welcome the offers." After all, he had instructions in such matters. No, the ministry could not tell the social insurance funds how to invest their moneys; but when deputies were involved (and Bayonne meant Garat), conciliate, conciliate. Dalimier signed the letter. He knew nothing of Bayonne and its sordid secrets; the ignorance that exonerated him from criminal complicity just as surely convicted him of professional permissiveness. But sometimes he stayed in his office until one in the morning signing letters, and there were limits to a minister's vigilance. Besides, Dubarry was a friend.[51]

The friend gave the letter to Alexandre, who erased Dubarry's name as addressee but not his title—the abstract "Monsieur le Directeur"—and so gave the document the appearance of a ministerial circular to the social insurance funds, and by extension to anyone else, touting the bonds of the crédit municipal of Bayonne. He and his friends at La Confiance put the letter to good use. They added it to their growing package of promotional materials—to the earlier letter to insurance companies, to the decrees founding the crédit municipal of Bayonne, to the prefectoral approvals. The secretary general of the social insurance funds, seeing Dalimier's seal, bought 20 million francs' worth. The bonds in circulation began to climb, from 110 million in September, before Dalimier absently signed his name, to 148 million at year's end, to many more before it was all over.[52]

Truly Dubarry was worth his weight in gold.

In December Alexandre finally bought *La Volonté*. He conjured up a new publicity company called the Société Anonyme de Publicité, d'Impressions et d'Editions Nouvelles de la Seine, SAPIENS for short, to run it. Most of its named shareholders were as ghostly and elusive as those who had lent their own names to launch the Foncière back in 1929, but the million francs that Alexandre discreetly put up were real enough to take over *La Volonté*. Several million more followed. From being Stavisky's benefactor Dubarry became his salaried appointee, his managing director, at ten thousand francs a month and another five thousand for expenses. He kept his freedom to decide the paper's political line. But Alexandre, of course, could control the financial pages and the braided, merging lines of what they reported and what they advertised. Above all, he could command Dubarry's influence.[53]

"I'm through with the job of bank messenger!" Dubarry told Prefect of Police Jean Chiappe, yet another friend. They had met almost forty years earlier, as the Panama scandal was ending, when both were young journalists in Corsica. "I'm going to become my paper's own director," he explained, since he thought fondly that his money worries were over. Chiappe knew of Stavisky, of his intermittent skirmishes with the prefecture and its Police Judiciaire, but only enough to caution his friend Dubarry. "Stavisky is capable of anything," he told him. But Dubarry did not mind. And why would Chiappe insist? As far as he knew, Stavisky's money came from the Foncière, and Dubarry's friendship was worth keeping.[54]

Chiappe's counterpart at the Sûreté Générale, Thomé, had also learned of Alexandre's acquisition of *La Volonté*. An inspector had got wind of the transaction and told him of it. Neither he nor Chiappe bothered to tell their common superior, Minister of the Interior Camille Chautemps. But Dubarry did. He called on Place Beauvau, told Chautemps of the takeover, and reassured him that he would retain editorial control. He was protecting his supply lines: the ministry subsidized *La Volonté*.

It was early December 1932, and the Chamber hotly debated reparations and interallied debts. Prime Minister Herriot's government fell, then Paul-

Boncour's, quickly; would Chautemps form a government? The consummate parliamentarian, dubbed by Léon Daudet "urbane and shadowy," maker of majorities and consensus, was too absorbed to pay much attention to Dubarry's story. Besides, the ministry could not regulate the ownership of all the country's newspapers on a daily basis. There were too many of them, and unless the police found criminal or suspicious foreign connections, the government could not lightly obstruct a private transaction. There had been the casino business in the spring. But Stavisky had been reinstated. For the second time Chautemps let him through, and a satisfied Dubarry left Place Beauvau. *La Volonté* began appearing with six pages instead of its usual four.[55]

In such small ways did editors of the day avow their weakness and demonstrate their strength. Need drove them toward finance, influence toward politicians. In ceding control of his newspaper to an unknown financier, Albert Dubarry had done no more than bow to the realities that had sent his confrères in similar directions—*Le Figaro* to François Coty in the perfume business, *Les Débats* to François de Wendel in steel, *Paris-Soir* to Jean Prouvost in textiles. The new magnates of the press craved less the profit that their factories already brought than the importance that ownership of a paper conferred, the connections, the influence, the access to a minister's office. Never enslaved, but always obliged, the editors in their pay were inspired to arrange some of the countless little compromises that bound together the elites of this Republic and that Stavisky too had learned to activate; with Dubarry his hour had come.[56]

To Arlette, Sacha seemed jubilant when Dalimier's letter came through. Jokingly, she asked him how much it had cost. He was taken aback. "Never in my life," he said.[57]

They were living in the Claridge, on the Champs-Elysées. That summer they had moved out of the villa in La Celle-Saint-Cloud and into the Hôtel Napoléon on Avenue de Friedland, leaving now and again for Nice, Biarritz, and Saint-Jean-de-Luz. Now they were to reside at the city's most fashionable address. Framed by fluted pilasters, the Claridge's grand entrance opened onto a mirrored foyer of glass and light displaying furs, handbags, ties, and beautiful books. Expressionless servants in livery stood by and innocent music floated out of the tearoom. An elevator cage, hiding ugly machinery, rose to the fifth floor where Stavisky, Arlette, their two children, and Camille the governess lived in suites 501, 502, 503, and 504. Indeed, much of the floor was theirs. The weekly bills came to five thousand francs. Their cellar burst with sporting articles, skis, sleds, golf clubs, and a million toys. Stavisky, king of the Claridge, showered the personnel with extravagant tips, so compulsive was his generosity, so ardent his craving for status. Rumor had it he was planning to buy the place, and when he went by in silk suit and dazzling white shirt he left behind an alluvium of hearsay, whispers, and awe.[58]

A jade green Hispano-Suiza, the pride of Bortchy-Melnikoff, rested outside, polished to a fine sheen. Bortchy disapproved of young Claude, who left fingerprints on the coachwork, which were immediately removed. Stavisky's insufferable companion Hayotte had a black Hispano of his own and a dark blue Bugatti *faux-cabriolet* to boot, and Arlette too now had her own green and black Marmon 879, a nice little sedan with four doors, four windows, and four seats.[59]

To lunch — since the mania for appearances extended to restaurants, the emblem of a financier's style and the sign of his worth. "Pay particular attention to the menu," M. Alexandre would ask the owner of the Auberge du Père Jean on Rue des Volontaires, and would arrive with beribboned guests whom he deferentially addressed around a remote table as "mon général," "cher maître," and "cher docteur." Afterward, he would leave lavish tips as he made his way to Bortchy-Melnikoff and the waiting Hispano. He took his friends and prospects to the Café de Paris on Avenue de l'Opéra, to Larue by the Madeleine, and to a private room at Drouant where, one day late in 1932, he asked the chasseur to go cash a check for thirty-two thousand francs. Ever attentive to the menu, he conspicuously displayed the exacting standards of a refined gourmet. But once, the maître d'hôtel saw through him. Bring me some other oysters, Alexandre asked with studied superiority, these ones are no good; and when the cunning maître d'hôtel returned with the same ones from the kitchen five minutes later, his demanding customer pronounced them excellent. It was all an act.[60]

The Thirst of the Press

Albert Livet, editor of *Le Cri du Jour,* picked up the Cannes casino story in September, months after *D'Artagnan* had first run it. A few days later, M. Alexandre called on him.

"I am Serge Alexandre," he said, and explained that he preferred an amicable discussion to a libel suit, since they had common friends.

Livet knew Cazenave, for example, the lowly accountant who had lent his name to the Foncière. Ten years earlier he had written the editorial column for Dubarry in *L'Ere Nouvelle*. He had also written, at about the same time, the poisonous "Red Devil" column in Georges Anquetil's scandal sheet of the day, the *Guignol Enchaîné*, and had blackmailed with him the owners of illegal brothels and gambling clubs. Now he edited his own rag, *Le Cri du Jour.*

M. Alexandre asked for a correction of the Cannes casino story, and Livet pleasantly obliged. But he complained that the casino owed him a thousand francs for the previous year's advertising. Alexandre paid him, and came up with another thousand for the casino in Deauville.

"It's taken care of," he told Livet a little later. "Every time you have amounts like this from casinos I frequent, hand them to me, I'll see to them." He also said that he would soon be able to take over the publicity for *Le Cri du Jour*. Livet listened with interest, and the two began to meet and talk about it.[61]

The connivance was spreading. Joseph Kessel, a larger figure than Livet, met Serge Alexandre at dinner in the spring of 1932 in a fine restaurant in La Villette. His host seated him near Dorn y de Alsua, the old Ecuadorian diplomat whose name somehow dignified the Compagnie Foncière and the stable of racehorses in Maisons-Laffitte. Dorn's mummified perfection fascinated Kessel—the tapered gray whiskers, the nearly precious speech, the rigid, formal bearing unchanged by five or six cocktails, wine, and prodigious liqueurs. Hayotte was there as well, and left the usual execrable impression on Kessel. The novelist found him bovine. Lightly Alexandre touched his shoulder. He asked about reporting, and Kessel in reply extolled his part-time trade.[62]

"It interests me too," Alexandre said. "I've been thinking of it for a long time, but I can't quite see how . . ."

A little later, Alexandre took Joseph Kessel's brother and fellow journalist, Georges, to lunch. Casually he proposed twenty million francs to start a daily newspaper. His guest, who had founded *Détective* and *Voilà*, politely refused, explaining that his ambitions did not extend beyond illustrated weeklies. Then let me contribute one or two hundred thousand francs to a new one, as a shareholder, Alexandre said pleasantly. "Which for me is nothing" he added.[63]

Later, at Père Jean, he renewed the offer to Joseph Kessel. Hayotte was there again, and so was Gilbert Romagnino, a dark, energetic man in his late thirties whom Alexandre introduced as his secretary. He had a hooded look, and his functions were obscure. Before the war he had sold jewelry for Van Cleef & Arpel on Place Vendôme, but when, in 1915, his three brothers were killed at the front, a compassionate command sent him to a comparatively irenic Morocco. Now over lunch he spoke nostalgically to Kessel of that country, of its villages, mountains, and fierce loyalties. After the war he had managed to buy a hotel in Le Tréport on the Channel, and there one day he met Hayotte, and through him Stavisky, and before long he had joined their P'tit Pot caper. But, after the disasters and arrests of 1926, he fled to Nice, where for several years he eked out a difficult existence in rooming houses inland and travel agencies on the Promenade des Anglais. Now he was back, manning the offices on Place Saint-Georges, one of the few who went up to the suite in the Claridge without being announced, a daily presence at his resurgent master's side.[64]

While Romagnino talked of Morocco, Alexandre ordered lavishly and pressed interminable courses on Kessel with Oriental, nearly sadistic hospitality. Typically, hypochondriacally, he ate little himself and scarcely touched the wine. The afternoon lengthened. Alexandre showed photos of Arlette and their children and talked of casinos and gambling and of colossal wins and losses.

"And so, the paper?" he suddenly asked Joseph Kessel.

Kessel agreed to meet him on Place Saint-Georges. There Alexandre kept his word and gave him a check for twenty-five thousand francs, the first quarter of his share. But he had Romagnino sign it. He did not want his own presence announced.

"When you issue the rest of the stock," he said, "let me give you some advice. . . . I know more about it than you do." He smiled swiftly, somewhat diabolically.[65]

Kessel never did launch the weekly, and in the bar of the Claridge one day he returned Alexandre's contribution to him. Crestfallen, Alexandre asked Romagnino to accept Kessel's check. But he and Kessel became friends. When Alexandre spoke vaguely but grandly of plans to settle war debts in Eastern Europe, Kessel detected in him delusions of grandeur, a conviction that he could save France and all Europe from the world's deepening economic crisis. He had emerged from the shadows, thought Kessel, into the glare of Paris society, and seemed to crave honor and respectable fame above all else, confident that his ends justified his means. Meanwhile, he flaunted his wealth. From time to time Kessel's brother Georges saw him at racetracks, at Chantilly and Saint-Cloud and Longchamps, where one day Alexandre proudly showed him one of his remaining hopes, a fine horse called "Prétentieux."[66]

In the late summer of 1932 Alexandre read Kessel's reports on the Nazis and the plight of von Papen's government, and asked him to write for *La Volonté*. Kessel was returning from Königsberg and East Prussia, Alexandre from Bayonne and the Côte Basque. Kessel suggested *La Liberté* instead, edited by his friend Camille Aymard. Alexandre was delighted. Here was a paper on the right, a nice complement to Dubarry and *La Volonté* on the left. Kessel brought Aymard to lunch at Larue.[67]

Like Dubarry, Aymard had come to Paris from the provinces—from Loudun, in the Vienne—and had tried his hand at law, politics, colonial adventure, and journalism. And like Dubarry, he had come to grief in all but the last vocation. Debarred before the war as a lawyer in Paris, suspended during the war as a notary in Saigon, rejected after the war as a Bloc National candidate in Versailles, Aymard had finally thrown his lot with *La Liberté* as editor and principal shareholder. He did not look like Dubarry—the editor of *La Volonté*, some ten years older, was short, round, and volatile, Aymard more angular and reserved. They did not share each other's politics either, and Aymard excoriated in *La Liberté* the very Radicals, the very *cartellistes* on the left, whom Dubarry extolled in *La Volonté*. But, like his rival, Aymard needed money, and had been known to practice the same sort of journalism. Once, counting on their reasoned generosity, he had threatened to campaign against gambling clubs. He too lived by subsidies and loans and expedients, and when, in 1927, the monthly deficit of *La Liberté* reached two hundred thousand francs, it was only thanks to Pierre Taittinger and his archconservative Jeunesses Patriotes that the paper stayed afloat. He was no better off now, even though he sat lunching in a private room at Larue with Kessel and their engaging host, Serge Alexandre.[68]

They bantered over the meal, discussed nothing serious. Two months later at the Claridge they met again. Alexandre, who had read Aymard's angry editorials in *La Liberté* about reparations, expressed his conviction that countries, like people, should honor their word. Aymard found such scruples incongruous in a financier. Alexandre also spoke to him, as he had to Kessel, of far-reaching international finance projects. Aymard paid little attention.[69]

"How is your newspaper doing?" Alexandre asked. He wanted to help. He offered fifty thousand francs. Aymard accepted.

A few days later, Alexandre proposed taking over *La Liberté*'s publicity contracts from the Havas agency. This would allow him to publish anything he wanted, and he was prepared to pay handsomely for the privilege. He had just done as much for *La Volonté*. Aymard was tempted. *La Liberté* was the last evening paper on the right. The Radical deputy Louis-Louis Dreyfus had just bought *L'Intransigeant*, even though he had left its politics alone, and now more than ever Aymard sensed the wolf at the door. But he resisted. If you ever want to sell the paper, Alexandre said amicably, keep me in mind, and the two parted ways. But only for a while.[70]

Aymard knew nothing of Bayonne and the source of Serge Alexandre's river of riches. Like so many others, he chose not to ask. He was a polemicist, not an explorer, and like Dubarry he lived only by the words he brandished. Like him too, Aymard claimed to cherish his independence. He could console himself with the reflection that his pen rather than his opinion was for hire. But sometimes his patrons told him what to write, and one day Serge Alexandre would politely do the same.

Even while wooing new friends, Alexandre sought to neutralize old enemies. The threat that *D'Artagnan* had conveyed in its winter articles about Stavisky's exploits in the Cannes casino returned that autumn in the columns of the similar scandal sheet, *Aux Ecoutes*. Its creator, Paul Lévy, ran a weekly more scurrilous and less substantial than even Dubarry's or Aymard's daily. Still he shared with them a law degree, early disgrace, and a cavalier disregard for even the puny ethical code of their profession. In 1926 *Aux Ecoutes* had briefly exposed Stavisky as the doors of La Santé prison closed after him. It had hinted then that something might be rotten in the justice system. *D'Artagnan* picked up the theme in the winter of 1932. Now *Aux Ecoutes* gently returned to it.[71]

Alexandre, it reported, had been thrown out of the Bellevue Casino in Biarritz, after a dizzying game of baccarat at the open stakes table. Charles Kahn, a rich cofounder of the Galeries Lafayette and frequenter of casinos, had told *Aux Ecoutes* all about the incident. For years he had shared with his friend Lévy the closely observed sights of the high life. Out of such intelligence, freely embellished, Lévy produced gossip items, *échos*, in *Aux Ecoutes*. Now he was away on vacation, at the Hôtel Splendide in Châtelguyon, but as usual at such times a part-time assistant editor from *Le Journal* came over to the little office on Rue Volney to put out the paper. He duly transformed Kahn's report into prose of a sort and published it, adding that Alexandre was "the Stavisky of the false Hungarian certificates"—an allusion to vague new rumors beginning to fly around town.

A week later, the assistant editor published another vignette from the sojourning Kahn. This time, a friend of Stavisky's, one Baron Empain, had been slapped by an angry Norwegian lady in the same casino and thrown out. Stavisky, himself back at the baccarat table, had managed to reinstate him. The story was harmless enough. But Stavisky's camp began to stir.[72]

Who, they wanted to know, was behind these stories? Garat the deputy and Dubarry the journalist also bridled at the attacks on their new associate. Reputation, in their world as in his, was all. A journalist in Biarritz aroused their suspicion. And well he might. Henri Mercadier had been campaigning against Garat in the Basses-Pyrénées for years, in newspaper articles and even in a vituperative book about him. Had Mercadier learned of the Alexandre connection? He was a sinister-looking young man with a narrow face and round glasses, a deserter and pimp, scribbler and propagandist. A chasseur from the Café Anglais called on him at his apartment in Biarritz. A Monsieur Myr would like to see you, he announced, and Mercadier went down to the café, which stood not ten meters from the casino on Place Bellevue.[73]

Myr Chaouat was Dubarry's secretary and *homme de confiance,* as handy and willing a servant as Stavisky's Romagnino. He had come to France from Tunisia in 1922 and moved about in the shadows of gambling clubs, banks, and newspapers until 1929, when Dubarry took him on as nominal editor of his biweekly theater review *La Rampe.* When Alexandre began frequenting Dubarry and the offices of La Volonté on Rue de la Michodière in the spring of 1932, he wandered into Myr's office and asked him what he did. That was how the two met. Now Myr had an aperitif with Mercadier in the Café Anglais. Then he took him outside onto the terrace and showed him the gossip items from *Aux Ecoutes.* Mercadier denied authorship. Dubarry is in the casino now, Myr said, and would like to see you later.

The rotund editor of *La Volonté* duly arrived and they all moved next door to the Café de Paris and dined on the terrace. At home with emperor and urchin, Dubarry was on good terms with Mercadier, who even contributed occasionally to his paper. But Mercadier was innocent of the irksome *échos* about Alexandre appearing in *Aux Ecoutes.* And, driven by a partisan hatred for Garat, Mercadier politely declined to moderate his attacks on Alexandre's local ally. Myr Chaouat extracted a thousand-franc note from a bulging wad and paid for their meal. A liveried chauffeur arrived in a fine car and drove him and Dubarry to the station and the blue train for Paris. Mercadier went home.

Dubarry made another attempt. He tried luring Mercadier away from his native habitat to Paris, where the disoriented creature might be more susceptible to pressure. But Mercadier would not bite. They would have to neutralize *Aux Ecoutes* some other way.[74]

A few weeks later, Paul Lévy, its editor, received in his office a calling card with a note on it: "Serge Alexandre, about the formation of the *Le Rempart* company."

In xenophobic, nearly fascist language, Lévy had announced *Le Rempart* in the spring. It was to be an independent weekly, freely fighting the forces of the foreigner, the demon anti-France. He appealed patriotically for subscribers and shareholders. Now Alexandre appeared at the door and offered his support. He had greatly admired Lévy's journalism, he said. Might a hundred thousand francs help launch *Le Rempart*? They began to talk.[75]

Quickly, through a publicity agent's good offices, they reached an agreement. Pierre Curral, son of a senator from Haute-Savoie, had gone down in flames as a pilot during the war and now directed publicity at *L'Intransigeant*, one of the most influential advertising agents in town. Earlier that year a jeweler, a mutual friend, had introduced him to Alexandre during an intermission at the Miracles Cinema on Rue Réaumur. Now he lived on the sixth floor of the Claridge, just above Alexandre and Arlette. They were neighbors, and passed each other often amid the reflections in the hotel's lobby. He's my best friend, Alexandre told Lévy grandiloquently, and over two lunches he and Curral acquired exclusive rights to advertising in the forthcoming *Le Rempart*—for three hundred thousand francs the first year and six hundred thousand the next. Alexandre set up yet another company—the Société Anonyme Parisienne d'Editions et de Publicité, or SAPEP, and Curral quietly withdrew for the time being. He would lend his advice but not his name to the operation. This annoyed Alexandre. But Curral had not yet outlived his usefulness.[76] Lévy published no further disparaging *échos* about Alexandre in *Aux Ecoutes* or anywhere else. What an affable and worthy man he is, Alexandre remarked to his lawyer Guiboud-Ribaud. And his arm is even longer than Dubarry's. Over at *La Volonté* Alexandre had asked an assistant editor to monitor the press for malicious reports. "Another canard coming out," the loyal employee warned him one day. "What is this *Rempart* going to be?"

But Alexandre was not worried. "I'm on good terms with Paul Lévy," he replied with a smile.[77]

Like Perseus, Alexandre kept hacking at the snakes on the Gorgon's head. Just as Paul Lévy lowered his head, Pierre Darius, the mulatto from Martinique, raised his.

With his elastic gait, photogenic smile, and speckled bow tie, Darius looked more like a tap dancer from the *revue nègre* than the editor of the weekly scandal sheet *Bec et Ongles*. At the age of five, thirty years earlier, he had lost his parents in Saint-Pierre, Martinique. Mount Pelée had buried them, along with thirty thousand others, in volcanic ash. But, since then, the Republic had taken good care of him. It had brought him to Paris and sent him, as a state scholarship student, to the Lycée Saint-Louis, the Lycée Montaigne, and the Faculté des Lettres at the Sorbonne. He was a writer of sorts—a dabbler, the author of a bad novel called *The Roses in the Stained Glass,* of some equally bad poetry, and of *Love in Morocco,* a tour of the brothels of Casablanca and Marrakesh that evoked lascivious dances, bejeweled limbs, and ornate ceilings with golden triangles, but that rarely rose above the tritest pornographic portraiture. Darius was also something of a crook. Before embarking on his literary career, he had sold rugs, wines, and agricultural machinery, leaving behind him a trail of lasting ill will and charges of swindling. But that was all past. Since then, when not absorbed by his literary oeuvre, he had managed theaters, including the Avenue, the Ambassadeurs, and the Apollo, had run for deputy in the fifteenth arrondissement and lost miserably, and had written for two of the city's beloved gossip rags and blackmail sheets, *La Griffe* and *La Rumeur.* He lived on Rue de Hauteville, not far from the Gare de l'Est, and frequented, nearby at the Porte Saint-Martin, cafés pullulating with prostitutes who called him "Pierrot le cendré"—ashen Peter.[78]

He founded *Bec et Ongles* in 1931. An ecumenical weekly, it attacked politicians, actors, athletes, and fashion models indiscriminately. Darius spent about forty thousand francs a month on it, relying largely on prudent preemptive donations from Quai d'Orsay, Place Beauvau, Rue de Rivoli, and Matignon, and from vulnerable citizens, who paid him off in all manner of currency—railway passes, restaurant privileges, discounts on cars, wireless sets and, of course, money, for the most part disguised as advertising contracts. Some deputies and senators subscribed with checks for one thousand instead of the normal one hundred francs. Darius collected his rumors in the corridors of the Chamber and the Senate, on café terraces, by telephone, among friends, and published them without unduly tiring himself with verification procedures. He published perhaps a hundred such *échos* every week. When the curious story of the crédit municipal de Bayonne came his way, he had, most recently, been attacking Général de Castelnau, the Rothschild group, The Baths of Monaco and many, many others. Here was one more.[79]

Chauchat of *Le Petit Journal* had heard all about the Bayonne bonds in a train to Paris, dizzying stories of vast sums and Parisian brokers who asked few questions, he told his friend Darius in passing. A firm on Rue Grange-Batelière, called Esperronier, was placing them, he said. This was true; the insurance company La Confiance had retained it, among others, to help with the steady flow of paper issuing from the little southwestern town. Darius, stealing around the Chamber of Deputies as usual, made the link to Garat.[80]

"Bonds issued by a pawnshop in a large southwestern city are currently on offer in Paris under alarming conditions," he announced in his issue of 15 October, and wondered what might be wrong at the pawnshop. "The city council ought to oversee more closely the management of its crédit municipal."

In November Darius picked up the story again, under the heading "In Hock at Bayonne." This was closer to home, more aggressive. "Canvassers with shady pasts are offering at any price bonds guaranteed by the great southwestern town," he announced inaccurately. "The credit of the town is at stake."[81]

His town, his town's council, his town's crédit municipal—Garat was furious. He was in the Chamber of Deputies when his friend and colleague Emile Morinaud came up and told him about the stories in *Bec et Ongles*. Morinaud was the deputy from Constantine, and when he had been undersecretary of state for physical education Darius had attacked him too, so Morinaud knew all about him. He and Garat went at once to the Chamber library and read the veiled accusations in *Bec et Ongles*. Garat flew into one of his violent rages.

"It's abominable," he shouted. He knew Darius by sight, as a familiar apparition in the lobby and the corridors of the Chamber of Deputies. He would sue him now, he declared, for impugning the public credit. Morinaud tried to dissuade him. It will take forever, he said, the correctional court is badly backlogged. Garat would have none of it. He was adamant.[82]

Sometimes lawsuits intimidated pests like Darius. To silence them, seasoned defenders might brandish the law like a bludgeon and demand apologies, retractions, and declarations of good faith. Such now was Garat's furious intent. But in his rage he risked self-immolation. A legal challenge to Darius's insinuations might send the court's investigators into the vaults, account books, and bond registers of the crédit municipal of Bayonne itself, and Garat, though unaware of many of Tissier's and Alexandre's more eccentric habits, would happily pass up so intense an exposure. Better a published retraction from Darius.

Once again Dubarry provided his good offices. He and Darius knew each other; they had worked together two years earlier, when for a while Darius had edited the "Paris" page in *La Volonté;* Dubarry had even praised his books in writing. Darius still turned up from time to time in the offices on Rue de la Michodière. Now Alexandre asked Dubarry to intercede with him. A campaign against Garat was under way, he said, and a simple retraction seemed infinitely preferable to a court case with all the accompanying attentions of the Bayonne press. Dubarry called Darius. This Bayonne business consisted of groundless rumors, politically inspired, he told him, and Darius obligingly published a retraction.[83]

While the presses were running, at about six in the morning, an emissary from Dubarry arrived. It was Myr Chaouat, *en mission* again for his employer. On the spot, he salted Darius's retraction with vainglorious yet contrite words. "Our well-known impartiality obliges us to clarify matters," he inserted, and added: "The establishment implicated operates normally. The Bayonne pawnshop is a good pawnshop." Two versions went out to the city that morning, one scribbled out by Darius to please Dubarry, a second duly doctored by Myr Chaouat. Thus did *Bec et Ongles* assert its editorial independence. But it did not matter. Darius did not care, as long as Garat withdrew his suit.[84]

This Garat proceeded to do, but not before fulminating a little longer at the impudent Martiniquais. Just as Audibert, an investigating magistrate in the financial section of the prosecutor's office, acting on his complaint, was issuing instructions to investigate the Bayonne bonds made public by Darius's loose tongue, Garat finally withdrew the suit. "M. Garat continues to disturb me,"

Darius had just written darkly to the judge, "I regret it for his sake." He was threatening to retaliate. And, pacified by Darius's retraction, swayed by Alexandre's entreaties, Garat consented to write the affair off as a tempest in a teapot. He had what he wanted. The magistrate Audibert closed the case.[85]

Nothing obliged him to do so. Once initiated, a legal proceeding became a public action governed by the public interest, not an expedient to be manipulated at will by a powerful citizen, to be adopted and just as easily discarded once it had worked its minatory magic. By no stretch of juridical imagination could the withdrawal by a plaintiff, especially from litigation involving bonds and the public trust, entail that of the public action; in a way, it heightened the incumbency on the magistrate, invited his vigilance and his tenacity. But Audibert thought Garat's complaint a vulgar case of failed blackmail, a sordid squabble between the usual suspects. Had he pushed on, had he discovered Stavisky's presence in Bayonne, had he only perused the files of the financial section or requested those of the Police Judiciaire—but Audibert saw no need. Everyone seemed happy.[86]

Once again, the law, alerted by the press, had turned a deaf ear. Two years earlier, the public prosecutor's office, in the distinguished person of Albert Prince, had dismissed Mennevée's doubtful ramblings in *Les Informations Politiques et Financières* and had observed a measure of caution and restraint that approached judicial capitulation.[87] Neither *D'Artagnan* nor *Aux Ecoutes* nor *Bec et Ongles* woke the palace from its torpor, and when Audibert closed the file on Darius, Garat, and Bayonne, he unknowingly ceded the field to Stavisky yet again.

That a blackmailer like Darius should come blindly knocking at the door of truth, only to be turned away by its ordained servants in the Palace of Justice, that he should threaten, and they protect, the swindler—that inversion of roles, if only it had attracted any attention, invited sustained, possibly hostile scrutiny of the Republic's vital institutions. It was a small matter, a trivial episode. But how easefully the deputy had exploited the law, the magistrate ignored its intent, and the journalist toyed with its workings. Darius had revealed to Audibert his source, then threatened Garat through him, and finally received his absolution. Then, a few months later, he traded away his freedom to Alexandre himself.

The two met in the corridors of *La Volonté*. "How happy I am to see you," Alexandre said warmly, and complimented Darius on his latest book. Then he proposed taking over the publicity for *Bec et Ongles*. Alexandre boasted of *La Volonté* and *Le Rempart,* and of the presence of the well-known publicity agent Pierre Curral at his side, and in no time he acquired control of the advertising space in *Bec et Ongles* for the modest sum of fifteen thousand francs a month, the price to pay for the silent goodwill of Pierre Darius the Martiniquais.[88]

Late in the winter of 1933 Pécune returned to the charge in the "A Little of Everything" column of *D'Artagnan*. He wondered where M. Alexandre's money came from, and marveled at the tycoon's progress since his abject arrest in Marly-le-Roi in 1926. Promptly Alexandre proposed a publicity contract. Promptly Pécune accepted. The trusted Romagnino, now everywhere at Alexandre's side, handled the arrangements. For twenty-five thousand francs a month, their new consortium, SAPEP, bought the rights to the advertising space in *D'Artagnan*. Pécune stopped his stories and even began introducing Alexandre to highly placed friends in the Ministry of Finance.[89]

Darius then complained that SAPEP was only paying him fifteen thousand francs a month for *Bec et Ongles*, ten thousand less than Pécune. To redress the injustice M. Alexandre told Romagnino to give him an extra month's bonus. "Yes, in the end that will give him a baker's dozen," he said.[90]

Livet sold *Le Cri du Jour*'s publicity to SAPEP as well, for 14,600 francs a month. Paul Lévy of *Aux Ecoutes* took 300,000 francs for a year's publicity in *Le Rempart,* which was still only a gleam in his eye. Alexandre went to *Cyrano* and *Charivari* and to anyone who would listen to tell them about SAPEP, a veritable Agence Havas for the lowly, scandalmongering periodicals of the capital.[91]

On the street with Romagnino one day late in 1932, he met Georges Anquetil, the bearded blackmailer now fallen on hard times, convicted of extortion against Marthe Hanau, in ill health, at loose ends. Alexandre complimented him effusively on his journalistic talent, and asked him to contribute some *échos* to the newspapers he now controlled. He also expressed interest in a new advertising concept that Anquetil was peddling, a setup requiring the use of a black velvet background to lend a third dimension to publicity photos. Early in the new year, Anquetil received a check from Serge Alexandre for three thousand francs. Two months later came another one for five thousand. The web of influence was growing.[92]

Through Albert Dubarry and *La Volonté*, Alexandre had already reached Camille Chautemps; through Camille Aymard and *La Liberté,* he boasted, he had access to the Radical leader's rival on the right of the of the Chamber, André Tardieu. Strictly speaking, this was untrue. But people believed him. Now and again, Aymard appeared in the glittering lobby of the Claridge.[93]

"The mass press is expensive," Alexandre complained to Romagnino one day, and he never gave up trying to buy it. He began calling on Chauchat at *Le Petit Journal* on Rue Lafayette, taking him to lunch at the Café de Paris, questioning him about the newspaper and its costs, and concocting grand publicity projects. He took aim, just as unsuccessfully, at Emile Buré and *L'Ordre*. In time he reached the editorial offices of *Le Matin* on Boulevard Poissonnière and persuaded the great daily to call off its campaign against a social insurance fund director who happened, incidentally, to have taken 10 million francs' worth of Bayonne bonds. But it was too late. The director had to resign.[94]

It was a harrowing business, this composing with blackmailers and gratifying of editors, a forward flight of accelerating compromises, each provoking the next. The attentions Serge Alexandre lavished on editors seemed at times to dwarf those demanded by parliamentary lawyers, civil servants, officers of the law, and assorted figures of influence. But the threat of exposure, more immediate than that of prosecution, drove him forward in a way that suggested he had lost control of the game. When might compromise lose its appeal for his persecutors, and how much of it in the end could the Republic take?

Alexandre cut his way through the tangled skein of the Parisian press, pausing now and then to collect his wits and time his moves. *La Volonté* was his base, his redoubt. Around noon on most days Bortchy-Melnikoff drove him to the paper's offices on Rue de la Michodière. He went up to the third floor, and there was Mme Dubois the secretary, the short, stout editor Dubarry, and the smooth young lawyer Guiboud-Ribaud. Once, Guiboud-Ribaud had helped set up the Foncière; now he helped manage the money at *La Volonté*. Alexandre had given him seven hundred thousand francs to start operations, and on the fourth or fifth of every month Dubarry handed over to him the secret funds that he had collected from the government ministries. He took care not to offend or upstage the imperious little editor. Alexandre went to his own office at the end of the hall on the right, read his mail, and chatted with Dubarry. At about one o'clock he went downstairs and settled again into the emerald car with the headlamps so huge that by night they could illuminate, all alone, the narrow little street that was home to *La Volonté* and its band.[95]

One day, a visitor asked Dubarry who the elegant man was who had just left. Serge Alexandre, Dubarry replied, head of a publicity firm with millions behind it. "They're madmen," he said, "They squander the funds."

And he turned back to enjoy the business at hand, the business of the press, and his lot in life, that of imaginary freedom. His curious mixture of power and weakness, of the menace proffered and dependency assumed, expressed the ambiguities of his trade and, indeed, of a political culture that sanctified the conflicting freedoms of expression and of commerce.

"But I," Dubarry added proudly to his visitor, "have retained all my political freedom."[96]

THE LIMITS OF PRETENSE

Perfectly aware that one is only seen when one tries to hide, I contrived to make all my faces known [to the police inspectors], to make them famous—but not my very own—and I only truly cheated [by hiding] my own true face and my own true name. —Sacha Guitry, *Mémoires d'un tricheur*

"What do you think of Stavisky, as a name?" Serge Alexandre asked his new friend Joseph Kessel one night.

He and the novelist were dining at Korniloff's Russian restaurant, near Place de l'Etoile. With mounting surprise, Kessel listened to him as he identified the delicacies, the *ogourtzi, stchouka,* and *seliodka,* in hesitant but perfectly stressed Russian. "It's the call of the ancestors," Alexandre had said earlier in the evening, and now, drinking for once, he seemed to surrender to his past, as though he could not escape it.[1]

Once in a while he encountered revenants who knew him as Stavisky. Paulette Luc, for one, sighted him outside the Bar Basque in Saint-Jean-de-Luz. She had met him in the Café Cardinal in 1922, given up her yellow Citroën, and had lent him fifteen thousand francs, which he never repaid. Now she sent word to him at the Miramar, and within an hour he emerged with a check for twenty-five thousand. At the Palais de la Méditerranée in Nice, he ran into old "Castel," the impresario who had been at the Marigny theater on the Champs-Elysées in 1909. He had covered the bills left by the young Stavisky's ruinous three-week tenure there that winter. Now, in Nice, Alexandre repaid the debt and charmingly held out hopes of a job for the aging showman. He went back to Salvatore Zelli's nightclub on Rue Fontaine to settle an old debt, older even than his check-forging caper there in 1923. Reproaches faded, reconciliations bloomed, but Stavisky's old friends from the street, in their opportune advance, in their hint of threat and coercion, darkly resembled his new ones in the press. Henri Poulner, the old prison mate at La Santé, emerged, and his former partner in crime gave him several thousand francs to go forget himself in the Pyrenees. Later Poulner returned and lunched with him and Arlette in the Brasserie Universelle on Boulevard des Capucines, hoping for a job, but he was too conspicuous, too dangerous. Alexandre feared Stavisky.[2]

But the name "Stavisky" meant nothing to Kessel at dinner in Korniloff's restaurant. Loosened up by vodka, his host expatiated freely on his past, mixing fact with fancy. He had spent eighteen months in prison, he said. He had married Arlette there. His enemies had put him there, but the courts had cleared him of all charges. That filthy Galmot had betrayed him to Pachot—and he began cursing, in a dialect so violently at odds with the ele-

145

gance of his dress and his surroundings that Kessel imagined for a minute that he was observing the long-concealed inner man.

"Eighteen months of prison," Stavisky said. "You can't imagine how I suffered. If I'd stayed in any longer, I would have put a bullet through my head."[3]

He recovered himself, however, resumed his normal manner, and the two ended the evening in Montmartre. Stavisky had appeared through Alexandre, coarseness through finesse, and scandal through success: behind image lurked interest. Kessel did not yet grasp the unfolding double plot. But Alexandre's brief demise over dinner portended that of his many allies as well, the stiff-necked dignitaries who might sense in his exposure their own, and turn on him, only to incur the wrath of a once-generous world.

French Officials against Hungarian Bonds

As the number of Bayonne bonds in circulation climbed, the seemingly endless prospect soon dissolved into a new vista, the widest and grandest yet. Alexandre's talk of Hungarian bonds, international agreements, and reconstruction projects, which now and again startled his lunch guests, did not spring from vivid fancy alone. With the millions from Bayonne, he planned to buy up the internationally recognized claims of many thousands of Hungarian landowners expropriated after the war. Then he planned to resell them as bonds on the French market, to finance vast construction projects. The resulting riches would dwarf any of his ventures up to now, and even pay off the Bayonne bonds once and for all. Legitimacy and standing would be his at last.

At the Cadet-Roussel he had exploited personal charm, at the Compagnie Foncière the names and titles of others, at Bayonne the prestige of public institutions. His progress, ever dependent on pretenses of varying fragility, now rested more than ever on the appearance of official goodwill and governmental approval, since the Hungarian venture required both to succeed, to make him a captain of commerce, and to complete his passage from local thief to international financier.

He had first caught wind of the Hungarian land claims in the summer of 1931, when the Bayonne crédit municipal was just under way. At once he seized on the idea.[4] The Treaty of Trianon had given large swatches of Hungarian land to Yugoslavia, Romania, and Czechoslovakia, which had just as quickly summoned the unhappy inhabitants to accept their new nationality or move to their truncated homeland. Uprooted and dispossessed in this way, some seven hundred families, for the most part rich, kept their Hungarian citizenship but lost their lands, their livestock, and their castles. By 1930, international accords in The Hague and Paris had set up an "agrarian fund" to compensate them. Soon the signatories authorized the fund to issue bonds to the expropriated landowners as a guarantee of eventual payment.[5]

At the mention of bonds, Stavisky sat up, for if he could persuade the dispossessed Hungarians to part with their claims he might then resell the bonds from the agrarian fund, boasting the cachet and the security of an international agreement, on the French market. This scheme called for another lawyer, one with the best connections—another deputy.

Romagnino, Stavisky's right-hand man, took to calling on his employer every morning at the Claridge, and there he often saw, on the landing, in the suite, or in the lobby, a short and ghoulish-looking creature called Gaston Bonnaure. "Gastounet," as Stavisky called him, had been SIMA's legal counsel when the Foncière took it over in 1930, and had never left his powerful client's orbit. No service was too small for him to perform. With unseemly haste, in the summer of 1931, Bonnaure had carried cash to Basel to pay off the bonds from Orléans held by the insurance company La Zurich. He had approvingly looked over the Bayonne statutes. He had set up the SAPIENS operation to buy *La Volonté,* finding directors and shareholders of doubtful authenticity— his hairdresser, his father-in-law, a sculptor, his fiancée. And he had prospered.[6]

Like Dubarry, Aymard, and so many others, Bonnaure came from the provinces and mixed law, politics, and journalism in his ascent. He had come to Paris in 1919 from Le Puy, where his parents sold enough wine on Rue Delaizon to send him to the local school and the law school in Montpellier. In Le Puy he practiced law, joined the Radical Party, and of course, the Lay Friends Union, and married the daughter of an artillery officer. But unlike Garat, Boyer, Puis, or any other of Stavisky's parliamentary outriders, he deserted his provincial stronghold. When he inherited and sold his parents' business after the war, he took the proceeds to Paris and a large apartment on Rue Beaubourg, where he began receiving clients as well as potential voters. He divorced his wife and married his secretary, perfected his Radical credentials by writing for *L'Oeuvre* and *L'Ere Nouvelle,* and by presiding over the Lay and Republican Youth; he began testing the electoral waters of his own third arrondissement, and soon ran for electoral and then national office, but the voters would have nothing to do with him.[7]

With his short stature and oversized head, Bonnaure looked like a music hall villain or circus tumbler. He was forty-six in 1932, and that year, when he ran again for deputy in his arrondissement, his rich client Stavisky subtly acquired the status of patron. While the candidate made speeches attacking the budget deficit, unemployment, and military spending, and while Camille Chautemps came into the neighborhood to lend his support and recall his youth and the first stirrings of the Radical Party there, Stavisky quietly financed the campaign. He paid for Bonnaure's electoral newspaper, *Paris-Troisième,* with money diverted from SAPIENS, ordered a tailcoat, a smoking jacket, and a vest for him from Lachaize, and placed Bortchy-Melnikoff and the Hispano at his disposal. In the streets of the arrondissement, in the neighborhood around Place de la République, and on the edges of the Marais, they called on shopkeepers and café owners, and the little man climbed out of the wide touring car with pride and authority, as though confident he could at last impress the voters.[8]

"Hello! Gastounet's elected!" Stavisky exclaimed to Hayotte over the telephone on Place Saint-Georges on election night. "Bravo . . . excellent . . . we haven't wasted our time." He ordered Bortchy-Melnikoff to call Bonnaure "Monsieur le député," but adopted a more informal stance himself, at once friendly and protective, tapping him on the shoulder and calling him *tu*. From Fouquet's on the Champs-Elysées that night, Stavisky also sent out telegrams of congratulations to any victorious candidates he happened to know. But, apart from Garat, Bonnaure now became his most precious parliamentary asset.[9]

Sometimes they dined as a foursome, with Arlette and Bonnaure's wife. Bortchy-Melnikoff fetched "Gastounet" at his new offices on Rue de Ponthieu, or at Stavisky's on Place Saint-Georges, or at the Café du Rond-Point des Champs-Elysées, or at Cyro's restaurant on Rue Daunou; and once he took him an envelope full of banknotes. Stavisky paid him well—almost 8 million francs before it was all over, and most of that soon came from his help with the Hungarian venture.[10]

There was nothing illegal about it, as Bonnaure gladly told Stavisky when asked, and by the time of his election the two had already visited Budapest together.

Bonnaure went armed with a letter from the Quai d'Orsay. It was October 1931, and he was not yet a deputy, but Briand's chief of staff gave him a banal letter of introduction, a courtesy to a citizen of some standing, carefully explaining that he came on private business. It did not greatly help. At the embassy in Budapest the chargé d'affaires, Beauverger, received them. Bonnaure introduced his traveling companion as "M. Serge Alexandre, banker in Paris." Beauverger listened politely while they talked vaguely of their projects and while Alexandre dropped the names of Edmond Boyer, deputy, and Victor Boret, senator. The diplomat was not impressed. He sent them to the commercial attaché, whom they took to lunch at the Ritz, but who was also not impressed. Twice he asked Alexandre what firm or group he represented, and twice Alexandre evaded the question. Beauverger cabled Foreign Affairs in Paris for guidance. Prudence and reserve, advised the Quai d'Orsay; we know Bonnaure, but not the other one; our letter of introduction was a polite formality. After that, Bonnaure and Alexandre stayed away from the embassy.[11]

On the Orient Express a year later, they met the French ambassador. He was returning to Budapest from leave. In the corridor of a sleeping car, Bonnaure, now a deputy, introduced him to two others—Hayotte and Alexandre—but in the roar of the great train the ambassador could not catch their names. Bonnaure and the elegant one talked of Budapest, business, and the last elections. The ambassador retired to his compartment. In the morning, as they pulled into Budapest, he exchanged pleasantries with the trio. But he found them suspicious and, once they parted ways at the station, he painstakingly avoided their company.[12]

In Paris, Bonnaure was a neighborhood politician, a name in the third arrondissement only, of little consequence among the career diplomats across the Seine. But in Budapest he represented the Palais Bourbon, and there Stavisky, for whom aura was all, made the most of him. The status-seeking financier dropped titled names and extravagant tips to impress his Hungarian hosts, but more often than not deferred to his friend the deputy, who spoke convincingly of his Radical connections.

By day they turned their rooms at the Hotel Duna-Palata into a command post, alive with the jangle of telephones, the rattle of typewriters, and the comings and goings of ephemeral new associates. By night they dined at the finest restaurants and stopped at the best clubs, and sometimes in the early hours of the morning gypsy orchestras escorted M. Alexandre to his car. He contrived to dazzle. In time he acquired his first claim on the agrarian fund.[13]

It belonged to Count Eugène Karacsonyi, a dispossessed and indebted landowner who ceded his claim to them for 90 percent of its nominal value. Such a demonstration of solvency might sway even incredulous claim holders, and as word spread, the pace of transactions began to pick up. On paper, the nominal worth of the claims passed from their holders to Alexandre—some 150 million gold crowns, or about 800 million francs. But he persuaded the claimants to accept far less than that in cash, 18 million francs or so, and by the summer of 1933 he was asking them to accept bonds from the crédit municipal of Bayonne. "These bonds aren't worth much," one of them remarked bitterly, "but they must be worth more than my claim."[14]

The claimants had lost faith in their claims. But sitting in the Bela Hoffmann bank in Budapest, as yet unpaid for, the claims meant everything to Alexandre. He had title to them, could promote them now at their full nominal worth on the French market—and why explain that he had paid till now only a fraction of their real value? Or that the agrarian fund had not yet issued any bonds in settlement of them? Lawful until now, his operation began inexorably to resort to pretense, hyperbole, and falsehood.

A latent affinity for spectacle and illusion, childlike make-believe writ large, had drawn Stavisky to the little Marigny theater in 1909 and to the Cadet-Roussel cabaret at the end of the war; in Budapest one night, it awoke again, at a performance of the musical comedy *Katinka*.[15]

He went with Hayotte. That night the two befriended the show's author and composer, a Hungarian student; the next day they began bargaining for the foreign rights to *Katinka* with theater agents on Barasster Street; and a few days after that, Alexandre announced in his rooms in the Ritz that his train was leaving in fifteen minutes, handed the astonished student-composer a first payment of twenty thousand francs in cash, and left.[16]

Hayotte fancied himself a theater director, a conceit Alexandre gratified with unlimited funds for a French production of *Katinka*. Back in Paris, Hayotte hired translators and the songwriter Saint-Granier to work on the score

149

and libretto while he busied himself with the casting. Through an agency in Berlin he found a German beauty dancing in Vienna called Rita Georg, brought her to Paris for an audition, and hired her for the title role. Sixty other dancing girls came over from London, shipped out by Max Rivers, the theater agent on Rupert Street. With money from Alexandre, Hayotte rented the Empire theater on Avenue de Wagram and took on hundreds of workers to rejuvenate the old music hall, to enlarge the stage and the orchestra pit, and to install the most revolutionary electrical equipment in Paris. Then he fired the opening salvos of an extravagant publicity campaign. *Katinka* was coming to town. He even paid off the organizers of the six-day bicycle race at the Vélodrome d'Hiver to anoint Rita Georg its reigning queen that year. No outlay was too lavish to ensure the success of the production, and Hayotte offered wages and threw sums into the air with such abandon that he frightened off even some interested actors. This was not serious, they thought, not in these times of slumping productions and unemployed professionals of the stage. A producer backed out, a singer from the Opéra-Comique decided to stay on at his trusted old employer. And they recoiled at the misbegotten musical arrangement — only one duet, only one waltz, and a finale that smothered the audience as well as art. Hayotte did not impress them either. Unlike Alexandre, he spared no feelings and paid no compliments. But he loved the theater.[17]

Hayotte lost his head over *Katinka*. For the rehearsal party, he brought in an orchestra and a hundred bottles of champagne for everyone from technician to star, and deliriously charged around the theater in a custom-made suit and a bowler hat askew on his head. Rita Georg's glamour intoxicated him. He showered her with gifts and exhibited her like a window display, blind to her quintessential mediocrity. She allowed his attentions but thought him something of a joke.[18]

Behind Hayotte migrated Stavisky's coterie, drawn along by his forward flight. Soon the offices on the fourth floor of the Empire housed a makeshift yet contented brotherhood of newcomers. Old Desbrosses, the disgraced treasurer from Orléans, turned up behind the cash register; Romagnino, the dark and versatile assistant, helped in accounting; Pierre Curral of *L'Intransigeant* took over the publicity contracts. Hayotte was happiest. He paid himself handsomely and took the lion's share of the original author's rights. With them he rented a town house on Rue Marbeau — next to that of former president Raymond Poincaré — and added to it an immense mahogany bar, carpeting, wood paneling, and a telephone in every room. Just seven years had elapsed since he had lived in a small flat on Rue Damrémont, had endeavored in vain to promote an imaginary consommé called Le P'tit Pot, and had tasted for eight months the bread of La Santé prison. Now he rejoiced with vulgar display in his takings and trusted witlessly in their everlasting source, his friend Serge Alexandre.[19]

During *Katinka*'s six-month run, the Empire became the hub of a varicolored social universe. Down the avenue, cafés and restaurants began filling with the new production's train of friends and followers, with actors, producers, and transient opportunists of doubtful provenance and uncertain design; once or twice the Marseilles gangsters Carbone and Spirito appeared in Cotti's restaurant, opposite the theater. Cast and crew mingled in a comfortable promiscuity, shared with the English dancers. Romagnino took up with one of them, Miss Cecilia Nono of Camden Town, and eloped with her for a weekend to the Savoy in London when *Katinka* closed for the summer. Hayotte blundered after Rita Georg. Sometimes he and Stavisky took her to fashionable cabarets after the show, and from time to time another came for her from far away, in a car with diplomatic plates—her titular lover, the Swedish consul in Vienna. Rita Georg was not up to the role, the critics sniped, but she savored her fleeting taste of stardom, and when *Katinka* closed in October she stayed on to sing and dance in a new musical, *Deux sous de fleurs.* Hayotte's party at the Empire continued.[20]

From opening night, on 23 February 1933, the audience was studded with *le Tout Paris*, guests of Serge Alexandre. Free tickets sprang from him like a river, irrigating the worldly milieus of his affections. Whether friends or indirect acquaintances of his, deputies, journalists, and government officials came to the spectacle, as did guests hitherto unknown to him but just as welcome, including the children of the employees of the prefecture of police, and the prefect's wife, Mme Chiappe, whose official black Renault sat parked outside on Avenue de Wagram on opening night. *Katinka* and *Deux sous de fleurs* became for Stavisky a celebration of his social destiny, the finale to a fancy glimpsed at the Marigny theater many years before; but in its madness the extravaganza at the Empire hinted too at his undoing.[21]

It cost too much. Hayotte was squandering twenty-five hundred francs a day for the theater, four hundred thousand for the deposit; forty thousand a month for Rita Georg, eighty thousand for her publicity stunt at the Vélodrome d'Hiver; more for the dancers, more for the orchestra, more for the advertising. Such lavish outlays, mindlessly funded by Stavisky, dwarfed revenues from tickets, songs, and recording rights—dwarfed them eventually by 6 million francs, a loss manageable enough had not the Hungarian venture that started *Katinka* gone sour that autumn of 1933, followed even more threateningly by Bayonne itself.[22]

▩

A new company, CADRE, appeared, as flimsy as the Foncière, to issue new bonds on the basis of the Hungarian claims. Alexandre staffed it with big names—an honorary prefect, an ambassador, a Belgian senator, his friend Pierre Curral—the well-known publicity agent from *L'Intransigeant*—and Romagnino, his right-hand man, who became a straw man, a secretary general, like Cazenave at the Foncière.[23] Their prospectus, as misleading as the Foncière's, declared the bonds of the agrarian fund unsinkable. The French government had not even ratified the accords. The agrarian fund and the Hungarian government complained: the promotion was dangerous and illicit, they insisted.[24]

In Paris the ministries began to stir again. Finance and Foreign Affairs invited each other to take charge. Investigate, Justice finally instructed the Paris prosecutor's office. Investigate, the prosecutor's office told the Police Judiciaire. It was 11 August 1933, and Inspector Cousin picked up where he had left off in Orléans two years earlier.[25]

■

Now as then, Alexandre deployed his hidden agents in the world of influence. He found grand lawyers to plead his cause and vouch for his integrity. Maître Vinson, a distinguished lawyer on the Conseil d'Etat and a former secretary of President Doumergue's cabinet, presented him with a twenty-two–page analysis of the Hungarian claims. They enjoyed the guarantee of the French state, he concluded obligingly, and the social insurance funds could certainly take them. Dalimier's ministerial epistle had claimed no less for the Bayonne bonds, and Vinson's own contribution, as easily reproduced and disseminated, won him just as much gratitude and recognition. No inner voice of conscience held Vinson back; in six hours, in two sittings with texts and precedents at hand, he wrote his brief and casually placed his association with the Conseil d'Etat, guardian of the public interest, at the service of Alexandre and his entourage. Twice he went to lunch at the Boeuf à la Mode with them, even though he found Alexandre unpleasantly foreign.[26]

The Foreign Ministry's lawyers dismissed Vinson's arguments almost out of hand, in a brief crisper than his own. The ministry disliked CADRE, and hastened to say so to inform Monsieur Alexandre and the distinguished members of its board.[27]

Instinctively, Alexandre tried to reach around the Foreign Ministry. Guiboud-Ribaud, the ambitious young lawyer now employed at *La Volonté*, asked Dubarry and Bonnaure as well if they could find him a position in the Ministry of Finance. Both were friends of Georges Bonnet, and when he became minister of finance in Daladier's cabinet in February 1933 he found a niche for Guiboud-Ribaud. The smooth young man became a *chargé de mission* without a mission, an idle dependent with an office on the ground floor, well away from the minister and his staff above, but an office nonetheless. He worked on a report about tax fraud and another about the pros and cons of returning to the gold standard. Otherwise he had little to do. He became Stavisky's eyes and ears, his fifth column, inside the walls of the ministry.[28]

But he never emerged with words of support for the agrarian fund and the Hungarian bonds, nor even with an introduction to the minister. Stavisky had managed to meet Georges Bonnet once before, through Gaston Bonnaure; he had eagerly accompanied the deputy-lawyer to a European conference at Stresa in May 1932, and had lunched there with the minister as Bonnaure's guest. For the most part, they talked about the coming honeymoon of Bonnaure's nephew and fiancée, also present. Bonnet left hurriedly to preside at the conference. Afterward, Stavisky boasted to Arlette that he had dined at Georges Bonnet's table at the Stresa conference. He seemed excited. But now, a year later, even with Guiboud-Ribaud clinging to the same minister's coattails, the Hungarian bonds met with skepticism and suspicion on Rue de Rivoli.[29]

Outside, Stavisky assembled more lawyers, more hallowed experts to overcome the resistance of officials. Gaulier, the obedient lawyer at his side since the days at the Cadet-Roussel theater, began calling up illustrious colleagues. He took Stavisky to the law offices of Etienne Flandin, former minister, who sent them away, and to those of Senator Odin of the Gironde, who cautiously lent his name to their endeavor. Odin, Stavisky's latest parliamentary conquest, resembled his predecessors—a self-made lawyer, Radical or as good as, child of a modest provincial family, a survivor in the jungle of the Paris bar. He was likable enough, a mediator between fractious Radicals on Rue de Valois, yet seen by them as a "fixer" always in search of a good deal, and when Gaulier asked him for help he did not refuse. He already knew Stavisky, thanks to a brief encounter in the lobby of the Empire theater, arranged by a minor journalist they had each befriended; soon Odin's friends began happily finding in their mail free tickets to *Katinka* and *Deux sous de fleurs*. Yes, said Odin, he would look into the Hungarian bonds and accompany Gaulier to the Ministry of Finance to see what he could do. Who spoke—the influential senator or the learned lawyer? The distinction, critical in the eyes of the law, proved as idle as it had proven for René Renoult, André Hesse, Gaston Bonnaure, and all the other parliamentary councillors whose proximity had dignified the ambitions of Serge Alexandre.

But the ministry rebuffed Odin and rudely cut CADRE loose. If M. Alexandre and his colleagues at CADRE issued any bonds, officials told Odin when he called, they were to say nothing of the agrarian fund and nothing of any imaginary guarantee from the French government. Odin did not insist. "The company concedes," the senator announced, as though speaking on behalf of CADRE, and withdrew.[30]

Deploying Trojan horses, Alexandre dispatched a retired ambassador, member of the new company's board of directors, to the Ministry of Labor to plead his case, Pécune, the newly conquered editor of *D'Artagnan,* to the Ministry of Finance, and Vinson, friendly lawyer at the Conseil d'Etat, to the agrarian fund itself, all to no avail; finally, he dispatched silken feminine charm, in the person of one Suzanne Avril, to the officials under her spell.[31]

Brunette, bejeweled, just short of showy, she sped about town in an olive green Ariès two-seater convertible and appeared, seemingly at will, in ministerial antechambers and parliamentary corridors. Georges Thomé, the cultivated, old-fashioned, and utterly naive director of the Sûreté Générale, received her in his office several times a month and grew increasingly fond of her.

"So you know Stavisky?" he asked her once.

"The way everyone does!"[32]

She had met Stavisky in Biarritz in the autumn of 1932. Mme Avril, who harbored journalistic aspirations and had first frequented the Chamber posing as a parliamentary reporter, extracted from him a promise of work at *La Volonté*. Soon they began meeting in Le Carillon, a small basement bar on Avenue de l'Opéra. They conversed earnestly, interrupted only by masculine voices asking for her over the phone; Alexandre said little about his businesses but much about his powerful friends, and pointedly asked Mme Avril about hers. "Lulu," as he called her, became his ambassador to an establishment just beyond his reach, and messengers from him bearing flowers, money, and paid travel tickets began to arrive perhaps once or twice a month at the door of her little flat on the second floor of a building on Rue de l'Assomption.[33]

"Most willingly," she replied in the summer of 1933, when Alexandre asked her to set up a dinner with François-Albert, the minister of labor, at the Café de Paris. She arranged meetings; that was her mission. The minister arrived in an official Renault driven by a chauffeur with a tricolor cockade on his cap. The minister was gray, in his mid-fifties, short, and frail-looking. He was a Radical, one of the leaders of the party, and came from an old family from Poitou that still lent substance to his infirm person. With him came her father's friend Gaston Hulin, deputy from the Vienne, self-made provincial lawyer, sometime journalist, briefly an undersecretary of state, now under a cloud of scandal. Hulin was a tall man with a long black beard, and he embraced Suzanne Avril's company with a warmth that transcended the usual obligations of family friendship. They dined in a private room, and as M. Alexandre told the minister of his projects, Hulin devoted his attentions to the young woman beside him.

But Mme Avril could not guarantee the outcome of the meetings she so graciously arranged. François-Albert listened while his host spoke of the economic crisis and of a grand plan to resuscitate the nation's commerce. His group, Alexandre explained, would issue bonds backed by the unimpeachable credentials of the agrarian fund, and would lend the proceeds on the most generous of terms to local authorities for civil construction projects. In this infallible way, idle money would circulate and infuse life into their languishing economy. Would the minister invite the social insurance funds to buy the bonds? Bemused, François-Albert promised to study the matter. It was two thirty in the morning. The dinner ended.

The next month François-Albert raised the matter with Hulin. They were at the Radical Party congress in Vichy. Prudence was in order, he thought; the whole agrarian fund business seemed doubtful. Hulin now became the trusted intermediary between him and Alexandre, bringing questions to the financier and soothing reassurances to the minister, a servant of interests he unhesitatingly sought to reconcile. But François-Albert held back.[34]

Then he died. But by then his disappearance did not greatly affect the CADRE project. Officialdom stubbornly withheld its blessing, and all the smiles and guile of Alexandre, the dinners hosted, emissaries dispatched, lawyers bought, and parliamentarians enlisted left the guardians of the national interest as hostile as before. This Hungarian affair, the Treaty of Trianon, and the tangled matter of eastern reparations touched too visibly on national prestige for them to yield to the unspoken rules of the influence game. The agrarian fund was not a crédit municipal, Basel was not Bayonne, and *raison d'état* suddenly had the better tune. Stavisky had pushed Alexandre too far.

Fourteen hundred million francs, he had said, obeying the laws and logic of megalomania, was what the Hungarian venture should bring. He could not stop now. They would start issuing the bonds anyway, without the cachet of the state. An initial 500 million francs of bonds, on the basis of a million francs' capital, might raise some eyebrows; but there was nothing illegal about it.[35]

Besides, they had little choice. It was November of 1933, and the situation in Bayonne was now desperate.

The Press against the Bayonne Bonds

All year they had scrambled to place new bonds, racing to put off the moment when so many of the old ones would fall due that the emptiness of the coffers on Rue Thiers would manifest itself in a flash.

One morning in May, coming out of his office at *La Volonté,* Dubarry met Alexandre on the stairs. Alexandre was anxiously awaiting word from the Banque Nationale de Commerce et d'Industrie (BNCI)—would they, he had asked, take 15 million francs' worth of Bayonne bonds? Dubarry agreed to add his word and his weight and Alexandre accompanied him as far as the bank on Boulevard des Italiens. But the bank's director resisted Dubarry's pressure. He knew of his ties to Alexandre, had heard stories about Orléans, and found 15 million francs exorbitant for a town as modest as Bayonne. "I have a memory," Dubarry told him angrily and added afterward to a friend, "in the end costs are always recovered." Alexandre was more philosophical. "Oh well, I'll ask others," he said.[36]

In June, for the first time, the crédit municipal of Bayonne paid out more for redeemed bonds than it took in for newly subscribed ones. The disparity was small but ominous, 15 million francs to 14. Garat, as president, proposed increasing the interest on new bonds to an irresistible 8 percent, a measure that the board of directors and the prefect duly approved.[37]

In July, Garat, now in his capacity as deputy, called on Charles Tissot, director of the social insurance funds at the Ministry of Labor. Garat brought Alexandre along and introduced him as the "authorized agent of the crédit municipal of Bayonne." Would the funds take 25 million francs' worth of bonds? Lucidly, politely, Alexandre explained how they worked, and how commune, department, and state guaranteed their soundness. Tissot promised to study the matter; Alexandre pressed, phoned, visited, took him to the Boeuf à la Mode and the Empire theater, even procured women of the night for him and his son. Garat spoke to François-Albert, the ailing minister of labor, in the corridors of the Chamber. Alexandre waited restlessly.[38]

He redoubled his efforts, renewed his rounds among protégés and obligés, as though to accelerate in that summer of 1933 the pantomime of professionals that had served him so well since Bayonne and even before.

In July, at the Coq Hardi restaurant some seven kilometers outside of Paris, Alexandre assembled a financier, a journalist, and a prefect for dinner. The first two he knew well: one was a Spanish adventurer who had promised to introduce him to the upper echelons of Madrid society; the other was Camille Aymard, newly befriended editor of *La Liberté* and occasional publicity man. But Alexandre wished to know the prefect, Armand Juillet, better; he had met him at lunch at Larue a year earlier, just when a ministerial ukase had ousted him from the prefecture of the Haute-Savoie. Immediately Alexandre proffered solace and support. "Listen," he insisted, "I have every means to settle this and it won't take long." He asked Louis Proust, the impecunious deputy who more than once had needed his helping hand, to intercede for Juillet with the prime minister; he hosted a party for the slighted former prefect at the Claridge, a lunch at the Café de Paris, and a soirée at the Empire theater; and now he sat opposite him among their little group at the Coq Hardi.[39]

They dined on the terrace, with Arlette and the Spanish financier's wife between them. Soon a violent summer squall drove them indoors, and during their flight Alexandre took Juillet aside, into one of the bay windows overlooking the grounds. Could he remember, he asked the former prefect, the size of the cash reserves in the social insurance funds of Haute-Savoie? Ten million francs, Juillet replied, and with intense interest Alexandre beckoned to Aymard the journalist.

"Do you know, old fellow, that the prefect doesn't know of the existence of the crédit municipal bonds?" he said, and with enthusiasm Aymard told Juillet all about them.

"He's a first-rate fellow," Aymard added to Juillet on their way back to Paris after dinner. "He has some wonderful projects."[40]

But even as Stavisky worked so feverishly to articulate once more the moving parts of the establishment, the first complaints about Bayonne came in.

In August 1932 l'Urbaine insurance company had bought 14 million francs' worth of Bayonne bonds. The company's directors, won over by the interest rate, the tax exemption, Garat's claim about state guarantees, and Dalimier's commendatory letter from the Ministry of Labor, had acted, they thought, in the best interests of their policyholders. Now, a year later, came word from Bayonne that repayment would be deferred. Pleas and pretexts came too, and promises to sell off if need be some 17 million francs of jewels from the vaults, but for the directors of l'Urbaine these did not matter: repayment would be deferred.

The sale of jewels brought in twenty-five thousand francs, not 17 million, and in the autumn Joseph Garat asked l'Urbaine for another delay. He wrote to other insurance companies as well. Bortchy-Melnikoff drove him to call on them door to door. Could they wait until December? Meanwhile Alexandre was visiting La Confiance several times daily. There, Guébin had helped from the start to funnel the bonds into the marketplace. Where now was the money to come from? Bonds were falling due, and the Hungarian venture was going nowhere. A director from l'Urbaine decided to call on Delamarche and Constantin at the Ministry of Commerce. Write to the prefect of the Basses-Pyrénées, they said, and tell him what you know. He did; and the prefect promised to look into the matter.[41]

Garat was furious at l'Urbaine—had he not promised repayment by December? But already he had begun to doctor, judiciously, the minutes of the first board meetings setting up the crédit municipal and its innovative modus operandi. There's been a mistake, he insisted to his secretary. Scratch out my name and replace it with that of Desbrosses—the cashiered treasurer. And the secretary did as he was told.[42]

In April Arlette had won the women's elegance contest at Cannes. She posed in the sun beside the Hispano-Suiza, which was bedecked in flowers, and *Le Can-can de la Côte d'Azur* published the photo in all its frivolity for a distinctive readership to admire.[43]

She knew little about her husband's business, she told an old family friend from Touraine. Jacqueline Vatin-Perignon had found her the job at Chanel back in 1925, warned her, when Arlette met Sacha Stavisky, against men's chronic infidelities, and then lost sight of her after the arrests and disasters of the following year. Now, in the spring of 1933, Mme Vatin-Perignon met her again at the races. He was involved in some Hungarian affair, Arlette added, but again knew little about it.

That summer she began learning that Sacha had less money at his disposal. They would have to cut down, he told her gloomily on several occasions. She often had to give him money herself, to tide him over. He rarely came on the weekends that year to join her and their two children at the seaside; the fine season seemed to pass him by; but once or twice he came to Deauville and went into the casino.[44]

One night in July there, he lost 2 million francs, covered by a bad check, but won them back the following day. If he hadn't, he said, he would have shot himself.[45]

Dubarry was in the casino in Deauville that night, and the two had angry words. After all he had done for Stavisky, raged the editor of *La Volonté*, after all the energy and influence spent for him in countless missions to ministries, the paper's new patron might at least live up to his financial promises and keep up the payments. This he had hardly done. Now here he was in Deauville, recklessly betting 2 million francs he did not have. Dubarry had seen enough. He broke then and there with Stavisky. "You're completely mad," he said, and ended at the casino in Deauville the friendship that had begun so auspiciously a year and a half earlier at the casino in Cannes.[46]

All that year Stavisky's rapport with the journalists, so carefully and so expensively established, had gone from bad to worse. He became a liability to his friends in the press and a target to his enemies, try as he might to woo them by the traditional tribute they accepted as their due, cash payments in the form of advertising contracts.

He gave Camille Aymard, editor of *La Liberté,* another fifty thousand francs for some useless publicity. "I have to please Aymard," he said. "I prefer having him in hand, because he could do us a lot of harm." That autumn Aymard sketched out some publicity for the Hungarian project. It promised watertight guarantees, he wrote, and returns free of taxes. What more could an investor want?[47]

Stavisky kept Darius the Martiniquais on his side too. The editor of *Bec et Ongles* displayed a kind of honor along with his usual bonhomie. He had denounced Bayonne before, he promoted it now. When La France Mutualiste refused to take any more Bayonne bonds, Darius took aim at the insurance company and its directors. One was an official in the Ministry of Agriculture, another a leader of the Federal Union of Veterans. Darius attacked both in his columns. And, like Dubarry, he undertook to win over a minister. But he had less luck. Henri Queuille, minister of agriculture, refused to give his blessing to the Bayonne bonds, and would not intercede with the official sitting on the board of La France Mutualiste. He sent Darius away empty-handed.[48]

One other time that summer, Stavisky's uncertain allies in the press took up the cudgels on his behalf, when Dubarry failed to induce the Banque Nationale de Commerce et d'Industrie to accept any Bayonne bonds. Livet in the *Cri du Jour,* Darius in *Bec et Ongles,* and Pécune in *D'Artagnan* all attacked the bank in unison. "But what is going on in this establishment?" they asked, and called one of its directors "a small-time Mussolini."[49]

But, more often now, they turned on him, or dropped him as Dubarry had. Blackmail could not continue indefinitely, especially when the victim was running short of money; and this one, thanks to the government's obstinacy over the Hungarian bonds, had less and less to give. Newcomers too kept entering the pack, enticing others in turn to join the circling predators.

The first was Jean Sartori, editor of *La Bonne Guerre,* a scandal sheet as mediocre as any other, sent to four or five thousand parliamentarians, financiers, and magistrates. "Serge Alexandre alias Stavisky," he began erroneously but ominously, "had decided in La Santé prison in 1927 to take over a newspaper upon his liberation. He has been free on probation for six years, the item added—"we'll say on what terms."[50]

In the spring of 1926, while Stavisky was on the run, Sartori called on a rich banker, Charles Neuburger. I am the editor of *La Bonne Guerre,* Sartori explained, and it will cost you ten thousand francs to become "one of my friends." Neuburger refused, and Sartori left, trailing words of warning. One night a few weeks later, Neuburger stepped off the train from Biarritz in the Gare d'Orsay with a woman unmistakably not his wife. From the platform Mme Neuburger took aim at her with a pistol, missed, and wounded another traveler. She had been tipped off. Three days later Sartori called.

"I've come to demand something," he announced to Neuburger.

"Monsieur, you've chosen a very bad moment to bring up business matters with me," Neuburger answered. "You're not unaware of my present troubles."

"On the contrary," said Sartori, "this is just the time to discuss them."

Then he published articles about the Banque Neuburger in *La Bonne Guerre*, lacing them spicily with allusions to the Gare d'Orsay and "the pistol of Lady Neuburger." The last of these he sent to the banker and embellished it in his own hand with the words "last notice."

They finally met in a private room at La Pérouse. Neuburger ordered a bottle of champagne.

"How much?" he asked

"A hundred thousand," answered Sartori.

He left with the first twenty-five thousand, a half-crushed bundle of banknotes. Minutes later he was arrested. Neuburger had brought in the police, and Superintendent Pachot himself had listened to their rendezvous from an adjoining room. Dangerous for adulterers, conspirators, and traitors, the thin walls and partitions of La Pérouse were manna from heaven for the inspectors of the prefecture of police.[51]

Sartori distilled in his person all the poison of an odious profession. He pried, threatened, and attacked indiscriminately, trafficked in what shameful secrets he could unearth, and damaged reputations when he could no longer exploit them; and now he attacked Stavisky and his friends.

He attacked Dubarry, "Stavisky's man," Aymard, editor of a "pro-Tardieu daily" taken over by a "band of adventurers," and Romagnino, a salesman, he said, of a "worthless ointment to cure hernias." He threatened to reveal the names of Stavisky's many friends, "however high up they may be." He denounced the "false Hungarian bonds." Finally, he trumpeted a front-page warning to his readers. "Warning to the honest," it read. "Serge Alexandre, residing in the Hôtel Claridge (apartments 501, 502, and 503) is really Stavisky, indicted for swindle before the thirteenth correctional chamber."[52]

They silenced him soon enough. Stavisky's faithful Romagnino and a few hirelings resorted to strong-arm tactics that left Sartori bloodied and indignant, decrying in his paper with typical self-importance a failed assassination attempt. An amicable settlement soon followed, and *La Bonne Guerre* lost interest in Stavisky alias Alexandre. But the damage had been done. People were beginning to talk about the articles. Fellow editors read them. An employee at *La Volonté* asked about them. Gaston Bonnaure, the deputy who had given his all in Budapest, now tried to help in Paris. On Wednesdays Camille Chautemps received deputies at the Ministry of the Interior, and Bonnaure raised Sartori's campaign at one of their meetings. Ignore it, Chautemps replied. He's waged campaigns against me too. There's nothing you can do about it. It was the third time Chautemps had heard Stavisky's name, but it was not the last.[53]

Next came Paul Merle, editor of *Le Pays*. His rag was even punier than Sartori's—some issues were printed on one side of the page only—but it reached as many readers of note, as many deputies, chiefs of staff, magistrates, police inspectors, and journalists as *La Bonne Guerre*. In his weekly column, called "It's on the Level," with the factitious air of intimacy that such publications habitually employed to flatter their readers, Merle started in on the beleaguered financier. "Alexandre Stavisky, alias Serge Alexandre," he revealed in a three-line *écho* culled from rumors overheard in the usual bars and cafés, had lost 1.8 million francs in the casino in Cannes. That was all. But such campaigns always started that way, the soft opening notes of a crescendo. Then Merle went to Bradstreet's financial information agency and published the contents of their dossier on Stavisky, including the press coverage from 1926 of his encounters that year with the law. Threatening phone calls began. He published the stories about the postponed hearings before the thirteenth correctional chamber, and soon after that, on the terrace of a café on Avenue de Marigny, several men accosted him and rewarded him as they had rewarded Sartori. After that, *Le Pays* fell silent, and Merle discovered the virtues of friendship.[54]

One of the men in the Café Marigny was the ubiquitous Romagnino. Another was a foreign legion deserter and former convict called Joseph Hainnaux, also known as "White-haired Jo" and "Jo the Terror." A third was Niemenczynski the boxer, Niemen for short, who retired from the ring in 1925, acted as an extra in René Clair's silent film "The Roofs of Paris" in 1929, and now gave physical education lessons every morning to M. Alexandre in his rooms at the Claridge hotel.[55]

The three became his defenders and enforcers, musketeers of the boulevards and back alleys, undisciplined yet loyal. The recourse to creatures from the border regions of the underworld betrayed a sense of desperation and, to the growing numbers in the press who knew Alexandre's identity as well as his past, marked a return to his original milieu of swindlers and petty criminals. But the physical attacks stopped, and Stavisky still looked to the subtler game of influence to subdue his tormentors. In the café where he still met his old friend from the Sûreté Générale, Inspector Bayard, he complained about the blackmailers. What can you do about them, he asked the inspector. Nothing, Bayard replied.[56]

It was true; there was nothing he could do. "Will there be a Bayonne crédit municipal bonds 'affair'?" the *Journal de la Bourse* suddenly asked in July. The editor had taken to calling on insurance companies and found to his astonishment that they held 78 million francs' worth of Bayonne bonds—and he had not even called on all of them. The bonds amounted to 5 percent of the assets at Lloyd's de France, 5.4 percent at l' Urbaine-Vie, 66 percent at L'Avenir Familiale. Had the services of the Ministry of Labor looked into this? It was all very odd. Insurance companies could lawfully place their funds in such bonds, the

Journal de la Bourse granted in August, but no governmental guarantees assured their recovery. What would happen if Bayonne could not repay its bondholders?—for that, the editor feared, appeared to be the case.[57]

Another gossip sheet, *Commentaires*, quickly picked up the story. The editor, Fernand Raucoules, had noticed Sartori's stories in *La Bonne Guerre* in May and found them wanting, insubstantial. But the new revelations seemed well documented. Raucoules went to the Ministry of Labor, in its converted archbishop's palace on Rue de Grenelle, and there an official in the office of insurance oversight took out the law of 1901 to demonstrate that insurance companies could indeed take crédits municipaux bonds, as many as they liked. The official declined to comment on the soundness of the Bayonne bonds. That was up to the Ministry of Commerce, he said. Raucoules went over there, just down the same street, to meet with M. Constantin, the inspector of crédits municipaux devoted to Alexandre since their meeting over lunch at Drouant's in 1929, devoted to Garat since hearing the deputy's promises of promotion in 1930, and devoted to the crédit municipal of Bayonne since his first official visit there in 1931.

"These certificates are guaranteed as much by the city of Bayonne, which assures their integrity, as by the state," Constantin told Raucoules.

"If a problem arose, who would pay?" the journalist asked.

"A problem is impossible."

Raucoules went away, leaving M. Constantin a copy of the *Journal de la Bourse* article that had aroused his curiosity.

At L'Avenir Familiale, in over its head with the crédit municipal of Bayonne, the securities employee confidently told Raucoules that the company was well protected, well covered. This the prying editor came increasingly to doubt. Soon he picked up word of the dubious Hungarian bonds that Alexandre ardently sought to place on the market.

"Hum . . . By golly! There are already, in the paper reserves of our insurance companies, 100 million francs of the 'cashier's bonds of the crédit municipal of Bayonne,'" Raucoules observed in *Commentaires* that August, and in his piety prayed that the companies had not added new Hungarian to old Bayonnais obligations.[58]

The *Journal de la Bourse* had set off *Commentaires;* now *Commentaires* set off the others. Stavisky had borrowed 2 million francs from the casino in Deauville, the new biweekly *Juvenal* reported incorrectly in September, and could no longer honor his obligations to the papers he owned. This the editor, Maxence Thomas, knew firsthand, since he had worked with Darius on *Bec et Ongles* at Stavisky's short-lived newspaper trust SAPEP, and had seen it die for lack of funds. Like Dubarry of *La Volonté,* he had taken his leave. Now his new *Juvenal* bore on its cover an epigraph taken from the second-century poet's fourteenth satire, devoted in part to the dangers of greed: "No need to worry whence come the riches, being rich is enough." Thomas reprinted *Commentaire's* revelations about the Hungarian bonds; he declared Rita

Georg of *Katinka* to be Stavisky's Hungarian mistress; and he warned darkly that he might soon reveal the mysterious financier's high-level political friends. Two weeks later he reprinted the *Journal de la Bourse* revelations about Bayonne, as an innocent question to its mayor and deputy, Joseph Garat. Then *Juvenal* fell silent. Thomas had received a satisfactory answer from Stavisky and Garat.[59]

Meanwhile Paul Lévy of *Aux Ecoutes* had seen the articles about Stavisky in *Le Pays.* An employee on his new paper *Le Rempart,* the same that Stavisky had agreed to finance in return for its editor's silence, had shown them to him. "It's blackmail," he concluded, as though in moral revulsion; but in September, unpaid like Dubarry, he abandoned Stavisky's ship as well.[60]

Such was the microcosm of the boulevard press, spinning with brief encounters and adroit betrayals. The trick for anyone guarding a secret was to keep it there, away from the wider world of the mass dailies. They too observed loyal silences, depending on their patrons and politics, ran aggressive campaigns, depending on their friends and foes, and minutely sifted through the intelligence that came their way: and sometimes it came from their disreputable relations on the boulevards.

Only recently, the Aéropostale affair had begun that way. Some curious documents about the troubled aviation company changed hands among scandal sheet editors on the street, drifted into the newsrooms of major dailies and the halls of the Chamber, and set off a scandal that broke briefly and died, as scandals often did, in a courtroom.[61] The Hanau affair had started in much the same way as well. Stories about the banker began appearing in the financial weeklies and gossip sheets, telling of hidden losses, imaginary profits, elaborate swindles, and much else besides. The police came for her, and the scandal blew over. It left few casualties but much discomposure among her illustrious friends. And what if the scandal should spiral upward and threaten everyone in its eye, including the journalists themselves? As a matter of fact, they varied little from one affair to the next, and the editor who had set off the Hanau storm was none other than Fernand Raucoules of *Commentaires,* the same who now trained his sights on Sacha Stavisky alias Serge Alexandre.[62]

Everyone against Alexandre

"It's a political cabal," Garat answered when Joseph Anthelme, subprefect of Bayonne, asked him about the articles in *Journal de la Bourse* and *Commentaires.* The two were on close terms; Anthelme had even worked on the deputy's reelection campaign in 1932.

"Look Garat, rumors are circulating, they're speaking of one Alexandre . . ."

"It's all politics," Garat said again, evasively.

Then Prefect Mireur asked him about the articles. "A jumble of rubbish and balderdash," Garat said, and he denied knowing anyone called Stavisky. He lied; by then he knew the reality behind the fiction of Serge Alexandre, and his mendacity betrayed his panic.

Walking out of the town hall, Léon Béhoteguy, a retired shopkeeper in Bayonne and member of the board of directors of the crédit municipal, asked about the stories as well. "My leg is tired," the limping mayor said as they reached the Café du Théâtre, "let's sit down here." It was blackmail, he explained. "I'm overwhelmed with work and worries. Trust me, I'll take care of it back in Paris."[63]

Garat was playing for time. He could no longer ignore what he had avoided knowing before, that his crédit municipal ran on fraud and forgery, its inaugural anomalies in 1931 a mere prologue to Stavisky's enormities since. Garat's own salvation urgently required that they pay off the bondholders, silence the rumors, and somehow salvage the lost vessel of his local dreams. He, more than elusive Alexandre, lowly Tissier, or any of the others at the crédit municipal, stood vulnerably on a pedestal, a temporary idol daily inviting iconoclasm. Already he had amended the minutes of the early crédit municipal meetings to erase his own presence, a crime—falsification of public documents—composed of perfidy as well as fright.[64]

Now he ordered Tissier to remove the few remaining genuine jewels, engaged by unsuspecting locals, from the vaults of the crédit municipal. Give them to Alexandre, he said, and Tissier, docile as ever, passed on the word to old Digoin, the retired police inspector, to go down to the vaults. "All right," Digoin replied, and shortly afterward faithful Romagnino turned up, the jewels in hand, at T. H. Sutton's, a jeweler and pawnbroker on Victoria Street in London. By such desperate expedients did Stavisky and his miniature hierarchy of appointees stave off disaster for Garat and for themselves. Hayotte too took the last of their honest jewels to Orléans, where Farault, who had once appraised their dubious emeralds for generous loans, agreed again to the operation—since the crédit municipal there, unlike its fellow in Bayonne, still had money to lend. The marionettes seemed to come to life one more time, as though in a finale or encore; but the play could not go on indefinitely.[65]

The deputy went through his motions as well. Garat called on the regulators. Why could not Constantin of the Ministry of Commerce play his part and come down to Bayonne for another inspection, to reassure the world that all was well at the crédit municipal on Rue Thiers?

In October *Deux sous de fleurs* opened at the Empire. The art was mediocre but the production sumptuous; the audience came not to listen to music or verse but to look at costumes and the decor. Paris had never seen a musical like it. During its run, *Deux sous de fleurs* brought in 2 million francs and cost over 5 million. Just as quickly, Hayotte's source of funds dried up: Stavisky stopped paying. He had had enough of Hayotte, he told Arlette. Hayotte borrowed frantically, engaged his wife's jewelry, paid the cast from day to day, and watched the bills pile up. He saw less and less of Stavisky.[66]

Neither Stavisky nor anyone else paid Bortchy-Melnikoff's wages. But the faithful chauffeur thought the crisis temporary. Money for the upkeep of the Hispano came now in hundred- rather than thousand-franc notes. Gasoline became a constant worry. Sometimes he arrived at the Empire with the tank empty.[67]

And by November Stavisky and Arlette owed the Claridge thirty-five thousand francs.[68]

■

Investigate, the public prosecutor's office had told Inspector Cousin in August, as the Hungarian bond venture set off alarm bells here and there. "Stavisky typifies the high-level industrial adventurer," he reported the following month, and, when he read the disobliging articles in *Commentaires* about his man, he pronounced them "perfectly accurate." At the Ministry of Labor he had learned that some insurance companies held a hundred million francs' worth of Bayonne bonds, and in the financial milieus where he routinely picked up rumors, Cousin heard talk now of bonds totally unsecured, perhaps 49 million francs' worth. The Orléans scheme writ large, he thought, and reported this too; and he added, as though to lament the rogue's uncommon powers of evasion, that in Orléans Stavisky had slipped through their fingers.[69]

Inspector Cousin's old superior, Superintendent Edmond Pachot, had left the scene at the beginning of the year, retired and gone back to his books. He had left with the esteem of his superiors, yet not fully honored by them for his exploits, since the distinction he had coveted—the title of divisional superintendent—had eluded him to the end. Stavisky was still at large. Pachot's successor, Léon Ameline, was every bit as cultivated; he had taught at the Lycée de Bourges before joining the police, had learned his finance law to a fault, and had written a comprehensive guide to the bewildering world of the Republic's police. He was a cold but urbane man, dark-haired, of medium height, well liked by the magistrates and prosecutors of the public prosecutor's office, in their nearby quarters at the Palace of Justice. Then Ameline donned Pachot's mantle, and with it descended like a curse the sign of Stavisky.[70]

When he read Cousin's report, Ameline sent it up the line to the prefect of police. He did not bother to inform the public prosecutor's office; let the Ministry of Finance, he thought, investigate the insurance companies awash in Bayonne bonds, since the prosecutors in that office had no grounds for going down there and asking the treasurer to open his books. He had notified the public prosecutor's office of Cousin's findings about the Hungarian bonds, and had even called in Stavisky for a brief and unproductive interview about them; but about Bayonne he remained bureaucratically passive, curiously inert, unlike his predecessor Pachot; as did Jean Chiappe, the prefect of police.[71]

Chiappe knew about Stavisky; he had even met him. Earlier in the year, when Dubarry and Stavisky were partners, the editor of *La Volonté* had brought his new patron to the prefecture to meet the prefect, his friend of forty years. Stavisky complained about the stories in the press about him, fed, he charged, by leaks from the officials and inspectors of Quai des Orfèvres. Send me a report, Chiappe suggested, and the two left. On their way out, Chiappe took Dubarry aside and warned him about Stavisky.

"Watch out, he leaves a bad impression on me," he said. The meeting had lasted all of five minutes. It had been frosty, yet that night Stavisky exulted to Arlette over its warmth, over the prefect's effusions. Now, in the autumn, Chiappe glanced at the latest report and sent it back to Ameline at the Police Judiciaire. There was little to be done. Bayonne was far from Paris. Let the gentlemen at the Sûreté Générale look into it—and take on Joseph Garat, if they wished.[72]

As it happened, the Sûreté Générale had already acted, gingerly and warily. The articles in *Commentaires* had crossed the desk of its director, Georges Thomé—the same kindly civil servant so captivated by Stavisky's friend, Mme Suzanne Avril. He duly informed the minister of the interior, Camille Chautemps, who now heard of Alexandre yet again, this time as Sacha Stavisky.

Ask the prefecture of police about him, Chautemps suggested, as though proposing a revolutionary departure from convention. The financial inspectors of the two services ran into each other at the Bourse, and regular meetings united the two at the ministry, but cooperation between them was no more eager now than it had been in 1931, during the investigation of the Foncière and of Orléans. At that time, the prefecture had failed to share its information about Stavisky with the Sûreté; now the Sûreté declined to share its knowledge with the prefecture. An inspector traveled from Rue des Saussaies to Quai des Orfèvres to retrieve and examine the Police Judiciaire's latest report on Stavisky. He did not, by way of gift exchange, tender his own bureau's fat dossier on the man, which lay at the Sûreté in a small mahogany cabinet in the office of a divisional superintendent. So triumphant, once again, was the bureaucratic parochialism that no captain in the Republic's impressive security forces concentrated the scattered but extensive disclosures about their common quarry, the swindler Stavisky. No captain cared to. Stavisky still had connections.[73]

Ask the prefect of the Basses-Pyrénées to look into the allegations, Chautemps also suggested to the director of the Sûreté Générale. But the minister asked that the inquiry be "discreet"—the injunction that had so mesmerized Albert Prince and the magistrates at the public prosecutor's office when they undertook delicately in 1929 to investigate the Foncière. At the time, the distinguished gentlemen on the new company's board had inspired the better part of valor in the investigators; now Joseph Garat alone did so, a deputy but hardly a power in the Chamber. Thomé complied; he asked Prefect Mireur of the Basses-Pyrénées to inquire "discreetly," and in so doing gently sent the unwanted vessel out to sea again.[74]

Back it drifted in November. Another revenant from Stavisky's past turned up to haunt him, a disbarred lawyer by the name of Paul Comby, who earned his keep by occasional swindles, blackmail, and even small-time treason, whenever, as during the war, the opportunity arose. By the early 1920s he was moving, consequently, in Stavisky's circles, a small man with a pointed beard living in a furnished room next to a cinema. In 1926 he was indicted along with Stavisky in the Labbé stock theft that still lay pending in 1933 before the thirteenth correctional chamber. Such a circumstance vexed Comby no end, and now he, like Stavisky himself, added on occasion the parenthetical but strategic role of police informer to his other vocations: he reported all he knew about Bayonne to an inspector of the Sûreté Générale, an old friend. "Would you be interested in looking into a 250 million-franc swindle?" He mentioned Garat the president and Tissier the treasurer. But the Sûreté was not interested. A superintendent, John Hennet, ordered his inspector, and by extension their mean informer, to keep out. I am already well informed about this, he said. "I'm not looking into it, and I have my reasons." Comby himself tried to see the minister of the interior, but Chautemps's chief of staff sent him back to the Sûreté, where Superintendent Hennet reaffirmed his indifference. He sent Comby away.[75]

Hennet was a short but solid man with a thin mustache, in caricatural contrast to the unsubstantial and unreliable informer who had just left his office. Twenty-seven years in the police, all but the last two in the provinces, had brought him finally to the Sûreté, where he enjoyed the trappings of high office and the esteem of his superiors. "A civil servant with long experience, very solid in judgment, entirely loyal, courageous and devoted," noted his immediate superior the month before the meeting with Comby. "M. Hennet directs our services with authority and deserves all the confidence of the administration." How ironic that a Comby should threaten Stavisky, a Hennet protect him, that poacher and gamekeeper should silently exchange roles once again — since that carnivalesque inversion had happened before. The distinguished Albert Prince, now far away on the benches of the court of appeals, and de Chevert, Stavisky's much less estimable accomplice in Orléans, had enacted just as diverting a spectacle two years earlier, the magistrate resisting, the turncoat pressing. Later, the Republic's most disreputable journalists had denounced Stavisky, and its most committed servants had reacted sluggishly or not at all. Influence, radiating most often from elected officials, had worked its magic, and Hennet no less than his predecessors now sensed the hovering aura. In Bayonne, a deputy-mayor held sway, and Hennet's own superiors had just deftly unloaded on the prefect there a highly charged investigation. So Hennet sent Comby away. Besides, he had nothing but contempt for the informer's ways. He was, after all, a professional police official.[76]

Quietly and unobtrusively, obeisance by civil servants to the power of Parliament subverted the liberal doctrine of the separation of powers. Deputies and senators routinely interfered with the promotion rotations of government ministries, asking for an appointment here, a transfer there, in timely notes handwritten on Palais Bourbon or Palais Luxembourg stationery: "I would be very pleased to learn that so deserving a civil servant . . ." Long before Stavisky cast his occasional shadow over the Sûreté, Superintendent Hennet sought from parliamentary patrons the magic formulae that helped his ascent, from a post in Toulouse to better ones in Clermont-Ferrand, Dijon, Orléans, and finally Paris. His colleagues sought them too.[77]

So personal a sense of obligation could only deepen a senior police official's deference to the electoral class as a whole. Paralysis might ensue, the price of security. So might temporary satrapies, composed of allegiance, rivalry, and the albatross of ideology. Hennet's friends, his political patrons, were on the left, southwestern Radicals from his long years at Toulouse; they included, by a cruel coincidence, Auguste Puis, the senator from Tarn-et-Garonne, whose financial survival Stavisky had thoughtfully helped ensure by favors in Orléans. The friends of Prefect of Police Chiappe, as everyone knew, were on the right. Cooperation between the Sûreté and the prefecture, never healthy, did not thereby flower. A year earlier, Hennet had traveled to central Europe to investigate the political connections, if any, of the assassin of President Paul Doumer, the crazed Gorguloff. He had discovered no communist connection, much to the annoyance of Chiappe and his right-wing friend André Tardieu who, as prime minister at the time of the murder, had so labeled the murderer. Hennet never forgave the two their carping. He had provoked the politicians, honor though they might the independence of the police.[78]

Now another political matter had fallen on him, the crédit municipal of Bayonne and its president Joseph Garat, as southwestern and as Radical a deputy as his own old patrons. Hennet backed off, content to leave the investigation to the prefect there. Once again the system protected Stavisky, and put off by its meandering and Byzantine ways the day of judgment; but not for much longer.

In the gathering crisis Garat grasped at the panacea of official benediction. Throw the articles from *Commentaires* into the wastebasket, said docile inspector Constantin of Commerce to Prefect Mireur. He was parroting Garat. Mireur did not insist; his "discreet inquiry" came to an end; once again the regulators had yielded deferentially to the regulated.[79]

Still there was l'Urbaine insurance company, asking politely about its unpaid bonds. And still, by way of reply, Garat wanted an inspection by the obliging Constantin. But Commerce thought Finance should look into Bayonne. The civil servants resumed their rondo, renewing the sequences that had allowed Stavisky to slip away unseen from Orléans two years earlier.[80]

A circular motion emerged among them, driven not by dishonesty but by deference, modesty, and doubt, and by the familiar phrases of bureaucratic evasion. You inspect the accounting, Commerce proposed to Finance. You carry out a full inspection instead, Finance replied to Commerce. Ask the board of directors at Bayonne to reassure l'Urbaine about the unpaid bonds, Commerce proposed to Garat. Send Constantin down for an inspection, replied Garat. Ask Finance instead, replied Commerce. Sometimes Prefect Mireur shuttled among them bearing their replies. Two months went by.[81]

Rumors floated in and out of the cafés of Bayonne, and reached the ears of Henri Cohen, the jeweler who had helped at the Etablissements Alex and in Orléans. He had since succeeded his late father, Samuel, as appraiser, of sorts, at the crédit municipal of Bayonne. Now he resigned in fright, citing ill health. Tissier the director talked him into staying on. But he warned him not to accept any valuable gages from local borrowers. There was no money left to lend them.[82]

On 15 December Garat and Prefect Mireur sat down in Paris with Constantin's old superior at Commerce. Is the director of the crédit municipal reliable? Delamarche asked. Garat turned to Mireur.

"You appointed him," Garat said. The rush for the lifeboats was beginning.

Mireur obediently vouched for Tissier's integrity. As if to demonstrate his own unyielding stringency, the prefect reminded his listeners that he had turned down Desbrosses, the cashiered treasurer from Orléans, before agreeing to Tissier.

Desbrosses — with a start Delamarche remembered the name from Orléans. Are there any other links to that affair, he asked incredulously. An Etablissements Alex, for example? Garat shook his head, then seemed to reflect for a moment.

"Our treasurer may indeed have a canvasser, an agent by that name," he said finally.

With mounting agitation Delamarche implored Prefect Mireur to call in Tissier and interrogate him. Make sure that Finance carries out a real inspection, he insisted. And he phoned Paul Maze, president of the Association of Crédits Municipaux, to tell him that Garat was in his office and that the two urgently needed to meet. Anxious or composed, Delamarche saw administrative responsibilities distributed almost at random around him, a marbled surface of uncertain design, a vision he might invoke should the matter at hand, the crédit municipal of Bayonne, ever invite scrutiny of himself.[83]

"What are those people all about?" Garat said four days later when Maze in turn asked him what he knew about the Etablissements Alex — for he, too, remembered the Orléans affair.

"Don't you know someone called Alexandre?" Maze continued.

Garat appeared to search his memory, as though straining in good faith to put a face to a name.

"There is indeed, I think, an agent of the treasurer's called Alexandre. Personally, I don't know him."[84]

It was 19 December. For four days Jules Maximilien Sadron, the treasury receiver in Bayonne, had been going over the books in the crédit municipal. He had oversight powers over the accounting, no more, and in the past had found nothing amiss. But this time he arrived spurred by his superior. "Be stern and inquisitive," the paymaster general had told him, alert to the rumors circling about the place. So Sadron arrived more as inquisitor than inspector, appearing at the door on the 15th not, as was customary, before opening or after closing time, but in the middle of the afternoon. He noticed with suspicion six blank bonds, already signed, on Tissier's desk. "If you'd come at five P.M.," Tissier said resentfully, "you wouldn't have found them."

Patiently, for five nights running, Sadron went through Tissier's monotonous registers and their unvarying, serial chronicles of several thousand bonds. In the mornings he returned the books. Five hundred thousand francs' worth of bonds were immediately redeemable, Sadron concluded. But he searched the crédit municipal's treasury in vain for the five hundred thousand francs to repay them. The next day the subprefect in Bayonne, Anthelme, told him, in passing, that l'Urbaine insurance company demanded repayment of 8 million francs of bonds. Of these Sadron, poring over the registers in the silence of the night, found no trace. They were fakes. But who had issued them?[85]

It had been three months since Camille Chautemps, as minister of the interior, had instructed the Sûreté Générale to look discreetly into the affairs of the crédit municipal of Bayonne. Sadron from Finance had finally stumbled on the fraud only because Subprefect Anthelme simultaneously remembered l'Urbaine's complaint and thought to mention it to him. Each soon claimed credit for the discovery in Bayonne, as did Delamarche at Commerce, who had urged others to investigate where he had feared to tread, and Hennet at the Sûreté Générale, who had unloaded the inquiry onto Prefect Mireur, and Mireur himself, who had inquired so discreetly that few traces of his vigor could be found, and almost everyone else, including Camille Chautemps from his lookout at the height of the system.

But if only Stavisky had not overreached himself and attracted such attention, had managed his takings so as to pay off the Urbaine as the demand arose, the crime of Bayonne might never have been discovered at all. Had the Hungarian bonds not threatened the prestige of the French state, and thus rendered the insolvency of Bayonne all but inevitable; had his profligacy not loosened the tongues of the blackmailers in the press, and thereby alerted even the most timid of civil servants; had he not undone the source of his success, Stavisky might not have turned his salvation into his ruin. Such simple inferences, once they were made and openly shared, might escalate into presumptions of a complicity so universal as to damn the most sacrosanct of establishments—if the conditions were right; and four governments had already fallen that year.

How many had protected Thérèse Humbert, the false heiress of the Belle Epoque, while she dined for a decade with presidents and kings? Only an empty coffer, opened with fanfare by the police, had exposed her swindle. Who had allowed the Banque Industrielle de Chine to go on trading in the early 1920s, its coffers empty as well and its debts out of control? Its downfall and bankruptcy seemed almost fortuitous, brought on more by personal animosities than by the laws of the market. Why was Meg Steinheil, former mistress of President Felix Faure, not brought to justice for the murder of her husband and mother for almost a year, in 1909, and then finally acquitted? Scandal lurked in every unsolved crime, every inconclusive fait divers or investigation gone astray. A Republic founded on virtue invited indignation, recognized no gray areas where neither good nor evil boldly marked the terrain; and of all the mysteries raised by Sadron's discovery at Bayonne, none was more suggestive than the crédit municipal's recent charmed immunity from justice and all its auxiliaries.[86]

"Let's stroll a bit," said Garat, back from Paris, when Sadron confronted him that afternoon. They were standing outside Sadron's office in the subprefecture. He was surprised to find the president of the crédit municipal there, as zealous and officious in his attentions as Tissier the director. Eight million francs of unrecorded bonds, Sadron told him as they strolled side by side under the arcade of the town hall. Garat, a man of violent reactions, was silent. They stopped and Sadron grasped him by his lapels.

"M. Garat, do you hear me? There are forged bonds. I order you officially to open proceedings in the prosecutor's office, against person or persons unknown."

Garat paled and said in a toneless voice, "Continue with your investigations."[87]

The next day Tissier confessed. Garat was meeting with the board of the crédit municipal to announce in shock that Tissier—their director!—had been issuing false bonds.

"What are you going to do to me?" Tissier asked Sadron when they met in the subprefecture. He was smartly dressed; cocky, thought the treasury receiver.

"Send you to prison," he replied.

"You won't do that. The scandal's too big. If you set it off, it will destroy you." Tissier began a wild tale of a villainous deputy and mayor and Hungarian bonds and much more besides. Sadron listened, incredulous. The local prosecutor arrived and a police officer led Tissier away.

How many fake bonds had they issued, the superintendent wanted to know as they walked through the prison gate. Tissier raised his arms into the air. "That many," he said abjectly. And then, with sudden violence, "I'm going to prison today, that's true, but tomorrow Garat will join me!" The Stavisky affair was beginning.[88]

◾

Two nights earlier, Alexandre had called from the Auberge du Père Jean in Paris. By prearrangement, he called the Café Glacier in Biarritz, asked for a M. Petit, and waited for Tissier to come to the phone. Alert as hunted prey to the dangers of high visibility, he tried to melt into the landscape. But it was too late.[89]

A hidden equilibrium, intrinsically fragile, was coming into view—the press that concealed and now revealed, the administration that ignored and now investigated, the insurance companies that asked no questions and now clamored for the light of justice and, incidentally, for their money back. How many others, how many lawyers, notaries, bankers, accountants, and assorted professionals of the liberal Republic had Stavisky once befriended? And how many others might now anxiously demand his head, not because he had robbed them, but because he had enriched them?

Stavisky was keeping up appearances. A few days before calling Tissier, he had called on the director of the crédit municipal in Bordeaux. A journalist of the usual variety, sometime swindler and editor of a local rag called *La Vérité* and employee of Dubarry's at *La Volonté,* had acted as intermediary and set up the meeting. In the director's office Alexandre was elegant and winning, the journalist seedy and withdrawn. Alexandre produced two rings from the watch pocket of his vest. How much will you lend for them, he asked. Twenty thousand, the director replied. They are worth sixty, Alexandre said with a sardonic smile. But he did not insist. He took his leave politely. Orléans and its emeralds had come to this. On the way out, he boasted to the journalist that the rings were worth a hundred thousand each. They lunched at Chapon Fin.[90]

A few weeks earlier, he had dined with the writer Colette in the Poisson d'Or. She too lived in the Claridge. Joseph Kessel, her fellow novelist and his friend, came along. He had noticed a fixed and alert expression in Stavisky lately—the pressures of success, he thought. That night, unhinged by the presence of Colette, Stavisky labored with all the affectations and mannerisms at his command to impress her. Yet he watched. He smiled with his mouth only, even as he studied with expressionless eyes the diners in the room and the newcomers as they arrived. Again megalomania darkened the studied social persona. He launched into his financial plans for the salvation of Europe, blind to his guests' incuriosity and boredom, and when he escorted Colette back to the Claridge he talked to her about his idée fixe all the way.[91]

In the elevator lobby of the Claridge, the night before Tissier's arrest, Kessel and his brother Georges ran into Stavisky again, all starch and smiles. He chided them for not coming to see him, and insisted on dinner the following week. "Happy Christmas Eve!" he cried as they moved off.[92]

The next day Bortchy-Melnikoff, unpaid and cap in hand, found him conversing as affably as ever with a visitor in his office. "Yes, yes, don't worry," he was saying. "Everything will turn out well."

The caller left and immediately an anxious, haunted look crossed Stavisky's face. Suddenly he noticed the chauffeur and forced a smile. "Romagnino will pay you," he said, and went out by a side door.[93]

NINE

FAME

The last months of 1933 had shrouded France in a strange twilight of murder. One sign in the darkness, toward Christmas, the Lagny rail catastrophe, which left two hundred dead. . . . And we learned in a few lines, in the papers, that a humdrum swindle implicated the Crédit municipal of Bayonne. —Robert Brasillach, Notre avant-guerre

The Flight

It was Saturday afternoon, 23 December 1934, and Tissier had been arrested in Bayonne that morning.

"What does this mean? Is it a felony? Do I risk forced labor?" Stavisky cried. He was beseeching his lawyer, the same clever Guiboud-Ribaud who had helped keep the law at bay in the past, to hold out hope again, and he appeared near hysteria, unhinged once more by the prospect of prison. Only the day before, he had seemed for a moment self-assured, still in control of his emotions. He had calmly answered a few lingering questions about the stillborn Hungarian bonds in the offices of Léon Ameline at the Police Judiciaire. No, he reassured one of the superintendent's assistants, he would not issue them without proper authority; yes, he was merely a financial adviser. Now, not twenty-four hours later, Tissier had broken the seal on Bayonne's secrets and Stavisky was a pitiful wreck.[1]

"My wife, my children. No, I won't go to prison. I don't want the penitentiary," he went on as Guiboud-Ribaud told him that the criminal court would probably play host to Tissier and his accomplices some day. The smooth young lawyer did not yet apprehend that he himself might number among the guests. "I'll never go," Stavisky insisted wildly. "I'll leave. If I can't cross the border, I'll kill myself."[2]

They were meeting in a ghost of an office on Rue Marignan, sometime home of the Hungarian bond venture. Romagnino came, as did Hayotte and René Pigaglio, a minor employee at *La Volonté* and then at the Empire theater, devoted to Stavisky, a votary among hypocrites, moved now by his benefactor's distress. Once, Stavisky, dispensing the largesse that won him so many temporary converts, had gone out of his way to help Pigaglio care for a sick daughter. The grateful hireling did not forget the gesture now. Stavisky asked to accompany him to Servoz in the Alps for his annual winter vacation. Yes, replied Pigaglio, adding apologetically that the chalet was not very comfortable. Stavisky did not mind. No one thought it necessary to point out the proximity of Servoz to the Swiss and Italian borders.[3]

172

"If I ever sense the hand of the police coming down on me, I'll commit suicide," Stavisky declared, and, since gun dealers were closed on Saturday afternoons, he quite logically asked Romagnino to lend him the Browning 6.35 millimeter that the faithful factotum had bought the year before at Meyer's on Rue de Rome, and that he kept under lock and key in his own office on Place Saint-Georges.[4]

■

Suicide, in this Republic, resembled the theatrical convention, the staple device, of some spectral dramatist scripting the plot of scandal. The intrigue was always the same. Why would he take his own life? Was it really suicide? Assisted suicide? With its why and its what-if, its urgent invitation to speculate, suicide handily engaged the citizenry in a public melodrama of crime and punishment. It raised endless possibilities, if only the spectators were willing to entertain them; and more often than not they were. Suspicious of state power and its secrets, they applauded each parable of foul play in high places, and gave the measure of their credulity as well as of their skepticism.

Cries of murder came from all sides when a maid found a scandalmongering, debt-ridden, violence-prone nationalist deputy by the name of Syveton dead in his armchair, the gas turned on and the chimney blocked with that day's newspaper—*L'Intransigeant* of 8 December 1904. The right accused the left, the left accused the right, some even accused his wife, the mistress, they whispered, of another nationalist leader. Letters of denunciation arrived in the morning mail at police stations. Postcards of Syveton went on sale. As always, the Palace of Justice came under fire, now guilty, cried its enemies, of covering the escape of Syveton's assassins. He had killed himself. But the fiction of murder survived for a while longer, so long as the enthusiasts came forth. Five hundred came to the commemoration of his death in 1907, one hundred in 1909, forty in 1910. By then the scandal had died, not with a dramatic finale, an indispensable resolution, but as they all did, in unanswered questions, deepening indifference, and finally oblivion.[5]

Apparent suicide, rather than obvious murder, gave the Republic's scandals their mandatory element of mystery. Real suicide set off rounds of speculation, mechanically invited by a practiced press, and no shortage of such incidents deprived the citizen-spectators of the chance to indulge in political fantasy and exercise their dark imaginations. During the Dreyfus affair, one forger's suicide eclipsed another's, when first Lemercier-Picard took his own life and then, more resoundingly, Lieutenant Henry followed suit. Swindlers and the less orthodox industrialists and financiers, in particular, chose to make their exit that way. The suicide of Baron Jacques de Reinach, the banker in the Panama Canal disaster, following that of the ruined aluminum financier Denfert-Rochereau, flamed wild speculation linking their two deaths. But they shared only the melancholy sequence of shattered empires, the violent encounter between dreams and reality. In 1932 the Swedish tycoon Ivan Kreuger watched his own empire of matches, forests, and loans to stricken governments dissolve in the general credit crisis and the debacle of the German and Austrian banks. The quiet, taciturn entrepreneur arrived by boat train off the Ile-de-France one Friday in March, back from the United States, went to his apartment on Avenue Victor-Emmanuel III, and shot himself. Consternation followed, *Le Matin* reported. Prime Minister Tardieu received the Swedish ambassador. Scandal threatened, and passed; Kreuger had done more good than harm, *Le Matin* allowed, and *Le Temps* wrote him off as a casualty of the world situation; but for the government it had been a close call. How long now before a Hanau, a Rochette, a Stavisky played the macabre role assigned them? "The scandal is too big," Tissier had said just before they took him away, and for once he had used good judgment, panicked but prophetic.[6]

The ultimate irony lay in the Republic's self-imposed martyrdom. The regime that had given the vote to all male citizens and almost unlimited freedom of expression to all newspapers now endured their gratitude, periodically suspected of the one crime of which it was no more capable than its liberal cousin to the north of the Channel, the crime it had imputed to more than one of its detested despotic predecessors, the crime of political murder.

Reluctantly Romagnino agreed to part with his revolver. He took out the keys to his office on Place Saint-Georges and gave them to Stavisky.

As an afterthought, he asked his distraught employer about all the check stubs in the office, the copious traces of countless small operations they had carried out together. As secretary, Gilbert Romagnino had routinely cashed hundreds of checks, made out to him and endorsed by him, but providentially recorded on the stubs as "Gil—office." The stubs might absolve where the checks damned, might exculpate him from the charge of personal enrichment, spare him grave embarrassment and worse. Romagnino at least was keeping his head.

"Keep them," Stavisky told him cryptically the next day as he handed over a heap of old check stubs, "they might yet be useful to you." It was lunchtime in the Auberge d'Artois, and they were waiting for Arlette.

Stavisky had taken them from Place Saint-Georges, along with the revolver. Others he had burned in the fireplace at the Claridge. Not until later, sifting through the several hundred stubs, did Romagnino understand Stavisky's remark. Most bore the anodyne inscription "Gil—office." But others displayed startling names scribbled in Stavisky's own hand: "Proust," the Radical deputy, "Queuille," the former minister of agriculture, "Chauchat," editor of *Le Petit Journal* and, less legibly, "Tardif" or perhaps "Tardieu"—the former prime minister.[7]

Here, unknown to Romagnino as he sat in the Auberge d'Artois, was the secret document, the instrument of revelation that, like suicide, allowed minds to speculate and scandal to flourish. Here was the Henry forgery from the Dreyfus affair, the list of *chéquards,* of deputies on the take from the Panama scandal, and the cache of secret notes taken by Masonic observers on Catholic officers from the affair of 1904. Each, counterfeit or genuine, concentrated by its sensible presence the passions that fed scandal, and, once revealed on the front pages of daily newspapers, held out the captivating promise of more to come. Sometimes the secret document, when it did not exist, had to be invented, inspired by available precedents. In 1903 Maître Labori, the lawyer who had ridiculed the army's talk of secret evidence during the Dreyfus affair, loudly demanded it be produced during the trial of his client, the false heiress Thérèse Humbert. It was never found. But in the Chamber the opposition took up the cry. That year Rochette, the enterprising banker whose first scandal broke in 1908, had kept a list of deputies in his pay, Panama-style, and a cache of private papers at a friendly journalist's apartment, so rumor held—but he had erased one and burned the other, it went on, nicely rendering the fiction invulnerable.[8]

Such games could get out of hand, as Gaston Calmette discovered in 1913 after he published in his *Figaro* Joseph Caillaux's adulterous "ton Jo" letter, and promptly fell victim to Mme Caillaux's pistol. Calmette, Caillaux's political foe, had wanted the scandal, if not quite in its final form. Someone always did, and secret documents circulated until they reached the hands of the happy person who had much to gain and little to lose from divulging them. Romagnino took the check stubs and left the Auberge d'Artois.

Presently Stavisky also left and rejoined Arlette at the Claridge. With Tissier's arrest two days earlier, her world had finally fallen apart. She had given Stavisky her last three bracelets, her earrings, and a diamond, and they had moved out of the Claridge and into a hotel nearby, the Château Frontenac. It was better that way, he had explained, better too that she find a small furnished apartment and wait out events there with the two children and their governess. He would go to Bayonne to find out what was going on, he said. Back and forth she went in taxis loaded with trunks and cases hastily bought at the Magasins Réunis, and sent her drivers first toward the Gare de l'Est, then toward the Gare Saint-Lazare, and finally to a *Résidence* on Rue Pierre-1er-de-Serbie. She feared being followed. To Stavisky she brought two suitcases, one yellow, the other green, and a black coat with a mink lining and an otter collar.

Later that day—Sunday, Christmas Eve—they met again. He was waiting for her in a taxi on Place de l'Alma, and they went to dinner in a small Russian restaurant nearby. All was lost, he said. His life was over. He had ruined everything and he begged her forgiveness. They would never take him alive; he would never go to prison; he would never inflict such a disgrace on her and the children.

Almost eight years earlier, Arlette had given birth to Claude as Stavisky entered La Santé prison. Now she displayed the same fidelity to his person and the same indifference to his profession that had lent wings to their union, the same self-preserving incuriosity that, happily for her, the law found natural in a wife but implausible in an accomplice. She tried now to galvanize his morale and lift him out of his despair. But their giddy ride was ending, in the same eighth arrondissement where it had started—the eighth arrondissement of

Coco Chanel and his father's apartment on Rue de la Renaissance at the beginning, of the Café de Paris, the Empire theater, and the Claridge at the end. Arlette was poor once again.

They parted at eleven. He left her at the Claridge without giving an address, without leaving a clue; but in the taxi he took the two suitcases with him. At the Porte de Champerret, in the Café des Coupoles, the loyal Pigaglio was waiting. He had his car. The two left the city shortly after midnight on Christmas Day and drove south toward Fontainebleau, in the general direction of the Alps, Pigaglio's chalet, and the Franco-Swiss border.[9] They spent the night in Fontainebleau, in the Hôtel du Palais, as Pigaglio always did when driving to his chalet. In the morning, as they drove on, Stavisky began talking vaguely of the developments that had forced his flight. Pigaglio had read *La Bonne Guerre* and all the other blackmail sheets, but now he listened with emotion as his employer and benefactor told his story.

The weather was bad. In rain and snow they abandoned the car in Laroche-Migennes and boarded a train for Dijon. There they lunched at Cochet, before proceeding by trains large and small up to Saint-Gervais in Haute-Savoie. On the evening of the 26th they finally reached his chalet in snowy Servoz, almost a kilometer up the side of Mont Blanc, only to find the pipes frozen and the boiler burst. Resourcefully, Pigaglio rented another chalet, named, as though for Stavisky, Les Argentières, and paid the owner in advance. Pigaglio was a true friend. They settled in.[10]

Tissier was saying nothing about M. Alexandre. He sat in his cell in the Villa Chagrin in Bayonne. They had charged him with theft, forgery, use of forged documents, and embezzlement of public moneys. He had retained a lawyer. Garat knew everything, Tissier had said at his arrest, but now he silently awaited his fate, soon to appear in the person of Victor d'Uhalt, the town's investigating magistrate.[11]

D'Uhalt was a local *béarnais,* pure Basque. One forebear after another had embraced the region and infused clannish pride into the original Duhalt name, as a justice of the peace, a lawyer in Parliament, an equerry, an officer in the *chasseurs basques;* and when his father introduced a Gallic apostrophe into the ancient patronymic he left intact its sound as well as its sense—"by the mountain torrent." D'Uhalt himself, at the age of thirty-six, was fiercely attached to his native land. He spoke its language fluently. More than once he had annoyed his superiors by requesting posts in the southwest, and four years earlier Barthou, as minister of justice, had threatened to strike him from the promotion lists altogether. But he had survived. He was conscientious as well as hard-working, and no one challenged his professional qualifications. Stout, of medium height, clean-shaven, free of fashionable affectation—d'Uhalt was a stubbornly rooted provincial, as different from Stavisky as day from night.[12]

Tissier he let languish for the time being. He needed information before he could interrogate him. With a court recorder d'Uhalt went into the crédit municipal and placed seals on the account books and the safe, on the doors and passageways leading down to the vaults. Bachacou, the concierge, found himself promoted to quasi-judicial status, ordered to guard the precious documents until the law returned with its experts to sift through the silty residues of Sacha Stavisky's passage through Bayonne.

Then d'Uhalt turned to Henri Cohen, the Moroccan jeweler who had succeeded his father as appraiser in 1932, had lived handsomely for a year and a half, and had tried to resign in November when he sensed danger. Plucky as ever, he produced a copy of his resignation letter. He regretted ever coming here, he told d'Uhalt. Yes, he had heard rumors, had seen an alarming article in a financial newspaper. Tissier, he knew, was somehow trafficking in forged bonds, along with a financier from Paris, one Serge Alexandre.[13]

"Track down on Paris financial market," d'Uhalt cabled the Sûreté Générale in Paris, "all transactions involving bonds of crédit municipal Bayonne and persons connected to such transactions, notably one Serge Alexandre."[14]

The name began to issue from official lips. Why had no warrant been issued for his arrest? Léon Delamarche at the Ministry of Commerce wanted to know. It was late in the afternoon on Christmas Day, and Mireur, the prefect of the Basses-Pyrénées, was calling from Pau. Garat was insisting that the crédit municipal be reopened, he reported. As usual, the docile prefect complied without judging, conveyed without commenting. As usual, Delamarche insisted that others take action. Mireur agreed that Stavisky alias Alexandre should be arrested. But that was up to the judicial authorities in the Basses-Pyrénées. He would talk to the prosecutor in Pau that night, he promised.[15]

Two more days went by. D'Uhalt in Bayonne told the prosecutor in Pau of "possible activities of Alexandre Stavinski"; the prosecutor in Pau told the Ministry of Justice in Paris of "a Stavinski of Paris said to be mixed up in this affair"; and the Sûreté Générale reassembled its well-traveled biographical material on Alexandre Stavisky. D'Uhalt received their report on the 28th, in reply to his earlier telegram, and waited no longer. He issued over the wireless a general warrant for Stavisky's arrest and a physical description of him to every port and border post in the land, to every police force in Europe, and, on a rumor, to vessels steaming across the Atlantic to South America.[16]

But Stavisky, of course, was nowhere to be found.

Renown

"Search Continues for Swindler Stavisky," *Paris-Soir* announced in its New Year's Eve issue. The story appeared on page 3, swamped by continuing front-page coverage of a catastrophic train wreck in Lagny-sur-Marne a week earlier.[17]

Along with some of the other papers that day and the day before, *Paris-Soir* had picked up a dispatch from the Havas wire service. The short item even surfaced on the front page of the socialist *Le Populaire,* engulfed by news of Lagny, the disarmament talks in Geneva, and the assassination of the Romanian prime minister. *Le Temps* inserted it into the crime column, above news of a robbery on Boulevard Poissonière and the arrest of two crooked bankers on Rue Vivienne. Havas had noticed the arrest warrant, and the Sûreté Générale had shared some of its harmless secrets with the usual reporters at the door—a Russian-born adventurer by the name of Alexandre or Stavisky, was wanted in connection with fake bonds issued in Bayonne. He had disappeared. A story seemed in the making, though where it might lead no one could yet say.[18]

A few days earlier, a small financial paper, the *Agence Technique de la Presse,* had learned of Tissier's arrest and had begun talking excitedly of a "big story," occult influences, and suppression of the truth. Its editor, Jacques Landau, who had frequented Stavisky's Cadet-Roussel cabaret in 1917 and had spent eight subsequent years in prison for his treasonable wartime journalism, had sensed the possibilities. After the arrest warrant went out, the *Journal de la Bourse* was quick to remind its readers that it had first sounded the alarm back in the summer. But these were slim rags. The mass dailies were stirring, and the financial weeklies could only bid farewell to Stavisky. He had served them well. Landau's voice, a blackmailer's swan song, was soon drowned out by the clarion calls of the mighty city editors.[19]

The blackmail press lived by publishing just enough of the truth to profit from withholding the rest. From limited disclosure it withdrew into conditional silence, accepting its small ransom as virtue's reward. But it did not often lie. *D'Artagnan, Aux Ecoutes, Commentaires, Juvenal, Bec et Ongles,* and all the others had published small truths about Serge Alexandre and threatened larger ones, wielding accuracy like a weapon. The mass press lived by publishing a full and continuing story, preferably true—but sometimes the story needed help, and sometimes the truth was left on the cutting room floor. On New Year's Eve, Stavisky's story was passing from one press to the other, and once his name leaped out at passersby from kiosks and corner newsstands, Landau and all his colleagues could only bow out. Their day was over.

Here, for the editors of the mass dailies, was a crime, a fait divers, of quality. A mysterious Russian swindler on the run, tales of millions in fake bonds, rumors of arrests to come—a serial novel, in as many installments as possible, seemed to spring out of the late December air. Besides, word quickly spread that the swindler had connections, political friends. That was how a fait divers became a scandal.

In the process, the producers of scandal vied fiercely among themselves for the privileged revelation, the scoop. Already intense, their rivalry had grown in urgency with the deepening economic crisis. Even if circulation held, profits might not. *Le Matin*'s circulation hovered around half a million, but its profits were plunging as costs went out of control. For 1934, profits would amount to a third of those the year before. The paper never recovered its financial health, never enjoyed again the halcyon days of the 1920s. The wire services fared no better; Havas, citing crippling losses, pursued its subscribers for bills they did not pay even as the agency's tickers pulsated in their newsrooms with the day's life-giving news and information. The pressures to innovate, to increase revenues in any way possible, intensified.[20]

Advertisers now suffered as much as everyone else, and held back today what they might have paid out yesterday. Along with the chiefs of staff in government ministries, they were the only source of revenue a newspaper publisher had, outside of subscriptions and newsstand sales. For favored advertisers, unmistakable prospects of editorial control ensued, tempting them now and then to overrun the page, to leave their promotional squares and rectangles and infiltrate the narrow columns of the printed word. In 1929 Gustave Téry, editor of the solid Radical daily *L'Oeuvre,* suggested to other papers a roving series of interviews with the heads of Europe. "Obviously," he proposed to assure Citroën, Delage, Renault, and all the other automobile manufacturers that might provide cars for the journalistic tour, "your firm would be mentioned in the columns of the various papers from the start. Furthermore, the name would be apparent on photos reproduced." Such indifference to professional independence, such confusion of journalism with publicity, rarely saddened the editors or the sponsors of *L'Oeuvre.* When the organizers of the International Aeronautical Exposition at the Grand Palais sent the paper fifteen hundred francs and asked in return for friendly coverage of the event—"in the form of articles or in any other form"—and for a warm reception for its press releases, the editor promptly agreed. They would not specify the length of the articles, the organizers of the exposition magnanimously announced. "We trust you."[21]

In the struggle, reporters fell over each other. The race for discovery, for the buried treasure that would enthrall their readers and enrich their papers, pitted them against each other, foot soldiers in their employers' contest for readers, advertisers, and profits. Their life was not easy. A regular reporter, lucky enough to be hired at the Radical *L'Oeuvre* thanks only to a recommendation from a Daladier or a Chautemps, might earn forty francs a day, but under conditions so exacting and tenure so precarious that he might soon doubt his good fortune. If assigned to the faits divers columns, he would arrive every morning at about eleven thirty, spend the afternoon on reporting assignments, return, and stay till eight, return again after dinner and stay by the press till the paper was put to bed, at about one o'clock in the morning. To leave earlier was to court reprimand or even dismissal. After a while the assistant editors might demote him to free-lance status anyway and pay him forty centimes a line—if they published his story at all. It all depended on what he brought in.[22]

Speed was of the essence. Now, as the Stavisky fait divers flowered into scandal and reporters headed for Bayonne, editors began clamoring for fast news. They wished to be first with the news of d'Uhalt's interrogations of Tissier and Cohen, and of any other suspect in the breaking story. "Cohen declarations received 10/40 [10:40 A.M.] already published in Le Matin," the Agence Havas wired its man in Bayonne on 3 January, chiefly to "recommend" that he inform the agency more speedily about the crédit municipal business—especially about any witnesses called to testify.[23]

On New Year's Day the editors of Paris-Soir moved the Stavisky story to the front page. They had sent a reporter to Bayonne, and he had phoned in a muddled account of the events there, which they ran under an imposing headline. They added an equally muddled biography of Stavisky, "the most prestigious operator and the most extraordinary swindler that the twentieth century has ever known." He was a seducer, a compulsive storyteller, and had acquired, they knew not how, a kind of lasting impunity. "A truly Balzacian character," Le Figaro called him. But where was he? Bound for Venezuela, L'Oeuvre reported, on a ship he had boarded in Lisbon. Hiding in the suburbs of the capital, Paris-Soir speculated one day, only to guess at Budapest the next. No one knew. And around him the story began to grow.[24]

Hayotte was financially incompetent, Stavisky was saying. It was 28 December, the day the warrant for his arrest went out. He was out walking along the road from Servoz to Passy with Henri Voix, an employee on Place Saint-Georges who had joined him the day before. Pigaglio had just left. Hayotte squandered 20 million francs of mine on horses, Stavisky complained aloud, and the Empire theater was an utter folly.[25]

Voix did not quite understand what he and Stavisky were doing up there. He had worked for him for three and a half years, first at SIMA demonstrating the Phébor machine for as long as it was credible, then at the Société Foncière doing whatever was asked of him, running errands, fetching cigarettes, carrying train tickets and small amounts of cash to Stavisky's enchanting female conduit to men in power, Mme Avril on Rue de l'Assomption. Like Romagnino, Pigaglio, Cohen, and so many others who had drifted into the entourage of M. Alexandre, Voix was an underling who had won his master's confidence; sometime champagne salesman, real estate promoter, and bookmaker, he had finally found stable employment of sorts in the offices on Place Saint-Georges. They had sent for him, and he had come. "What are you doing here?" he had asked when he finally found Stavisky in the chalet called Les Argentières. "Things are going badly," Stavisky had replied, "I'll explain." And he had given him a month's salary.[26]

Voix was an unattractive man. He was tall and gaunt and resembled a buzzard, with aquiline nose, bony face, and hollow cheeks. When they reached Passy, Stavisky had him buy *Le Petit Dauphinois, Le Journal,* and *Le Matin.* But there was nothing.[27]

On the 31st Pigaglio returned. He brought with him the Paris papers, the dailies trumpeting that the hunt for Stavisky was on. He had been unmasked. Stavisky remembered aloud the shattered dinner party in Marly-le-Roi in 1926. At the time, Galmot, his friend and ally, had betrayed his whereabouts to Superintendent Pachot, even as a car waited to take him to Switzerland. He feared such treason again, by his friend the journalist Camille Aymard, whose own newspaper *La Liberté* was now brazenly carrying stories about him, by his lawyers Bonnaure and Guiboud-Ribaud, who had sent word with Pigaglio to give himself up, by all who had lived off his dreams and schemes and who now, irreproachable and above suspicion, displayed shock and dismay.[28]

This time the Swiss border was close by—a short trip down to Annemasse, a shorter tram ride across to Geneva. But he did not have the right passport for a prolonged stay abroad, only one he had thoughtfully taken from Niemenczynski, the retired boxer who had given him early morning physical education lessons in the Claridge. Inexpertly Stavisky had substituted his own photograph for Niemen's. It was inadequate. Besides, the last three letters of the name might arouse suspicions, now that his own name had traveled across the wires from Bayonne and Paris to every port of departure in the land. He spoke for a while of returning to the suburbs of the capital, close enough to rein in the turncoats. In the end he decided to leave Servoz and move on to Chamonix.[29]

There, just outside the mountain resort, at the end of a snowy trail bordered by pine trees, stood Le Vieux Logis. It was a large empty chalet with four bedrooms, and it looked onto the glistening northeastern face of the highest peak in Europe, Mont Blanc. A young married couple wished to spend their honeymoon there, Pigaglio explained to the owners, and he introduced Henri Voix and an attractive young woman, a brunette in her late twenties. They signed the rental form as M. and Mme Fargeas.[30]

The woman, Lucette, was Voix's mistress, and had joined him in Servoz after throwing a tantrum at his sudden departure from Paris. She too was a drifter. In the capital she had modeled, typed, and sold women's shoes at Véronique's on Rue de Clichy; she had left one lover, who had run a theater agency near the Gare Saint-Lazare and fathered her child, for another—Henri Voix; now the two lived together, a source of some annoyance to Voix's estranged wife. Therefore they prudently signed in at Chamonix as Fargeas. Pigaglio left again.[31]

Voix said little to Lucette about the mysterious guest who now joined them in Le Vieux Logis. His name was M. Maurice, he explained—the first name on Niemen's errant passport—and he required looking after. Lucette found M. Maurice strange. He secluded himself in his bedroom at the far end of the chalet, and during the meals she had prepared he would sometimes break down in tears for no apparent reason. He was thinking of his wife and children, he explained. Lucette's suspicions grew. Maurice powerfully resembled the Stavisky whose face she now saw on the front pages of the newspapers they brought him. Voix told her not to meddle. "You don't need to get involved in politics," he said rudely.[32]

Every day Voix went into Chamonix and brought back seven or eight francs' worth of newspapers. "Garat will be indicted," Stavisky said, and complained of the mayor of Bayonne's lack of sangfroid. Garat had only discovered the full truth toward the end, he explained, and then had panicked. They might still have arranged matters. Even now, from time to time, Stavisky seemed to hope that everything might blow over. But more often despair took hold of him.

Give yourself up, Voix urged. Never, replied Stavisky, for the sake of his wife and children he would kill himself rather than go to prison; and once he even sent Voix to the pharmacy to buy some potassium cyanide.[33]

When, on 28 December, the magistrate d'Uhalt finally interrogated the prisoner Tissier in his office in the Palace of Justice in Bayonne, he asked all about Garat. M. Alexandre had introduced them in 1931, Tissier explained, and the domineering deputy-mayor had instructed him to do exactly as he was told. So Tissier obediently had the comptroller Piet sign blank bonds, made them out as generously as M. Alexandre wished, and recorded them for the trifling amounts that put the directors on the board to sleep. There was abundant collateral anyway, he thought, and it was all for a good purpose, something to do with Hungarian bonds for the ever-absent, ever-gray M. Alexandre—"the great," as they sometimes called him.[34]

D'Uhalt sent for Garat. The mayor denied all knowledge. He had trusted Tissier, trusted Alexandre, trusted everyone. He was shocked, he would bring suit. The little magistrate was not impressed. Garat did not intimidate him. D'Uhalt sent for him again a few days later. Garat was back in the capital; the mayor in Bayonne had become the deputy in Paris; he boarded the *rapide* at the Gare d'Orsay and left it for a car in Dax in the middle of the night, to throw off hostile onlookers and intrusive reporters. The next day, at half past two, he arrived at the steps of his town's modest Palace of Justice. A policeman bowed, beret in hand. Garat walked confidently, jauntily, up the steps and through the doors. Two gendarmes stood outside d'Uhalt's office.[35]

Outside a small crowd gathered. Some reporters waited, and about twenty idlers and strollers joined them. Some in Bayonne were angry, not at Garat, but at the Parisian Alexandre who had swindled them and their crédit municipal. "So! Monsieur le reporter from Paris," a shopkeeper told a journalist from *Paris-Soir,* "the provinces will show you what kind of wood they put in their fire." Garat had been careless, that was all, but Alexandre was the villain, and who in Paris had protected him, and why was he still free?[36]

Evening fell. The crowd grew to about fifty. From time to time a silhouette moved about in a rectangle of light on the leprous wall of the old palace. D'Uhalt was pacing. Toward nine o'clock Garat emerged pale from the palace, between three gendarmes. For six hours he had prevaricated. No one had ever warned him about Alexandre. He knew very little about the workings of the crédit municipal. No, he could not explain the several erasures of his name from the minutes of the board meetings. At length d'Uhalt asked about the article in *Bec et Ongles*, in which Darius had attacked the crédit municipal and then fallen silent under Garat's threats. "Since you intend to indict me," Garat said with his customary truculence, "I invoke the provisions of the law of 8 December 1897"—he was himself a lawyer, and knew that he was entitled to one. D'Uhalt indicted him for forgery, the use of forged papers, misappropriation of public funds, and complicity in swindling. The three gendarmes took him to a waiting taxi and escorted him in it to the Villa Chagrin, the prison where Tissier already languished, charged with the same crimes. The papers wrongly reported that Garat had confessed to everything. It made a better story that Monday, 8 January 1934.[37]

In Paris, the police began to fan out. D'Uhalt kept demanding news and information from them. Which insurance companies had taken the Bayonne bonds? Who had peddled the paper? What did the bank accounts reveal? Where was Hayotte, and where was Dubarry? Where was Arlette? Superintendent Hennet at the Sûreté handed the case to his trusted professional, his right-hand man, Inspector Bonny.

Pierre Bonny, after fifteen years with the Sûreté, had investigated some of the more spectacular crimes of the postwar era, including the disappearance of the American film star Jeanette MacDonald and the murder of the Breton departmental councillor Pierre Quéméneur in 1923, for which he helped send the unprepossessing and possibly innocent Guillaume Seznec to Devil's Island. He looked the part: dark mustache, hair parted in the middle, the inevitable raincoat. Bonny was a ferret, a compulsive searcher for detail, and a correspondingly effective police officer; but he was not above suspicion or reproach. Once, only a few years earlier, he had helped a Lithuanian financier stave off imminent expulsion from the country in return for modest considerations—a tailor's bill here, a small amount of foreign currency there. Bonny was venal.[38]

This new case held out a prospect of riches difficult to measure but also difficult to ignore. For some years now, Bonny had lurked in Stavisky's environs, aware of his existence but uninvolved in his doings. Along with everyone else at the Sûreté, he knew of the *Valdivia*, the steamer from South America that had lost its load of bonds to the swindler in 1925, and of the fugitive's postprandial arrest in Marly-le-Roi in 1926; he had heard the name from time to time since then, most recently that past spring or summer, accompanied by tales of debt and imminent bankruptcy; he remembered the name now, in December, as the news of Bayonne began to break. Then he began hearing other names—Garat, Bonnaure, Georges Bonnet, the names of Radical deputies, Radical ministers. The affair was political.

Bayonne itself was nothing. Expertly and energetically, Inspector Bonny began to investigate.[39]

He requested that the bankers, stockbrokers, and insurance agents of the capital, in a letter that went out from Rue des Saussaies six hundred times, produce records of any dealings with the man. He went into the suite on the fifth floor of the Claridge, where he found only an empty safe, and with an investigating magistrate into the offices of La Confiance insurance company, where he found 80 million francs' worth of Bayonne bonds. Workers carrying blowtorches and oxygen tanks preceded him into the offices on Place Saint-Georges. They blew open the safe on the third floor, and, with another magistrate, Bonny began patiently examining the correspondence that lay like debris in the deserted offices of the Compagnie Foncière et d'Entreprises Générales des Travaux Publics. Whenever they came out, even briefly, the press set upon them. Then they went back in and the newsmen sat back to wait.[40]

Bonny looked for Arlette. She had not traveled far. With the two children and their governess she had moved into a small furnished apartment on Rue Obligado, across Place de l'Etoile, opposite the Claridge; and there, on the evening of 30 December, Bonny found her name—"Arlette Simon"—on the register. He told the concierge to reveal her presence to no one, and to call him at the Sûreté if Sacha Stavisky ever appeared; a few days later, as reporters appeared in the street and rumors began wandering across the front pages of the dailies, he asked her to mark Arlette on the register as having left.[41]

For hours he interrogated Henri Hayotte, the inept, rakish manager of the Empire theater. That establishment had closed its doors. The company staged *Deux sous de fleurs* on New Year's Day but sent everyone home the following day. Disappointed ticket holders learned only that the mechanical curtain was stuck. Musicians and technicians left unpaid; Rita Georg, the star, returned to Vienna with her lover, the Swedish consul there; Max Rivers's dancing girls boarded trains back to the Channel ports and London's West End.[42]

Hayotte himself was drowning in debt. Once fervidly enthusiastic about the Empire, he now struggled frantically to meet its bills as well as his own. He pawned his wife's jewels and parted with his blue Bugatti and his black Hispano-Suiza, sleek vehicles from the halcyon days with his vanished friend. By night his wife began moving her furniture out of the town house they had refitted so extravagantly. The Empire was pronounced bankrupt, as was Hayotte. Then Bonny called him in. Hayotte gabbled incoherently, and Bonny found his story difficult to follow. They went together back to the offices on Place Saint-Georges, followed by a throng of reporters and photographers. "I don't understand," Hayotte lamented to them. "I have nothing at all to do with the Bayonne business."[43]

Bonny also went with two investigating magistrates into the offices of *La Volonté*. They found ten reporters already encamped in the antechamber of Albert Dubarry's office, and the rotund editor waiting inside. An editor at *Le*

Petit Parisien had learned of the impending visit from the law and had tipped his colleague off. Bonny and the magistrates found some fascinating correspondence, a year-old letter from Darius of *Bec et Ongles,* about a campaign against the crédit municipal of Bayonne that Dubarry had wanted stopped. The next day one of the magistrates sent for him to ask all about it. Dubarry arrived at the Palace of Justice as natty as ever, swinging a cane with a golden handle. "I've intervened on behalf of everyone," the investigating magistrate heard him explain. He emerged an hour later, bathed in the light of early morning and the camera flashes from the press photographers crowded around the palace's great gates. He smiled easily. "A bonus for the best photographer!" he cried, and went on his way.[44]

Very soon Bonny and the magistrates were overwhelmed. The sluice gates were swinging open. Just after Dubarry came Darius, his friend and colleague, summoned back to Paris from a winter on the Côte d'Azur. He stepped down from the train at the Gare de Lyon on the morning of 8 January and denied all rumors to the reporters lining the platform. He protested the publicity, the surveillance, the intrusion. But he turned up as requested at the Palace of Justice that afternoon and, in the office of an investigating magistrate, began answering interminable questions about *Bec et Ongles,* its advertising contracts, and the money he appeared to have received from Sacha Stavisky. As night fell Darius was still in the palace. The magistrate kept him. He was awaiting a telegram from d'Uhalt in Bayonne asking him to arrest Darius and to send him down at once.[45]

Each suspect revealed another, in a cascade of names and faces. Behind Darius was Camille Aymard of *La Liberté,* and behind him Paul Lévy of *Aux Ecoutes,* and how many others? When Bonnaure's name came up, magistrates in the palace began talking of prohibiting deputies from practicing law, and among themselves lawyers began worrying about Gaulier, Guiboud-Ribaud, and the honor of their profession. Every day brought its insinuations and tawdry revelations, heavy with threats even to honorable names. A day or two earlier a Romanian adventurer had suddenly turned up in Inspector Bonny's office. It was Sylvain Zweifel, Stavisky's old comrade-in-arms from the days of the Brunoy counterfeiting ring in 1926, eager as always to advance his own cause. He spoke of money, jewels, and, most important of all, check stubs—with sums and names, telltale check stubs he had heard of somehow and that Bonny, the very next day, 8 January, set out resolutely to find.[46]

That day Jean Chiappe, prefect of police, returned to Paris from Florence. He had abruptly cut short an Italian holiday. When the overnight *rapide* from Rome arrived at the Gare de Lyon, at nine forty-five in the morning, the reporters were waiting. So was a police guard. "Stavisky?" he replied, "But we've been watching him for ten years!" He angrily denied ever taking any money from him. He slipped away, past the photographers, and went straight to the

Pursuit: Police search the offices of *La Volonté* and interrogate its editor, Albert Dubarry. (Photo courtesy of Bibliothèque Nationale de France.)

Ministry of the Interior, where the prime minister, Camille Chautemps, was waiting for him.[47]

For two weeks, ever since Tissier's arrest in Bayonne, the Republic's appointed and elected officials had endured the free-spoken speculations of its press. Beset by rank rumors of malfeasance, they had reacted sluggishly, sometimes not at all. At first no one awoke to the imminent metamorphosis, quickened by a poisonous climate, of fait divers into scandal. At Commerce the minister's chief of staff dismissed Léon Delamarche, the exposed and alarmed inspector general of credit. Go away, the chief of staff replied in effect into the telephone. The minister was at home writing a speech. There was no need to bother him with stories about some provincial pawnshop. Delamarche should be worrying about international trade and finance, the chief of staff thought, he had his priorities all wrong.[48]

Perhaps; but the provincial pawnshop soon swamped any chosen order of the day. By the 29th, alarm already mingled with anticipation, and fact with fiction, in the corridors of the Chamber of Deputies. Stavisky had controlled Dubarry's paper! — and with money from the Bayonne bonds, which Dalimier, as minister of labor, had promoted; those two had dined several times a week at the Ritz, and seven or eight Radical deputies were compromised too. Chautemps had hastily left for an alpine holiday — the scandal, they said, loomed as large as the banker Oustric's three years before. Then Chautemps had artfully exploited the uproar to bring down his right-wing rival André Tardieu in a game that two could play.[49]

Chautemps did leave for the Swiss Alps that day, with his family, to ski in Crans-sur-Sierre. He had done so every winter for fifteen years. But how cruel, this time, that his journey should seem to converge with Sacha Stavisky's. Twice in 1932 the name "Alexandre" had reached his ear, both times from the lips of Dubarry, and once again early in 1933, from those of Deputy Bonnaure. Then, in September, the name sounded again, this time as "Stavisky," when not even the deaf could ignore the rumors about the Bayonne bonds. Now in December their paths almost crossed again, as though even in the alpine snow the personage could not shake the interloper.[50]

It was only a matter of time before a certain arm of the press connected their journeys. When Chautemps had left Paris on the 29th, Stavisky had been a name, a problem on a desk somewhere, dwarfed by the statesman's weightier obligations—a speech to the Chamber until two in the morning on the 24th, respects to the victims of the Lagny train catastrophe the same day, Christmas in Blois with his family the next, the disarmament conference, diplomatic notes, Italy's Mediterranean ambitions. When he returned on 3 January, *Le Populaire,* on the left, was insinuating that Chautemps's Ministry of the Interior had covered Stavisky's escape, and *Le Figaro,* on the right, was calling for a new leader who, like Clemenceau driving the defeatists from the councils of war, would clean out the Augean stables and save the nation. Chautemps was in jeopardy.[51]

Minister of the interior for the sixth time, though prime minister only for the second, Chautemps knew how to protect himself. He was a master of timely concessions and small betrayals; compromise and improvise, manipulate and ingratiate, were his unsentimental yet winning tactics, and Chautemps was nothing if not a tactician. Indefatigable and conniving, he cobbled together parliamentary majorities; courteous, polished, and articulate, he charmed them until they voted and went home. Even his enemies admired him. "Subtle, lacking in strength, but incomparably shrewd!" His face was narrow and pale, his gaze clear, his step smooth and supple. No outsider or parvenu, he moved among his fellow Radicals as naturally and confidently as any creature amid its own kind: Radicalism ran in his blood. His father the minister, his uncle the senator, and his brother the deputy, killed at the front in 1915 at the head of his company, had all endowed him with a birthright and an authority that by now, even in this Republic, signified dynasty. Chautemps the scion was not yet fifty. He had a future.[52]

Dalimier, his minister of colonies, presented the immediate problem. He was in Nice, on the Promenade des Anglais. Two years earlier, as minister of labor, he had delighted Dubarry and Stavisky and signed two letters. How many thousands of letters had he signed since? How could he remember them? But now, as Chautemps returned from Crans-sur-Sierre, *Action Française* published them; and so did *Paris-Soir* a day later; and so did others. Reporters arrived in Nice and at the Ministry of Colonies. Dalimier arrived in Paris, in Camille Chautemps's office at the Ministry of the Interior. Soothing communiqués issued forth about his good faith and the prime minister's good trust, but Albert Dalimier was fast becoming a liability. He might have to go.[53]

Cutting a minister loose, or better yet, accepting with chagrin his sacrificial departure, sometimes kept the predators at bay. Briand's departure from the Foreign Ministry in 1921 effectively ended the scandal over whatever official favors the Banque Industrielle de Chine might have enjoyed. But sometimes as well, such mea culpas rang hollow, and only provoked louder cries of indignation from the scandalmongers. Raoul Péret's resignation as minister of justice in 1930, forced by a careless association with the financier Oustric, for which the High Court later forgave him, could not save Tardieu's government. It fell. Chautemps would have to manage Dalimier's departure carefully.[54]

Besides, the former minister of labor was only part of the problem. By 6 January Chautemps had understood that the entire administration of justice was under attack — the courts, the magistrates, the police, even the ministers, since René Renoult's interventions on behalf of Stavisky back in 1926 had now leaked out onto the front pages. So had the reluctance of Pressard, the public prosecutor, to prosecute the Foncière company in 1931. Raynaldy, the current minister of justice, in turn cut short his stay in the Aveyron and returned in haste to the capital. He and Chautemps put their heads together; each ordered an official inquiry, one into the courts and the other into the police. Why had they not brought Stavisky to trial? The government wished to display unyielding rigor. But not everyone wished to wait, and on 8 January a small riot shattered the stately and ordered routines of the Palace of Justice. Down the Galerie Marchande came cries and insults and a large banner calling for the resignation of Pressard and of all the other protectors of swindlers. The palace guards, all maimed veterans of a different war, fell back, and the Republican guards came in to repel the invaders, to arrest a few and expel the others. The skirmish ended soon enough. But for a moment the palace became a sordid show ground of sedition, and provided a spectacle that, for anyone who cared to watch, betokened the coming of civil strife.

And on the 8th as well, as Prefect of Police Chiappe arrived in Chautemps's office and Inspector Bonny searched for the telltale check stubs, as Garat and Tissier languished in the Villa Chagrin in Bayonne, and as Darius tried to explain himself to an investigating magistrate — on the 8th, ten deputies were demanding answers in the Chamber. They were putting forward formal motions, the opening shots in the parliamentary battle. Would the government resign? Some of them thought so, as did some editors. But Chautemps saw matters differently. He called a meeting of the full cabinet for five o'clock that afternoon, and prepared to confront Albert Dalimier with the ire of the government.[55]

The End

Stavisky was here, Stavisky was there — spurious sightings of him all over the country now muddled the inspectors and superintendents at the Sûreté

Générale. Poor director Thomé, distinguished and befuddled, and in no way a police professional, did not know what to make of them. But on the 6th one of his two top aides, Superintendent Ducloux, sensed a breakthrough. It followed adventitiously on the theft in a train of a woman's suitcase.

Returning to Paris from Servoz, where she owned the villa called Les Argentières, a Mme Dusset reported the disappearance of her suitcase and, as an afterthought, mentioned a suspicious guest—highly suspicious, she thought, in view of all she had been reading lately in the papers. René Pigaglio, who appeared in Servoz every winter and who worked, she knew, in some way at *La Volonté* in Paris, had brought a mysterious and reclusive friend with him to Les Argentières. The man never showed his face, asked only for newspapers and two liters of milk a day, and left money on the table to avoid paying in person. Mme Dusset wondered if he might not be . . . and Ducloux sent three of his inspectors to Servoz that night.[56]

One of them, Marcel Charpentier, called the villa before leaving. The reclusive guest had departed on New Year's Day, the concierge replied, and so had another transient resident of Les Argentières, a man distinctive for his large red nose. That might be Henri Voix, Superintendent Ducloux conjectured alertly: the existence of Stavisky's ungainly employee was known to the Sûreté thanks to the indispensable and ubiquitous inspector Bonny, who had learned from an informer that a man called Voix had probably left to succor his runaway master some days earlier. If they could find Voix, Ducloux reasoned, they could find Stavisky; and he gave Charpentier a photograph of the man to take with him as he left for the Gare de Lyon. The clues were beginning to cohere.[57]

Indeed, the next day, arriving in Servoz, Charpentier and his two colleagues from the Sûreté found the trace of Voix's passage through town. The concierge at Les Argentières identified the photo, and Charpentier found his signature on the guest register; he also found Pigaglio and his entire family in the villa next door. Mme Pigaglio stood casually on the balcony, smoking a cigarette. But Charpentier found no sign of Stavisky.

With alacrity Pigaglio and his family left. Charpentier watched them slide by in a sleigh. He asked one of the other inspectors to follow them. It was all highly suspicious. They had stopped for an hour in a café in Chamonix while Pigaglio disappeared, he learned with interest in the morning. Then they had all taken the train for Paris. In Chamonix Charpentier, his two colleagues from the Sûreté, and a local gendarme sat down over lunch with the local guest registers in front of them. At a villa called Le Vieux Logis, on the night of 31 December, someone had signed in as "Fargeas"—but in a hand closely resembling that of Henri Voix on the register in Servoz, and seemingly accompanied by the same kind of identification, a press card. Charpentier's suspicions deepened.[58]

He was in plainclothes, inconspicuous. But word of the famous fugitive's proximity was spreading, shared among the apprehensive, the talkative, and the inquisitive. The mayor of Servoz had already reported the suspicious strangers' passage through town to the nearest gendarmes, who had turned up uniformed and enthusiastic at the door of Les Argentières, much to Charpentier's annoyance. He had sent them away, much to theirs. Worse, the press had found out. Two nights earlier a reporter from *Paris-Soir* had watched him board the train in Paris for the Alps, with his two colleagues. The paper had duly published the item the next day. So had *Les Allobroges*, a paper in nearby Bonneville. Today, the 8th, *Le Matin* carried it on the front page, and legions of scribblers were on their way. To take Stavisky by surprise Charpentier would have to act now.[59] Quickly he found Antoine Chatou, an elderly and respectable antique dealer, owner of the nearby villa, Le Vieux Logis. Through the curtains of his shop Chatou pointed to Le Vieux Logis in the distance. Yes, he recognized the photo of Voix alias Fargeas. But no, he did not recognize the other photo—Stavisky's. He had not seen that man. And no, he could not leave his boutique unattended. Charpentier pressed, Chatou yielded. They set off for the villa. It was two thirty on a Monday afternoon, 8 January.[60]

That morning Pigaglio stepped off the train at the Gare de Lyon and looked aghast upon "HANDSOME ALEXANDRE'S STAY IN SERVOZ" in *Le Matin*. His own arrest was imminent. At home he found the door broken open, the calling card of a sudden visit by the police. He went to Gaston Bonnaure, lawyer and friend to both Stavisky and himself, or so he thought.

He had known Gastounet, as Stavisky called him, since the 1920s, when the droll Radical lawyer from Auvergne had arrived in the third arrondissement to begin his ascent to the position of deputy. There Bonnaure had met Pigaglio, fellow enthusiast in the arrondissement's Lay Republican Youth. Once elected, the deputy rewarded the voter and supporter with friendship and connections, with services rendered for loyalty returned, with a job at *La Volonté*, just as Stavisky, a different sort of client, was taking over the paper. Of such minute local arrangements did the Chamber's backbenchers build their base. Now Pigaglio had returned from Chamonix in a panic. He held *Le Matin* in his hand and imagined policemen everywhere.[61]

Through Pigaglio, Bonnaure had already advised Stavisky on his mountaintop to give himself up. He had proffered no guiding or consoling words to his friend, still less any timely revelations to his government. Such timorous passivity now fulfilled a lawyer's obligations to his client just as nicely as the spirit of enterprise, the nights in Budapest and the calls at the Claridge, had once done. But by this Monday, the 8th, Bonnaure's name was in the papers, his reputation and perhaps his neck at stake. He decided to protect himself. Where exactly was Stavisky, he asked Pigaglio; and leaving the frightened underling in his office he went to the Ministry of the Interior and asked to see Camille Chautemps.

The prime minister about to sacrifice Dalimier had no time for the deputy about to sacrifice Stavisky. Instead, an undersecretary of state received Bonnaure, encouraged him ambiguously—"It's in your interest"—and then listened to the revelation, prefaced by billowing declarations of professional uprightness, that Stavisky was hiding somewhere within a thirty-kilometer radius of Servoz.

Bonnaure knew much more. Pigaglio had even given him a phone number—Chamonix 319. But Bonnaure's future, perhaps his freedom, hung in the balance. Therefore he had only half-betrayed, just enough, he hoped, to earn the government's gratitude but not the indelible stigma of the turncoat.[62]

It was a last act of ethical incoherence, a display of moral cretinism so complete as to steal the finale from the others, some more and some less qualified than he to compete—such as Garat the deputy, Guiboud-Ribaud the lawyer, Tissier the accountant, Dubarry the journalist, Constantin the civil servant, Dalimier the minister, Pressard the magistrate, Bayard the policeman, and so many others whose names in the press that day were merging, to the great indignation of their owners, into a prismatic spectacle of amorality.

At the Sûreté, Superintendent Ducloux learned of Bonnaure's garbled revelation early in the afternoon. He tried to get word to Charpentier in Chamonix. But the inspector was already on his way to Le Vieux Logis.

Bonnaure thoughtfully found a lawyer for Pigaglio, who was later arrested and charged with harboring an outlaw.[63]

"The lowly have the best hearts," Stavisky complained to Henri Voix as they sat in Le Vieux Logis. He decried the friends who had dropped him, especially journalists of the likes of Paul Lévy and Camille Aymard, who had taken his money and whose pharisaic professions of indignation now filled the columns of their own newspapers. There were too many deputies, it would blow over, Bonnaure could work something out with Dalimier, he had once hoped aloud; but no more.[64]

A hundred million francs in profits, all lost, he reflected. It was the morning of the 8th, and he was telling Voix all about what might have been. The Hungarian bond venture, Bonnaure's domain, would have filled some holes—he did not elaborate—and left him the bonanza besides. But it was all over. All he had left was the money he carried with him. He would go abroad, to Italy perhaps.[65]

The night before, they had celebrated Epiphany with Voix's mistress, Lucette. They had sat up playing cards until four in the morning. Now Stavisky, suddenly thinking of music to break the monotony, gave him a thousand francs and asked for a radio along with the newspapers. Voix left the house at about two o'clock.

Lucette, as suspicious as ever, went with him. To her, the mysterious resident of Le Vieux Logis was still "M. Maurice," but in Chamonix she saw that day's *Le Petit Dauphinois* and its story about Stavisky's rumored presence in the area. She grew agitated. Voix noticed the same story in *L'Ami du Peuple* and also observed the uniformed gendarmes in town. But he and Lucette went about their shopping anyway. They rented a small radio and returned it when the pharmacist ventured the opinion that it looked too weak; they called at the co-op, the fishmonger, and the coal merchant, where Voix ordered 150 kilos of coal and signed, reluctantly, as "Fargeas"; they went to a tearoom called La Potinière and sat down.

There was not much else they could do. Like Pigaglio, Voix had suggested to no avail that Stavisky turn himself in. He had tried the best he could to lift his master's morale. But it was no good, and recently he had noticed on Stavisky's night table, by the bed, a letter addressed to Arlette lying beside the revolver, Romagnino's Browning, that he kept on him all day and by him all night and that he refused to give up.[66]

Coming up the long snowy path toward Le Vieux Logis, Inspector Charpentier held back a few steps with his colleague from the Sûreté, Inspector Girard, while his other colleague, Le Gall, and the villa's owner, Marcel Chatou, led the way. Well away, out of sight, three local gendarmes brought up the rear.[67]

The doors were locked. There was no answer. Charpentier gallantly invited old Chatou to enter through an open window, unlock the door from inside, and let them in. The place was empty. At the far end a bedroom was locked from inside, but no sound there, no breath, no footstep, no involuntary sign of life, betrayed a human presence behind the door. Is the room comfortable? Charpentier asked very loudly of Chatou, and the others understood that the inspector was resorting to subterfuge, to the persona of a prospective tenant, for who else might lull the bedroom's silent occupant into a sense of security and out into the open? Then they made as though to leave, and afterward stood noiselessly by the bedroom door; and were still standing there when one of the local gendarmes turned up and told Charpentier that Superintendent Ducloux in Paris urgently wished to hear from him.[68]

From a nearby phone Charpentier obediently called his superior. Armed with Bonnaure's modest revelations of the day, Ducloux wished to assure his inspector that Stavisky was within a radius of thirty kilometers, and to enjoin him not to leave the area. To this sublimely useless disclosure Charpentier rejoined that Stavisky was probably a great deal closer than that, and when he had finished explaining the present impasse he asked into the phone for instructions.

Charpentier was a twenty-one-year veteran of the Sûreté, well acquainted with the protocol of waiting a man out. But this was different. He did not know who, if anyone, was in the locked bedroom. The press would be on them any minute like a horde of locusts. What should he do?

"Break the door down," Ducloux replied simply, and Charpentier returned with the others to Le Vieux Logis. Chatou stood behind him in the dining room, and the police surrounded the house.[69]

Charpentier tried the bedroom door again, and knocked.

"Who's there?" came a voice from behind the door.

"Police. Open up," replied the inspector, and when poor Chatou heard the shot he ran for dear life, out of his villa and back to the barn, while Charpentier

Nemesis: Stavisky at Chamonix, 8 January 1934. (Photo courtesy of Bibliothèque Nationale de France.)

and his men went outside, tore the shutters off the bedroom's terrace door, broke the glass, unlocked the door, and went in.[70]

Stavisky lay by the bed in navy blue ski clothes, unconscious but alive, blood pouring from his nostrils, bits of his brain on the floor. His right hand, still shaking, held a revolver. A bullet lay beside him. It had entered through the right temple, exited through the left, and ricocheted off the wall above. An ejected cartridge lay on the floor as well, beside a broken watch stopped forever at four o'clock. Inspector Le Gall took the revolver—a Browning 6.35 millimeter automatic—and placed it on the bed.[71]

"It's him all right," said Charpentier, and went to the phone. He called for a doctor, who arrived a few minutes later. They called an ambulance, the prosecutor in Bonneville, more gendarmes, and a photographer. Charpentier called Paris. Reporters began arriving in droves.[72]

Voix came trudging up the path with his *panier à provisions,* his grocery basket, into the falling darkness and the gathering throng of police and reporters. He had left Lucette back at La Potinière. One of the gendarmes stopped him and brought him in. "It was bound to happen," Voix said, and Charpentier had him stay until the prosecutor from Bonneville arrived.

In the tearoom Lucette hurriedly drank some herbal tea and left. She wandered wildly toward Chatou's antique shop, and there a gendarme found her too. She was very frightened.[73]

TEN

THE AFFAIR

"Of course," she told me, "this Stavisky is a swindler, he's just doing his job! But these gentlemen of the government . . ."—Newspaper vendor to Paule Henry-Bordeaux, *Le Figaro*, 26 January 1934

Assembling at the Ministry of the Interior on Place Beauvau just after five o'clock, the cabinet listened to Chautemps talk of the afternoon's events in Chamonix. Not far away, on the boulevards, the first of the special editions appeared, and around the city radio sets announced the news of Stavisky's apparent suicide. In the inner corridors of the Chamber small groups of deputies gathered around the bulletin boards to read the wire service dispatches as they went up. The Radical Party canceled the meeting of its executive committee, alarmed by mutinous mutterings among the rank and file, and some of its leaders prayed aloud that Herriot could find the way, the words, to dissipate the rising storm.[1]

Presently, before the gathered cabinet, Dalimier began speaking. He had done nothing wrong, he insisted. But a glacial silence greeted him when he finished. The ministers were in no mood to listen to his protestations of innocence. Finally Chautemps spoke up. Had anyone anything to say? he asked. Yes, said Eugene Frot, minister of the merchant marine, who then asked politely but firmly for Dalimier's resignation. Philippe Marcombes, Chautemps's own undersecretary of state, expressed his support for the idea. Later that night Dalimier sent over a letter of resignation to Place Beauvau. Chautemps accepted it with alacrity. But in a press communiqué he expressed his entire government's confidence in their fallen colleague's good faith.[2]

It was too late. Ministerial responsibility, in this Republic, rendered even a minor setback potentially deadly; and governments had fallen over lesser misfortunes than a minister's resignation. Such was the power of Parliament that an adroit motion or a hostile maneuver might deprive the country of its executive. A merely ambiguous vote in the Chamber had provoked the fall of Combes's government in 1905, then of Briand's in 1910 and again in 1911. Neither had even been voted out. Nor had Chautemps's; but another resignation or two might prove more than his government could tolerate.[3]

Besides, the nocturnal sacrifice of Dalimier lost all nobility in the harsh light of day, as scandal greeted each official word and deed with mockery and derision, and each revelation of a meal in the swindler's company with a vehement presumption of complicity.

"Stavisky commits suicide with a bullet fired at him at point-blank range," announced the *Canard Enchaîné* with sardonic glee. It added that perhaps

Dalimier, in view of the government's uncertain future and its praise for his ethical standards, should return as prime minister himself.[4] An orgy of self-indulgence now swept the papers, a celebration of skepticism and disbelief, and no sooner had the government announced the news of Stavisky's death and the minister's departure than it found itself retreating under a hail of questions, accusations, and insults.

It did not greatly matter which hue of the political spectrum the paper reflected. "The police affirm that he committed suicide," declared *Le Populaire* on the left, "but the affirmation doesn't fool anyone." In *L'Ordre,* on the right, Emile Buré announced "a revolution by contempt," and assured his readers that nobody believed the suicide story. The extremes mirrored each other, and not for the first time. Like the royalist *Action Française,* the Communist *L'Humanité* announced that the government had murdered Stavisky in Chamonix. Closer to the center, the editorialists moderated their tone, but *Le Figaro* still found the fugitive's death suspicious, his escape from arrest more so, and even papers as unimpeachably Radical as *La République* and *L'Oeuvre* seemed at a loss for words, supporting their men in power but calling for investigations. The police, symbols of the government's monopoly over legal violence, had become the visible symptoms of its vulnerability.[5]

Conflicting stereotypes of the police had long served the public imagination, conveyed by a press both servile and suspicious and by a literature that made heroes as well as villains of them. The nineteenth century opened with Minister Joseph Fouché, looking elusive even in his likeness on canvas; the twentieth opened with Prefect Lépine, solid and dedicated in the popular *Lectures pour Tous.* In between, novelists watched and wrote. Balzac's Vautrin recalled Vidocq, the escaped convict of Fouché's and Pasquier's police, and the Javert of *Les Misérables,* an exemplary and zealous servant of public order, expressed in part Hugo's hatred for the prefect of police who ushered him into exile, Maupas of the 1851 coup d'état. Balzac's policeman was human, a creature of passion and greed; Hugo's was scarcely plausible, a figure of such relentless devotion to duty that any self-doubt or sense of fallibility rendered his own life unbearable. Closer to earth and the man in the street, the foot soldier of the gutter police appeared in one case as the enemy of the working man, in the other as his protector. One day in 1841 Hugo defended a woman in the street against her persecutors among the police. The incident found its way into the first part of *Les Misérables,* and so did the woman, as Fantine. But later, *Lectures pour Tous,* again idolized the ordinary policeman Rossignol, poorly paid, often injured, always victorious in the crusade against street crime. "Police. Is always wrong," wrote Flaubert in the *Dictionnaire des idées reçues,* but the Larousse dictionary of the day, in a description as massive as Flaubert's was pithy, deemed any modern society unthinkable without them. Disfigured by its foes and beautified by its friends, the face of public order appeared as elusive and changeable as authority itself.

The renditions depended, in part, on their artists' attitude toward the regime of the day. Liberal or Radical opponents of the Second Empire resented the police as bitterly as did socialist, royalist, or Bonapartist foes of the Third Republic. In 1870 Clemenceau, as mayor of Montmartre, refused to turn over his Orsini bombs to the new prefect of police; in 1909 Clemenceau, as minister of the interior, was happy to be known as the country's top cop, *le premier flic de France*. Thus left and right played on the phantasm as they might. The conspiracy, intrigue, and uncommon power of manipulation they pretended to see in the police reflected more imagination than discernment. The reality was less exciting. Fouché had not contrived the downfall of Napoleon, nor Lépine that of Rochette, nor Chiappe that of Sacha Stavisky. But the phantasm was afoot again. Who would exploit it now?[6]

As luck would have it, the Chamber returned on the 9th from its Christmas recess. By then, eleven deputies had put forward questions delivered at various hostile pitches, and at once the familiar specter of ministerial crisis returned to stalk the Palais Bourbon. Would the varied socialists, orthodox behind Léon Blum, schismatic behind Adrien Marquet or Marcel Déat, support the government? Would the minority members of the cabinet, men outside the Radical fold such as Raynaldy at Justice or Frot at the merchant marine, close ranks? Radical backbenchers now denounced their colleagues André Hesse and Gaston Bonnaure, lawyers who had represented the scoundrel and brought odium on their party. Would the Radicals hold together?[7]

As if to render the questions and indeed the deputies irrelevant, about two thousand supporters of Action Française turned up that evening on Boulevard Saint-Germain, only to be turned away by police when they tried to force the barriers protecting the Palais Bourbon.[8] They were a fringe group, raucous enthusiasts for a lost cause. But the skirmish in the street, accompanying the voices in the press and the rising tumult in the Chamber, resounded faintly with historical memories—of government besieged, confidence destroyed, and a regime in crisis.

Next to the Panama Canal company forty years before, which had bribed hundreds of deputies and journalists and squandered the savings of hundreds of thousands of small investors, the crédit municipal of Bayonne invited at most a sympathetic tear for the bilked insurance companies rather than a general political crisis. Next to the guilt or innocence of Captain Dreyfus, which had brought fundamental concepts of right into conflict with each other, Stavisky's crimes called only for the prosecution of his accomplices, and perhaps a few resignations for laxity, not a climate of civil war. Yet already, voices predicted in the Chamber and proclaimed in the press a scandal worthy of the earlier two, a sudden paroxysm in the Republic's maturity to rival those of its youth.

More recently, Stavisky's spiritual kin had engaged in financial practices that had gravely embarrassed the political establishment. Yet none had set off a scandal of the magnitude now at hand. The fall of Albert Oustric's bank in the autumn of 1930 had provoked that of Tardieu's government, when his enemies in the Senate seized on the services, legal and otherwise, that his justice minister, Raoul Péret, had once provided to the unconventional financier. But the affair blew over, and Tardieu was back in office little more than a year later. In between, the Aéropostale affair had threatened Etienne Flandin, minister of finance: like Péret, he had once, when out of office, served as legal counsel to a questionable company, which was now trying to win government concessions for new airlines to South America. Dalimier had never done as much for Stavisky. But Flandin defended himself ably in a violent debate in the Chamber, and the scandal evaporated. The banker Marthe Hanau enjoyed a circle of political friends as wide as Stavisky's, but when she fell, at the end of 1928, the government survived, in spite of predictable attacks on the justice system and some angry columns in the newspapers. Such affairs stirred few memories of Panama or Dreyfus. Yet this one did.[9]

The secret lay not in Stavisky's misdeeds but in the country's climate: the scale of iniquity mattered less than the intensity of the ill will. Demonizing the police, and by extension the state itself, the scandalmongers in the Chamber, the newsrooms, and the streets quickly seized on modest abuses to stigmatize officialdom as a whole. This too followed an old pattern. In the late 1840s accusations of corruption or depravity had followed rather than preceded the troubles of the ministry and the monarchy. Critics had proposed drastic diagnoses out of all proportion to the ills unmasked; cynicism about the present had complemented recollections of past glory; incompatible malcontents unexpectedly joined arms. Now, in the gathering gloom of the 1930s, an intensely political culture allowed its celebrants to blame a swindler's success on a government's complicity, glibly diagnose the misfortunes befalling the country at home and abroad, and threaten the survival of a comparatively benign regime.

As the scandal broke, the cast of characters swelled into the dramatis personae of the liberal Republic itself. A journalist, a lawyer, an accountant, an insurer, a notary, a doctor—there seemed no end to the representatives of civil society who had lent Stavisky their good offices, no end to the parade of professions whose advent, not so long ago, Gambetta had hailed with that of the Republic itself. With each arrest and each revelation came lamentations about "rot" and "easy morals," dim stirrings of self-doubt largely absent from the scandals of the recent past. Now lawyers, journalists, and financiers denounced their own colleagues. A republican conscience accused a liberal society. But how, now that history, ideology, and tradition had invested the Republic's political institutions with deep moral purpose, could such accusations not come to rest on the vital representative institution, the locus of transparency and delegated sovereignty, the Chamber of Deputies?

Investigation into the Ruins

Covering her face in her fur collar, escorted by a police inspector from Lyons, Arlette arrived at the little station in Chamonix on the morning of 9 January. At about eight thirty the night before, she had learned that Sacha was in a coma in a hospital there. Over an hour had elapsed as he lay on the floor in Le Vieux Logis, while a doctor, a photographer, and eventually, through snow and ice from Sallanches, an ambulance came. At the hospital doctors tried to operate. They failed, and at two thirty in the morning, as Arlette traveled in the train from Paris, Stavisky died. "Suicide by bullet from a repeating revolver," concluded the autopsy that day, "fired by a right-handed man at short range."[10]

At the station a crowd of vacationers, newsmen, and local Savoyards turned out for Arlette. Shielded from their insatiable curiosity by police, she made her way to the hospital. With emotion she identified Sacha's body, and then kept vigil by him for a while as the sisters in white glided down the halls.[11]

Later she met with the investigating magistrate from Bonneville, who had arrived during the night. Stavisky had threatened suicide, she explained, the last time they had spoken. She was not surprised at what had happened. The magistrate removed an envelope taken as evidence from Le Vieux Logis and handed it to her. On it Stavisky had written "For my beloved wife." She opened it and found three letters, one to her and one to each of their children, three letters, as it were, from beyond.[12]

"My great love," she read, "I write these lines with a torn and broken heart . . ." Short pages in Stavisky's small, precise hand followed. He expressed no regret for his actions, only sorrow at leaving his family destitute and horror at the prospect of prison, the very word too dreadful to use. "The situation I find myself in is so serious that I see no way out. . . . To stay separated from you, my sole reason for living, is something I cannot resolve to do. . . . It would be criminal of me to impose so long a wait on you." He had decided to disappear. And he urged her to bring up Claude and Michelle "in the path of virtue," to make sure that Claude became "a good and loyal man," and that neither suffered from their surname—which he urged her not to change.[13]

Before parting with the letter, the investigating magistrate ordered photographs of it. Irony glimmered through the melodramatic farewell. The confidence trickster's testament, his penultimate act, shone for its sincerity, and he who in life had ruthlessly exploited the vanities of officialdom now in death delivered it from infamy with a document that, for all intents and purposes, absolved it of political murder.

The next day, leaving him in a temporary grave, Arlette boarded the train for Paris and returned to the little apartment on Rue Obligado, her obscure new home in the shadow of the Claridge. Waiting in the wings was Inspector Bonny of the Sûreté Générale and, though she did not know it, an even chance of having to answer to the magistrates for her bygone connubial bliss.

■

Inspector Bonny sent for Arlette the day after her return from Chamonix. Reporters mobbed the halls of the Sûreté. To elude them, Bonny brought her into the secretary's office adjoining that of his superior, the supervisor of judicial investigations, John Hennet. A typist and another inspector joined them.

Yes, she had met a few men of mark, she said, including Garat and Bonnaure among the deputies, and Dubarry and Paul Lévy among the journalists, and once her husband had been to Stresa and lunched there at Georges Bonnet's table. Jean Chiappe, the prefect of police? No, she had never met him, although she had seen him, and once her husband had come home speaking warmly of him after a meeting arranged by Dubarry. Stavisky had grandiloquently suffused the frosty five-minute encounter in February 1933 with a golden glow of fellowship; but this Arlette did not know.

When Bonny placed the typed transcript in front of her, she declined to sign it. She asked that he remove her allusions to Chiappe, which suggested familiarity with a man she had never met. Bonny went to Hennet's office; the door opened, shut, opened again; Bonny emerged to hand her a duly expurgated deposition, which she duly signed.

But he had made a separate note of her declarations about Chiappe. Hennet thought it a good idea too. Legally, as evidence, the note was useless. But politically, who could tell? The chance to embarrass the Sûreté's powerful rival at the head of the prefecture of police was too precious to abandon to Arlette and her memory. Behind Bonny's little maneuver lay a history of bad blood between him and Chiappe. His sympathies at the time lay on the left, Chiappe's on the right, and the inspector had never forgiven the prefect for blocking his career, stopping his ascent, back in 1927. Energetic and professional until now, keener and swifter than his colleagues, Bonny was crossing the same frontier into self-aggrandizement that so many other capable professionals had crossed in their travels with Stavisky during his life.[14]

The case now totally absorbed him. Four days earlier, as Stavisky lay in Le Vieux Logis, Bonny had called in Romagnino and listened to his tales of journalists, deputies, and *le tout Paris;* and the inspector in turn informed Romagnino of the news from Chamonix. The two developed a modus vivendi, an accommodation akin to that uniting a police officer to his informer.[15]

Hayotte turned himself in the next morning. He and Bonny had already met a few days earlier, but now a warrant was out for his arrest and Stavisky's clumsy friend refused to answer any questions in the absence of a lawyer. Bonny questioned Depardon, the lowly employee who had run errands for Stavisky at the Foncière. He had seen Deputy Bonnaure there, he said. Bonny questioned Niemen, the retired boxer and sometime film extra at Gaumont, who answered incoherently about the passport in his name found on Stavisky; he too had seen Bonnaure in Stavisky's company, at the Claridge, where he had tended every morning to his hypochondriacal employer's physical conditioning. But he knew nothing of Bayonne and not much of anything else. Bonny questioned Desbrosses, the old accountant who had helped launch the Orléans operation. He had taught Tissier, his counterpart at Bayonne, the tricks of the trade. Pierre Curral, Stavisky's neighbor at the Claridge and publicity agent for the Empire, came in too and told Bonny of names, especially parliamentary names, that he had heard Alexandre drop. The motley faces from Stavisky's circle now passed before the inspector's fascinated gaze. But who were the villains, who the victims? And who the casual associates, the indifferent birds of passage?[16]

Overwhelmed, Bonny called in help. From the Sûreté's financial brigade arrived the aptly named Inspector Peudepièce—"short on coins"— who busied himself calling on banks and examining the records of any accounts that Sacha Stavisky alias Serge Alexandre might have kept. Soon he began examining other accounts as well, including those of the journalists Albert Dubarry and Camille Aymard. He also searched among insurance companies and banks for traces of the Bayonne bonds, for their obscure paths through the channels of higher finance. But he did not look for Stavisky's telltale check stubs, the little secret that Bonny withheld from Zweifel, because he did not know of them. Those Bonny wanted for himself.[17]

The Magistrates against the Liberal Professions

Peudepièce and Bonny, like all their colleagues, were the eyes and ears of justice, looking and listening, transmitting their daily sensations. Justice was reacting in its spasmodic way, avid for facts yet fearful of error.

In Bayonne the magistrate d'Uhalt sat his two local captives, Garat and Tissier, down together. The prisoners faced each other between the gray bare walls of the Villa Chagrin's visiting room and conversed with incongruous decorum. Each stuck to his position. You knew everything and told me to do as Alexandre said, Tissier began. I knew nothing of the forgery and had every reason to trust you, Garat rejoined. It was pointless. But more prisoners were on the way to Bayonne from Paris.[18]

In the capital, the most prestigious public prosecutor's office in the land had assigned three investigating magistrates to d'Uhalt's investigation on the distant banks of the Adour. Voices were raised; he should relinquish the affair, they insisted, now Parisian, not Bayonnais, in scope. But, for the time being, the magistrates in Paris could only support their provincial colleague, wire him their discoveries, and send him their suspects. Soon Garat and Tissier had company from Paris.

There, in his office in the Palace of Justice, sat the magistrate André Ordonneau. He was in his early fifties, and, not surprisingly, still cut his beard and mustache in the prewar style. His narrow face suggested finesse, his broad brow intelligence, and indeed, his reserved, modest manner dissembled a powerful command of the law and its resources—especially in matters of finance. Like his wife, Ordonneau came from a family of magistrates in Périgord; he carried traditions within him, and, decorated and thrice wounded as an infantry lieutenant in Champagne and on the Somme, had many years before demonstrated an innate capacity for selfless service.[19]

He sat now, as night fell, with Darius of *Bec et Ongles*, querying the jaunty editor about his threats to Garat in the winter of 1932 and his subsequent accommodation with Stavisky. The sordid little episode suggested a knowledge of Stavisky's dealings that both editor and deputy now vigorously denied. Such intelligence was enough to prove *recel*, the knowing reception of goods or money of criminal provenance. That night Stavisky was dying. In Bayonne, d'Uhalt had already charged Garat with receiving stolen goods, among other misdeeds; in Paris, Ordonneau now considered the mulatto with the spotted bow tie sitting before him.

Where had the information for the item in *Bec et Ongles* come from? Rumors in the corridors of the Chamber of Deputies, Darius replied vaguely. How could he publish so damning an item and then accept an advertising contract, and even promote, in the summer of 1933, the Bayonne bonds themselves? Because he believed all the assurances given him by Garat and Alexandre, the editor insisted. And so it went, Garat's blissful ignorance on the Adour replicated just as blithely on the Seine—I knew nothing, he knew all. To prove prior knowledge in a court of law was no easy matter. But Ordonneau quickly had Darius placed under arrest. The next morning, flanked by two inspectors from the Sûreté Générale, Darius boarded the train for Bayonne. In Dax they took him off, fearing crowds on arrival. But no crowds came, and, unnoticed by all but a few reporters at the gate, Darius entered the Villa Chagrin, where Garat, shivering and depressed, had just moved to a sunnier cell and received the miserable gift of a heating stove.[20]

Two more journalists followed, their household names revealed to Inspector Bonny and then to the magistrate Ordonneau by the newly voluble Romagnino. At Ordonneau's request, a colleague in the palace began probing Albert Dubarry's jovial, arrogant defenses. When had the editor of *La Volonté* met Stavisky? What favors had he performed for the new owner of the paper, what missions to Dalimier, to Chiappe, to Darius, to anyone else, and how could he possibly ignore the tainted source of Stavisky's riches? Now an arrest warrant arrived from d'Uhalt in Bayonne. Two inspectors found Dubarry seated before the remains of a large breakfast in a hotel near the Opéra. As usual, reporters had learned of the warrant and milled eagerly around the doors. "I had hoped to see you sooner," Dubarry said amiably to the inspectors, and, twirling his golden-headed cane, he followed them, all smiles, to a waiting taxi.

The night before, Ordonneau had called in Camille Aymard, the former editor of *La Liberté*, whose name the busy magistrate had also heard issue from eloquent Romagnino. Aymard had dined with Stavisky; had accepted money from him; had sketched out for him some advertisements, which the police now seized in the offices on Place Saint-Georges. Duly informed, d'Uhalt wired a warrant for his arrest as well. In the morning, as Dubarry breakfasted in precious liberty, three inspectors appeared at Aymard's door on Rue de Lille. He received them politely in a dressing gown. A political machination, he told the assembled reporters, and, cigarette in mouth, drove off with the inspectors in his own car.

"Receiving stolen goods! It's inconceivable!" exclaimed Dubarry, emerging from the investigating magistrate's office in the Palace of Justice. There was Aymard. "We meet under singular circumstances," said the editor of *La Liberté* to his colleague from *La Volonté*. He extended his hand. Only their shared plight could explain such a burst of camaraderie among journalists of right and left; or perhaps a secret sympathy, deeper than the clash of creeds or the intermittent rancor of rivalry. Under guard on the same train to Bayonne that night, they resembled captive members of some elusive species. Each stayed, caged but respected, in his own compartment of velvet walls and varnished woodwork; Aymard slept, Dubarry did not; as dawn broke in Les Landes, they emerged and met in the corridor; and in Bayonne they drove with their captors past photographers at the station, down sleeping streets to formalities in the Palace of Justice, and on to the cold cells awaiting them in the Villa Chagrin.[21]

That made three representatives of the press in the dank prison; how many more might join them? Curral's fate hung in the balance; behind him bustled the editors of Stavisky's hopes and the blackmailers of his fears, Pécune of *D'Artagnan*, Livet of *Le Cri du Peuple*, Sartori of *La Bonne Guerre*, and Paul Lévy of *Aux Ecoutes*, whom one of Ordonneau's colleagues now called in and questioned. Yes, he conceded, he had taken money from Stavisky for a new weekly, and had lunched with him. But no, he had never done his ephemeral sponsor any favors; besides, the affair had proved a disaster. And, added Lévy, "I have always had the highest conception of my calling."[22]

Ordonneau and his colleagues held off for the time being. Suspicion was one matter, proof another, and criminal complicity required a precise demonstration. To put an editor on trial for the way he financed his paper, for his dealings, however shady, with known transgressors, was to court cries of persecution and censorship as well. Already Aymard was playing victim: the editor on the right, he insisted, was offered up as a sacrifice to the government's supporters on the left. In 1902 the courts had charged the editor of *La Guerre Financière et Politique* with theft and receipt of stolen goods for his transactions with the doubtful banker Boulaine, in prison for embezzlement at the time. He cried foul and his paper survived. Tainted funds, a poisoned well, did once bring a newspaper down, but that was in 1917, the paper was the *Bonnet Rouge*, and the crime was not receipt of stolen goods but treason.[23]

Structural reforms came to nothing, remaining the stillborn recommendations of a deputy or a commission. In 1912 the parliamentary commission looking into the Rochette affair thought publicity budgets should be more transparent; if newspapers had a stake in a financial venture, the commissioners thought, its readers, the potential investors, deserved to know. They might in that way smell a rat, an unduly enthusiastic editorial promotion. The Chamber thought so too; it passed a resolution; and nothing changed. Full transparency, even written into the commerce code, was too difficult to enforce, and editors in Stavisky's day were no more exposed to scrutiny than those in Rochette's. And if they transgressed as citizens, by colluding with doubtful sponsors, they might yet enjoy protection and even immunity as journalists, shielded by the law of 1881, the carapace of liberalism.[24]

So too might lawyers, obliged to defend their own clients and allowed to set their own fees. Guiboud-Ribaud's and Gaulier's fees looked suspiciously high. Legal counsel or criminal complicity? Faces more familiar than theirs studded the parade of lawyers grown rich at the felon's side. As elected politicians, they mixed at one time or another their office's sash with their profession's robe. Minister of Justice René Renoult, Senator Jean Odin, Deputies André Hesse, Anatole de Monzie, and Gaston Bonnaure had all added the aura of the Parliament to the fellowship of the bar. Who among them had trafficked in their influence, who had received stolen moneys? Each action, for the prosecution, was an elusive crime, doubly so when the suspect, a lawyer, enjoyed a measure of professional immunity; triply so when he enjoyed parliamentary or ministerial immunity to boot.

The founders of the Third Republic, authors of the constitutional law of 16 July 1875, had prohibited legal action against sitting deputies and senators, unless their fellow parliamentarians voted to suspend the immunity. With memories of the Second Empire still fresh in their minds, the legislators had hoped in that way to protect the representatives from vengeful ministers or spiteful rivals. No regrets accompanied the unspoken assumption that justice could be manipulated at will, only a firm resolve to shield the representatives against its misuse. The chambers rarely refused, once asked, to lift the immunity of one of their members. Sometimes during the war, the deputies even displayed more enthusiasm than justice itself for pursuing colleagues whose patriotism they doubted. Still the requirement gave the prosecutors pause. They hesitated to incur accusations of political partiality, especially if an election was pending; and usually one was pending, in this Republic of cantonal, municipal, and legislative contests. What if an acquittal in court followed a defeat at the polls?[25]

Now two investigating magistrates, Ordonneau and d'Uhalt, contemplated indicting several elected representatives, most of them members of the governing majority. Politics hung heavily over their heads. No matter that the charges pending were politically indifferent, achromatic on the ideological spectrum: to prosecute was to persecute, as Joseph Garat's supporters in Bayonne were already crying outside the walls of the Villa Chagrin. Open justice portended politicized justice, since, in a regime of liberties, defendants as well as prosecutors could exploit a trial, leaving public opinion the ultimate judge of winners and losers.

In the capital, indignation at parliamentary lawyers was rising. It erupted first among their own colleagues, who poured out their anger as though to wash away their profession's sins. Anxious and agitated, the lawyers in the palace swarmed through the galleries in their black robes like ants under siege in a colony. Early in January two hundred of them signed a petition banning deputies from the bar. It was too virtuous by half; the lawyers were depriving themselves of the political influence that allowed them a say, indirectly through the Ministry of Justice, in the appointment of magistrates. But no one went so far as to suggest that fees be regulated. Naturally, accusations flew among the self-righteous, the holier-than-thou paragons of probity. On the stairs leading from the cloakroom down to the Galerie Marchande, the deputy and lawyer André Hesse came to blows with just such a colleague, a self-appointed knight who, beating the drums of virtue, had ordered him out of the palace. "Go away," he had cried, and the ensuing set-to left Maître Hesse's robe in shreds, a tattered vestige of its former self.[26]

For the moment, Ordonneau and d'Uhalt decided to pursue Bonnaure. Once again, Romagnino had sung. He had told Ordonneau how Stavisky had paid Bonnaure's campaign expenses in the third arrondissement in 1932; he had told him of the deputy's bill at Lachaize the tailor, which Stavisky had kindly seen to as well; and Ordonneau had told d'Uhalt. Days earlier, the energetic magistrate in Bayonne had arrested one deputy, Joseph Garat, but now that the Chamber was in session he needed a lifting of parliamentary immunity before he could go after another. This the Chamber duly passed. Very well, the droll little deputy insisted, he had nothing to reproach himself for; yes, he had been Stavisky's lawyer, and would explain himself to d'Uhalt—as long as he did not violate the confidentiality of his client relationship.[27]

Followed by two inspectors of the Sûreté who had accompanied him all the way from Paris, Bonnaure walked briskly up to the palace in Bayonne. He obligingly imparted his identity to the magistrate d'Uhalt on the second floor, heard his host indict him for receiving stolen goods, and emerged with his two escorts from the doors of the palace, silent, unruffled, and still at liberty—but for how long? Heady wines and aromatic cigars awaited him at his hotel. He lunched well with the two inspectors, and later boarded the night train with them for the Gare d'Orsay and the lingering pleasures of the capital.[28]

Two weeks later, d'Uhalt sent for him again. Wearily now, with lawyers at his side, Bonnaure ascended the steps to d'Uhalt's office. "Cordial relations with an important client, that's all," Bonnaure told the magistrate. Yes, he had handled important business for Stavisky, primarily the Hungarian affair; had accepted accordingly high honoraria, some six hundred thousand francs in all; had never doubted the Bayonne bonds. His defense system was clear, a happy union of ignorance and professional pride. As the afternoon wore on, a crowd of several hundred gathered outside the walls of the palace. No, he had known nothing of Alexandre's past, and yes, Stavisky had paid his tailor's bill. When Bonnaure finally left the palace by a side door after dark, the crowd chased him into a nearby haberdasher's. "To jail! To jail!" they cried. In their minds, the story seemed already to pit an avenging magistrate against a reprobate deputy. For the moment d'Uhalt was a hero, Bonnaure a villain. The public trial was under way; justice had company.[29]

The State against the Civil Servants

Turning on the police and the magistrates, the government now pursued the pursuers. How had the criminal escaped prosecution for so long? Why had he not been arrested, who had let him go? Through a show of implacable rage, Chautemps's government might ride out the storm, even emerge purified.

Chautemps, as minister of the interior, asked one inspector general of administrative services to investigate the conduct of the Sûreté Générale in the sorry affair, another inspector general that of the prefecture of police, and a third that of Commerce, Labor, and Finance; meanwhile, Raynaldy, as minister of justice, ordered an inquiry into the nineteen successive postponements of Stavisky's hearing before the thirteenth correctional chamber.[30]

Such searching attentions unhinged the occupants of the five ministries and their services, scattered over the city from Interior and Finance on one side of the river to Commerce and Labor on the other, with Justice in its island palace aptly commanding the center. Added to a criminal investigation that threatened one or two of their own already, so public an inquisition into the civil servants' virtues and vices struck them as a witch-hunt. Mutterings of pharisaism, protestations of innocence, and mutual recriminations greeted the inspectors general, whose intrusions deranged an already troubled esprit de corps.

Summoned to explain their incuriosity about Orléans or Bayonne and their insouciance about Stavisky, the beleaguered officials in the various services more often than not blamed each other. At Commerce Léon Delamarche insisted as vigorously as ever that administrative oversight of the crédits municipaux fell to Interior through its prefects, and accounting oversight to Finance through its collectors and inspectors. At the Sûreté Générale Superintendent Ducloux argued that the magistrates of Justice, not the police of Interior, had shrugged off Bayonne and sent up a smokescreen of laissez-faire over the new enterprise. The prefecture of police and the Sûreté Générale abandoned Stavisky to each other, happily surrendering responsibility for his surveillance and thus for his escape. Such pervasive abdications left the inspectors general unmoved, even exasperated.[31]

Each civil servant had restrained his appetite for administrative empire, a bureaucratic self-denial as characteristic under these circumstances as self-indulgence under others. Stavisky had exploited both the voracity of ambition and the abstinence of self-protection. At Commerce alone, he had exploited Constantin's hope of status and Delamarche's fear of bureaucratic trespass, gaining the favors of the one and the lame acquiescence of the other. At each of his ports of call in officialdom he had mined the vanities and the modesties of power, until, bemused by his successes, he had offended both.[32]

The inspectors general deplored the culture of evasion and passivity they found, condemned or reproached its most prominent practitioners, and proposed to the government reprimands, disciplinary hearings, and forced retirements. Of corruption or complicity they said nothing at all. No one had enriched himself, no one had so sacrificed the public interest to his own as to barter his influence for profit at the late swindler's side. The law had no grievance here, save perhaps against Constantin of Commerce, whose kindnesses in Bayonne the public prosecutor's office now began to scrutinize. The fault, the inspectors general saw, lay in bureaucratic paralysis. The administration of the Republic lacked the material means for its mission, and often the moral means as well, the hidden reserves of conscience. The inspectors identified the symptoms, but left the diagnosis to others. Why the deficiencies? Were they the price of fiscal austerity, a circumstantial cause, Or that of subservience to an omnipotent Parliament, a structural cause? About such questions the inspectors general, themselves creatures of the administration, maintained a prudent silence.[33]

Meanwhile, careers crashed, the human wreckage floating in Stavisky's wake. Vulnerable and restive, the personages marked by the scandal ignored the administrative inquiry and set about identifying visible culprits.

At Commerce, even before the inspectors general began knocking at poor Léon Delamarche's door, his days were numbered. The minister, Laurent Eynac, was about to issue a self-serving communiqué commending his director of credit—since Delamarche had in the end sounded alarms about Bayonne—when Chautemps intervened. "Delamarche must be dismissed," the prime minister insisted. "Responsible," Chautemps called him five days later in a packed Chamber of Deputies. There would be hearings. But Delamarche's career was over.[34]

At the police, Inspector Bonny, exploring the terra incognita of Stavisky's inner circle, amassing secrets and half-truths that only he knew how to use, suddenly found himself suspended. He was listening to Desbrosses talk about Orléans when Ducloux, his superior at the Sûreté, called him in and took him off the case. Chautemps had set the procedure in motion on 15 January, before any inspector general had questioned Bonny. "Unacceptable," the prime minister called his interrogation of Arlette, with its unofficial yet unmistakable insinuations about the prefect of police, Jean Chiappe. Conveniently, three days later a superintendent in the rival prefecture of police produced a six-year-old charge of corruption against Bonny, a matter of accepting bribes from a Lithuanian businessman unwanted on French soil. "Suspend Bonny before dismissing him," ordered Chautemps the next day. The doubtful inspector, ever a dark horse, had become a liability to the government, a possible threat and a needless figure of controversy. He stepped down. But he continued free-lance—continued his personal quest for the telltale check stubs.[35]

And at Justice the highest magistrates suddenly shattered the calm of Albert Prince. As head of the financial section, he had gingerly inquired into the

Compagnie Foncière until, worn and exasperated, he had moved gladly in 1931 to the benches of the court of appeal. For three idyllic years he had heard nothing of Serge Alexandre or Sacha Stavisky. Now, on a Monday afternoon in January, the fugitive lay dying on the floor of Le Vieux Logis and the judge sat in session in a red robe on the dais of the criminal court. An errand boy came up. The judge was wanted urgently in the office of Eugène Dreyfus, presiding judge of the court of appeal.

What did you do, Dreyfus asked Prince as he walked in, with a report all about Stavisky sent to you in 1931 by one Inspector Cousin of the Police Judiciaire?[36]

President Dreyfus knew about scandal. As an Alsatian Jew starting out in the magistracy in 1893, he had suffered almost at once from the affair that bore his patronymic. He had waited seven long years for a mere lateral move from Le Havre to Rouen, and seven more just to rise in rank there. He had presided in 1910 over the trial of Henri Rochette, whose frauds and friendships dimly foreshadowed those of the fugitive in Le Vieux Logis. One of his earliest supporters in the Chamber, Maître André Hesse, was today best known as the fugitive's friend. At the end of his irreproachable career, scandal dogged Dreyfus as it had at the beginning. That Monday, Raynaldy, the minister of justice, had asked him and the prosecutor general, Donat-Guigue, to find out how on earth Stavisky's hearing could have been put off nineteen times. Gomien, the advocate general, joined them, as did Pressard, the public prosecutor. At once, Donat-Guigue produced the Cousin report: in it the inspector had warned of Stavisky and expressed surprise at the postponements of his trial. The agitated magistrates sent for Prince. When he arrived no one offered him a chair.[37]

For all his reserve, Prince was an emotional man. Startled and distraught, unable immediately to recollect the Cousin report, he nevertheless grasped the stratagem of his former superior, Georges Pressard—to proclaim his own ignorance and Prince's negligence. The public prosecutor knew of no Cousin report because the head of the financial section had never told him of it. There, happily, lay the blame.

"Do you know who's to blame in the Stavisky affair?" Prince asked his wife at a dinner they hosted at home that night. "Well, it's me! I see they want to place everything on my shoulders!" His guests found him pale and preoccupied. He began searching his memory that night, and later his papers as well. "Between Pressard and me it's hatred unto death," he told a friend in the Café de Flore one evening.[38]

Then the Gripois report of 1930 surfaced. In it Cousin's older colleague at the Police Judiciaire had enumerated the oddities of the Foncière and the transgressions of Stavisky. And it too had gone to Prince, who now went hastily to look at it. Twice he returned. "The Gripois report is just what I thought," he told a fellow judge of the court. "I don't understand all the fuss about it. It's not as important as they think and the financial section has nothing to reproach itself for." He was sounding defensive. To a lawyer he encountered in the palace several days later, he again played down the report. "I attached no importance to it!" he said. "No more than to the dozens and dozens of reports constantly coming into the financial section."[39]

Like Delamarche, Prince faced crucifixion for the sins of the system. Four years earlier, as a willing colleague, he had complied and conformed. Moved by extramural influences, the velvet-footed hierarchs of the palace had blighted the investigation of the Compagnie Foncière. Now the most spineless among them, Georges Pressard, hid behind a veil of ignorance. He had never seen the reports, he insisted. He had so, Prince replied. It did not matter. Pressard had known of them, even if he had not seen them. He had known of the affair. But how could Prince prove it, prove that his own error of judgment was everyone else's too?[40]

In the palace, word of the dispute quickly leaked out. In the galleries and shadows, lawyers stopped each other to denounce Pressard. He had refused to cover his former subordinate. Honor had fled the palace. Combined with the recriminations over parliamentary lawyers and over Stavisky's perenially postponed trials, the latest dereliction plunged the ancient seat even deeper into crisis. Not since the early years of the Third Republic, when the government purged the magistracy of suspected royalists and Bonapartists, and when resentment poisoned the air, had the palace known such strife. Often enough the magistrates had defended themselves against assailants from outside their walls. The most resounding faits divers of the Republic provoked reflexive cries that the magistrates had colluded with the guilty or the government or with occult forces of evil that lurked about the place. Disingenuously or not, even the adversaries of the Republic espoused liberalism and positivism in demanding that the administration of justice shut out ideology and politics and, to a degree, the conflicts and interests of society at large. But now such familiar hostilities, common enough beyond its walls, had broken out inside the palace itself.[41]

Where was justice? On the side of the strong. The proposition was almost as ancient as political philosophy itself, advanced by the sophist Thrasymachus in Plato's *Republic,* a work subtitled by its Alexandrian editors "Of Justice." The notion had so impressed opposition movements in France that it became a rallying cry, familiar to anyone who lived long enough to watch one regime replace another. It sounded before the Revolution in the legal briefs that denounced arbitrary noble privilege, during the Second Empire in the liberal or Radical attacks on the emperor's magistrates. It sounded again in the scandals of the Third Republic, whenever a minister, prefect, or deputy was spared the indignity of a trial or a conviction. "Equality before the law is perhaps not as absolute as it might be," declared, gently, a newspaper from the Saone-et-Loire when the courts dropped charges against Deputy Wilson and Prefect of Police Gragnon in the first major scandal of the Republic, set off in 1887 by a traffic in presidential decorations. Public opinion in the department held the same view but expressed it more violently, the police explained. "One has to be kind to investors," they were saying at the same time in the Tarn. Conversely, a minister, once threatened by the law, could raise the same cry: justice was the weapon of his enemies. Caillaux's friends in the Human Rights League said as much of his trial for treason after the Great War: "The whole trial stems from the hatred on the part of the Ministry of Foreign Affairs, just as the Dreyfus affair stemmed from the hatred on the part of the Ministry of War." The novelists of the Republic tirelessly exploited such fears, portraying judges as jackals and justice as injustice—Alphonse Daudet in *Port Tarascon,* Zola in *La bête humaine,* Giraudoux in *Bella*—so that the liberal Republic at its start provoked some of the same indignation as the absolute monarchy at its end.[42]

Amidst the mounting agitation, the designated victims raised thin voices of protest. Among the lawyers, Hesse invoked his duties to his client. Among the judges, Fillaire, who had granted the most postponements in the thirteenth chamber, spoke of standard operating practices. And, among the prosecutors, Prince gathered his recollections with visible anxiety. "You must watch out," said one of Mme Prince's friends to him at her weekly reception. "Fortunately, I'm not the only one to know what I know," he replied, "otherwise I wouldn't have any illusions, my life wouldn't be worth much."[43]

Factions against the Government

It was all about capitalism, said Georges Monnet on the left of the Chamber, all about the morality of its state; about magistrates and men, said Dommange on the right, men like Georges Pressard; about protecting republican liberties, said Bouisson from his perch above the assembly. The Chamber of Deputies, on the afternoon of 11 January, resounded with diagnoses and prescriptions from all sides. Until the roll of drums that convened them, the deputies had huddled in animated little conclaves in the Salon des Quatres Colonnes and the Salon de la Paix. There, safe from the spectators and journalists who flowed through the halls and packed the galleries, they whispered, argued, and speculated about the unfolding scandal. Tempers flared, insults flew, and in this feverish hour Minerva's statue in the lobby seemed all but forgotten, a goddess of reason watching over a house of passions.[44]

Long after nightfall the debate still raged. Untouched themselves, the government's opponents castigated the overnight villains delivered to them by the scandal. Avalanches of extenuating minutiae poured back. The debate began to flag. At length Chautemps mounted the tribune. The born orator spoke without notes, the born conciliator without malice or rancor. The inspectors general had barely begun their inquiries, but already the prime minister diagnosed the ill—an obsolete organization of police and justice. There would be reforms, there must be new laws, the press must rid itself of its crooks. And with what conviction he promised to sacrifice family and friends, his own career even, to purify the poisoned atmosphere that now hung over the country—it was, even to his critics, the night's winning performance.[45]

When he had assumed office two months earlier, Chautemps had managed in extremis to push some budgetary measures through the Chamber. For eighteen months of economic crisis, the insoluble contradictions of Radicalism had exposed themselves to the world: between its heart on the left and its wallet on the right, between principles and practice, tradition and necessity. Herriot, Daladier, and Sarraut had tried to cobble together majorities and ministries by pleasing friends and propitiating foes, each anxious to preserve his base even as he preached fiscal austerity. Each had failed, thwarted along the way by the working of the institutions. Chautemps had emerged as a newcomer at the helm, his five-day stint there in 1930 forgotten, and had swiftly capitalized in the Chamber on brief hopes of renewal and lasting fears of the unknown, of crisis. He had pushed through 6 billion francs in spending cuts. But the economy was no stronger, the government's majority no stabler, and Tardieu had neither forgotten nor forgiven his defeat in the elections of 1932. Away with Radical impotence, an end to paralysis, called the right; defend the workers, protect the victims of fiscal austerity, came the answering cries from the left. Talk spread of a new way out, a government of national unity. On this state of siege the Stavisky affair broke.[46]

The crisis set alight fringes of discontent and alienation, the disillusioned patriots, the champions of radical reform, the die-hard enemies of democracy and of any kind of pluralism. At a distance, a political philosopher might even discern a process of degeneration endemic to democracies. Political parties blind to any interest other than their own; the slow descent into factionalism, and with it the colonization of the state and its administration; the recourse to leaders notable for their insignificance or for their aversion to unsettling initiative: classic symptoms of a democracy corrupted by its own inner spiral of competition and compromise. In a parliamentary democracy untended by a powerful executive, a constitutional monarch, or the heavy hand of custom, partisan contest might one day so thoroughly fill the public space as to leave no institution untouched by its spirit or uncorroded by its bitterness. Then institutional paralysis would threaten.

Stavisky had played on the vanities, appetites, and hypocrisies of the contestants for influence. He had exploited the prestige of deputies, the weakness of officials, and the ambitions of both. Now, to their collective dismay, his name was linked to theirs, and unimagined hatreds from the outer world came their way.

As Chautemps spoke, awnings burned and flower stands went over. Gratings, trees, benches, urinals, lampposts, and street signs lay strewn across Boulevard Saint-Germain, Rue du Bac, and Rue Royale across the bridge, like wreckage from a hurricane. Man-made barricades, they dammed the traffic and disrupted the cordons of police and Republican guards protecting the approaches to the Palais Bourbon and the deputies within. "Down with the Stavisky government!" "Down with the sellouts!" Four thousand of them ran through the streets and mobbed the entrances to metros and cafés. Violent clashes and mounted charges left hundreds injured, and, in the police buses that took them away defiant, insurgents continued to chant and jeer. Public order had broken down.[47]

Even before they began hearing of Stavisky, the people of Paris had taken to greeting their elected representatives with seditious glee. In December, while twenty-eight cinemas were showing Pagnol's *Fanny*, and while *Deux sous de fleurs* was playing at the Empire, the Comédie Française put on Shakespeare's *Coriolanus*. Audiences applauded the royal tirade against the plebes, universal suffrage, and the tribunes who issued from it. "The devil!" wrote one of the critics. "We lend an ear, hearing already the drums of Brumaire."[48]

Coriolanus was still playing as Chautemps stood at the tribune of the Chamber and rioters savaged the city. At the Théâtre Albert-Premier, *Olive Labasse* ridiculed deputies and the political class in general, taking up where *Topaze* had left off six years before. As yet, only the fervent yet disciplined extremists of Action Française and the Jeunesses Patriotes had carried the challenge from the stage to the streets. But passersby joined in, and from various parts of the country came disquieting reports of agitation in parks and cafés, especially where Stavisky was rumored to have passed through—in Perpignan, where the Compagnie Foncière once owned a meager lot, deputies, lawyers, and a justice system said to be shot through with political influence provoked open scorn. In Bayonne, Stavisky became synonymous with Paris. Local pride required it. Even Garat's enemies rallied to the defense of their mayor, and attributed to the corruption seeping from the capital the misfortunes of their picturesque town. In nearby Pau, taxpayers seized the occasion to threaten open revolt. Talk of a crisis of the regime became a self-fulfilling prophecy.[49]

Easily confused with antirepublicanism, such antiparliamentary sentiment was as old as the regime itself. But it had never driven a government from office. Parliament itself had sufficed for that. In 1871 Thiers had repressed the Communards; between 1887 and 1889 Rouvier, Tirard, and Floquet had resisted the Boulangists in the streets, but not their own foes in the Chamber; likewise, several years later, the governments of Loubet and Ribet had survived the Panama demonstrators but not the Parliamentary Commission of Inquiry. Not once had riot or sedition brought down a ministry, not even during the Dreyfus affair, when passions turned violent but Brisson and Dupuy fell according to the rules of the game. Now the streets were stirring again, all around the Chamber, and this time the government appeared exposed and shaken.[50]

Once in a while discreet incursions, from bishops and bankers among others, had diverted the course of politics. Monseigneur Dupanloup had his say in the governmental crisis of May 1877, the regent of the Banque de France his in that of July 1926. But they had acted for the most part behind the curtain, respectful of appearances. Now too, extraparliamentary interests were stirring, only no longer so discreetly. Pushed by economic crisis and deflation, civil servants, taxpayers, shopkeepers, and veterans hectored the deputies and by extension the cabinet, and unwittingly carried ministerial responsibility beyond the confines of the Palais Bourbon. Sometimes they intervened in the legisla-

« Fermeté et justice » (C. Chautemps)

L'ENQUÊTE...

(Dessin d'Herms)

Politics: For the antisemitic, anti-Masonic, and antiparliamentary *Je Suis Partout* (20 January 1934), Camille Chautemps ("firmness and justice") is a hypocrite, the investigation a shame, and Marianne—the Republic—a murderess and a whore.

tive process; and now, they sometimes joined with the demonstrators in the streets.[51]

Many came from the right, from the leagues and their supporters. But the most splenetic victims of the depression included many in the lower middle classes, the small farmers, shopkeepers, and entrepreneurs who made up an essential Radical clientele. They were growing louder, and mixed anger at the party with scorn for the parliamentary accommodations it had come to incarnate.

The press emboldened them. A weapon as well as an entertainment, the Stavisky story ministered to the varied needs of fiercely competitive newspapers. Along with colorful speculation about his friends in the Chamber, lackeys in the public prosecutor's office, and murder in Le Vieux Logis came somber reflections about institutional failure and even the end of the regime. In time, these eclipsed the story itself.

On the right, all bemoaned decay and decline. Otherwise they did not shine for their choral harmonies or concordances. *Le Figaro* spoke inconsistently of maladies, moral one day, physical the next. Where are the honest men, the moralist asked; septicemia of the regime, the pathologist decreed. *L'Intransigeant* depicted amorality descending from the summit, *Le Quotidien,* scandal rising like a tide; *Le Temps* and *Le Matin* denounced *l'Etatisme corrupteur,*

Spectacle: A curious public reads that "they are covering up the Stavisky affair." (Photo courtesy of Bibliothèque National de France.)

L'Ordre, liberalism and its incoherencies, *L'Action Française* alone, democracy itself. Most wished to save an ideal Republic from the "the traffickers' Republic," as *Le Matin* put it, and, warning of imminent doom, clamored for drastic yet obscure measures of national renewal.[52]

On the left, *L'Humanité*, as apocalyptic as *L'Action Française*, pilloried the country's leaders indiscriminately. All were Stavisky's accomplices, the Communist daily revealed, sounding more and more like its royalist counterpart. Quite naturally, they had murdered him. When *L'Humanité* was not attacking the government, it was attacking the Socialists, who in *Le Populaire* were themselves busily proclaiming the guilt of the regime—not of the Republic, but of capitalism. The left blamed social, and the right political, institutions, but together they confirmed old illusions of deception in high places and contrived in that way to deepen the crisis of confidence. The swindler's act, the country's partisan press suggested, had been a mere curtain-raiser, prologue to a masquerade of false appearances across the public stage. *Le Figaro* summed it up as "parliamentary facade," *L'Humanité* as "turpitudes of the ruling class." Stavisky, in death, had set off a generalized search for subterfuge.[53]

In the Radical press of the center left, the government's friends raised weak voices of moderation. Do not mix justice with politics, they said; think of the regime and the nation. Stavisky had evaded prosecution, *L'Oeuvre* insisted, under governments of the right and left alike. *L'Ere Nouvelle* worried about French prestige. Enough suspicion and psychosis, declared *Notre Temps:* "The insurance companies have been robbed. But the towers of Notre Dame are still there."[54]

The journalists and editors were themselves too much part of the ailment to diagnose it accurately. The same who took exorbitant fees in 1929 to advertise the Foncière's issues in their newspapers now cried with no saving hint of irony: "Down with the robbers!" They belonged to liberal society, the competitive order of which Parliament was only the most potent symbol. Success in this contentious community was individual, often at another's expense, and Stavisky was no stranger to its ways. He had reserved his greatest assiduities for visible deputies and invisible officials. But he had also accosted their fellows in the liberal professions of private society, and there he had easily found members — lawyers, journalists, accountants, notaries, doctors — whose sense of the public interest was hardly stronger than his own. Upon this the journalists did not dwell. From the liberal professions, especially from the lawyers, came most of the Republic's elected officials, often men of words rather than action, and of ambitions rather than ideals. Their professional class as a whole had suffered the least from the economic crisis, a circumstance unlikely to enhance their general popularity in these times of scarcity. On this the journalists did not dwell either. They burned with curiosity about Stavisky's conquests in the political order but not in their own. That the two were of a piece did not concern them. They wrote of government alone, and conveyed to their readers a troubling sense that the values of the Republic had served only to disguise the interests of its servants. In their anxious, self-righteous columns, another old phantasm now surfaced, that of forfeiture by the nation's governing class, the same tenacious suspicion that had stalked monarchies in 1830, 1848, and 1870, and that now floated around the Republic's own crown, its Parliament.

The vicinity of the Chamber was quiet when debate resumed the next morning. The demonstrators had left trees, benches, lampposts, and multicolored debris behind, and their flares had melted the tar in the streets; but they themselves had gone. The deputies orated. Public rancor had stirred, said Marcel Déat at the tribune. But the violence of the previous day, he added, had not measured up to any great *journée parisienne,* any descent of workers from their own districts to the city center. "It will come!" came shouts from the Chamber. "It will come!"[55]

For the government's opponents in the Chamber, yesterday's riot was today's opportunity. They saw the climate of civil war as their chance to bring down the government, and slid easily from patriotic indignation into the black arts of slander. No desertion or dereliction seemed too vile for their imaginations, no complicity too improbable. Ybarnegaray, a fellow Gascon and rival of the unfortunate Garat, climbed to the tribune to revile the government as the assassin of Stavisky and of justice itself. Franklin-Bouillon, renegade Radical, rival of the late Briand, preoccupied solely with French weakness and the eternal German question, condemned an administration abandoned en bloc to a professional blackmailer named Albert Dubarry. André Tardieu, rival and equal of Camille Chautemps, warned him that the government's shaky majority could never assure the course of justice in the land. In so doing, Tardieu dropped any pretense of trust in the separation of powers; and he then demanded, in a fine strategic move, the appointment of a parliamentary commission of inquiry.[56]

"A bit of light and truth," Chautemps had promised the day before, and, as he spoke, inspectors general were knocking on doors in ministries on both sides of the Seine. But a commission of inquiry? Made up of deputies from every side of the Chamber? It would perpetuate the scandal as surely as the commissions of the past had breathed life into the fallen figures of Rochette or Oustric. Chautemps opposed it. A little more than three years before, however, he himself had called for the Oustric commission, much to the annoyance of the prime minister then in office—André Tardieu. This was different, Chautemps insisted: then the minister of justice, Raoul Péret, had lied to the Chamber about his dealings with Oustric. But today the public indignation is incomparably deeper, rejoined Louis Marin from the benches of the right-wing Union Républicaine Démocratique. Chautemps had blundered. A suggestion of hypocrisy now followed him like a shadow. "Oustricards against Stavicrates," scoffed *L'Humanité*. Toward midnight, his smooth and accomplished image already tarnished, Chautemps put the matter to a vote. The Chamber rejected the commission of inquiry. Chautemps's majority had held; he had survived. But not for long.

Outside, the streets were quiet. It was raining, and the demonstrators had stayed away. But not for long.[57]

"Justice has been set in motion," Philippe Henriot was proclaiming at the tribune. They were supposed to be debating the budget. "Justice has in fact been so set in motion that she is going in circles." Who better than he, mesmerizing orator of the right, to bring down the government? Tardieu, champion of insincerity, had too much of the world-wise traveler about him. Why was Bonnaure still free, Henriot asked. Why, when Stavisky had been arrested in 1926, had Paul-Boncour gone to Arlette's side? What had another minister, Anatole de Monzie, done for the swindler? Why had Superintendent Simon not acted on the revelations of the informer Comby in 1933?

Above the din Henriot went on, diffusing his secrets into the shouts and tumult of the Chamber. What had Stavisky been doing in Stresa with Georges Bonnet, and what had Guiboud-Ribaud been doing in his ministry? With innuendo, exaggeration, and intimations of more to come, he damned an entire administration and provoked cries of outrage. From his perch, Fernand Bouisson furiously sounded the presidential bell and rapped violently, uselessly, with his letter opener on the brass fittings of the desk.[58]

There could be no doubt: well-wishers in the police or the prosecutor's office or some strategic ministry had been nourishing the Bordeaux deputy's predilection for ghosts in the attic. They had fed him their secrets. Arriving late in the Chamber, Chautemps himself said as much. How unwittingly Henriot himself betrayed a weakened, balkanized administration, and how generously the unfolding scandal once again demonstrated the very abuses it condemned—he ranted on.[59]

The demonstrators were out again, as many as during the first debate a week earlier, marshaled as before by Action Française. Every day now Boulevard Saint-Germain, the stock exchange, and the *grands boulevards* resounded with cries of "Down with Chautemps! Down with the robbers!" The climate was execrable. One night, while the police and the Republican guard were expelling the royalist Camelots du Roi and their friends from one street around the Chamber, only to see them emerge in another, and while the trams stood immobile along rails short-circuited by firecrackers, new faces besieged the town hall across the river. Municipal employees, many from the socialist CGT, were protesting salary cuts. On a construction site nearby on Place du Châtelet, the Communists held an impromptu rally and harangued the crowd. Cries rang out. "Our wages! Our wages!" "Down with the robbers! Down with Chautemps!"[60]

It did not greatly matter what "the robbers" had stolen or what "the sellouts" had sold, or how exactly Chautemps had profited from Stavisky, or how municipal workers stood to gain in salary from what the government might lose in moral capital. An obsession with chicanery had invaded the city. With studied dismay, the press reported the degradation of public mores. "I know that, today, to please the public you have to bring dishonor upon a man a day," sighed Emile Buré in *L'Ordre*. He called for a strongman to save the regime from itself. In *L'Oeuvre*, Marcel Déat called for "a complete examination of contemporary political mores." And *Paris-Soir* gravely recalled Panama. " 'Names! Names!' " it quoted. "This doesn't make us any younger. Political history has its recurrences."[61]

Even as it played public censor, the press resisted any policing of its own morals. Chautemps, making good on promises of reform, had proposed that libel and defamation in the press, about which he could now speak with some assurance, be sanctioned in the correctional rather than the criminal courts. The absence of a jury would facilitate convictions. Intolerable, replied the press. "The jury! The jury! The jury!" cried *Le Figaro*. So did *Le Temps*, less hysterically: trial by jury in such matters was, it announced, the very touchstone of a liberal democracy. So indignant was the fourth estate that it largely ignored the government's companion project, a new law on the corruption of public officials. Reforms could wait. The urgent business at hand, for many of the nation's editors, was to rid France of its government. Insurrection, *Le Figaro* reminded its readers, was a republican duty.[62]

With the clarion calls of sedition sounding in his ears, Henriot returned to the charge. On 23 January he again attacked the Palace of Justice—"den of deals and tricks"—this time in the person of the minister himself. Until now the scandal had left Eugène Raynaldy untouched, but Henriot chose the moment, as the waters rose rapidly around the government, to unveil an obscure episode from the minister's past. Once, when neither a deputy nor a senator, but nonetheless a former minister, Raynaldy had sat on the board of a doubtful holding company set up by another fallen financier by the name of Sacazan. Although no Stavisky, Sacazan had thought like so many others to succeed by dint of his connections rather than his gifts. Raynaldy had accepted 250 shares from him, and, once a minister again, had held on to some of them. Henriot's knowledge seemed encyclopedic. Some suspected Chiappe, whose sympathies for the right were as extensive as the secrets at his command in the prefecture of police, of educating the fiery deputy. An investigating magistrate called on the ministry on Place Vendôme. Raynaldy was hardly at fault. But on the 27th he resigned anyway.

It was a Saturday morning. The Chamber was usually quiet that day of the week. But today the Salle des Quatre Colonnes was pullulating with deputies. Among themselves they exchanged endless rumors of crisis. A prefect arrived at the Ministry of the Interior, walked past the journalists in the courtyard, and asked to see Chautemps. "Today, impossible," replied the doorman. "May I return Monday?" "Pointless, by then." Georges Bonnet, minister of finance, came and left, looking pale. Paul-Boncour, the foreign minister, followed and chatted awhile with the reporters. "It's not as nice as Quai d'Orsay," he told them. "There I put in a museum and central heating." Later, Chautemps left the ministry and went to hand in his resignation to President Lebrun at the Elysée. The situation was hopeless. All the parliamentary majorities in the world could not govern the situation. But he had made progress. His first ministry, in 1930, had lasted five days, this one sixty-two.

At the Palace of Justice all was silent. "Nothing to report," the employees there told a reporter from *Paris-Soir,* who did not believe them.[63]

The Riot

"What are your Christian names?" It was the director general of the Ministry of Fine Arts, and he was asking his old friend Georges Thomé, director of the Sûreté Générale, for the most baffling particulars. "What are your university degrees?" he went on.

"What's this all about?" Thomé asked. "What are you getting at?"

"You've not heard?"

"Heard what?"[64]

That Saturday morning, 3 February, the new government had tried to put the scandal behind it and succeed where Chautemps had failed. "Fast and firm, such is our will," Daladier had said. President Lebrun had turned to Jules Jeanneney in the Senate, Fernand Bouisson in the Chamber, and old Gaston Doumergue in his retreat near Toulouse in Tournefeuille. Each had declined to form a government. Three days went by. On the *grands boulevards* a bus burned, and chairs, bottles, and saucers flew from café tables. Finally Daladier agreed, and cobbled together yet another cabinet out of yet more familiar faces from the center and center left. "We wish to restore confidence, order in people's minds," he announced, and in so saying, met with his new minister of the interior, decided to move some top officials around, and ignited, even with his light touch, the Parisian powder keg.[65]

"We talked of you, this morning, at the cabinet meeting," the director general told Thomé.

"Of me?"

"Yes, you're leaving the Sûreté Générale. You're going to the Comédie Française."[66]

Like the other personnel moves thought up by the new government, Thomé's transfer to the great state theater was more political than punitive. It might impress the doubters. So might exiling Chiappe, the capital's other chief police officer. Daladier had read the reports by the inspectors general: they had spared the two directors, especially Chiappe, but not the two police organizations, and how better to demonstrate a will to renewal than to turn out the old guard? Besides, many on the left wanted Chiappe's head, and the socialists were withholding their support from the new government. Therefore, Chiappe would go to Morocco, and, in the general rotation, Thomé, as its new director, would go to the Comédie Française.[67]

But neither accepted.

"There would be hilarity all over Paris the next day," Thomé told the new minister of the interior over the phone that evening. He would not go. "No one would understand how I could leave the house on Rue des Saussaies for the house of Molière." He stayed.

Chiappe refused as well, over the phone to Daladier himself. Daladier heard him say, "I'll take to the streets"; Chiappe heard himself say: "I'll be on the street." Confrontation followed. Meant to appease the left, Daladier's maneuver only enraged the right. But he could not back down now. Chiappe left, and quickly became a symbol.[68]

Two ministers from the center hastily resigned. The press on the right denounced a coup on the left. Two thousand Action Française sympathizers took to the *grands boulevards,* four thousand Croix de Feu veterans to the Champs-Elysées: the veterans, embittered by the lost victory of the Great War, had joined the fray. Spectators at the Comédie Française interrupted *Coriolanus* and improvised speeches from balconies, loges, and the forestage. Afterward, outside on the Place, they clamored their support for the theater's displaced director, Emile Fabre, a sudden martyr of the scandal. Militants around the city pasted up new multicolored posters on walls and sidings every half-hour: "The Country in Danger," "Enough Scandal," "Appeal to the People of Paris." Veterans and activists called new demonstrations for the afternoon and evening of the 6th, when Daladier would ask the Chamber for its vote of confidence. The ministers appealed for calm and warned against professional agitators.[69]

218

The people of Paris had been invading representative assemblies since October 1789. The tradition, by now, had a pedigree. But never in the history of this Republic had the Chamber become the target of such concentrated fury as on the afternoon of 6 February 1934. As the deputies assembled, so did the massed demonstrators—"What will happen tonight?" asked *Paris-Soir*. It might more serenely have wondered why the approaches to the Palace of Justice were so quiet. The demonstrators were ignoring it, withholding even the honor of their insults. A scandal set off by a failure of justice had culminated in an assault on the legislature. Threatening to monarchs, alarming to republicans, a fully independent judiciary had never, save for a moment during the Revolution, seen the light of day in France. It had remained an auxiliary, its marginal status as evident to Stavisky as to the malcontents who now bypassed it and marched on the true guarantor of their open society, the Parliament.[70]

"Long live Chiappe!"

"Murderers!"

Walking in a daze past enraged and bloodied rioters on the Champs-Elysées, Stavisky's old friend Joseph Kessel made his way toward the pitched battle on the Concorde.

"They opened fire!" Each had his atrocity to proclaim, his example of police brutality to condemn.

"I saw three go down."

"It's a massacre."

Buses and newsstands were flaming in the evening's glacial fog, and on Rue Royale a café had become a field hospital. A scent of burning floated through the streets.

Inside the Chamber Daladier sat calmly but melancholically on the bench, with his arms folded before him.

"Resignation! Resignation!" he heard from the right of the Chamber.

"The Soviets! The Soviets!" came from the far left.

"Leave!" Franklin-Bouillon shouted at him from the tribune. Pandemonium had already broken out when Scapini, the blinded veteran with the patch over his eye, announced from his seat that the Republican guards on the Concorde had been ordered to fire on the demonstrators. During an intermission, the deputies peered out toward the Concorde from behind the gates of the Palais Bourbon. The noise from the street overcame the tumult in the Chamber; the session ended and the lights went out; the deputies stole away. Many had bravely voted their confidence in the new government. But some avoided the conspicuous metro station by the Chamber and made instead for the Solférino station, where, with an injured demonstrator, a scarred war veteran, they boarded the metro for home and safety.

On the Champs-Elysées Joseph Kessel reached the Claridge hotel. The French windows were shattered, and, in the foyer, glass from the display cases

Politics: A bus burns on the Place de la Concorde during the riots of 6 February 1934. (Photo courtesy of Bibliothèque Nationale de France.)

lay on the floor. Guests and employees wandered through the wreckage, speaking in low voices. Suddenly a vision of Serge Alexandre appeared on the scene to Kessel. He looked impeccable as always, and seemed to the novelist intent on keeping the rendezvous they had made there just before Christmas.

"See you soon," Kessel's Alexandre said, as he vanished again.[71]

ELEVEN

SACRIFICIAL MAGISTRACY

Since February excitement in France has been intense. On all sides they're agitating, assembling, preparing for an awful civil war.—Roger Martin du Gard to his daughter, Christiane, in French West Africa, Nice, 6 April 1934

Time goes by . . . this confusing, troubling news; these newspapers, which I can't avoid perusing, and which are vile, untrustworthy. They can't not sully my mind, extinguish all joy, and make me fear for the future. A real rot . . .—Eugène Dabit, journal entry for 9 March 1934

"Mutilated corpse," the general secretary of the Paris prosecutor's office repeated into the phone. He was taking notes in his office in the Palace of Justice. Other magistrates and two superintendents from the Sûreté Générale came in and out. In his office nearby, the public prosecutor, Georges Pressard, appeared agitated.[1]

In itself this was not surprising. In the fifteen days that had elapsed since a riot on 6 February had driven Daladier from power, the press had not for a moment lifted its siege of the Palace of Justice and the men of law within.

In the beginning, a cartoon in *Le Canard Enchaîné* showed two policemen taking a jewel thief away. "You can release me at once," he tells them. "I'm retaining as a lawyer the minister of justice." The distant services to Stavisky of René Renoult, former minister, had leaked out.[2]

Every day some new face of renown flickered across the scandal's screen, and many belonged to men of the robe or their auxiliaries—to lawyers, magistrates, or police. Among them flitted the profile of a minister called René Renoult, a senator called Odin, who had given legal counsel about the Hungarian bond venture, and deputies called Garat, Bonnaure, Proust, and André Hesse, who had helped in their distinctive ways with the Foncière, Bayonne, or the Hungarian bonds. Images recurred of strangely passive magistrates such as Pressard and Prince, and jaded policemen such as Bayard and Bonny, travesties of their calling, an unfolding caricature of the Republic's justice.

For the right especially, the palace and its dependencies made a perfect target. To savage the only ministry bearing the name of a virtue in a Republic so devoted to its cause, to uphold an elevated, purist conception of the state while suggesting that their foes knew no interest higher than that of self, to attack, in the men of the bar, the Radical Party, which counted so many of them—here was an opportunity no conservative could miss. Socially strong yet politically weak, they chafed at their recurring exclusion from the governments that resulted from universal suffrage. Justice was a scapegoat, a surrogate for their re-

sentments. But on the newly galvanized left few leaped to its defense. Some
even renewed the attack. Justice was an instrument of the rich, an oppressor of
the poor, and memory and tradition alone kept them from its side.

One denounced anarchy, the other inequality, and the hostility between the
holders of social and political power, between plutocracy and democracy, shed
its disguise. Justice was politicized, justice was weak; justice was the servant
rather than the master of liberal society. Once again, the highly symbolic figure of justice, one of the oldest expressions of public power in the land, had set
off warring conceptions of the collective ideal, at one only in their deep suspicion of the diversity of interests that the liberal order seemed to uphold. Few
pointed out the inconsistency in subjecting justice to a representative assembly and then requiring it exercise sovereign detachment. But who, in the current climate, could fret over such pedantries?

Georges Pressard, the public prosecutor held responsible for Stavisky's impunity, was awaiting a timely transfer to the court of appeal. Daladier had decided on it in the ill-fated personnel shuffles at the beginning of the month. As
the brother-in-law of Camille Chautemps, Pressard had become a useful symbol of an imagined Radical stranglehold on the palace. He had more reason
than most to tire of the attacks, to resent the status of scapegoat. But this
Wednesday morning he was unnerved by the news of a corpse announced by
the adjoining office of the general secretary. "It's dreadful," he said, and, to his
designated successor as prosecutor, he added: "Take care of this matter at
once," since the body in question, found mangled by a train on the tracks near
Dijon, was that of his old colleague, the former head of the financial section of
his public prosecutor's office, and currently a judge on the court of appeal: Albert Prince.[3]

Albert Prince, during those past two weeks, had not been idle. Shaken by his
former superior's attempt to blame him for Stavisky's escape from the law, he
had endeavored to demonstrate a broader base of responsibility for the judicial indulgence that had shone on the swindler.

"I'm going to free my conscience," Prince had said dramatically on the 15th to
Lescouvé, who as presiding judge of the Cour de Cassation had taken over the
investigation of all that had gone wrong in the judicial branch. Prince insisted
that he had shown Pressard the Police Judiciaire reports about Stavisky. He
seemed so shaken that Lescouvé suggested that he withdraw, calm down, and
write a report instead.[4]

To his friends and family, Albert Prince the bon vivant still thrived, gregari-
ous and welcoming, happy at the prospect of his son Raymond's forthcoming
marriage. "Isn't it fun to think that soon we may be grandfathers and grand-
mothers," he said to a friend at a reception only two days after his agitated call
about Lescouvé. They made plans to see *L'Homme invisible* at the Cinéma
Bonaparte the following week. On Monday the 19th, he took Raymond and his

fiancée to the Brasserie Lipp for lunch and then to a session of the criminal court. And he made plans with his wife to buy a small farm in the country, a refuge in the storm.[5]

But to most of his professional colleagues, Prince in those days seemed a magistrate unhinged, determined to save a professional honor that scandal now held up for the world to mock. "I won't give up, I'll go all the way, and we haven't seen the end of this," he told friends. "My job is becoming unbearable," he added to them a few days later. The Stavisky affair obsessed him.

"It's as serious as the queen's necklace affair," he told Paul Caujolle, the accountant investigating Bayonne for the courts. He had done his duty, he said. The two were sitting in the Café de Flore. "Everything that should have been done was," he said of his actions in 1931. He also retaliated. To Caujolle, and to his fellow magistrates as well, Prince spoke of his accuser Pressard's own culpable lapses. He spoke of how, before the High Court in 1931, Pressard denied knowing what Prince himself had told him, that the fallen minister of justice Raoul Péret had once counseled the fallen banker Albert Oustric. Strategic amnesia, Prince implied, and, to damn him once more, he spoke finally of convincing evidence, of two letters from Pressard furnishing irrefutable proof that three and even four years earlier he had known all that Prince had known about that dangerous and infamous swindler, Sacha Stavisky.[6]

"They must neither stray nor be taken from me," he told Caujolle, and he asked the accountant to have the letters photographed at the prefecture—oddly, for why could Prince himself not take or send them there? Magistrates from the palace always did so. But Caujolle agreed, and Prince promised to bring them to the Café de Flore on the evening of the 20th.[7]

He also promised to bring his report for Lescouvé to the palace on the 21st.

Caujolle waited at the Flore until eight and finally left. Prince never came. Lescouvé never received the report.[8]

Prince had left earlier than usual that morning for the palace. Shortly before eleven, the phone rang and Mme Prince answered. It was a Dr. Hallinger, calling from Dijon: Prince's mother there, he announced, had fallen ill, and her son must come at once. Under no circumstances was she to accompany him. Minutes later Prince himself appeared at the door. He had forgotten his wallet. Hearing the news from Dijon he packed a bag, overcame her insistence that she come along, and left by metro for the Gare de Lyon. He phoned his wife before boarding the train, to wish that, in the end, she had come along, and from the station in Dijon late that afternoon he cabled her: "Arrived all right. Going to the clinic. Consultation six o'clock. Dr. Hallinger declares condition as normal as possible. Albert."

Toward nine o'clock in the Perrigny depot, near Dijon, the horrified engineer of delivery train 4805 noticed blood and possibly brains on the front of his locomotive. Later, two station employees came upon a man's decapitated and mangled remains strewn along the rails near La Combe aux Fées, two kilometers away. A tattered stretch of rope circled one of the ankles. Beside the rails lay a bit more rope, an open yellow briefcase, a bloodstained knife resting on 397 francs in cash, and a visiting card in the name of Albert Prince, judge at the Paris court of appeal.[9]

The Affair Revived

At close to eight o'clock the next morning, before any magistrate or investigator, a journalist arrived on the scene. He was from the Dijon newspaper *Le Bien Public*. A source at the Paris-Lyon-Méditerranée rail company had just told him of the body found crushed by a train. The gendarmerie had added helpfully that it appeared to be that of Albert Prince of the Court of Appeal of Paris. Two gendarmes had stayed the night at the spot, but only now, as day was breaking, had they informed the Dijon public prosecutor's office of the discovery. By the time the magistrates arrived, the reporter had come and gone. Soon he returned with a photographer. In the afternoon, more reporters turned up, from the major Paris dailies and the smaller, angrier partisan press, and mingled freely with the investigators, inspectors, and gendarmes by then milling around the railroad tracks at La Combe-aux-Fées.[10]

Just six weeks after Stavisky's death in Chamonix, a renewed contagion of conjecture swept the press. "Mysteriously murdered," *Le Figaro* announced on the right. "Mysterious murder," *Le Populaire* echoed on the left. "Murdered in a police ambush," *L'Humanité* more confidently informed its readers. "M. Albert Prince, drawn into an ambush, was killed, and his body was then carried onto the railroad tracks," concluded *Le Petit Parisien*. Why? To eliminate a witness, perhaps; to seize the judge's diary, rich with six years of secrets about the Stavisky affair; a crime of vengeance or greed or fear, no one could quite say. But in a rare meeting of minds, all agreed that the late judge had met with a violent death, undeniably the victim of murder most foul.[11]

All agreed, that is, save one or two thoughtful members of the profession, who timidly expressed their doubts and confusion. "Murder," they said in the newsroom of *L'Ordre* when the word arrived. But one of the editors held back. If Prince had been such a threat, he wondered, why wait until now to eliminate him? And why, if ambushed, had he sent his wife the telegram from Dijon? At *Le Matin* a columnist noted "oddities that baffle." Nothing made sense, he complained. If the murderers had gone to such elaborate lengths, why had they done nothing to disguise the identity of their victim?[12]

◼

But the murderers were nowhere to be found.

Their traces, almost too brazen to be true, led nowhere. Albert Prince's mother had not fallen ill and no doctor had phoned her son's home. Someone in Paris had made the call. Prince had indeed sent the telegram from the Dijon station, but had not been seen after he left his suitcase at a nearby hotel minutes later. Someone had bought the knife in the Bazar de l'Hôtel de Ville, the department store next to city hall, several days earlier, but the salesman could remember nothing more. In any case, the body showed no signs of stab wounds. The autopsy revealed no traces of an anesthetizing drug or of prior violence. There was the stretch of rope—but how could you tie anything or anyone to an embedded, unbroken rail line? As *Le Matin* said, it all made no sense.[13]

The magistrates of the Dijon public prosecutor's office had neither called in experts to examine the human traces on the locomotive, nor taken fingerprints from the knife before removing it, nor examined his personal belongings before returning them to his wife. They had botched the case, thought two superintendents from the Sûreté Générale when they arrived from Paris. The Dijonnais magistrates resented the Parisians' presence and told them so. The investigation had begun badly.[14]

Honoring tradition, the newspapers hired their own investigators. For many years they had played Sherlock Holmes to the police's Watson. As faits divers in their columns began to command a mass following, their reporters hastened to the scenes of crimes of promise, arriving sometimes before the officers of the law. And the law of 1881 allowed them what that of 1897 forbade the magistrates, the right to interrogate a suspect without a lawyer at his side. In 1908 a reporter from *Le Matin* and another from *L'Echo de Paris* extracted a pseudo-confession from Meg Steinheil, the former mistress of President Felix Faure, then suspected of murdering her mother and husband. The next day the police arrested her; each newspaper claimed credit. In 1927 *Le Journal* announced the imminent arrest of the banker Rochette, and the coming of a second Rochette scandal, the very day it occurred. The Police Judiciaire was bathed in camera flashes even before Rochette was inside. Now, in 1934, *Le Matin* hired the former brigadier Riboulet, famed for helping catch the Bluebeard Landru, and *Paris-Soir* hired the equally celebrated Georges Simenon as well as three retired inspectors from Scotland Yard, all to succeed where the police and the public prosecutor's office had failed, and to solve the mystery of the death of Albert Prince.[15]

Meanwhile, headlines and editorials sounded the national alarm more urgently than ever. Often they spoke confidently in the name of a public that they alone represented. "Public opinion is calling for light," announced *Le Petit Parisien*. "Public opinion expects it. Public opinion is ready to demand it." Opinion was what the papers chose to make of it. But nearly everyone spoke of crisis. The Prince affair, for *Les Débats*, was the nadir, the final demonstration of moral and administrative laxity tantamount to criminal complicity. Vague and drastic proposals for remedies concluded the jeremiads, especially in the papers of the right. The public, declared *Le Figaro*, was "resolved . . . to impose the renaissance of France." And for Gustave Hervé at *La Victoire*, salvation was at hand: "If you're incapable of managing your household and keeping it clean, get a man, Marianne, get a man!" Prince's demise took the place of Stavisky's, and the affair started up anew.[16]

CHAPTER 11

The affair, for the investigating magistrates d'Uhalt in Bayonne and Ordonneau in Paris, meant twelve or fifteen hours of toil a day, watched by the ministry, the Chamber, and the press.[17]

What was the link between Orléans and Bayonne? To whom were the bonds given? By whom? How were they placed? What had Stavisky done with the proceeds? And who among the recipients knew of their tainted source? From its Bayonnais beginnings the inquiry expanded luxuriantly, each invaded walkway opening onto another.

In Bayonne, the lights burned in the crédit municipal as gendarmes stood guard over its unplumbed mine of documentation. At the Palace of Justice, d'Uhalt called in prisoners from the Villa Chagrin, released some, returned others. In Paris his counterpart Ordonneau skipped meals. His health began to suffer. Two other magistrates arrived to help; secretaries requisitioned from other ministries typed furiously; accountants sifted, book by book and bond by bond, through the archival traces of Stavisky's ephemeral empire. Arrests, in both the national and the Basque capital, continued to punctuate the winter and early spring.[18]

Guébin, the insurance director from La Confiance who had done so much to place and push the Bayonne bonds, was philosophical. He sat early one chilly morning in a deserted café in Bayonne, shrouded in the shifting grays of his topcoat, muffler, and felt hat. Beside him one police inspector drank a small rum, the other a black coffee. "Please follow us," they had said at the door of his handsome apartment in Paris the night before, as he was sitting down to dinner. Now they respected his silent reverie. Before lunch, while his two lawyers remonstrated in the Palace of Justice with d'Uhalt, Guébin stood on the jetty in Biarritz and watched the waves break on the Rock of the Virgin. D'Uhalt indicted him that day for using forged public documents and for complicity in swindle, and two weeks later imprisoned him as well. A small crowd watched a policeman gently push Guébin's portly figure through the gates of the Villa Chagrin, and a hateful voice called out after him.[19]

Gaston Bonnaure, yesterday gratified by the votes of the citizens and by the fees of Sacha Stavisky, was today comical, touchingly so. Already indicted, now no longer free, the little deputy, obscured by policemen and suitcases, arrived outside the Villa Chagrin in an old taxi adorned with archaic luggage racks. The crowd began to laugh, and Bonnaure posed with an easy smile for the photographers, full face, profile, or three-quarters profile, as they wished. Then he too disappeared into the shadows of the prison.[20]

In the end, Arlette restrained her indignation. Veiled, still in mourning, she left the apartment on Rue Obligado between two police inspectors sent to fetch her. "After my husband, they want to drive me to despair," she said, and entered the palace pursued by photographers. Ordonneau could not believe that she had known nothing of her husband's operations. He indicted her for receiving stolen

226

Pursuit: Arlette arrested, 2 March 1934. (Photo courtesy of AP/Wide World Photos.)

goods and, lest she flee the country, sent her to the women's prison of La Petite Roquette. She soon regained her composure, and called her children's governess with instructions. She did not expect to stay in prison for long.[21]

Arlette was mistaken; her detention was constructive as well as preventive, encouraging cooperation even as it precluded flight. Her captors would hold her in La Petite Roquette as long as they thought it useful, as long as she had intelligence to share. La Santé too was a powerful weapon in the hands of Ordonneau and his two colleagues, and in March they began to people its cells with shabby sycophants from Stavisky's entourage, mediocrities damned for their complicity but blessed for their knowledge. Inspectors in trench coats appeared unannounced in seedy hotels to extract Romagnino the trusted aide and Niemen the

Polish boxer; at apartment doors for Depardon the lowly front man of the Foncière and Guiboud-Ribaud the smooth-talking lawyer; outside the crédit municipal in Orléans for Farault the appraiser. And gradually the prosecution's case began to take shape. As if by magic, Stavisky's check stubs also reappeared.[22]

They appeared at suspended inspector Bonny's door one night, in the hands of the inebriated gangster called Georges Hainnaux, also known as "Jo-la-Terreur," a deserter from the foreign legion, thief, would-be murderer, and amnestied prisoner, who now spent his time in bars and dance rooms in and out of Paris, and who lived these days in a hotel with Romagnino in Montmartre. Bonny had been expecting him. That afternoon the gangster had called. Would you like Stavisky's check stubs? he had asked.

Alert to the value of the fabled missing stubs, Bonny had never stopped searching for them, even after his suspension in the middle of January. He still frequented his old informers, and finally, the best among them delivered the prize that might restore to citizen Bonny the standing and title of inspector. Romagnino had already given generously of his time and his knowledge; now, facing arrest and imprisonment, he had given of his possessions as well. He had left in the hotel room most of the stubs, wrapped in paper and tied with string, had given his lawyer a few others sealed in a yellow envelope, and had told Hainnaux to take both packets to their mutual acquaintance, Inspector Pierre Bonny.

Late into the night Bonny, the investigating magistrate Ordonneau, and another police commissioner pored over the stubs. The drunken Hainnaux had arrived late and tried to toss them into the fire. The public prosecutor, Pressard's successor, had come and gone. Ordonneau had not eaten all day. Toward three in the morning Bonny opened a bottle of champagne; it was all he had to offer, and Ordonneau drank the sole selection, but, for the disgraced inspector, the libation marked rehabilitation. For good or for ill, Bonny was back.[23]

After the check stubs came the missing jewels, the few genuine ones from Bayonne that Stavisky, desperate for cash, had taken and engaged in the autumn. Slowly the traces of his passage through society were telling their tale. The jewels had stayed where Romagnino had taken them, at T. H. Sutton's in London, where late in March Inspector Peudepièce of the Sûreté and a counterpart of his from Scotland Yard duly arrived to retrieve them. Next to the worthless baubles of Henri Cohen's extravagant appraisals, they spoke volumes to expert jewelers back in Paris, who soon established that some had traveled between Orléans and Bayonne. The plot kept widening.[24]

It had long since overrun its primary Bayonne setting; inexorably, Ordonneau came to supersede d'Uhalt as the dominant protagonist among the magistrates; and finally, the capital city took formal control away from the provincial town. D'Uhalt relinquished control, and one morning sent Ordonneau a yellow leather suitcase, sealed, guarded by five police inspectors, and containing the fruits of his labors — sixty kilos of reports, depositions, and transcripts. For a moment d'Uhalt had enjoyed among his fellow Béarnais the status of small-town hero, the intrepid provincial magistrate challenging the mighty of

Pursuit: A constable outside Sutton's on Victoria Street, London, in March 1934, as French police search the premises. Here, several months earlier, Stavisky had pawned the few genuine jewels left to him. (Photo courtesy of AP/Wide World Photos.)

the capital. He now returned to a more lasting obscurity, overtaken by the affair but quickly rewarded for his services with a judgeship in Bordeaux, promoted in rank yet still close to his beloved Basque homeland.

In Paris Ordonneau's travail was only beginning. By early May he and the other two magistrates had indicted twenty-seven suspects and were investigating twenty-one others. But the attorneys in the public prosecutor's office knew that receiving stolen goods and peddling influence were notoriously difficult charges to prove. Who, how many, would in the end stand trial? Neither Ordonneau nor his colleagues could yet say, but all around them people demanded to know. They also demanded to know why no one had yet found the assassins of Albert Prince.[25]

Justice Politicized

This was highly unwelcome to the new government.

Encouraged by the kindly old figure of Gaston Doumergue, talk of national unity had briefly chased away the shouts of 6 February. With left and right now serving in the same cabinet, surely the truce might prevail? Surely Tardieu would not now undo Doumergue from inside the cabinet as he had undone Chautemps from outside, and the magistrates might continue their investigations of Stavisky's assorted accomplices in peace?

Such naive hopes were dashed almost as soon as the new minister of justice, Henry Chéron, moved to Place Vendôme. The son of a salesman in Lisieux, once a lawyer there himself, Chéron brought to high office some of the reputed values of the provincial middle classes: common sense, financial orthodoxy, a belief in the market and also in agriculture, which led him to proclaim more than once that "wheat is gold." Nearing seventy, Chéron, with his massive bulk, gray goatee, and briefcase under his arm, was a caricaturist's delight, a good-humored Norman who had represented Caen in the Senate for twenty-one years. Now assuming ministerial office for the ninth time, this old hand of the moderate right was far more attached to his Parliament than to his party; he had served once in the Radical Paul-Boncour's government, much to the annoyance of his friends on the right, and now naturally entered the government of national unity. But he had little respect for the confidences of judicial office and none at all for the independence of the magistracy. From Place Vendôme to the Palace of Justice there soon flowed a river of pettifoggery, of requests to verify a rumor, photograph a document, send over a report, and, above all, speed up an indictment. "We've arrived at a time," he would declare, "when the public consciousness craves closure"—always the public, as though magistrates had to march to the beat of Chéron's restive voters. "I cannot insist too much on the necessity of hastening the resolution of these affairs . . . for the sake of public peace," he said. He would sometimes temper his exhortations with hollow reverence for the sanctity of judicial freedoms: "Without intervening in the least in the investigation, over which the magistrate remains freely sovereign . . ." Sometimes the prosecutor general protested weakly that Ordonneau would investigate at his own pace. But Chéron only clamored more loudly and sanctimoniously.[26]

Politics drove his anxieties, the unstable politics of coalition government and chronic electoralism. Was it true, as Tardieu had asked, that Suzanne Avril—seductive intermediary between Stavisky and the government—had been a drug dealer, or that a sister of Niemen the Polish boxer had been Stavisky's secretary, or that Inspector Bonny had divulged details of the check stubs before Ordonneau had even seen them? It was not? Tardieu had demanded to know. How to assuage an angry deputy from the Ardennes, who complained that one of the magistrates in Paris was prying into his bank account in Charleroi, and who threatened to raise the matter in the Chamber?[27]

Chéron also fretted about the daily attentions of forty-four deputies sitting on a parliamentary commission of inquiry. The new government had bowed to necessity and accepted the measure that Chautemps had refused; it had agreed to a commission, empowered to call and hear witnesses, and enjoined to present its findings in three months. Presently three months became six, and six became nine, and, as 1934 ended and the new year came in, the deputies were still exploring the dead ends and sinuous passages of the labyrinth they called "the Stavisky affairs."

Commissions of inquiry had a troubled past, and now provoked the sarcasm of the jaded as well as the enthusiasm of the naive. An early concession to liberalism and open government under the Restoration, they had since become the instruments of pacification, exoneration, or oblivion. With the advent of the Third Republic, the Chambers began habitually to appoint them, and as the regime settled in so did they, yet another expression of the powers concentrated in the representative assembly. With each passing legislature they grew more familiar, a way for scandals to expire in an overabundance rather than a dearth of detail. Sometimes the commissions identified underlying problems, but they never solved them. They usually absolved the elected while condemning the appointed officials. After one of their own, President Grévy's son-in-law Wilson, was found trafficking in decorations in 1887, the members of the commission complained of gross slander and exonerated most of their fellow deputies. After Panama, they denounced the attempt to turn the Parliament, and with it the Republic, into a scapegoat. Negligent magistrates were to blame for the rise of the false heiress Thérèse Humbert, the commissioners of 1903 claimed. Those of 1914, after examining for four years—almost the entire session of the legislature—the circumstances of the banker Rochette's rise and fall, passed resolutions forgotten as soon as adopted, including a call to sequester justice from politics. Critics of commissions of inquiry called them useless, the weapons of political warfare. As the Stavisky commission convened, skeptics captiously recalled its most recent predecessor. In the winter of 1931 a commission of inquiry, instigated by the left, had investigated Albert Oustric's financial dealings and had helped send the minister of justice, Raoul Péret, before the High Court, which had acquitted him. Would today's commission, instigated by the right, prove any more consequential? Would it do anything more than once again poison the atmosphere around the government in office?[28]

Almost as soon as they sat down in a specially appointed room in the Palais Bourbon, the deputies of the commission assailed Chéron with demands for every word, every transcript, deposition, and background report the magistrates had generated. Chéron complied, over the prosecutor general's protestations about confidentiality and practicality, and soon paper flowed back through the minister's open channel to the eager commissioners. When Ordonneau ordered Stavisky's grave opened for a second autopsy—which laid to rest rumors of his murder—four members of the commission demanded to be present. They began suggesting new investigations to Chéron. As their witnesses filed past, transgressions only dimly linked to Bayonne or Orléans came to light, opening up new possibilities of prosecution, which Chéron dutifully passed along to the public prosecutor's office. Such proposals often followed violent quarrels inside the commission itself. The members on the right bitterly resisted moves to make too much of Senator Odin's testimony, which had revealed his own modest role in the Hungarian bond venture. Members on the left tried to protect their fellow Radical, the lawyer André Hesse, from the attentions of the justice system, and, when they failed, turned on the right-wing journalist Paul Lévy of *Aux Ecoutes,* whose brief encounters with Stavisky now came to light. Chéron raised his arms to the ceiling. "There's nothing in this affair," he said of the case against Lévy, substituting his own judgment for that of the magistrates. And his gesture betrayed his plight, that of a political actor in a judicial drama.[29]

Some proposals the prosecutors took up, others they discarded. So it was that the distant, questionable services that Senators Renoult and Puis and Deputy Louis Proust had rendered to Stavisky now returned to haunt them in the form of an indictment for influence trafficking, while those of Senator Odin and Deputies Hulin and Hesse faded into history: the facts were too equivocal, their services too professional, for the prosecutors to seek a conviction before a skeptical jury in the criminal court. But, indicted or not, the exposed parliamentarians could jettison any aspirations to renown or higher office. Their careers were ruined. Expelled from the Radical Party or from the bar association, or both, most withdrew into obscurity and advancing age, and when a pale and silent Renoult appeared in the Galerie Marchande of the Palace of Justice, his fellow lawyers, swathed in black, greeted him with cries of "Stavisky!" "To jail!" and an impromptu rendition of the old Revolutionary song "Ça ira."[30]

Pushed by the politicians, Chéron was also hounded by the press. Its audacity alarmed him. Reporters made off with the secrets of an interrogation, and photographers caught suspects and witnesses in magistrates' antechambers. The minister flailed about wildly. Powerless to sequester or to speed the investigation, he still hoped to bask in its occasional successes, and he followed avidly its coverage by an invasive, inaccurate, and riotously indiscreet press.[31]

The papers reported that Stavisky and Rita Georg, star of *Katinka,,* had been German spies; that Arlette had hidden the check stubs; that Stavisky had operated a gambling club on the Champs-Elysées; that the government had covered the escape of the guilty and contrived to deflect the investigators from their chosen paths. An unbridled enthusiasm for the sealed book of mystery accompanied a cavalier disregard for judicial secrecy. "So what are the awful secrets they want to hide from us?" asked *La Liberté du Sud Ouest.* Many still refused to believe in Stavisky's suicide. "We have never accepted the easy theory of suicide," declared *La Liberté* in September, long after the second autopsy had failed to find any of the telltale signs of murder crowding the columnists' febrile imaginations. New rumors disposed of old ones, and when the "A. Tardi——" on one of the check stubs turned out to be a decorator and not the former prime minister, the editors could turn to the next, because word of each stub somehow leaked out, fuel for their speculations.[32]

Chéron would ask the magistrates to verify each rumor and false report, further swelling the flow of paper between Place Vendôme and the palace. Sometimes the commission of inquiry would ask him about an article, and he would pass that along too. But gradually the editors tired of the banal complexities of bonds and their bearers, and relegated to inside pages the lengthening chronicle of an arcane crime. In the empty space, they placed instead the mystery of the death of Albert Prince.

With the Prince affair, Chéron dropped any lingering pretense of respect for the independence of the judiciary. The government, the commission of inquiry, and the press returned to the charge against Justice, and the minister, his domain invaded once again, mounted a disastrous counteroffensive.

He sent in Inspector Bonny, once demonized, now eulogized, to help with the investigation. Reinstated after his discovery of the check stubs, Bonny seized a new chance to advance his career. When informers convinced him that the criminal underworld had lent a hand in the death of Albert Prince, the opportunistic inspector rashly pulled in from Marseilles a trio of the milieu's best-known gangsters, Carbone the Corsican, Spirito the Sicilian, and de Lussatz the Monégasque. But none had been anywhere near Dijon on the day or night of Prince's death, and each was released after a month, leaving the mystery darker, the press angrier, and Bonny deeper in disrepute than ever.[33]

Chéron stamped the fiasco with his own antics. As though possessed by the affair, he pressed on the magistrates in Paris and Dijon any tip or clue, any signed or anonymous letter that came his way. Once, he made the investigating magistrates in Paris send police inspectors all the way to Cahors to verify the unverifiable claims of a local seer. He wished immoderately for closure, and when, in June, Ordonneau took over the case and added Albert Prince's dossier to the rich inventory of the Stavisky investigation, he too encountered the redoubled zeal of the minister of justice.[34]

As usual, Chéron evaded the pressure from politicians and journalists, his office continuing to serve as the meeting place between the newly liberal order and the age-old imperative for justice. The deputies on the commission of inquiry wandered from the Stavisky affair into the Prince mystery, thinking, not unreasonably, that the two were connected. They asked Chéron for the magistrates' findings, and complained when they did not receive them at once. Even Chéron raised the matter of confidentiality, and reminded the members of the commission that Léon Bourgeois, minister of justice during the Panama scandal in 1893, had chafed as well at the violation of judicial secrecy. But Chéron gave in.[35]

How, in any case, could he withhold from the commission secrets that he could not keep from the press? Every day, the newspapers published word of a breakthrough or of an impasse, of an imminent arrest, interrogation, or revelation. No matter was too delicate, no rumor too improbable, to appear in their columns. Within days reporters picked up murmurs in the palace and the Chamber about a parallel life led by Prince, a dark underside to his luminous public existence, spent in secret assignations with prostitutes in Paris and Dijon. Indeed, the investigating magistrate in Dijon, Rabut, had interrogated a prostitute who confirmed the rumors and confidently identified Prince from a photo. But such rumors led nowhere. Papers in Paris and Dijon revealed Bonny's ill-considered report about the Marseilles gangsters almost as soon as he had written it. Once, a journalist insinuated himself into Ordonneau's office and claimed to represent Mme Prince. The magistrates sent him away, but the impostor's ruse revealed the desperate lengths to which the frustrations of the press might drive it.[36]

Complain though he might about the journalists' indelicacy, Chéron himself did little to cool their ardor. In intemperate declarations the minister of justice turned the Prince investigation into a national crusade against unnamed penumbral villains. "We have to find the assassins of ill-fated Judge Prince," he urged. "The country has fallen prey to a gang of ne'er-do-wells who will stop at nothing to carry out their misdeeds. The band must be tracked down and punished." Chéron, determined to restore confidence in the administration of justice, only prolonged its agony, for even as he pressed and pushed the Palace of Justice, the conviction took hold that there were no murderers to be found, and that Albert Prince had taken his own life.[37]

■

Strange assassins! Who phoned their victim at home after his departure for the palace, assumed that he would return and take the first train and that he would dissuade his wife from joining him as well, lured him all the way to Dijon and then waited three hours to dispatch him to a highly visible spot, on a railroad in full view of a heavily traveled national highway. And who then left the instruments of their crime by the track, a bloodstained knife and a thin stretch of cord, ignoring the most elementary precautions after executing the most elaborate and hazardous of abductions. And who finally vanished, leaving only unverifiable tales told by bogus witnesses, the parvenus of every public mystery.

And strange victim! Who accepted the urgent message without question, without returning the call; and who, within minutes of arriving in Dijon, sent reassuring information to his wife, which he could scarcely have had time to receive; and who then went to a hotel, while the boarding house lodging his supposedly stricken mother was only a kilometer away.[38]

Entertained at first by a few skeptics in the press, but dismissed by most others, the possibility of suicide became over time a political as well as a forensic matter. A suspicion of murder floated conveniently over the Radicals, and their most audacious foes, the enemies of the regime itself, accused Georges Pressard of masterminding the crime. The public prosecutor, brother-in-law of Camille Chautemps, had silenced his rebellious subordinate in the only way possible. Seditious as always, Léon Daudet did not mince words in L'Action Française. "The magistrate," he revealed, "was killed by Masonic order, not without police complicity, at the instigation of Camille Chautemps and his brother-in-law Pressard." More thoughtful observers questioned the motive. Prince had no secrets to reveal; none were found among his papers, and the letters he had spoken of mysteriously in the Café de Flore were never found; why go to such spectacular lengths to remove him? His role, distant and occasional, hardly justified such attentions. The Radical paper *L'Oeuvre* soon came to doubt that he had been murdered. Others observed a prudent silence. When the inspectors hired by *Le Matin* and *Paris-Soir* quickly despaired of ever finding any assassins and left Dijon, their employers decided not to publish their implicit conclusions. Prince's death, like that of Stavisky, had become a partisan matter.[39]

Magistrates, pushed by the incessant clamor, lost all sense of reserve. Chéron, as minister of justice, had already publicly prejudged the matter when the Dijon magistrates followed suit. They called it murder. The advocate general in Dijon, placing his personal obligations before his professional ones, insisted that his close friend, the late Albert Prince, would never have taken his own life. And with unseemly haste the young magistrates ruled out suicide altogether. In Paris, the presiding judge of the Cour de Cassation, Lescouvé, made headlines when he appeared before the deputies on the commission of inquiry. "Without knowing it," he said of the day Prince came to him to challenge Pressard's account, "he had just signed his own death warrant." It was, for one of the country's highest magistrates, a reckless declaration. The climate invited it.[40]

But at the Palace of Justice in Paris, doubts were growing. By May 1935, when the magistrate assigned to the case, Pierre Lapeyre, left for the court of appeal and handed it over to Ordonneau, he had abandoned his initial suppositions and concluded firmly that Prince, no longer master of his own mind, had committed a suicide disguised as murder. By then a new official from the Sûreté, Divisional Superintendent Guillaume, had taken over from the disgraced inspector Bonny. Several weeks later, much to the annoyance of the Dijon public prosecutor's office, he reached the same conclusion.

Superintendent Guillaume was a faultless professional, his career never held back by an administrative reprimand or advanced by a parliamentary recommendation. Like the magistrate Lapeyre, he had at first deemed murder the more plausible explanation of the death of Albert Prince. No strong affinity for the Radicals compelled this conservative, practicing Catholic to spare them the embarrassment of a seemingly political murder. But the circumstantial evidence in Dijon, he felt, left him no choice. The traces on the coupling hook of the locomotive, nearly a meter off the ground, and the disposition of Prince's remains around the tracks strongly suggested that he had been seated, his back to the locomotive, at the moment of impact. Other experts subsequently confirmed this finding, which contradicted the hasty judgment of the Dijon public prosecutor's office that he had been tied across the rails. The thin rope found by the tracks, Guillaume demonstrated with the help of another locomotive, had never been used to tie down Prince, around whose ankle, furthermore, there were no signs of pressure or struggle. Freely seated, he must have been conscious, willing.[41]

But a second autopsy contradicted the first and concluded that Prince, under duress, had inhaled some undefined "volatile substance," which had left him living but unconscious at the moment of impact. Not so, answered a third and prolonged chemical examination, which found no traces of any known narcotic substance in the viscera, and confirmed unequivocally the findings of the first autopsy. Chemical and histological findings nullified each other, but the circumstantial evidence remained. And Superintendent Guillaume's doubts grew.[42]

"Dr. Hallinger," for so the mysterious caller that morning of 20 February had named the physician of Prince's mother, was an imaginary physician, an evident misnomer for her real one, Dr. Ehringer. Oddly, on his arrival in Dijon, Prince had committed the same small travesty. His telegram of the afternoon repeated the error of the morning's phone call.

More oddly still, a waiter at Lutétia, which Prince frequented regularly, saw him, on the morning of the phone call, head toward the telephones in the basement of the famed café, not five minutes from his apartment on Rue de Babylone, where, after leaving that morning, he reappeared.[43]

In Paris, Lapeyre and Guillaume's colleagues at the Sûreté Générale concluded that Prince had staged his own death. He had concocted the letters from Pressard to clear his name and establish a motive for his own murder; he had called as the doctor "Hallinger" to preclude his wife from calling his mother's real physician as an afterthought; had returned home in seeming innocence and left again. He had phoned from the Gare de Lyon and cabled from Dijon to reassure his wife, left his suitcase in a hotel room, and proceeded to La Combe aux Fées for the macabre staging of his death, the violent denouement of his life and career.

But why? His motive remained as obscure as that of his supposed murderers. The glare of scandal now shone on his conduct three years earlier, but neither secrets nor shame emerged. He had committed errors, but fewer than many who had crossed Stavisky's path; his career might now suffer, but perhaps not for long. His act made no sense. Such doubts drove Superintendent Guillaume to look into the persistent rumors about the distinguished magistrate's private life. In the brothels of Montparnasse he found traces of Prince's passage, women who claimed to remember him as a strangely silent, apprehensive client. If true, their accounts revealed a master of dissimulation, for not one of his friends suspected any double life, salacious or otherwise. But the reports led nowhere. Why had Judge Prince take his own life?[44]

■

Almost as soon as Superintendent Guillaume handed in his findings to Ordonneau, at the end of August, the press published them, and, in a final paroxysm of public controversy, the Prince affair expired.

A sense of duty, *Le Matin* informed its readers, forced it to publish a summary of Guillaume's report. It did not reveal the source of the leak. But evidently someone friendly to the Radicals within the police, eager to lay to rest the myth of murder and promote in its place the presumption of suicide, had passed it on. *L'Oeuvre* published a summary as well, *Paris-Soir* the full report.

"The Guillaume affair begins," announced *Le Quotidien*, since the press on the right now vilified the hapless superintendent, whose methods and findings conspired to undermine their cherished conviction in the murder of Albert Prince.[45]

Into the storm now blundered the deputies on the commission of inquiry, who added the Prince affair to their existing burdens, and demanded from the Chamber full judicial powers to investigate. They saw nothing improper in so annexationist a demand, no overt threat to an officially revered separation of powers. The keenest among them, whose sense of purpose shone through the tenacity of his questioning, defended the notion: Georges Mandel now behaved toward the magistrates and the police as his mentor Clemenceau had toward the supporters of a negotiated peace. He sought to make them pay for their ways. This time, he said, he and his colleagues on the commission would not transmit dossiers to the chancellery and merely hope for results. They would watch over the public prosecutor's office and the Sûreté and, said this purist of the late Third Republic, would make sure that they took action. In his ardor, he incarnated the old absolutist notion that the sovereign had delegated the administration of justice and could take it back at will; now the sovereign was the people, and Mandel was its representative.[46]

The commission never did acquire the full judicial powers it wanted, but took up the Prince affair undaunted, and soon strayed from Stavisky's pathways and inroads to the "mutilated corpse" of La Combe aux Fées. Justice took its course anyway, and the Prince investigation moved inexorably toward closure and the archives. No assassins were ever found. From the beginning, politicians and journalists had made the mystery their own affair, with each individual appealing to his own public. The aging Voltaire had done no less in 1762 when he launched his campaign to rehabilitate Calas and brought public opinion to bear on the closed, secretive justice of the ancien régime. The idea that openness might thwart arbitrariness seemed evident to all who called for it, but it was less evident that openness might also wreak havoc on the separation of powers in a representative democracy. No matter how liberal the hour, transparent justice, in the hands of a docile judiciary, was also penetrable justice. Since the Revolution, no regime had so sheltered the magistrates or their auxiliaries from scrutiny or interference as to assure their immunity from the vicissitudes of national politics. The empire had not wanted to, the Republic had not dared to. And the founders of the Third Republic had proceeded to a purge, determined to perpetuate among the magistracy the pliancy from which they themselves, in less happy times of opposition, had been the first to suffer. Now, in the Prince affair, a travesty of open justice was coming to an end. Journalists, deputies, and ministers had substituted their own judgment for that of the magistrates, and in the blizzard of words all had lost their way.

Chéron declared absurdly that he had nothing to do with the Guillaume report. But he no longer spoke of assassination, only of a "tragic death." His days at the ministry were numbered, ended by the Prince affair and his own excesses. It had not been the most successful of his nine trips into ministerial power. Now, after the sweetness, he encountered the bitterness of high office, and in some dismay he retired to Normandy and his native Lisieux, where, still mayor, he died a year and a half later.[47]

The Republic Torn Apart

In February 1935 Ordonneau sent the public prosecutor his rulings about Stavisky's accomplices. They filled two volumes, and distilled the yearlong labors of justice and its auxiliaries—seventeen thousand pieces of evidence gathered, seven thousand pages of expert reports commissioned—into his final word about the guilt or innocence of all the suspects, captive or free, awaiting their fate.[48]

He proposed sending nineteen of them before the criminal court, appraisers and accountants alongside deputies, journalists, lawyers, and a former model, now famous, bankrupt, and imprisoned.

Ordonneau also proposed dropping the charges against twelve others. Had Niemen the former boxer, however shady a character, or Boyer the former deputy, or Aymard the editor of *La Liberté* known the nature of the moneys Serge Alexandre had paid them? Had Proust the sitting deputy trafficked in his influence, sold his authority for Stavisky's cash? Not demonstrably enough, thought Ordonneau, but such cases were moot, and the public prosecutor insisted on retaining at least a charge of receiving stolen goods against Proust and Aymard. In the end, the Chamber of Indictments threw out the charges against Proust but kept those against Aymard, so that in early June twenty of Stavisky's associates, his wife included, found themselves formally accused of crimes and misdemeanors ranging from swindling to forgery. Of their assorted misdeeds, fabricating or using false public documents were crimes brought before juries, swindling or receiving stolen property only misdemeanors brought before the professional judges of the correctional courts—the same that had so often failed to try Stavisky himself. But the magistrates had taken too much abuse to risk again the mockery of the press and its readers. Best to bring all the accused together, the public prosecutor's office reasoned, before the popular judges called jurors, and hold this most public of trials in the most public of jurisdictions, the criminal court in Paris.[49]

Once already, the deputies on the commission of inquiry had trampled on Montesquieu and requested just such a trial by jury. The public deserved one, they said. They were concluding their hearings. Ordonneau and his colleagues had taken much too long, the deputies complained, ignoring their own deliberate pace—they had held 185 sessions over 432 days, and had not yet assembled their conclusions. When they finally did, a year later, they called fondly for a more independent judiciary.[50]

For the last time, the deputies had denounced an ill that their own power exemplified. For most of 1934 and part of 1935, they had searched tirelessly for the failings on the part of the executive that had allowed Stavisky to flourish. They had found some; but, creatures of parliamentary politics, they stopped short of questioning an imbalance of power that generously favored their own legislative branch.

They inveighed against Hesse and Bonnaure and the rest of Stavisky's parliamentary friends, not because they were deputies whose influence had so often carried the day for him, but because they were lawyers who placed their client's interests above all else. "Excuse me," Commission President Guernut asked ingenuously as the commission looked into the success of Stavisky's lawyers in putting off his hearings, "above the lawyer's interest . . . isn't there that of justice? Doesn't that interest also have its advocates?" And Mandel, not known for his naïveté, expressed shock at Senator Renoult's approach on behalf of Stavisky in 1926. "If I have understood you correctly, Monsieur le juge," he said to Prouharam, the prosecutor whom Renoult had pressured, "you find any effort on the part of a lawyer normal?"[51]

They decried regulatory incoherence but never the weak executive it betrayed. Delamarche, the beleaguered official from Commerce, exasperated them. "I am asking you, which is the overseeing body?" one of them finally asked as he lost his way through the administrative jungle enveloping the crédits municipaux. The regulators obeyed the regulated, Mandel said. "Exactly," replied Montabré, the inspector from the gambling section who had watched Stavisky gamble away millions in the casinos on the coast. President Guernut even hailed the subordination of the executive to the legislative branch, untroubled by its crippling of the prefects in Orléans and Bayonne: "No democracy has ever known a sovereign prefect. He reports to a ministry, which can, in consequence, issue him orders at any time."[52]

They doubted the virtue of selfish interest but never the liberal ethos itself, nor its relevance to the country's somber circumstances. One of them was shocked that prosecutors could lose interest in Stavisky as soon as he paid off his victims. They acted, he said, like collection agents rather than society's advocates. Another saw the birth of the Foncière as a symbolic triumph of the financial over the public interest. And, at the press and its habits, several professed alarm or disenchantment—at its advertising budgets, secret subsidies, and indifference, yet again, to the wider interests of society. They wanted to know why Mennevée, the editor who had threatened the Foncière, had not shared all his secrets with the authorities. "Do you think," he retorted, "that I replaced the Sûreté Générale or the Police Judiciaire?"[53]

In censorious asides and occasional preachments, the deputies of the commission condemned the predators of liberal society but never the logic of liberalism itself. The republicans had not deserved the law of 1881 freeing the press, said Astruc, Stavisky's onetime publicity agent. "But there are people with enough wit to profit from it," replied Guernut pointedly from his seat on the commission. Beyond that he would not venture. The higher interest to which the deputies kept alluding could only be that of the Republic, but how might it prevail over the liberal society epitomized by their own parliamentary regime? They did not say.[54]

239

As Ordonneau sent in his rulings and the commission concluded its hearings, the press was slowly losing interest. News of the affair now came erratically in its columns, like the aftereffects of a violent storm. The propaganda sheets of the antisemitic far right resolutely kept Stavisky's name before their readers, and occasionally the mass dailies lent their columns to the ever-popular hounding of magistrates. They told of the night of the check stubs, months earlier, when Ordonneau, tired and thirsty, had drunk Bonny's champagne as though from a poisoned chalice. They also carried sporadic news of police hunts, like that for Stavisky's old associate Henri Poulner, fraternizing lately with swindlers and counterfeiters in Casablanca. Another Stavisky affair? they asked hopefully, before dropping the story. And on impulse they pursued the ruined and the forlorn. *Paris-Soir* thought it might publish the memoirs of Inspector Bonny, United Press International those of Arlette. "I am given to understand," the managing editor of UPI wrote her in her cell at La Petite Roquette, "that some financial assistance might be of use to you and your family at this moment." But nothing came of the ventures. Until the trial opened, the Stavisky affair had lost its news value.[55]

It gave way to a chronicle of civil strife. Consensus had eluded the government of national unity, born to the shots and shouts of riot and called to the task of pacification and reform. For a moment the truce had held, as leaders of the right and left moderated their passions and tried governing together. But the street did not follow. A cycle of demonstrations and counterdemonstrations set in; battles raged in the Latin Quarter; the Popular Front was in the making. Old Doumergue could no more hold the government than the country together, and in July Tardieu, abandoning all pretense, accused Chautemps before the commission of inquiry of every malfeasance known to man. Doumergue gave up in November, and abandoned to shaky successors the hopeless task of accomplishing a meeting of minds in a country now polarized by ideology.

Stavisky, like a sorcerer, had conjured the reciprocal hatred between right and left, and made latent hostility a real passage of arms.

On the right, the Jew, the foreigner, the parvenu, had set off fitful fears of disorder, decadence, and social upheaval; the left they saw as the midwife of all three, the menacing face of chaos. Justice they chose as the symptom, the sign that authority had to be restored, the country renewed, the parties brought to heel. The path to recovery, for the right, was political, and to preserve their society they proposed to evict from power the agents of anarchy and decay, strike the proper balance between liberty and authority, and rebuild the institutions of liberal government before it was too late.

But the conquering nabob, the artist of influence, had revived on the left in these distressed times a loathing of the rich and a passion for social and egalitarian justice. In his charmed circle they detected the corrupt ways of privilege and precedence, in his impunity the injustice of the established order. To reform liberal society they proposed to keep the right from power, protect the

Politics: For Socialist demonstrators in February 1934 ("prison for Stavisky's friends"), the scandal demonstrated the iniquities of capitalism. (Photo courtesy of Bibliothèque Nationale de France.)

existing institutions of government in order to use them, and bring about in their day a measure of social reform that their enemies would never introduce on their own.

Neither could afford to sweep away the existing order altogether. From it the conservatives, resistant to undue policing, had profited handsomely. Today they denounced its justice in their press; tomorrow they would exploit it in their boardrooms. Likewise the left, through all its tortuous rationalizations, welcomed the institutions that might give it power and a measure of satisfaction. Behind all the invective, a sullen convergence of interest had in the end spared the country a coup d'état, revolution, and civil war.

But the affair had set the promise of liberalism against its practice. The right proposed to save society but change its governance, the left to change society but save its governance. One condemned liberal politics, the other liberal society; each struck at the other's base of power; and in their deafening confrontation Stavisky's name faded like a distant echo.

Suicides

The scandal had unhinged men as it had the country, setting off crises of conscience that sometimes led them to contemplate ending their days.

On the morning of 5 March 1934, Henri Hurlaux, an assistant prosecutor in the Paris office, theatrically produced a small vial of poison before his superiors in the Palace of Justice. Once, hoping for promotion, the middle-aged

241

magistrate had asked a flourishing Stavisky to put in a word with the prime minister. But once, he had also granted Stavisky one of his many trial postponements. Sequence did not prove consequence. Nonetheless, he faced dismissal for his imprudence. He struggled with his colleagues over the poison. "If the minister of justice dismisses me," he cried, "he'll dismiss a dead man." Doctors led him away to a clinic, where, his career at an end, he recovered.[56]

On the 8th of the same month, leaving Ordonneau's office late at night, Maître Raymond Hubert made straight for the Seine. From his own windows a month earlier he had watched in distress the riot of 6 February. Barely forty, already famous, the gifted lawyer had saved famous murderers from the guillotine. Now he was defending Romagnino, and had held for a while some of the fabled check stubs that his wary client had entrusted to him. But the affair raised fears of the apocalypse in him. "We'll all be carried away by the storm," he kept saying. "The end of the world is at hand. Where are we going?" Riddled by doubts about his own legal role now that Ordonneau was asking him about it, Hubert jumped from the Pont de Solférino into the icy river. "I lost control over myself," he said in a convalescence home a month later.[57]

Early on the 16th, about to testify for a second day before the commission of inquiry, Emile Blanchard, official at the Ministry of Agriculture, left the city. Years before, he had foolishly accepted Stavisky's invitation to join the board of SIMA, and then of the Foncière, and after that to write an occasional article in *La Volonté*. Now he was under indictment for corruption and complicity in swindle, and had greatly embarrassed the minister. To him Blanchard proclaimed his good faith, and to his wife he bade farewell; with the help of a knife and a vial of Gardenal he took his own life under the arch of an aqueduct spanning a valley near Fontainebleau.[58]

And Prince took the train to Dijon. Here and there an inflated sense of honor and shame had elevated venial into mortal sins, and set off the internal clamor of a private scandal. All around them, prosaic abuses had stirred uncommon passions, so that the distress of the country was mirrored in their own and in the most excessive act of all, the suicide of Albert Prince.

TWELVE

A LIGHT IN THE COURTROOM

The real shame is that man's justice always arrives too late; it punishes or stigmatizes the acts, incapable of reaching higher or farther than the one who commits them. — Georges Bernanos, *Journal d'un curé de campagne*

Presiding Judge Barnaud, growing animated, went on telling the jurors of the criminal court about Stavisky; his silver hair and white ermine shook; now and then a clerk brought up a dossier from the great gray vault, untied it, and waited while the aging magistrate paused to glance at it.

Once, Barnaud called Stavisky's women his useful allies, and Arlette, among the accused on the bench, brought her black gloves to her face. But the presiding judge did not dwell on her late husband's character. Remember instead, he told the jurors, the fake jewels and bonds, the subterfuge at the heart of the crimes before us.

And, to illustrate the point, clerks hoisted sheets that named the charges against the twenty accused and referred the jurors to corresponding questions already handed to them about each — 1,956 questions in all, one for each count of fraud, forgery, or receipt of stolen property. The sheets fluttered overhead like a giant pair of wings, and murmurs ran through the courtroom. "Come on! Come on!" said Barnaud. "I have a bell. Be silent!"

Barnaud's new bell had replaced an oak gavel. It resembled the one Fernand Bouisson had sounded with such fury and futility in the Chamber that night in January 1934, as the deputies drowned his calls for order with insults and invective. How pious was Barnaud's wish now, in November 1935, for the law and nothing more! Few had come to talk merely of jewels and bonds and the finer points of fraud; many among the journalists, lawyers, witnesses, and accused meant to place on trial a government, a society, or an era; and Barnaud's bell, the ring of the magistracy, became instead the symbol of its solitude.[1]

The Other

The old treasurer from Orléans — Desbrosses, short and bent, in a black suit, wing collar and bow tie — stood sweating at the bar. His glasses reflected the light, hiding his eyes.

"I was perhaps an imbecile," he said.

"Oh no! You weren't an imbecile, you were a forger," Barnaud exclaimed.

He was bearing down now, and Desbrosses's system of defense was fast falling apart. The statute of limitations had expired on the jewelry swindle in Orléans, but not on the forged bonds that had followed, and their connection

243

was, to Barnaud, a matter of fascination. If Desbrosses had believed so much in the authenticity of the emeralds, why had he, in extremis, given Alexandre the false bonds to raise the money to redeem them?

Desbrosses told of how a distraught Alexandre had threatened theatrically to shoot himself. "I wanted no such scene in my office," Desbrosses explained, to laughter in the court. But what of the twenty other forged bonds? Had Alexandre brandished a revolver for each? "I wanted to save my organization."

"By turning out forgeries?"

"Who wouldn't have done the same?" asked Desbrosses to renewed laughs. When it was over, he returned to his place on the bench. Suddenly, with a belated flash of wit, *l'esprit d'escalier*, he turned back. "How could I mistrust this man," he asked, "who knew so many deputies, senators, who dined with ministers?"

"Which ones?" asked Barnaud. "Which ones?" asked one of the lawyers.

"Names! Names!" the deputies had cried at the time of Panama. The search for scandal took well-traveled paths, those leading into the world of occult, highly placed complicities. Who had helped the lay nun, Sister Candide, skim off millions from her charities? the scandalmongers had asked in 1910. Fearing a new Panama, the government had brought her to trial in this same courtroom, and waited for the anticlerical passions and counterallegations about "high notables of the Republic" to subside. Who had helped Thérèse Humbert pull off the most elaborate inheritance hoax of the Belle Epoque? Which deputies? She had dined with *le tout Paris*. So persistent a fantasy, discerning an illicit shadowland behind the glittering facades of power, could only spring from ancient fears. And indeed the fantasies of the liberal Republic revived those of the absolute monarchy, when the Parisian advocates of virtue wished to see Versailles as a house of secrecy, corruption, and vice. Stavisky, for all his boasts, enjoyed only a few friends among the deputies and none among the ministers; he had resorted to intermediaries, with mixed results; still the fiction of the camarilla weighed like an incubus on the minds in the courtroom. Who were all Stavisky's powerful friends?

"I couldn't know all of them," Desbrosses replied. "I was told . . ."

"Who told you?"

"He himself," Desbrosses said lamely. Once again, laughter erupted in the court. He returned pathetically to his seat.[2]

Later Hayotte took up the theme. As usual, he made an execrable impression. Stavisky's old friend, his partner in Orléans and the ruin of the Empire theater, came down from his seat in the third row, posed and swaggered among his fellow accused, and replied volubly to the presiding judge's questions about jewels engaged, bonds cashed, Bugattis driven, and suits tailored. Once the silver-haired Barnaud told him sharply not to interrupt. "I'm going to give you some advice right at the outset, don't interrupt me like that, I hate it." But even he could not slow Hayotte down. What impressed you so about Alexandre, one of the lawyers asked Hayotte. His entourage, he replied.[3]

At once, the lawyers picked up the scent. What entourage? asked Jean-

Charles Legrand, the provocative enfant terrible of the bar, close in his politics to the royalist far right. Who? Where were they?[4]

As though in choral response, his client Tissier entered. He, at least, confessed all. He had already done so almost two years before, when the district tax collector had discovered the false bonds in Bayonne. But now as then the director of the crédit municipal meant to take the president down with him. Garat had given him orders, he had carried them out.

"If Garat had told you to go and kill," asked Barnaud, "you would have done so?"

"That's not the same thing. But if he'd asked me to hand over the treasury, I would have handed it over."

He spoke in well-rounded phrases that, together with his silver mustache and upright posture, lent him an incongruous air of assurance. But while imprisoned in the Villa Chagrin, he had sometimes sung for hours on end in his cell. In the courtroom one or two wondered whether he was altogether sound of mind. "Your Honor, did I receive a single centime? . . . Luxury has never interested me. I never go to cafés, I only wish for one thing, a walk in the open air." Once again derisive laughter swept the floor.

And once again Maître Legrand asked about Stavisky's mysterious entourage. The jurors needed to know, he said. It consisted, Tissier replied, of obliging officials from all over, from the ministries and the police and the prefecture of the Basses-Pyrénées. "We the accused are willing to pay, but we are not willing, Gentlemen of the jury—I am speaking for all, am I not—to pay for those who aren't here."

As though on cue, one of the lawyers rose and said, "The innocent have no intention at all of paying for the mistakes of others."[5]

No one had yet identified "the others." Their renown grew daily, but, bashful deities, they remained faceless and anonymous. Then Romagnino stood to defend himself, and soon began reciting names as though announcing the arrival of long-awaited dignitaries at a reception.

Stavisky's factotum was elegantly dressed, his hair brilliantined, and he spoke quietly and intelligently, sometimes glancing at a note to jog his memory. He talked of itinerant jewels and promenading check stubs, of blackmailers and gamblers, and of a revolver he had lent Stavisky one Christmas Eve nearly two years before. Stavisky's connections were those of any prominent banker, Romagnino observed simply. They included deputies, senators, ministers, journalists, chiefs of staff; and he even named some of them, exposing the people of a half-hidden land of influence.[6]

It was true; Stavisky had briefly flourished there; and the defendants kept pointing to it, as though to some lotusland of the Republic, whenever Barnaud challenged the worldly misdeeds that had brought them into his court.

The People

Heavyset, jowled Farault answered Barnaud in tones of outraged innocence. Of course he, the appraiser in Orléans, had believed in the authenticity of the jewels. "Do you think I would have taken pebbles from the Loire in return for loans of 10 and 15 million?" Of course he had known nothing of any substitution of fake for real emeralds. "But really I don't know whom you take me for?" Laughter erupted; and when Barnaud revealed that the only three real ones had somehow found their way back to the jeweler the day after their engagement in Orléans, even Arlette bent over with a wild laugh.[7]

Farault was playing the card of humility, the people deceived by the elite. He came, his lawyer later explained, from the honest and industrious race of peasants that gave France her strength: he had been duped, that was all.[8] Complementary myths, of occult influence and now of popular goodness, of darkness and light, suffused the trial, lending to the proceedings the didacticism of a morality play.

At least as old as the prerevolutionary attack on "the nobles" in pamphlets and caricatures, the myth of common goodness sanctified the people even as it vilified the aristocrats and above all the courtiers. The Janus-like myth kept changing one of its faces, that of evil, as Jesuits, Freemasons, Jews, capitalists, communists, and foreigners came under attack; deeper than any conceptual artifacts of left or right, but equally adaptable to both, it passed freely from one camp to the other; and always the binary opposition between the wholesomeness of the many and the poison of the few came into play. Such Manichaean thinking flourished in times of crisis or tension, and now it appeared again in the criminal court.[9]

The confusion between innocence and populace reached new heights in the humble appearances of Cohen the appraiser and Digoin the sales agent. Pathos, here, assumed the guise of comedy. Such small defendants for so grand a defense! Had such jejune creatures nearly brought down the regime?

Like Tissier, Cohen the little Moroccan jeweler confessed to his misdeeds, but in terms that delighted his audience. Yes, he had obeyed orders in Bayonne to overvalue jewels—"more or less fake," he called them. "Yes, Your Honor, I had this failing. . . . I limited my failing, I draw your attention to this, I limited it to 15 million." Stavisky's charm had conquered; the devil, that day, had the better tune. "Had he talked with you, Monsieur le Président . . ."[10]

Emile Digoin, looking gray and shriveled, slapped his forehead and laughed like an imbecile. The former police employee, who had kept the Etablissements Alex at Le Touquet one summer in 1928 and had recorded the engagements in Bayonne three years later, answered feebly and inarticulately. But his piteous bearing served his lawyer and unmanned his persecutor. Where was the line between servant and accomplice? Barnaud began to relent. "I do in fact have the impression that you were simply Stavisky's man," the presiding judge said at the end, "and that they made you do what they wanted; so I won't insist further."[11]

Timid Depardon, the former employee at the Foncière, notable for his insignificance, only deepened the mystery. Where were the mighty? Poor Depardon! His wife had gone mad upon his arrest and now lived in an asylum. He had only learned of the identity of M. Alexandre when he passed a newspaper stand near the Bourse in 1933 and bought an old copy of Sartori's blackmail sheet, *La Bonne Guerre*. So by then everyone knew who he was, Maître Legrand quickly observed, and his meaning was clear: Stavisky had friends in high places.[12]

So catchy was the theme that even Hattot, the old actor who had once added his gifts to Stavisky's and posed as the emissary of the emeralds' owner, took it up as well. "If everyone had done their duty, he wouldn't have been free to get us in trouble today."[13] If the mighty of the Republic had not doubted Stavisky, how could he, Hattot, a naïf, an aging and unemployed actor?

Guébin, the insurance executive, said much the same; the bourgeois as well as the bohemian could tamely follow the lead of officialdom. Why should I have verified the Bayonne bonds, he asked. His health had been ruined by his incarceration, and he elicited sympathy. With his long salt-and-pepper beard and feverish eyes, he looked stricken with grief and disbelief. Do you check the signatures on treasury bonds or on the paper from the Banque de France? he asked. Why, added Maître Ribet, should his client have doubted bonds he believed guaranteed by the state?[14]

For a moment Guébin too assumed for the jurors the improbable features of Marianne, the common people contending with the duplicity of power.

And for fifteen minutes, still in hat, scarf, and gloves, Arlette personified innocence exploited. She had known of Sacha's visits to Bayonne, she said, but nothing of his doings there; had known too of his medical concerns but nothing of the trial postponements they allowed; of his sudden riches but nothing of their source. "I still love him," she said, and Moro-Giafferi, her lawyer, was so satisfied with her performance that he had nothing to add.[15]

The Arbitrariness

As the trial wore on, the defendants took to enacting the myth that set the people of light against the powers of darkness: they challenged with growing confidence the magistrates of the Republic.

Such high fees for such small services? Barnaud asked of the lawyers in the dock. "My services were not that expensive," Bonnaure the lawyer said of all the fees he had taken for his services to the Hungarian bond venture. There was laughter in the court. The droll, heavy little man seemed eternally condemned to amuse. Gaulier, Stavisky's oldest lawyer, looked worn and frail; Guiboud-Ribaud, his youngest, was petulant and aggressive, a latter-day Rastignac who had dreamed of conquering Paris with the help of the all-too-fleeting Stavisky. Both defended their past fees. And by what right did the court pretend to regulate the fees that lawyers accepted for their services? No liberal profession could concede such powers to the public authorities.[16]

The question of liberties hung in the air. Had the lawyers, like the journalists, exercised or abused their privileges? They stood accused of receiving

Nemesis: Arlette in the dock, December 1935. (Photo courtesy of AP/Wide World Photos.)

stolen goods. Did the court expect the accused to identify the distant sources of every advertising payment or legal honorarium that came their way? What, then, of their professional freedoms, so emblematic of the values of this Republic?

"I was arbitrarily arrested," Albert Dubarry complained. The editor of *La Volonté* waved his short arms and turned his small stout frame this way and that. "Where are the responsible officials from Justice? I don't see a single one on these benches." Justice was an accomplice, guilty too of provoking a public uproar that had brought the country within a shot of civil war. Of his own kindness to Stavisky he had little to say. Yes, he had rendered services, as he had for so many others. It was in his nature—and in his journalist's calling, he seemed to say. But that did not constitute receiving stolen goods. Besides, added Maître Loewel, he had informed the minister of the interior, Chautemps, and the prefect of police, Chiappe, about Stavisky's takeover of *La Volonté,* and still the funds from the government flowed to the paper—and Maître Legrand jumped in.

"We're all going to develop hypotheses—troubling hypotheses—the first will be that there was an understanding between those who should have been prosecuted and the office that should have prosecuted them. This hypothesis," he added disingenuously, "is evidently improbable."

"It's an outrage to the prosecutor's office," shouted the advocate general, Louis Gaudel. He had a white handlebar mustache, and had risen livid with indignation from his place beside Barnaud. "No, no, I won't stand for this!" The lawyers, Legrand foremost among them, began shouting back. "For three days we've been covered with mud," Gaudel went on, "I never reacted but this is too much." He was about to leave the court when Fernand Roux stopped him. The prosecutor general was sixty-six and gray. Only rarely did a head of the public prosecutor's office join a trial. Fernand Roux's predecessor, Donat-Guigue, had done so to dignify the trial of President Paul Doumer's assassin two and a half years earlier; now Stavisky's associates enjoyed the same rare mark of respect.[17]

"I'll answer," he said. The magistrates were emerging from their stoic reserve, finally galvanized into action by the insolence of the bar. "If a few mistakes were made," Fernand Roux went on, "is that a reason for not judging all those who took money from Stavisky for one reason or another?" The defense was advancing a juridical absurdity, the request that all or none face trial. And the prosecutors had braved this public and collective trial, Roux reminded the defense, instead of bringing Dubarry before the correctional tribunal, where he would have stood alone without codefendants and without a jury. "We've come before you courageously. . . . We wanted you to challenge us and we wanted to go through with this daily crucifixion."[18]

Their crucifixion, as Roux called it, became a daily rite, performed usually at the end of the afternoon, and soon known as "the five o'clock incident."

"I'll cut down M. Chéron," shouted Paul Lévy, editor of *Aux Ecoutes* and of the ill-fated *Le Rempart,* which Stavisky had financed. For four hours he had accused justice and the police of arresting him, an editor on the right, to offset the equally sacrificial Dubarry on the left. In particular, he blamed Chéron, the minister of justice, for his own presence in the court.

"Please, please," said Barnaud urbanely.

"M. Paul Lévy!" exclaimed the prosecutor Roux more emotionally.

"I cannot stop you from speaking but there are words that shouldn't be spoken," added Barnaud, and everyone laughed; had the leaders of the Republic taken this furious little editor so seriously? He leapt and turned, like a fish in a net, and so conveyed his animus and rancor as to tire and finally exhaust the court.[19]

But when another editor on the right, Camille Aymard, took his turn and answered for his friendship with Stavisky, and for the traces it had left in his bank account, he renewed Lévy's attack. So did the lawyers. Why had the public prosecutor's office gone after Aymard?

"A concern for political balance," answered one of them.

"It's proportional representation, my dear friend, let me assure you," answered another.[20]

When Bardi de Fourtou asked why he alone among the directors and board members stood in the dock that day, the lawyers murmured their approbation. The old general had once graced the Foncière with his name and title and had negotiated without question the bonds that Alexandre had given him; now, in a stentorian voice, he declared that others had done the same, and that the public prosecutors who had spared the Foncière were persecuting him instead.[21]

"There are two reports by the head of the financial section," interjected the general's lawyer in an allusion to Albert Prince and the Foncière, "and he refused to prosecute." Next to his younger, more abrasive colleague Legrand, Maître Maurice Ribet, with his elegance, moderation, and hair as white as a wig, shone for his moderation.

"Let us not shift subjects!" implored Barnaud.

"Nor responsibilities!" rejoined Maître Pierre Loewel, whose literary pastimes and drama criticism now led to his defending the journalist Dubarry.

"Now the trial begins!" added Dubarry's other defender, Maître Dominique.[22]

The lawyers' trial had indeed begun. A motley crew physically as well as spiritually, they nevertheless pursued in soldierly unison their strategy, and sought to turn the jurors against the magistrates, the people against the government. Once again, as during the Prince affair, justice drew fire from all sides, and concentrated within itself the passions of the affair; but no one went so far as to blame the Chamber and its friends for enslaving justice.

Young inspector Cousin, deferential yet firm, and volcanic old superintendent Pachot, were called to the witnesses' stand by the defense. For hours the magistrates withstood the two police officers' vocal recollections of a pursuit cut short in the palace by the hesitations of Albert Prince and his colleagues.[23]

They also called Georges Thomé, the former director of the Sûreté Générale, whose good faith and charming inadequacy had already delighted the press. He took the stand, elegant, cultivated, and lost. His career was over, a casualty of a disabled Sûreté. The derelictions were not of his making, he said.

"Who protected Stavisky?" Maître Freyssenge asked.

"Not I," he replied.

"Say who protected him," persisted Freyssenge.

"You tell me that it's not your fault," added Maître Legrand. "I agree with you, it's not your fault. But in that case, why was Stavisky protected, and who protected him?"

"Who are the lightning rods?" asked Freyssenge.

"How can I answer a question like that?" protested Thomé.[24]

More sinister police took the stand too, as useful as their honorable or amiably incompetent colleagues. Inspector Bonny walked painfully to the bar in overcoat and muffler, jaundiced and feeble, his jet-black hair flecked with gray. Three months earlier, he had left the same courtroom with a suspended sentence for unrelated acts of corruption. Behind him trailed his unorthodox antics in interrogating Arlette, searching for the check stubs, and arresting the Marseillais gangsters. Everything about him was dark and indecipherable, save his bitterness of spirit. Like Inspector Bayard, who had hired Stavisky as an informer, Bonny epitomized the gutter police, but like his mirror images Pachot and Cousin, he served to deflect attention and blame from the accused onto the administration and its agents. His two shining colleagues cast justice in a bad light, while he held out its evil arm.[25]

The lawyers meant to absolve their clients in the dock by damning their counterparts on the bench, and reached an acme of audacity during their defense of Joseph Garat.

No longer president of the crédit municipal of Bayonne but still a deputy, Garat declaimed where Digoin, his employee, had mumbled; he rambled compulsively where the other had shrunk from speech and its strategies. He appeared diminished in all but his native bombast, physically ruined by twenty-two months in the murderers' wing of the Villa Chagrin but temperamentally still as game and gruff as ever. He stood shakily in the back row in a suit now too large for him and rested one hand on his cane. "They won't get me!" he had said to the guard by his side, and for four days he harangued with a wounded and hunted look the crowded courtroom before him.

Had he known the past of Serge Alexandre? Of course not. And the fraud in Bayonne? It was Tissier's doing—presidents did not draw up bonds. The administration of the Republic—the ministers who approved, the prefects who oversaw, the officials who inspected the crédits municipaux—and not the son of Gascony had failed the country. How could mayors promote the public good, bring lasting benefit to their communes, when anarchy reigned in the nation's administration? The deputy and mayor pretended to avenge the elected representatives of the people, and, by extension, the people themselves.[26]

On the third day of Garat's hearing, they came to his brief encounter with Darius of *Bec et Ongles* at the end of 1932. Darius had threatened, Garat had sued for defamation, Darius had retracted. And Dubarry had lent his good offices to the peace settlement. Now all three joined company in infamy. The episode proved my good faith, Garat insisted. Or your guilty knowledge, suggested Barnaud. Once Darius fell silent, you lost all interest in his accusations. It was up to the prosecutor's office to prosecute, retorted Garat, its failure to act was not my fault. "Someone will have to find out whose shoulders bear the blame."

"Think carefully about what you just said, M. Garat," warned Barnaud.

The lawyers leaped to their feet and flapped their black sleeves. "We will all think about it," said Maître Ribet. "And many of us will pursue it," added Maître Freyssenge. Why had the prosecutor's office abandoned its pursuit of Darius? Why had it tamely followed the plaintiff? The lawyers demanded a reply.

"I don't answer interrogations," said Prosecutor General Fernand-Roux on Barnaud's right. The mustaches and ermine of the advocates general stirred at his sides.

"It's easier that way," retorted Maître Ribet.

"The prosecutor general has not yet crossed over to that side," Barnaud interrupted, pointing toward the benches of the accused.

"It's the prosecution of the prosecution," said Maître Freyssenge simply.

Almost every day, the scene repeated itself. Lawyers rose to their feet to point at the magistrates on the dais and shout insolent questions. "Please, gentlemen," Barnaud would say, "sit down, and believe me, my job is tiring!"[27]

He looked for guilt, the lawyers for negligence. The men in black reproached the men in red for their past incuriosity about Stavisky, they in turn reproached the accused for the same, and the trial unwound like a double helix, its twin strands circling and spiraling as the days and weeks went by.

The clamor, the spectacle of courtroom strife, told a story larger than Stavisky's own. The magistrates in their royal colors, potently emblematic of an ancient state and its administration, confronted a motley assortment of lawyers, journalists, and deputies, members of a younger, more liberal order symbolized by its Parliament. Each side reproached the other for its failings. Eighty years earlier, Tocqueville had gloomily concluded that administration and Parliament in France would never learn to live together; sixty years earlier, the founders of the Third Republic, crafters of an enduring compromise, had hoped otherwise. Their settlement had held; but now and again its fissures and ambiguities invited the likes of a Stavisky, who exploited the ambitions of the younger side and the reticences of the older, and divulged in his ruin the reciprocity of their resentment.[28]

The Confusions

Yet the trial slowly undid the very antagonism between old state and new society that the lawyers sought to exploit. More often than not complicity rather than rivalry came to light, blurring and even inverting roles, and revealing a heterodoxy at the heart of this, as of every, scandal.

"When you're out in the open," Barnaud advised Constantin, the official from Commerce who had shown such indulgence toward the gentlemen from Bayonne, "and you meet people who boast of their connections, kindly beware: those who have them don't boast of them."

What was wrong with lunching with Constantin? Garat asked testily.

"Come on, Gentlemen! Please." Presiding Judge Barnaud objected. "And let's put a stop to these stories of lunches!"[29]

But M. Alexandre had entertained Constantin at Drouant, and Garat had toasted him in Bayonne: these stories of lunches seemed to symbolize the fellowship of financier, deputy, and civil servant.

"One of the great culprits of the Stavisky affair is camaraderie," one of the lawyers remarked, "camaraderie as de Jouvenel described it in his 'Republic of the Pals.' "

In 1914 Robert de Jouvenel had portrayed, with a pen only barely satirical, the balance of expectation, reticence, and reward that regulated the higher friendships of French republican society, the ties that united deputies, ministers, magistrates, senior civil servants, and journalists in a tacit pact of mutual assistance. "Few big scandals and many small ones, little corruption and much indulgence," as he had put it, marked the triumphant regime; eclipsed by its finest achievements, in peace and then war, such accommodations now emerged like a nemesis in Stavisky's wake.[30]

The regime of favors and recommendations, declared Albert Dalimier on the witness stand, had allowed Stavisky's impunity. The former minister of labor had signed the precious circular recommending the Bayonne bonds. Relieved not to be speaking from the box of the accused, he nevertheless appeared spiritless and weary. Dubarry had asked the favor of him and he had signed absently, one letter among thousands. Inevitably, the talk turned to the role of favors in the Republic of the Pals, and Dalimier showed some signs of life.

"It's the plague of the regime," he said. "It's a custom threatening to undo the magistrates themselves. We have to end this system."

"You've just heard, Gentlemen of the jury," interjected Cohen's defender, Maître de Poorter, "we're nearing the true guilty parties in the Stavisky affair. It's not the cupidity of the magistrates, for whom we have the greatest respect."

"One wouldn't think so," broke in Judge Barnaud.

"It's something more serious linked to the regime."

Barnaud found the remark intolerable and said so. De Poorter had come close to impugning the parliamentary regime itself. But Barnaud himself had enjoyed the patronage of senators and ministers—including that of Gaston Doumergue—early in his career. Such practices exemplified a form of collusion between legislative and executive, ever condemned, ever renewed.[31]

Later, Maître Appleton expanded on the theme. As one of the lawyers for the plaintiffs—the social insurance funds, cooperatives, and insurance companies that had taken the Bayonne bonds—he sided with the public prosecution against the defense. "Why all this negligence, why all this weakness?" he asked, and immediately answered, "because we're living under the confusion of powers." Deputies hobbled the administration while ministers came and went, leaving behind forlorn civil servants, once guarantors of standards and continuity, now helpless hosts to daily intruders. How could a prefect act when he risked displeasing a powerful deputy, how could a magistrate investigate when he could not rid himself of a politician disguised as a lawyer? "Without a firm executive power," he concluded, "free of parliamentary influence, how do you expect to protect the savings of the public, which we here represent?"

At such moments, Stavisky became at most the agent of revelation, the bearer of scandal. Likewise, the collusions he had courted in the press exposed the hollowness of its liberty and the source of its power. Appleton also decried the blackmail press. So, disingenuously, did Paul Lévy of *Aux Ecoutes*. But Darius described it affectionately; he celebrated with undisguised delight his livelihood as well as his mission. The editor of *Bec et Ongles* stood at the bar, a mulatto in bow tie and double-breasted suit, and revealed gaily that hundreds of deputies and senators subsidized his paper. His patrons were everywhere. Even as he had languished in La Santé prison, the Ministry of Agriculture had kept its promise and distributed decorations—the Mérite Agricole—to his friends, the friends of *Bec et Ongles*. The pungent vapors of camaraderie pervaded the courtroom.[32]

Nemesis: Darius, editor of *Bec et Ongles,* on trial, November 1935. (Photo courtesy of Bibliothèque Nationale de France.)

"Exactly, all my political friends," Bonnaure the deputy acknowledged regarding the barber, father-in-law, and secretary's husband whom he had placed with Stavisky's money on the board of SAPIENS. With the financier's money, the deputy had concluded alliances as promiscuous as those of the journalist. But why the reproach? Stavisky's payees, he insisted, would have filled the recently demolished Trocadéro palace and more. Laughter erupted once again.[33]

More somberly, to a hushed and deferential courtroom, Camille Chautemps said almost the same thing. The former premier came to the bar a week before Christmas, and spoke eloquently, without notes, as he had in the Chamber almost two years before when his government's fate hung in the balance. More even than a decrepit and archaic administration, the indulgence of postwar France was to blame for Sacha Stavisky's protracted immunity from prosecution. Chautemps mentioned the press; he mentioned finance and "ignoble money"; he mentioned the loose morals of postwar France, the pervasive greed that allowed even the most honorable of men to dine with scoundrels.[34]

Before he left the stand, Chautemps put in a word for Albert Dubarry. The editor had told him of Serge Alexandre's acquisition of *La Volonté*, and now the premier defended the good faith of his fellow Radical from the press. "Never in the last two years have I been so moved," Dubarry said tearfully to his lawyers. Other witnesses of note had done as much for Dubarry. As Prefect of Police Chiappe had left the courtroom, he had given him a friendly and encouraging tap on the hand. Joseph Caillaux came out of retirement, monocled, bald, and aloof, to declare Dubarry incapable of swindle. Years earlier, Dubarry had taken up in his columns the cause of the once-powerful Radical minister, who resided then, accused of treason, in La Santé prison. Now, with their fortunes reversed, the ties still bound.[35]

Was this what Chautemps meant? Caillaux had often been reckless in his choice of friends, which had included journalists more disreputable even than Dubarry. Indiscriminate fraternizing had dishonored the country's elites, Chautemps had told the court, providing by his own kindness to Dubarry a manifest case of the ailment.

Public identities faded; deputies and senators doubled as lawyers; ministers deferred to reporters; generals, ambassadors, and prefects left high office only to enter the shabbiest of private enterprises. Even institutions at times looked curiously hybrid, especially the Republic's crédits municipaux, entrusted with a public mission but operating at times like private enterprises. And in this very courtroom the bar exchanged roles with the public prosecutor's office: the lawyers accused and the magistrates defended, a parting reminder of the confusion of administration with representation, and of authority with interest, that had borne fruit in the Stavisky affair. Even as state and society vied in the courtroom, their traffic with each other came to light. Such an inversion sinned against the commonwealth as provocatively as the immemorial role betrayals of heresy, treason, or sexual deviance. It had become the modern form of scandal, the expression of a republican culture that forbade what it could not prevent.

Demagogy

A crowd turned out for Arlette. Women predominated, in hats that shook with Roman *bersaglieri* feathers and African ostrich plumes. Their finery contrasted with Arlette's own modest dress. And they were disappointed; she said so little.

Already the public that had braved the wind and rain had begun to dissolve. Few faithful remained at the back of the court, other than the woman with the green corsage, who still arrived first every morning, and a jovial, aged mulatto soon known as "Darius's grandfather." Monotony had set in, unrelieved by even a single sensational revelation. Was this what they had come to hear? No scandalous exposé greeted them, only quibbles over evidence and a lengthening litany of administrative reproaches.

"The Stavisky trial?" a reporter mused, as crestfallen as his readers. "No, there's no longer any Stavisky trial." They had hoped for a denouement to the affair and had been treated instead to its dissolution. What, then, was it all about? And, wondered the reporter, would this tedious trial end by Christmas?[36]

The prosecution called in accountants and jewelers, whose pedantic dissections and demonstrations drove other reporters in the courtroom to distraction. "Monotonous, without any high points," one of them had complained only four days into the depositions. "There are only about 240 others, which promises us much pleasure."[37]

On the dais, the prosecutors began now and then to attend to their routine correspondence. The jurors resented their lengthening confinement, and finally threatened to strike unless their allowances were raised from twelve to fifty francs a day. Hayotte and Romagnino took to passing out lozenges among the accused in the dock. On the floor, artists sketched, photographers set off flashbulbs, and reporters with leather portfolios vied to extract drama from the longest trial in modern memory. Ennui crept over the courtroom.[38]

Sometimes the orators played to the gallery, to the public at the back, and to the streets beyond.

"But all this is normal," said the enfant terrible of the trial, Maître Legrand. "Cases are put off? That's normal. Lawyers don't defend in court? They pay visits and work out arrangements? That's very normal." Laughter and applause were rising in the court. "The police don't arrest? That's normal. Inspectors don't inspect? That's very normal. Reports are buried? That's normal." And they, the humble French citizens, bore the cost. "We turn to the state and the state tells us: 'Why, your pockets are empty, taxpaying citizens, but that's altogether normal!' " The crowd approved.[39]

What ailed France? The foreigner? Now and again, the Stavisky scandal had provoked outbursts of xenophobia mixed with antisemitism, notably on the far right and in the columns of *Action Française* and *Je Suis Partout*. Such phobias, fed by immigration, diplomatic impotence, and economic stagnation, expressed a free-floating fear of decadence. Now they surfaced intermittently amid the clamor and quibbles of the trial.

De Chevert stood at the bar in monocle and bow tie, a music hall traitor. Of Stavisky, the man he had betrayed in Orléans, he had much to say. "This naturalized citizen, who became French, came to us from some static horde between the Urals and the Volga. He had smooth black hair and a glowing complexion. When tired, his eyes dimmed. He was Asiatic, barely Judaized."[40]

Fifty years earlier, antisemites, led by Edouard Drumont, had accused Jews of bringing down the Catholic and therefore French Union Générale bank. Three Jewish financiers of Panama—Arton, Herz, and Reinach—had come to epitomize the cosmopolitan and the predatory; Cornelius Herz, especially, had seemed to foreshadow a new and rootless seeker of influence, plying the waters of press, Parliament, and finance. By the Belle Epoque the stereotype had entered the courtroom. In 1909 Lemoine, an elegant swindler and forger of diamonds, stood trial in the tenth correctional chamber. "He has a bizarre accent," a court chronicler wrote of Lemoine, in an oddly premonitory description, "at once Russian and Italian, with odd intonations. He seems to belong to unknown Oriental lands, and to have come to Paris one knows not whence to do one knows not what. He bears the aura of strangers coming from indefinable nations."[41]

When Paul Maze, president of the association of crédits municipaux, took the stand in the criminal court, he sounded the theme again, picking up where de Chevert had left off. He spoke of the day Stavisky had called on him. "He conveyed the impression of a foreign financier," he recalled, "rather than a man likely to be involved with crédits municipaux, public French establishments."[42]

But the demon was gone, and reports of Stavisky's collusion with English or German intelligence services, or with faceless international conspirators, had soon vanished along with him. A reporter in the court thought that Desbrosses, the treasurer in Orléans, looked Chinese. Otherwise, few tilted at the specter of the alien within or took up a crusade dear to the far right but of little use to the defense.[43]

An echo of the far left sounded late in the trial. "These scandals stem not from administrative, governmental, or constitutional structure," Maître Alexandre Zévaès argued. "They are rooted in a social and economic milieu where royalty goes to the primacy of money." The bearded old socialist, who had nevertheless defended the assassin of Jean Jaurès in this courtroom, delivered a summation mixing revolutionary aspiration, historical allusion, and institutional insolence. He attacked speculation, capitalism, corruption; he recalled the lost millions of Panama, the scandal of his youth; and he held out the defendants to the jurors as the victims of a vast and impersonal capitalist order.[44]

But demagogy generally preferred the streets; outside the palace, the passions set off by the affair had long drowned out its arcane particulars.

The right-wing leagues agitated, and the Chamber voted to dissolve them; the government decreed economic austerity, and the Popular Front demanded social justice; the left denounced fascism, and the right condemned warmongers. The climate of civil war deepened.

On the day Arlette stood before the criminal court, Giraudoux's *The Trojan War Will Not Take Place* opened at the Théâtre de l'Athénée with Louis Jouvet as Hector. The play warned of war and of the blind, fanatical, or vain leaders who would start one, and it drew the same applause as Coriolanus's assault on demagogy on the stage of the Comédie Française at the height of the Stavisky affair almost two years earlier.[45]

In between, Edouard Bourdet's *Difficult Times* had opened at the Théâtre de la Michodière, in the very building that also housed Dubarry's *La Volonté*. The play excoriated the bourgeoisie and the political class, to the delight of critics who saw it as a comment on the times. "Already, pressing events," wrote Jacques Copeau in *Les Nouvelles Littéraires*, "leave little room for the fictions of the theater."[46]

France first, said the far right; class struggle, said the far left; contain the powers, said the Radical center; and, in the courtroom, yesterday's scandal played on.

Virtue

A moralistic note sounded in the prosecutors' summations, as though a republican conscience had to fill the void left by the courtroom's absent crucifix. In convicting the insurer Guébin, they claimed, the jurors would warn the business community against the temptations of fat commissions. In convicting the lawyers Gaulier and Guiboud-Ribaud, they would condemn the unworthiness of their professional attitude as well as the source of their honoraria. And as for Deputy Garat, Fernand-Roux, who, when indignant, flushed to a red deeper than his robes, could scarcely contain himself.

"M. Garat," he told the furious deputy from Bayonne, "I will tell the gentlemen of the jury what I think of you, and I will tell them that I have in front of me a guilty man, a guilty man, whose punishment I will call for."

"Then call for that of the magistracy!" retorted Garat.

Fernand-Roux had already defended his office. He quoted another magistrate, Montesquieu: "Republics live and flourish only through virtue."[47] But the *président à mortier* of the Parliament of Bordeaux might not have acknowledged his descendants in the prosecutor's office; nor, perhaps, would the author of *De l'esprit des lois* have recognized his fruit in this Republic. Like the first and second Republics, the third departed drastically in practice from Montesquieu's ideal of equilibrium between institutional powers, and perhaps also from his conception of a Republic, more moral than political, and in any case unlikely, he thought, to take hold in a nation the size of France. In quoting him, Fernand-Roux raised the question that had haunted the trial since its opening day: why the gap between the moral ideal and the political reality of the Republic of the day?[48]

The confusion of castes, revealed by the scandal and recalled in the trial, had awakened an old idea, absolutist and then revolutionary, that attributed every national misfortune to the corruption of general by particular interests. Belief had it that the elites had forgotten their mission and interlaced their functions because they had lost their way in a forest of private motives. With them went the higher good, source and object of ethical behavior. But what defined the higher good? Social justice? National greatness? In the streets, the collective ideals left the scandal behind, and provided a measure of the tenacity and the folly of the hope that any set of institutions could ensure the reign of virtue in human society.

▦

A thick fog enveloped the Palace of Justice, and rain continued to fall against the windows of the criminal courtroom. The Seine had flooded its banks and engulfed the quais. Crates of liqueurs floated away from the Halle aux Vins by the Pont de Bercy, the Zouave under the Alma bridge turned amphibious, and curious onlookers watched from the bridges as a few remaining barges attempted to negotiate the course of the swollen river.[49]

Once before, in 1910, the floodwaters had driven jurors, magistrates, and defendants from the recently added criminal court into the inner sanctuary of the ancient palace. Had the Seine continued to rise in the rainy winter of 1936, it might have put an end for the season to judicial oratory in the capital's most public court. But the trial was almost over.[50]

On 15 January 1936, workers wearing caps emblazoned with the arms of the city brought beds into the deliberation room behind the court. The next morning, the jurors moved in. At midday, they requested lunch from the palace restaurant. Word of dissension over the menu leaked out and gave rise to alarming rumors of a hung jury. Aperitifs arrived, followed by herring, a leg of lamb, salad, cheese, dessert, and assorted bottles of Beaujolais. In the afternoon, they sat down at a large round table and began their deliberations.

In the palace the accused had nothing more to do. Following custom, those still jailed awaited the verdict in the Conciergerie — Cohen played card tricks, and Garat sat sullenly in a corner. In the courtroom, the others, provisionally at liberty, chatted freely among themselves. Arlette asked Moro-Giafferi if she might go home now. "But don't think of it, my child," he answered, "you're still accused."

The next morning, the jurors came in, unshaven and deprived of sleep. They had reached a verdict in the small hours. "Guilty," answered their designated spokesman, a pharmacist from Boulevard Voltaire, for nine of the accused. The lawyers paled. Later in the day, the jurors returned to pronounce sentences. In the pervasive fog, the courtroom's lights shone dimly.

Tissier reaped seven years' hard labor for his pains at Bayonne, Hayotte seven years' confinement for his culpable loyalties. Tissier broke down and Hayotte begged for mercy. Three of the others were sentenced to five years' confinement for their services to Stavisky — Cohen the plucky little appraiser, who contained himself, while his wife began swearing loudly among the public at the back, Desbrosses the old accountant, who appeared lost in an indecipherable reverie, and the insurer Guébin, a groaning wreck, who exclaimed hoarsely, "All that's left is for me to kill myself."

259

The jurors, unmoved by weeks of eloquence, had resolved to make an example of the artisans and journeymen of the swindle, the crafters of its success. The appeals to sympathy for the weak and resentment at the strong had fallen on deaf ears. The jurors' presence alone, symbolic of popular sovereignty, had invited such tirades. Yet now they sensibly placed the penal above the political, and by their modest votes vindicated the prominence of the urn that crowned Justice on the stone steps to the criminal court.

The papers reported and quickly forgot the verdict, as though the crime, once stripped of the crisis, had lost its meaning as well. Rumors of injustice persisted, the afterlife of scandal. "It's a political affair, you understand," one of the jurors' wives told a reporter the next day, "so I understand nothing of it. Ah! If they had judged a crime . . ." Her husband and his eleven fellows had so judged. But it did not matter.

Three of the remaining guilty escaped with two years each. Hattot, the corpulent, unemployed actor who had posed so obligingly as the emerald emissary from distant lands, turned pale and rested his great head on his cane. General Bardi de Fourtou, paying more for his former rank than for his recent misdeeds, made a bitter sign to the crowd as if to say, "I told you so," and buried his head in his hands. Garat gave the jurors a long black look. They had absolved him of any criminal complicity in the swindle at the crédit municipal of Bayonne, but convicted him of falsifying the minutes there when, in the panic-filled autumn of 1933, he had discovered the truth. His anxiety had lost what his incuriosity had saved. He did not see matters that way. "Me, a forger! It's an infamy!" On the way out he hurled a chair through the door. But he had already served his time in provisional detention, and left the court a free man. So too did the other deputy, Bonnaure. The jurors sent him away with a suspended sentence of one year. His fees, unlike those of the other lawyers Gaulier and Guiboud-Ribaud, had been too fat for the popular judges to ignore. And he was a deputy, their presumed paragon of civic virtue. "They had kept the psychosis of two years ago," he said of them the next day. "They tried to get at Parliament through the Parliamentarians." For him as well, the trial was political.

The eleven others, the acquitted, came down the steps from the courtroom into the great vestibule. The four journalists and two lawyers among them had spent much of the past two years discerning a political plot behind their plight. They did not now thank popular justice for their deliverance. A correctional court, unfettered by a jury, might have convicted them on logical grounds alone. Were their takings less tainted than those of Bonnaure, or of Garat, who had not enriched himself at all? The jurors thought so. They expressed the wish that the guilty in government be pursued and tried. Professional liberties, they appeared to affirm, differed from those of deputy or general, even when exercised in the same sphere, and they did not see why Darius, for instance, should suffer for profiting from his échos when other editors, including Pécune of D'Artagnan, had not. In the open courtroom that tempered legal code with social context, the jurors, obliquely but consistently, had expressed society's reluctance to condemn itself.

The editors left the palace. Darius smiled; Aymard was jubilant, Lévy tight-lipped. Dubarry, looking happy and healthy, announced that for the rest of his days he would devote his pen to defending the sacred cause of liberty.

The others parted ways, out past Prudence, Justice, and the allegorical figures in between. Several of the acquitted, held until now in La Santé prison, returned there to retrieve their belongings. Digoin emerged from its gates in a black frock coat, high collar, and bow tie, a modest retired police official. Farault, the appraiser from Orléans, disappeared at once into a green taxi. Lucky Romagnino, in a shiny blue suit, pulled down the window of his own taxi and began declaiming King Lear's attack on sheltered, hypocritical officialdom.

Through tattered clothes small vices do appear
Robes and furred gowns hide all.

Even the magnanimity of the court could not discourage his parting shot at the magistracy.

At the Palace of Justice, Arlette, dressed in black, made her way through the vestibule and left. "She bears his name, she was his wife," her lawyer Moro-Giafferi had told the jurors. "That's her crime, there's no other." She walked away past a crowded newsstand and prepared to leave a few days later, under her maiden name of Arlette Simon, for Le Havre, on the steamship *Ile de France,* and a new life in the United States. It was still raining. The affair was over.[51]

EPILOGUE

Many years later, when Arlette returned permanently to France, her son, Claude, was earning a living as a professional magician, and François Mitterrand was approaching the second, scandal-plagued term of his presidency. It was 1988, and she was eighty-five years old.

"Understand that my husband alone was more intelligent than all the journalists of the world put together," she told a reporter for *France-Soir*, and withdrew once again into her silence.

In 1936 she had not stayed long in the United States. A music hall impresario had hired her, and so had a fashion designer, but by October she was back in Paris. She sold her jewels and her furs, designed dresses without a license, and paid the rent with some trouble. For a while, during the difficult years of the Occupation, she moved in with Darius. After the liberation, she married a U.S. officer and lived comfortably with him in Puerto Rico.

One night in 1960 she reappeared, at the Triumph Circus near Bordeaux. She had come to watch her son perform as "Prince Frankestas" the magician. Claude had spent most of his life since 1934 in and out of mental asylums, expelled from the Claridge and the giddy years of his early childhood. His occasional circus employers had tried to market the name that his mother no longer used, but its infamy could not compensate for his ineptitude. He rarely lasted long. Police once arrested him for vagrancy. He had eight francs in his pocket.

"Stavisky," a call from the past, had sounded often enough over the years to ensure an unhappy kind of recognition for Claude. A few more trials—of Senators Puis and Renoult, who were both acquitted of influence peddling—and a few more cries from defrauded insurance companies had kept the name before the public of the1930s. The futile investigation into the death of Albert Prince dragged on, intermittently troubling the country's collective memory. In 1937 it was called off, and for a while no more was heard of the affair that had once threatened the regime.

Then, during the Occupation, fanatics tried to link it to all they reviled in the late Republic: the deputies, the Jews, the decadence. To some extent they succeeded. In March 1942, as Vichy placed the former leaders of the country on trial at Riom, a play about the affair, "The Pirates of Paris," opened at the Ambigu theater. "A Jew from the ghetto!" *Le Petit Parisien* recalled. "This great corrupter could have become a minister! The regime allowed that!" And *Je Suis Partout*, even more zealously, reminded its readers that "the gigantic swindle of the Jew Stavisky is a critical chapter in the Jewish corruption from which our unhappy nation nearly died and by which she remains wounded and gasping." Eight years earlier, few papers had bothered to point out that Stavisky was Jewish. Most had called him a naturalized Russian immigrant. Now, after the Popular Front, the defeat, and the miseries of the Occupation, the free-floating xenophobia had crystallized into a doctrinaire antisemitism, preached by the regime and parroted by the press.

Thirty years later, Alain Resnais's period piece about the affair resurrected it again, in cinemas. This time, a stern left-wing ethos pervaded the story, indicting the evils of capitalism even while seducing the public with the fetching, hypnotic luxuries of interwar France. Bizarrely, Resnais used Leon Trotsky's presence in France in 1934 to suggest some sort of alternative society, suffusing the film with the delusions of May 1968. *Stavisky* returned, inevitably, on television screens every few years, and conferred on the affair its final role as one more coffee table book about the past, *la petite histoire.*

In retrospect, however, the Stavisky scandal had been the last and the loudest of its kind. A miscarriage of justice provoked a crisis in the regime: here, writ large, was the script of most of the scandals of the Third Republic. An unscrupulous financier had for a while played on the languor of the justice system, only to learn at the end that even his impunity had its limits. Boulaine, Rochette, Hanau, and Oustric had fared no differently. But neither journalists nor deputies suffered the imperfections of justice gladly, and all happily hectored the courts during occasional treason trials and frequent faits divers. Finally, much against his will, Sacha Stavisky ignited an explosion that briefly engulfed the entire system of government. His affair had inverted Captain Dreyfus's, substituting a guilty man gone free for an innocent one sent to Devil's Island, civilian for military justice, and a defensive for a missionary Republic. But each expressed the conflict between ideals and realities that had plagued France since the Revolution, and that in this regime accounted for the frequency of scandal.

The problem might arise whenever the dignitaries of state and society appeared to exchange roles. Prefects, generals, and ambassadors presided in corporate boardrooms; lawyers, financiers, and journalists traveled the corridors of government. Such modern role reversals scandalized as mightily as heresy or apostasy in a bygone age. They set off fantasies of subversion and subterfuge, a vision of the public interest secretly enslaved—to capital, to the foreigner, to the Jew, to some malevolent force depriving society of its servant, the state. Usually, the feverish gaze came to rest on the administration of justice.

This was surprising: the Third Republic faced problems far more daunting than the timidity of its courts. Even in 1934, their inadequacies preoccupied minds as powerfully as economic stagnation or diplomatic impotence. The symbolic and ancient manifestation of sovereignty, even more than the real aftereffects of the recent war, awakened competing visions of the collective ideal, at one only in their hostility to the pretensions of particular interests. But this Republic had given free rein to such interests, celebrated them in its press and its Parliament, and even in its most distinctive court, the criminal court, which had brought abstract law face to face with reality, circumstance, the public, and the jury, it had combined code with equity. Only the tenacity of the collective ideal could sustain the indignation that even minor violence to the justice system aroused, and explain the incidence of scandal in a Republic hardly more corrupt than previous regimes in its own country, and drastically less so than most contemporary ones elsewhere.

The Stavisky affair was the last scandal over justice to threaten the regime, the last to insist so intransigently that the reality of the Republic conform to its ideal. So pressing was the exigency of virtue, so shrill the cries of selfish society for selfless government, that holier-than-thou competitors for power lost all respect for one another. Consensus, so elusive throughout the nineteenth century, unraveled again, revealing three rivals for the country's future. The first rejected the Republic in favor of a bleak and archaic uniformity. The second defended the representative regime as the vehicle of social justice. The third called for an executive regime, a republican monarchy of sorts, to guide the destinies of the nation. The first had its day in 1940, the second most durably in 1946, and the third in 1958 and 1962. Each proposed its own prescription for the common good, but acceded to power only thanks to the hazards of war, foreign or colonial.

After Stavisky, no miscarriage or misapplication of justice threatened the stability of the country's institutions. Occasions did not want; justice, no more emancipated than before, merely exchanged masters under each new regime, and submitted tamely to the de facto authority of Vichy, the legislature of the Fourth Republic, and the executive of the Fifth. André Bruzin, the magistrate at the Paris prosecutor's office who had questioned Stavisky's Foncière in 1931 and given up, also resisted serving at the Riom trial in 1942—and again gave up. He drafted the indictment against Daladier and his fellow accused, and Cassagnau, one of the two advocates general who had helped prosecute Stavisky's accomplices, signed it. The founders of the Fourth Republic envisaged an independent magistracy, eventually free from any governmental interference, but the deputies shrank from the prospect, and the Fifth Republic removed it altogether. "The magistrates of the prosecutor's office," declared article 5 of the organic law of 22 December 1958, "are placed under the authority and oversight of their hierarchical superiors and under the authority of the minister of justice." Forty years later, timid attempts at reform had yet to bear much fruit.

The attendant abuses, commensurate to the growth of government and its means, dwarfed those of Stavisky's day, yet provoked none of the same anger. Investigations into political murder, electoral finance, insider trading, personal corruption, and every imaginable misuse of power seemed now and again to wither on the vine, as though justice had quietly expired. Such untimely demises seemed oddly to coincide with the imminence of a presidential reelection campaign. What had happened, just before de Gaulle's campaign of 1965, to the investigation into the disappearance of Ben Barka? Or, before Giscard d'Estaing's of 1981, that into the death of the Prince de Broglie? Or, before Mitterrand's of 1988, that into the 80 million francs that had vanished from the Carrefour du Développement, the agency ostensibly set up to promote development in Africa? Stavisky's fleeting impunity had shaken the Third Republic to its foundations. Where now was the political and institutional crisis?

Curious calls for a rediscovery of the Republic issued from politicians and intellectuals, some of them belated converts to a cause once deemed conservative or unfashionable. But they warned more of Europe or the United States, cultural pluralism or the tyranny of the free market, than of "the affairs" and the corruption of public interests by private. More often than not, the latter-day republicans encountered hostility or derision, stigmatized as anachronistic or even backward, nationalists in an age of globalization.[1]

Others, usually in positions of power, belittled the magnitude of the problem. "We're living in more moral times than those of the Third Republic," François Mitterrand declared early in January 1992, as investigating magistrates called at the headquarters of the Socialist Party to probe the intricacies of its electoral finance.[2] The France of his presidency, he seemed improbably to believe, was stricter than the France of his youth, intolerant now of practices it would have condoned then. A fond fallacy, typical of a time of moralistic words and amoral deeds: secret and systemic flows of money now generously bathed the politics of the Fifth Republic, dwarfing the touching exchanges of the Third and unmasking intermediaries more artful and determined than any in Stavisky's day. They revealed role reversals between state and society as disconcerting as ever: at times, government itself was privatized. Yet they provoked no reaction as violent, no prescriptions as drastic, save a renewed insistence that justice root out abuses and control rather than serve the other branches of government. More dispassionate than indifferent, the measured response itself calls for an answer: has the state lost its sanctity and the collective ideal given way to the personal?

ABBREVIATIONS

ADCdo	Archives départementales de la Côte d'Or
ADP	Archives de Paris
AMJ	Archives du Ministère de la Justice
AN	Archives Nationales
AN MI	Archives de l'Intérieur (Fonds Panthéon)
APP	Archives de la Préfecture de Police
Ars. Ro.	Bibliothèque de l'Arsenal (Fonds Rondel)
CAC	Centre d'Archives Contemporaines (Fontainebleau)
CC	Commissaire central
CD	Commissaire divisionnaire
CE	Commission d'enquête chargée de rechercher toutes les responsabilités politiques ou administratives encourues depuis l'origine des affaires Stavisky
CE (6 February)	Commission d'enquête sur les origines des évènements survenus le six février 1934
CGRJ	Contrôleur Général des Recherches Judiciaires
Comm.	Commissaire de police
Comm. sp.	Commissaire spécial
Gds	Garde des Sceaux (minister of justice)
Insp.	Inspecteur
Insp. gén.	Inspecteur Général
JI	Juge d'instruction (investigating magistrate)
JO	Journal Officiel
PG	Procureur Général
PJ	Police Judiciaire
PR	Procureur de la République
SG	Sûreté Générale
USNA	United States National Archives

References to interrogations are usually given as follows: archival source (name and title of interrogator/name of suspect or witness, date).

References to the trial, 4 November 1935–17 January 1936, are given as follows: archival source [AN 334AP 68 through 71] (name of accused, witness, lawyer or prosecutor, date).

References to appearances before the parliamentary commission of inquiry are given as follows: CE volume: page number (name of witness, date of appearance).

NOTES

PREFACE

1. See, for example, Serge Berstein, *Le 6 février 1934* (Paris, 1975), and Maurice Chavardès, *Une campagne de presse. La droite française et le 6 février 1934* (Paris, 1970).

2. See, for example, Ralph Schor, *L'Antisémitisme en France pendant les années trente: Prélude à Vichy* (Bruxelles, 1992), and Paula Hyman, *The Jews of Modern France* (Berkeley, 1998).

3. Pierre Nora, "La République," in *Dictionnaire critique de la Révolution française,* ed. François Furet (Paris, 1989), 391. Translations are my own.

CHAPTER 1. A SHADOW IN THE COURTROOM

1. I have relied heavily on the invaluable work of Katherine Fischer Taylor on the architecture of the Palace of Justice: *In the Theater of Criminal Justice: The Palais de Justice in Second Empire Paris* (Princeton, 1993); and "The Palais de Justice of Paris: Modernization, Historical Self-Consciousness, and Their Prehistory in French Institutional Architecture (1835–1869)" (Ph.D. diss., Harvard University, 1989), 7 vols. Cf. also Jacques Charlot, "A la découverte des symboles dans le palais de justice de Paris," *Histoire de la Justice* 8–9 (1995–96): 149–74. To a lesser extent, I have also relied on François Gebelin, *La Sainte-Chapelle et la Conciergerie* (Paris, 1931); Henri Stein, *Le Palais de Justice et la Sainte-Chapelle* (Paris, 1912); René Benjamin, *Le Palais et ses gens de justice* (Paris, 1919); and Léon Werth, *Cour d'assises* (Paris, 1932).

2. For the opening of the trial I have relied on *Paris-Soir,* 2, 3, 4, 5, 6, and 10 November 1935; *Le Matin,* 5, 6, 7, and 21 November 1935; *Le Temps,* 5 November 1935; *Le Populaire,* 6 November 1935; *La Liberté,* 4 January 1936; *Le Petit Parisien,* 5, 6 November 1935 and 17 January 1936; *Action Française,* 5 November 1935; *Le Journal,* 5 November 1935; *Paris-Midi,* 19 October 1935; and AN 334AP 68 (trial transcripts, 4 and 5 November 1935).

3. Marc Martin, *Médias et journalistes de la république* (Paris, 1997), 166–70.

4. Pierre Birnbaum, *Le peuple et les gros. Histoire d'un mythe,* 3d ed. (Paris, 1995); Maurice Barrès, *Leurs figures* (Paris, 1902); Emile Zola, *L'argent* (Paris, 1891); Alain, *Eléments d'une doctrine radicale* (Paris, 1925).

5. Odile Rudelle, *La République absolue, 1870–1899* (Paris, 1986), 30–31, 47; Octave Mirbeau, *Le jardin des supplices* (Paris, 1898); Joris Karl Huysmans, *A rebours* (Paris, 1884); Henry Bataille, *Le scandale* (Paris, 1909), act 4, scene 2; AN BB18 2213 (Comm. de Police Bordeaux to PG, 9 March 1902); Henri Jeanson, *70 ans d'adolescence* (Paris, 1971), 93 (regarding speech of Moro-Giafferi at Bonapartist meeting); "Un baromètre de l'opinion," *Lectures pour Tous,* May 1900; "La Machine parlementaire," *Lectures pour Tous,* November 1901.

6. Marcel Rousselet, *Histoire de la magistrature* (Paris, 1957), 1:325, 389ff.

CHAPTER 2. A QUESTION OF CONFIDENCE

1. ADP 1320W102 (Delgay to SG, 15 September 1934); ADP D2U8417 (Insp. Bonny, 30 December 1933); CE 1:52–53 (Arlette Stavisky, 6 March 1934).

2. ADP 1320W102 (Delgay to SG, 15 September 1934); ADP D2U8429 (*Juge suppléant* [surrogate judge], Bayonne, 4 January 1934); ADP D2U8434 (JI Ordonneau to Arlette Stavisky, 4 December 1934; Arlette Stavisky to Ordonneau, 24 December 1934); *Le Journal*, 28 July 1926.

3. AN 334AP69 (Arlette Stavisky, 22 November 1935); CE 1:52–53 (Arlette Stavisky, 6 March 1934); ADP D2U8428 (Bonny/Niemen, 12 January 1934); ADP D2U8434 (Ordonneau/Poulner, 15 December 1934); ADP 1320W102 (Delgay to SG, 15 September 1934); AN MI 25377/85 (PJ report, 17 May 1926); *Le Journal*, 30 July 1926.

4. AN MI 25377/85 (Henne to Pachot, 1 April 1926).

5. *Le tas, c'est moi*: literally, "I'm the pile," play on "L'Etat, c'est moi"; *allez-graisse*: literally, "go-fat," play on the word *allégresse* (lightheartedness).

6. AN MI 25376 (Sûreté Générale file on Jeanne Bloch, 19 September 1921); AN MI 25377/85 (Henne to Pachot, 1 April 1926); *Aux Ecoutes*, 8 August 1926; Bibliothèque de l'Arsenal, Ars. Ro. 15844, press clippings on Jeanne Bloch, including some erroneously announcing her death in August 1916.

7. AN MI 25376 (SG to Comm. sp., Cannes, 18 February 1932); ADP D2U8417 (Bonny, 30 December 1933); AN MI 25377/85 (Henne to Pachot, 1 April 1926); CE (general report), 42–44; Bibliothèque de l'Arsenal, Ars. Ro. 15736 (Fonds Rondel); Marigny programs.

8. ADP D2U8424 (Max Viterbo, 7 August 1934); ADP D2U8434 (Ordonneau/Poulner, 15 December 1934); ADP D2U8441 (Emilienne Laquèvre, 20 June 1934); *Aux Ecoutes*, 10 December 1934; CE (general report), 50; AN MI 25303/11 (Comm. sp. Beausoleil note of 31 March 1918 in Landau/Goldski dossier); AN MI 25376 (note on opening of Cadet-Roussel, n.d.); APP, B/A 1590 (programs of Cadet-Roussel). Paul Lenglois's *Vie et mort de Stavisky* (Paris, 1934), affirms, without offering any proof, that Stavisky was selling drugs at the bar of the Cadet-Roussel (34ff.).

9. ADP D2U8470 (Tribunal civil de première instance Seine, twelfth chamber, 9 February 1921); CE (general report), 50–51; recollections of inspector Faralicq in *Excelsior*, 9 January 1934.

10. ADP D3U6179 (report of JI, 6 and 28 December 1917; correspondence of JI with the expert Poirier, 2 March 1918, and with Pereaux, 11 May 1918); CE (general report), 48–49.

11. CE (general report), 49–50.

12. ADP D2U8424 (note of 4 April 1934); AN F7 13981 (report on Kossecki, 5 January 1934).

13. AN MI 25377/85 (Henne to Pachot, 1 April 1926); CE (general report), 44–45; ADP D2U8424 (Paulette Luc, 26 September 1934); ADP D2U8470 (Tribunal civil de première instance Seine, twelfth chamber, 9 February 1921); ADP D3U6179 (Pereaux to JI, 11 May 1918).

14. ADP 1320W102 (Delgay to SG, 15 September 1934); ADP D2U8440 (Demay/Arlette Stavisky interrogation, 27 April 1934); *Aux Ecoutes*, 29 August 1926; Eugène Bortchy-Melnikoff, *300.000 kilomètres avec Stavisky* (Paris, 1934), 13; AN MI 25377/85 (1 April 1926). Technically, Stavisky *fils* did not become fully French until after his twenty-first birthday. The CE incorrectly stated that Stavisky attended the Lycée Jeanson-de-Sailly: CE (general report), 40.

15. ADP D2U8 417 (Bonny, 30 December 1933); ADP D2U8417 (Henri Hayotte, 11 and 30 January 1934); ADP D2U8428 (Sevestre et Cousin, 3 February 1933); ADP D2U8428 (Ordonneau/Hayotte, 1 May 1934); ADP D2U8428 (Tribunal civil de première instance Tours, 5 June 1924); ADP D2U8462 (Weitz to PR, 13 March 1934); CE 3:3091 (Camille Chautemps, 22 June 1934) and 3195–96 (Pierre Chautemps, 28 June 1934).

16. ADP D2U8462 (Weitz to PR, 13 March 1934); AN F7 16010/1 (note of 24 July 1924 on James Schenkel of Bradstreet's); AN F7 13978 (report of 28 June 1926, Hanau); AN MI 25372/80 (biographical note on Rochette, 9 December 1926); AN BB18 6745 (note on Oustric, PR to PG, n.d. but 1930; AN 334AP 68 (Hayotte, 6 November 1935).

17. AN MI 25377 (Insp. Clavel, 26 July 1926); AN MI 25377 (notice on Germaine Roy); AN MI 25379/87 (JI Demay/Ferrier, 30 April 1934); MI 25379/87 (JI Demay/Germaine Roy, 20 July 1934); CE 1:211 (Guiboud-Ribaud, 13 March 1934); Bortchy-Melnikoff, *300.000 kilomètres avec Stavisky*, 27.

18. AN 334AP68 (Hayotte, 6 November 1935); ADP D2U8462 (Weitz to PR, 13 March 1934); AN MI 25377 (anonymous letter from Pau to Comm. Peudepièce, 8 March 1934); AN MI 25379/87 (CC, Le Mans, to SG, 1 May 1934); *Le Petit Parisien*, 8 June 1926; AN MI 25377 (Insp. de police mobile Borel to SG, 9 March 1928).

19. ADP D2U8428 (Bonny/Zweifel, 13 January 1934); AN MI 25378 (Insp. Courtois to SG, 21 April 1934); CE 5:4715ff. (Sylvain Zweifel, 19 December 1934).

20. ADP D2U8420 (anonymous note on Zweifel, n.d., c. March 1933); AN MI 25378 (Insp. Courtois to SG, 21 April 1934); CE 5:4715ff. (Sylvain Zweifel, 19 December 1934); CE (general report), 73–82. Before the CE, Zweifel cast himself as an innocent victim.

21. CE 4:3892 (Benda, 24 July 1934); CE (general report), 51–56; AN MI 25376 (report of Xavier Guichard, PJ director, 12 January 1934); AN MI 25381 (Insp. Arrazat/Marcel Heskia, 19 April 1934).

22. AN CAC (SG dossiers returned from Moscow, 940469/376, dossier Poulner, 16/32401); AN MI 25381 (arrest warrant for Poulner, 29 December 1934); ADP 1320W132 (Insp. Delgay to SG, 22 December 1934); ADP 1320W132 (dossier Poulner); ADP D2U8434 (JI Ordonneau/Poulner, 15 December 1934); ADP D2U8417 (report of Insp. Bonny, 30 December 1933); ADP D2U8443 (JI Ordonneau/Himmelfarb, 17 April 1934); CE 5:5043–45 (Prouharam, 23 January 1935).

23. ADP D2U8443 (Ordonneau/Himmelfarb, 17 April 1934); ADP D2U8440 (reports on Cie. générale d'exportation et d'importation, s.a., n.d. but 1924); CE (general report), 57–60.

24. ADP D2U8440; see n. 21; ADP D2U8443 (JI Ordonneau/Himmelfarb, 17 April 1934); ADP D2U8441 (Emilienne Laquèvre, 20 June 1934); CE (general report), 54; ADP D2U8431 (Alex Lafont, 3 March 1934).

25. AN BB182340(1) (PG Paris to Justice, 9 November 1906); AN BB182536 (PG Paris to Justice, 22 May 1914); "Dernières prouesses de MM. les escrocs," *Lectures pour Tous*, June 1906; Pierre Delcourt, *Le vol à Paris* (Paris, 1888); Gilbert Guilleminault and Yvonne Singer-Lecocq, *La France des gogos. Trois siècles de scandales financiers* (Paris, 1975), 138–39.

26. AN F713978 (PJ report on Hanau, 28 June 1926); AN BB18 6732 (report of experts on *Gazette du Franc* for Tribunal de la Seine, 3 July 1929); *Le Journal*, 25 March 1908.

27. AN BB18 2632 (dossier on Banque du Foncier Français, April 1924–January 1931).

28. ADP 1320W32 (PR Seine, indictment of Vachet, 16 March 1936); ADP D2U8440 (Vachet, 27 March 1934); AN MI 25381 (insp. Bouscatel, 10 March 1934); CE 2:1456–80 (Vachet, 27 April 1934).

29. CE (general report), 96–112; CE 5:5190–5202 (Maurice Privat, 6 February 1935); AN MI 25379/87 (JI Hude/Privat, 15 May 1934); AN MI 25381 (Bouscatel, 10 March 1934).

30. CE (general report), 96–112; CE 5:5203–20 (Brouilhet, 13 February 1935); ADP D2U8440 (Brouilhet, 24 March 1934); AN CAC 940434/634 (dossier Brouilhet, 2/53011).

31. See n. 29.

32. CE 5:5228 (Cathelineau, 13 February 1935); see n. 30.

33. CE 5:5208 (Brouilhet, 24 March 1934); CE 2:1464 (Vachet, 27 April 1934); ADP D2U8440 (Vachet, 27 March 1934); ADP D2U8440 (Brouilhet, 24 March 1934).

34. AN MI 25326/34 (police notes in dossier Galmot); Blaise Cendrars, *Rhum* (Paris, 1930).

35. ADP D2U8428 (JI Ordonneau/Hayotte, 1 May 1934); ADP D2U8451 (Delgay to SG, 28 January 1935); CE 5:4716 (Zweifel, 19 December 1934); AN MI 25347 (note on Paul Lévy and *Aux Ecoutes*, 23 February 1926); AN MI 25326/34 (police note, 4 October 1919); AN MI 25339 (police note of 23 June 1922); AN BB18 6733 (dossier Anquetil, July 1929–December 1932).

36. See, for example, Georges Clarétie, "L'Affaire Marix," *Drames et comédies judiciaires. Chronique du Palais, 1909* (Paris, 1910); APP B/A 1254 (police note, 10 February 1911); Arthur Meyer, *Ce que mes yeux ont vu* (Paris, 1911), 230; Jean-Noel Jeanneney, *L'argent caché. Milieux d'affaires et pouvoirs politiques dans la France du XXe siècle* (Paris, 1982).

37. Summary of Stavisky's convictions before 1926 in AN BB18 6767.

38. CE (general report), 42, 52.

39. On Jeanne Bloch's police report, AN MI 25376 (19 September 1921; see n. 5), the following words appear in pencil: "Stavisky indic à Leroy [illegible initials: 'S.G.' for Sûreté Générale?]"; AN MI 25376 (Bayard to SG, 9 November 1923); CE 4:3903–4, 3907 (Benda, 24 July 1934). Bayard denied before the CE that Stavisky, at this date, was his informer (CE 1:533–51, 27 March 1934 and 4: 4265, 9 November 1934), but his behavior in the Valdivia affair, together with Benda's testimony and Bayard's later rapport with Stavisky, discredits the claim; CE (general report), 56–57.

40. Henri Deneux, "La responsabilité civile des notaires comme conseils de leurs clients" (doctoral thesis, Faculté de droit, Université de Paris, Beauvais, 1932), 9–10, 12–14, 22–23, 72–73, and 163–68; Raymond Hermant, *Sous la poussière des panonceaux* (Nice, 1955), 276–80, 295; E. Berton, *Les coulisses du notariat* (Paris, 1904) 9, 53–54; C. Lafitte, *Scandale, misère et cie* (Nogent-le-Rotrou, 1896), 91; AN BB18 2434 (dossier Duez); Robineau left no testimony anywhere, but his clerk did testify before the CE (5:5371, Delaire, 13 March 1935).

41. ADP D2U8447 (correspondence between JI Ordonneau and Gaulier, 25 April, 16 August, 6 September 1934); CE 5:5159 (Gaulier, 1 February 1935); Bortchy-Melnikoff, *300.000 kilomètres avec Stavisky*, 55.

42. Henry Bénazet, *Dix ans chez les avocats* (Paris, 1929), 16–18; Henri-Robert, *L'avocat* (Paris, 1923), preface and 75–77; Jean Appleton, *Traité de la profession d'avocat* (Paris, 1928), 406.

43. CE 1:958 (Glard, 13 April 1934); see n. 40.

44. AN BB18 6767 (Justice note of 13 January 1934 about Stavisky's release from the army); ADP 1320W132 (PR Seine, indictment of Vachet, 16 March 1936); CE 2:1456–80 (Vachet, 27 April 1934). It is not entirely clear from Dr. Vachet's varied testimony whether his observations antedate 1927, but he seems to allude to a long-standing chronic condition. See chap. 5, 71.

45. Louis Gardenat, *Traité pratique des fraudes* (Paris, 1923), 238–40; see AN BB18 6723 (report of PR Seine on legislation covering financial groups).

CHAPTER 3. THE LIBERAL PROFESSIONS

1. CE 5:4719 (Sylvain Zweifel, 19 December 1934); AN MI 25377/85 (Insp. Bayard/Loiseau, 31 July 1926); AN MI 25377/85 (Insps. Peres and Renault to Pachot, 2 April 1926); AN MI 25378 (note of Insp. Delgay, 7 April 1934).

2. ADP D2U8471 (eighth chamber, court of appeal of Paris, 25 April 1928).

3. Ibid.; AN MI 25377 (report of Insp. Clavel, 2 August 1926).

4. CE 1:734, 749–50, 763 (Lescouvé, 10 April 1934); Pachot gave a figure of 8 million francs in 1934, but this seems to include other misappropriations as well. See CE 1:20 (Pachot, 2 March 1934); AN MI 25377/85 (Bayard/Loiseau, 31 July 1926).

5. ADP D2U8420 (anonymous note on Zweifel, n.d., c. March 1933); AN 334AP68 (Ministère public c/M. René Renoult, trial transcript, June 1935); CE 2:1348 (Labbé, 25 April 1934). Grébaud, in his testimony in 1934, thought Zweifel had assumed the name of Martinelli; see CE 5:5078 (Grébaud, 23 January 1935).

6. ADP D2U8422 (suit of Banque Spéciale de Crédit, 1 April 1926); CE 2:1330 (Decante, 25 April 1934); CE 5:5228 (de Cathelineau, 13 February 1935).

7. Georges Petit, *De l'organisation du marché des valeurs mobilières. Bourses de valeurs et agents de change* (Paris, 1955), chap. 2; Olivier Moreau-Néret, directeur du Crédit Lyonnais, quoted in C. Farnier et al., *Les problèmes actuels du crédit* (Paris, 1930), 134–36; Marcel Proust, *A la recherche du temps perdu* (Paris, 1954), 1:143.

8. CE 1:733–34 (Lescouvé, 10 April 1934); Benjamin Martin, *The Shame of Marianne: Criminal Justice under the Third Republic* (Baton Rouge, 1990), 151, 175; Maurice Garçon, *Histoire de la justice sous la Troisième République* (Paris, 1957), 2:164.

9. CE 2:1351 (Abel Pouharam, 25 April 1934); CE 1:973, 975 (Cauwès, 13 April 1934).

10. CE 2:1330 (Decante, 25 April 1934).

11. CE 1:20, 28 (Pachot, 2 March 1934); AN 334AP69 (Pachot, 25 November 1935); Jean Belin, *Trente ans de Sûreté Nationale* (Paris, 1950); CE 3:3511 (Gripois, 11 July 1934); CE 2:1330 (Decante, 25 April 1934).

12. CE 5: 5072–84 and 5119–25 (Grébaud, 23 January 1935; and Beaurain, 24 January 1935); CE 1:5129–51 (Kleinaus and Guillaume, 29 January 1935); CE 1:667 (Xavier Guichard, 29 March 1934); AN MI 25377/85 (PJ report of 19 April 1926).

13. CE 5:5072–84 and 5087–92 (Grébaud and Flach, 23 January 1935).

14. CE 5:5120 (Beaurain, 24 January 1935); CE 5:5130, 5131 (Kleinaus, 29 January 1935).

15. See, for example, AN BB18 2213 (PR Cherbourg, to PG Caen, 18 February, 25 and 26 March 1902; PG Nancy to Gds, 9 and 17 February, 6 March 1902; PG Besançon to Gds, 6 January, 3 and 14 March, 14 April 1903); AN BB18 2225 (Boulaine affair, PG Paris to Gds, 12 July and 10 October 1901); *Le Nouvelliste de Bordeaux,* 20 November 1902; *La Guerre Financière et Politique,* 6 December 1902.

16. CE 5:5087–92 (Flach, 23 January 1935).

17. CE 5:5072–84 and 5087–92 (Grébaud and Flach, 23 January 1935); CE 5:5121 (Beaurain, 24 January 1935); CE 5:5160 (Gaulier, 1 February 1935); see n. 5 above.

18. AN 334AP69 (Pachot, 25 November 1935); AN MI 25376 (Pachot to SG, 2 April 1926); CE 1:20 (Pachot, 2 March 1934); CE 2:1330 (Decante, 25 April 1934). Zweifel claimed that Stavisky fled at a sign from Gaulier, a charge that the latter naturally denied: ADP D2U8432 (Guillaume/Zweifel, 20 April 1934).

19. AN MI 25377/85 (PJ report, 19 April, 6, 11, 17, and 21 May, 7 June, 2 July 1926).

20. CE 5:5161 (conclusions of the expert, M. Israel; Gaulier, 1 February 1935); ADP D2U8440 (JI Demay/Pierre Vachet, 27 March 1934); ADP D2U8440 (Jacques Marteaux, 3 April 1934); ADP D2U8420 (Gaulier to Ordonneau, 25 April 1934); ADP D2U8428, JI Ordonneau/Hayotte, 1 May 1934.

21. AN 334AP68 (Hayotte, criminal court of the Seine, 5 June 1935); AN MI 25377 (PJ reports, 17 May, 17 and 23 July 1926).

22. CE 2:1804 (Marcel Caen, 7 May 1934).

23. Rudelle, *La République absolue,* 210–32; Jean-Yves Mollier, *Le Scandale du*

Panama (Paris, 1991), 393–94, 417, 425; CE 2:1361 (Renoult, 25 April 1934); Meyer, *Ce que mes yeux ont vu,* 58: "Selon le mot de M. Charles Dupuy, elle [la France] entendait le pas du cheval, elle ne voyait pas encore le cavalier"; *Dictionnaire des parlementaires,* ed. Jean Jolly, 8 vols. (Paris, 1960–77), s.v. "Renoult," "Doumer," and "Floquet."

24. AN 334AP68 (criminal court of the Seine, 5 and 6 June 1935, biographical details).

25. Ibid., CE 2:1333 (Decante, 25 April 1934); CE 2:1804 (Caen, 7 May 1934); CE 2:1425 (Renoult, 26 April 1934); ADP D2U8402 (JI Ordonneau/Gaulier, 25 April 1934).

26. CE 2:1332, 1335 (Decante, 25 April 1934); ADP D2U8402 (Ordonneau/Decante, 18 July 1934).

27. CE 2:1418, 1425 (Renoult, 26 April 1934); AN 334AP68 (Hayotte, 6 November 1935).

28. CE 2:1425, 1430 (Renoult, 26 April 1934); AN 334AP68 (René Renoult, criminal court of the Seine, 5 June 1935); ADP D2U8402 (PJ report, 18 August 1934, Waldeck-Rousseau); Maurice Garçon in *Le Figaro,* 8 January 1934.

29. ADP D2U8402 (consultation with H. Donnadieu of Vabres, Faculté de Droit, Université de Paris, 18 February 1935; and supplementary consultation, 12 March 1935); Charles Bourgeois, "De la corruption des fonctionnaires publics" (doctoral thesis, Faculté de droit, Université de Paris, 1902), 92–104 and passim.

30. AN 334AP68 (summation of Me Ribet, criminal court of the Seine, 6 June 1935); CE 2:1363–64 (Renoult, 25 April 1934); AN 334AP68 (Renoult, criminal court of the Seine, 5 June 1935); ADP D2U8402 (Marcel Lévy, 6 October 1934).

31. CE 2:1364, 1368, 1414–15 (Renoult, 25 and 26 April 1934).

32. AN 334AP68 (Labbé, criminal court of the Seine, 5 June 1935; summation of Me Ribet, 6 June 1935; ADP D2U8402 (Lévy, 6 October 1934); CE 2:1369, 1429 (Renoult, 25 and 26 April 1934).

33. CE 2:1353, 1357 (Prouharam, 25 April 1934), and CE 2:1366–68 (Renoult, 25 April 1934).

34. ADP D2U8402 (Cauwès, 16 July 1934); CE 1:970–72 (Cauwès, 13 April 1934).

35. CE 1:970–72 (Cauwès, 13 April 1934); Cauwès, in his appearance before the CE, alluded to three missions to the High Court, but the third must have been later, since the trial of Raoul Péret took place after the Oustric affair of 1930–31; ADP D2U8 (deposition of René Decante, 18 July 1934); CE 2:1332 (Decante, 25 April 1934); AN 334AP68 (Prouharam, criminal court of the Seine, 5 June 1935).

36. AN 334AP68 (Prouharam, criminal court of the Seine, 5 June 1935); CE 2:1343 (Decante, 25 April 1934); AN 334AP68 (Cauwès and Decante, criminal court of the Seine, 5 June 1935).

37. It is more than likely that Gaulier knew where Stavisky was, but he denied this before the CE (2:1662, Gaulier, 3 May 1934).

38. CE 5:5277 (Pachot, 20 February 1935); CE 5:972–73 (Cauwès, 13 April 1934).

39. AN MI 25377/85 (PJ report to Decante and Pachot, 17 May 1926; PJ/SG report, 7 June 1926); AN 334AP68 (Hayotte, 6 November 1935).

40. Report of the mayor of Montigny-sur-Loing, 7 June 1926; AN MI 25377/85 (PJ/SG report, 7 June 1926).

41. AN MI 25377/85 (PJ/SG report, 7 June 1926).

42. *Le Journal,* 7 and 11 June 1926; *Le Petit Parisien,* 8 June 1926; *Le Matin,* 9 and 11 June 1926; *Paris-Soir,* 9 June 1926; *La Liberté,* 9 June 1926; CE 5:5192 (Maurice Privat, 6 February 1935).

43. Stephan Valot (editor at *L'Oeuvre),* "L'évolution contemporaine du journalisme," in Georges Bourdon et al., *Le journalisme d'aujourd'hui* (Paris, 1931), 55; Georges Bourdon (editor at *Le Figaro),* "Qu'est-ce qu'un journaliste," ibid., 20–40.

44. Léon Groc (editor at *Le Petit Parisien),* "La Chasse aux nouvelles," ibid., 53–68; AN F7 12551 (*L'Echo de Paris,* 26 November 1908); *Le Matin,* 22 and 26 November 1908, 20 January 1909; *Paris-Journal,* 27 November 1908.

45. *La Guerre Sociale,* 25 November 1908; *L'Humanité,* 24 November 1908; *L'Autorité,* 29 November 1908 and 20 January 1909; *Les Nouvelles,* 25 November 1909.

46. Francis Delaisi (Fédération Internationale des Journalistes), "Le Journalisme et l'argent," in Bourdon et al., *Le journalisme d'aujourd'hui,* 122–34.

47. AN MI 25377/85 (report of the mayor of Montigny-sur-Loing, 7 June 1926).

48. AN 334AP69 (Pachot, 25 and 26 November 1935); CE 1:21 (Pachot, 2 March 1934); *Baedeker's Paris and Its Environs* (Leipzig, 1924), 16, 23.

49. ADP D2U8434 (JI Ordonneau/Arlette Stavisky, 24 March 1934); AN MI 25377, report of Pachot and Bayard, 26 July 1926.

50. ADP D2U8434 (JI Ordonneau/Arlette Stavisky, 24 March 1934); ADP D2U8440 (Jacques Marteaux, 3 April 1934); ADP D2U8114 (JI Ordonneau/Hayotte, 1 May 1934); AN 334AP68 (Hayotte, 6 November 1935); CE 1:1138/18 (Philippe Henriot, 21 March 1934).

51. CE 1:21 (Pachot, 1 March 1934); AN MI 25377 (notices on those present in Marly-le-Roi); AN 334AP69 (Pachot, 25 and 26 November 1935).

52. AN MI 25377 (report of Pachot and Bayard, 26 July 1926); CE 1:533 (Bayard, 27 March 1934); CE 1:21 (Pachot, 1 March 1934); ADP D2U8440 (JI Demay/Vachet, 27 March 1934); AN 334AP68 (Hayotte, 6 November 1935); *Le Journal,* 28 July 1926.

53. *Paris-Soir,* 27 July 1926; *Le Matin,* 28 July 1926; *Le Petit Parisien,* 28 July 1926; *Le Journal,* 28 July 1926; Michel Nathan, *Anthologie du roman populaire, 1836–1918* (Paris, 1985), 345.

54. Eliane Tonnet-Lacroix, *La littérature française de l'entre-deux-guerres* (Paris, 1993), 152–57; *Le Journal,* 30 July, 5 August 1926.

55. *L'Intransigeant,* 8 August 1926; CE 5:192–93 (Maurice Privat, 6 February 1935); René Duval, "Ondes. Radio-Paris," in *Entre deux guerres. La création française, 1919–1939,* ed. Olivier Barrot and Pascal Ory (Paris, 1990).

56. AN MI 25347 (dossier Paul Lévy).

57. Ibid.; François-Ignace Mouthon, *Du bluff au chantage. Les grandes campagnes du "Matin"* (n.d., c. 1910), 1–32, 93–111.

58. *Aux Ecoutes,* 1 and 8 August 1926, 3 October 1926.

59. AN MI 25372/80 (notes of 15 and 26 November 1926).

60. AN MI 25326/34 (note of 4 October 1919); AN MI 25347 (notes of 23 June 1920, 23 February 1926).

61. ADP D2U8402 (director of prisons to Justice, 16 January 1935); CE 1:750 (Lescouvé, 10 April 1934); CE 2:1330 (Decante, 25 April 1934).

62. ADP D2U8402 (director of prisons to Justice, 16 January 1935); ADP D2U8434 (JI Ordonneau/Poulner, 15 December 1934); AN MI 25379/87 (note of Insp. de Police Mobile Arrazat, 25 January 1935).

63. ADP D2U8434 (JI Ordonneau/Poulner, 15 December 1934); ADP D2U8434 (Ordonneau/Mme Vatin-Pérignon, 7 December 1934; and Ordonneau/Arlette Stavisky, 24 March and 4 December 1934); AP D2U8440 (deposition of Dr. Vachet, 27 March 1934); ADP D2U8440 (Ordonneau/Arlette Stavisky, 27 April 1934); AN MI 25376 (note on Henri Poulner, n.d. but 1934).

64. CE 2:1488–89 (Dr. Paul, 27 April 1934); CE 2:1331, 1334–39 (Decante, 25 April 1934); CE 2:1814–15 (Caen, 7 May 1934).

65. CE 2:1814–15 (Caen, 7 May 1934); CE 1:735, 750 (Lescouvé, 10 April 1934).

CHAPTER 4. THE FALSENESS OF NAMES

1. AN MI 25377 (Decante to Insp. Peudepièce, 11 February 1928; Insp. Borel to CGRJ, 9 March 1928).

2. Ibid.

3. ADP D2U8424 (deposition of B.-L. Collange, 5 July 1934).

4. ADP D2U8434 (JI Ordonneau/Arlette Stavisky, 12 and 24 March 1934).

5. ADP D2U8435 (René Lachaize, 10 January 1934).

6. AN MI 25376 (Insp. gén. Plytas to Chautemps, 24 January 1934); CE 1:533 (Bayard, 27 March 1934); AN 334AP69 (Saunois-Chevert, 26 November 1935).

7. ADP D2U8440 (deposition of Lepage, 25 May 1934).

8. AN 334AP68 (Henri Cohen, 7 November 1935); AN MI 25382 (Eliane Cohen, 5 July 1934); *Le Journal,* 8 January 1934.

9. AN 334AP68 (Desbrosses and Hayotte, 5, 6 November 1935); ADP D2U8420 (court-appointed accountant on Optants Hongrois, 28 September 1934), 79.

10. ADP D2U8 (Paul Maze, 18 January 1934); "Le banquier des pauvres," *Lectures pour Tous,* November 1904.

11. AN BB18 6765 (Insp. gén. Rouvier, 19 January 1934); ADP D2U8425 (report on crédit municipal of Bayonne, 3 vols., 19 July 1934).

12. AN 334AP69 (Saunois/de Chevert, 26 November 1935).

13. AN MI 25382 (CD Orléans to PR Orléans, 27 November 1931); ADP D2U8417 (Insp. Bonny to CGRJ, 30 December 1933); ADP D2U8418 (Desbrosses, 15 December 1934); ADP D2U8428 (Bonny/Desbrosses, 15 January 1934, and note to CC Orléans, 6 August 1934); ADP D2U8431 (Desbrosses, 18 November 1931); *Le Populaire,* 6 November 1935; *Le Matin,* 6 November 1935; *Le Petit Parisien,* 6 November 1935.

14. AN 334AP68 (Desbrosses, 5 November 1935); ADP D2U8418 (Saunois/de Chevert, 17 March 1934); ADP D2U8431 (Pachot/de Chevert, 2 October 1931); ADP D2U8439 (JI Demay/de Chevert, 19 March 1934 and 18 April 1934); *Action Française,* 6 November 1935.

15. AN 334AP69 (de Chevert, 26 November 1935); ADP D2U8431 (Pachot/de Chevert), 2 October 1931.

16. *Le Journal,* 27 November 1935; *Le Petit Parisien,* 27 November 1935; *Le Matin,* 27 November 1935; AN 334AP69 (de Chevert, 26 November 1935).

17. ADP D2U8431 (Insp. Cousin, 21 May 1931); AN 334AP68 (Henri Cohen, 7 November 1935); AN 1320W32 (Mata and Meilhan to CC Orléans, 5 September 1929, forwarded to public prosecutor's office, 19 September 1929).

18. ADP D2U8431 (Pachot/de Chevert, 2 October 1931).

19. AN 334AP68 (Hayotte, 6 November 1935); ADP D2U8418 (JI Ordonneau/Hayotte, 19 September 1934; Ordonneau/Hayotte, 20 December 1934; Alfred Chiche, 6 October 1934).

20. AN 334AP68 (Hayotte, 6 November 1935); ADP D2U8418 (report on Emile Farault, 20 January 1936); *Action Française,* 6 November 1935.

21. AN 334AP68 (Hayotte, 6 November 1935); ADP D2U8418 (Georges Hattot, 6 September 1934).

22. CE 4:4245, 4248 (Hattot, 8 November 1934); ADP D2U8418 (Hattot, 6 September 1934); AN 334AP68 (Hattot, 6 November 1935); *Le Journal,* 5 and 7 November 1935.

23. ADP D2U8418 (Hattot, 6 September 1934); AN 334AP68 (Hayotte, 6 November 1935); AN 334AP68 (Hattot, 6 November 1935).

24. ADP D2U8419 (report of the expert-comptable René Jacob, 8 August 1934), 1:12, and chap. 5.

25. ADP D2U8418 (de Chevert, 17 March 1934 and 1 October 1934); ADP D2U8431 (Pachot/Chevert, 2 October 1931).

26. ADP D2U8418 (Henri Cohen and de Chevert, 5 October 1934); ADP D2U8418 (Hattot, 6 September 1934 and 28 December 1934); AN 334AP68 (Hayotte, 6 November 1935). In 1937 80 percent of civil servants earned less than twenty-three thousand francs a year; see Marc-Olivier Baruch, *Servir l'état français* (Paris, 1997), 31.

27. AN 334AP68 (Farault, 5 November 1935); ADP D2U8418 (Farault, 22 December 1934).

28. AN 334AP69 (Séror, 27 November 1935); AN 334AP68 (Hayotte, 6 November 1935); ADP D2U8418 (de Chevert, 5 October 1934).

29. AN 334AP69 (Séror, 27 November 1935); AN 334AP68 (Hattot, 6 November 1935); ADP D2U8418 (Farault, 18 September 1934).

30. AN 334AP69 (Séror, 27 November 1935); ADP D2U8418 (Henri Cohen, 5 October 1934).

31. AN 334AP68 (Hayotte, 6 November 1935); ADP D2U8418 (Hattot and Porquerel, 24 and 28 September 1934); AN 334AP68 (Hattot, 6 November 1935).

32. AN F7 12550 (Humbert affair, report of comm. sp. from Madrid, 23 December 1902); AN BB18 6731 (Hanau affair, police note of 14 December 1928).

33. AN MI 25382 (Comm. Delgay/Lelièvre, 4 October 1934); ADP D2U8441 (Delgay/Kuven, 5 May 1934).

34. ADP D2U8431 (Pachot/de Chevert, 2 October 1931).

35. AN MI 25382 (police note, 10 January 1934, and letter from Cazenave to Berthault); ADP D2U8431 (report of Insp. Cousin, 21 May 1931).

36. AN MI 25382 (police note, 10 January 1934, and letter from Cazenave to Berthault); ADP D2U8418 (report of the financial brigade and declaration of de Chevert, 2 October 1931); ADP D2U8428 (Sevestre and Cousin, 3 February 1933).

37. ADP (dossier Foncière, no file number, Edouard Cazenave and Aramis Lherbier [*sic*], 27 October 1934, and expert-comptable Février, 20 October 1934).

38. ADP D2U8431 (Cousin, 21 May 1931, and Guiot, 6 May 1932); CE 2:1782–94 (Hudelo, 7 May 1934), 1564, 1568 (Pierre Laval, 2 May 1934), 2280 (Bardi de Fourtou, 28 May 1934), and 2241 (de Monzie, 25 May 1934).

39. CE 2:2277ff. (Bardi de Fourtou, 28 May 1934); ADP D2U8467 (Bardi de Fourtou); ADP D2U8428 (report of Insps. Sevetre and Cousin, 3 February 1933); ADP D2U8418 (police report on Bardi de Fourtou, 22 December 1934); ADP D2U8431 (report of Insp. Guiot, 6 May 1932).

40. CE 2:2277ff. (Bardi de Fourtou, 28 May 1934).

41. CE 2:1782–94 (Hudelo, 7 May 1934).

42. ADP D2U8431 (Insp. Cousin, 21 May 1931, and de Chevert, 2 October 1931).

43. ADP D2U8428 (report of Insps. Sevetre and Cousin, 3 February 1933); ADP D2U8431 (report of Insp. Cousin, 21 May 1931).

44. AN CAC (dossier Charles Wurtz, 22/13470–940484/149); AN BB18 6723 (report of PR Seine on "legislation relating to financial organizations," 22 May 1920); CE 2:1616 (Paul Reynaud, 2 May 1934) and 2232 (de Monzie, 25 May 1934).

45. ADP (dossier Foncière, interrogation Baraveau/Hudelo, 17 November 1934); CE (individual reports, report of René Besse), 131, 137–39.

46. AN CAC (dossier Samuel Jean Henri Astruc, 1/23651–940432/256); CE 2:2438, 2439–42, 2449 (Astruc, 4 June 1934).

47. AN BB18 6723 (report of PR Seine on "legislation relating to financial organiza-

tions," 22 May 1920); AN 5AR 404 (correspondence of the Agence Havas, *Havas to Le Temps*, 30 October 1930); CE 3:2785 (Mennevée, 18 June 1934); CE 2:2444 (Astruc, 4 June 1934).

48. Emmanuel Berl, *Mort de la pensée bourgeoise* (Paris, 1929), 107–8; CE 3:2442 (Astruc, 4 June 1934).

49. CE 3:2441, 2449 (Astruc, 4 June 1934); AN BB 18 6722, expert's report, 10 October 1921; Jeanneney, *L'argent caché*, 168ff.

50. CE 3:2441 (Astruc, 4 June 1934); AN BB18 6733 (Hanau affair, Anquetil to GdS, 27 December 1932); AN CAC (dossiers Anquetil 1a/332–940433/4 and 1/17361–940432/185); *Les Débats*, 10–11 January 1930 (trial proceedings).

51. ADP (dossier Foncière, Augustin Dupuis, 16 August, 15 September 1934; Saulière, 16 October 1934; Eugène Barbot, 3 August 1934; mayor of Lux, 2 May 1934).

52. CE 1:72–74 (Depardon, 6 March 1934); ADP D2U8 417 (Insp. Bonny/Depardon, 11 January 1934), 418 (de Chevert, 17 March 1934), 431 (Insp. Cousin, 21 May 1931), 439 (JI Ordonneau/Depardon, 27–28 February 1934, 8 January 1935; reports of expert Mulquin, 2 January 1935; Insp. Courtois, 19 January 1935; and police note of 9 October 1934); AN F7 13981 (police note on Henri Depardon, 12 January 1934); *Le Journal*, 21 November 1934.

53. ADP (dossier Foncière, P. Angelini, 6 July 1934; Camisat, 22 January 1934; Marcellin Sève, 18 January 1934; Comm. de police, Brest, to PR, 15 February 1934); ADP D2U8431 (de Chevert, 2 October 1931 and report of Insp. Cousin, 21 May 1931); AN F7 13981 (police note of 17 January 1934).

54. Maurice Lorain, former inspector of finance, 14 February 1930, in Farnier et al., *Les problèmes actuels du crédit*, 23–24, 28; Olivier Moreau-Néret, directeur du Crédit Lyonnais, 5 March 1930, ibid., 116; James Harvey Rogers, *The Process of Inflation in France* (New York, 1929), 251–52, 261–62.

55. AN MI 25379 (police notes on Puis, 9 and 12 June 1934).

56. ADP D2U8438 (JI Demay/Mme Oury; letter from Puis dated 18 May 1930; Demay/Puis, 8 May 1934).

57. ADP D2U8438 (JI Demay/Puis, 23 March and 7 April 1934; JI Demay/Potier, 24 March 1934; police note on Potier, 21 April 1934; report of expert René Jacob, 13 April 1934); CE 1:346, 348 (Puis, 16 March 1934).

58. CE 1:346, 349 (Puis, 16 March 1934); JI Demay/Puis, 7 April and 8 May 1934; Rio, 12 April 1934; Demay/Hayotte, 29 March 1934, and Demay/Potier, 27 March and 4 April 1934.

59. ADP D2U8436 (Comm. Angers to PR Angers, report on Boyer, 9 March 1934); Bortchy-Melnikoff, *300.000 kilomètres avec Stavisky*, 125; *Dictionnaire des parlementaires*, s.v. "Edmond Boyer." AN MI 25379/87 (gendarmerie Bonny-sur-Loire, note, 25 June 1934); ADP D2U8436 (report of expert-comptables on Boyer et al., 28 July 1934); CE 1:415, 421, 429 (Boyer, 21 March 1934).

60. ADP D2U8439 (insp. gén. of agriculture to minister of agriculture, 22 January 1934); ADP D2U8418 (report of PJ, 2 October 1931); ADP D2U8427 (report of experts-comptables Février and Bleuville, 4 October 1934); ADP D2U8428 (report of Insps. Sevetre and Cousin, n.d., copy transmitted 3 February 1933); CE 2:2113 (Landau, 23 May 1934); CE (general report), 195–200.

61. ADP D2U8439 (insp. gén. to agriculture, see n. 57); ADP D2U8427 (report of experts-comptables, see n. 57); ADP D2U8428 (report of Insps. Sevetre and Cousin, n.d., copy transmitted 3 February 1933); ADP D2U8431 (PJ report, 21 May 1931); ADP D2U8431 (Bortchy-Melnikoff, 6 February 1934); ADP D2U8418 (report de Insp. Cousin, 4 December 1931).

62. ADP D2U8436 (report of expert-comptables on Boyer et al., 28 July 1934); CE 1:415–17, 423–24.

63. CE 1:313–14 (Victor Boret, 16 March 1934); *Dictionnaire des parlementaires*, s.v. "Victor Boret."

64. CE 1:315.

65. Bortchy-Melnikoff, *300.000 kilomètres avec Stavisky*, 17; ADP D2U8431 (Bortchy-Melnikoff, 6 February 1934).

66. ADP D2U8418 (report of Insp. Cousin on Sima, 4 December 1931); D2U8425 (accountant's report on placement of Bayonne bonds); D2U8439 (report of insp. gén. of agriculture, 22 January 1934); D2U8427 (accountant's report on SIMA, 4 October 1934).

67. ADP 1320W98 (letter from Moutot about Diagne, 20 November 1935); *Le Populaire*, 14 March 1934 ("Diagne, Député Tardieusard du Sénégal"); CE 1:188 (Guiboud-Ribaud, 13 March 1934).

68. ADP D2U8439 (Insp. gén. Laurent, 22 January 1934); CE 1:297–98, 302–4 (Blanchard, 15 March 1934); CE 1:314–15 (Victor Boret, 16 March 1934).

69. ADP D2U8438 (JI Demay/Rio, 12 April 1934; and Demay/Puis, 7 April 1934).

70. ADP D2U8428 (Comm. Delgay/Braunstein and Delgay/Derote, 5 December 1934); *Action Française*, 8 November 1935; *Le Matin*, 8 November 1935; Bortchy-Melnikoff, *300.000 kilomètres avec Stavisky*, 15, 40.

71. ADP D2U8428 (JI Ordonneau/Digoin, 28 July 1934).

72. AN 334AP68 (Emile Digoin, 8 November 1935); Léon Ameline, *Ce qu'il faut connaître de la police et ses mystères* (Paris, 1926), 32–33; APP (Minstère public c/Oustric et Benoist, 26–29, May 1933, criminal court of the Seine, deposition of Emile Barthélémy).

73. AN MI 25376 (Xavier-Guichard, 12 January 1934); CE 3:3517 (Gripois, 11 July 1934); CE 5:5139–42 (Guillaume, 29 January 1935); see chap. 2, 15, and chap. 3, 28.

74. AN 334AP69 (Emile Digoin, 8 November 1935); ADP D2U8428 (Insp. Peudepièce, 20 January 1934); the salary of an *inspecteur principal*, a higher rank than Digoin's, at the Police Judiciaire was twenty-five hundred francs a month—see AN MI 25376 (annex to report of Insp. gén. Mossé, 21 January 1934).

75. Bortchy-Melnikoff, *300.000 kilomètres avec Stavisky*, 1–9; ADP D2U8431 (Bortchy-Melnikoff, 6 February 1934); ADP D2U8428 (Bortchy-Melnikoff, 15 January 1934); AN MI 25376 (note of CD Guillaume, 9 January 1934).

76. Bortchy-Melnikoff, *300.000 kilomètres avec Stavisky*, 10–16, 131.

77. Ibid., 124–27; ADP D2U8431 (Bortchy-Melnikoff, 6 February 1934).

78. Bortchy-Melnikoff, *300.000 kilomètres avec Stavisky*, 41–42.

79. Louis Roubaud, *La Bourse. Foire aux entreprises. Criéé des valeurs. Maison de jeu* (Paris, 1929), 21–22.

80. Cf. Bortchy-Melnikoff, *300.000 kilomètres avec Stavisky*, 99: "Il avait l'air de s'amuser vraiment, ce qui est la suprême politesse."

CHAPTER 5. JUSTICE IN THE LAND OF FINANCE

1. Bortchy-Melnikoff, *300.000 kilomètres avec Stavisky*, 58.

2. APP (Ministère public c/Oustric et Benoist, criminal court of the Seine, 26–29 May 1933); AN BB18 6745 (PR Seine to PG), n.d. but April 1936 and 12 and 18 November 1930; Maurice Garçon, *Histoire de la justice sous la Troisième République* (Paris, 1957), 2:89–100.

3. Bortchy-Melnikoff, *300.000 kilomètres avec Stavisky*, 58.

4. Jean Tulard, "Les débuts du régime parlementaire," in Michel Bruguière et al., *Administration et parlement depuis 1815* (Geneva, 1982), 7–12; André-Jean Tudescq, "Parlement et administration sous la monarchie de juillet," ibid., 13–37; Vincent Wright, "La crise de 1871–1882," ibid., 49–57; Claude Goyard, "La critique parlementaire des administrations sous la IIIe République," ibid., 59ff.

5. Marc-Olivier Baruch, *Servir l'état français. L'administration en France de 1940 à 1944* (Paris, 1997), chap. 1: "L'héritage."

6. CE 3:1927ff., 1938 (André Hesse, 9 May 1934).

7. CAC (file André Hesse 8/12874 940451/151, including: SG notes Versailles, 26 March, 17 and 25 April 1902, SG note La Rochelle, 13 January 1909 and 2 August 1917), *Les Echos Parisiens*, 10 July 1924; *Dictionnaire des parlementaires*, s.v. "André Hesse"; Roger Martin du Gard, *Journal* (Paris, 1992–93), 2:28, December 1928.

8. ADP D2U8443 (JI Ordonneau/Himmelfarb, 17 April 1934); Henri-Robert, *L'avocat* (Paris, 1923), 60–61; CE 2:1933, 1937 (Hesse, 9 May 1934); CE 2:1807–8 (Caen, 7 May 1934); ADP D2U8453 (JI Ordonneau/Romagnino). In his first appearance before the CE, Hesse denied visiting Stavisky in prison (CE 2:1493, 27 April 1934). In his second, he could not remember whether he had visited him or not (CE 2:1929, 9 May 1934). But a letter to him from Stavisky (CE 2:1933) and the appearance of his name on a list of Stavisky's visitors in La Santé (CE 2:1809) leaves no doubt about the matter.

9. CE 2:1656, 1657 (Gaulier, 3 May 1934); CE 2:1948 (André Hesse, 9 May 1934).

10. CE 1:735 (Lescouvé, 10 April 1934); CE 2:1331 (Decante, 25 April 1934); AN MI 25377 (Insp. of Police Mobile to CGRJ, 9 March 1928).

11. See chap. 2, 23–24, and chap. 3, 26–27; AN MI 25381 (SG note on Vachet, 10 March 1934); ADP 1320W132 (indictment of PR Seine) of Pierre Vachet, 16 March 1936; CE 2:1488–92 (Dr. Paul, 27 April 1934); CE 2:1456–57 (Vachet, 27 April 1934); CE 2:1934 (Hesse, 9 May 1934).

12. Henry Bénazet, *Dix ans chez les avocats* (Paris, 1929), 29, 66ff.; Henri-Robert, *L'avocat* 62ff.; AN BB6 II 885 (personnel dossier of Theodore-Paul Lescouvé); in 1926 correctional courts in France acquitted 9.5 percent of those accused, the criminal courts 34 percent—see USNA, M1442/12 (U.S. consul to Department of State, 19 August 1930 and 13 November 1930, reports on French legal system).

13. JO (Chamber of Deputies, 18 January 1934, speech by Marcel Héraud); CE 1:734, 749–50, 763–64 (Lescouvé, 10 April 1934); CE 2:1331 (Decante, 25 April 1934), 1499 (André Hesse, 27 April 1934), and 1807 (Marcel Caen, 7 May 1934); Bénazet, *Dix ans chez les avocats*, 60.

14. CE 1:737, 790, 791 (Lescouvé, 10 April 1934).

15. AN MI 25376 (report of Insp. gén. Armand Mossé, 21 January 1934); CE 1:22, 34–37 (Pachot, 2 March 1934).

16. AN MI 25376 (Bayard to Insp. gén. Plytas, 10 January 1934); Plytas to Chautemps, 24 January 1934; CE 1:533–51 (Bayard, 27 March 1934).

17. CE 1:533–51 (Bayard, 27 March 1934).

18. AN MI 25376 (Comm. Badin/de Chevert, 29 August 1928); SG (report, 23 November 1931); AN MI 25378 (note by Insp. gén. Mossé, 20 February 1934); ADP D2U8424 (Desolneux, 7 May 1934); CE 2:533, 539–40 and 4:4263–64 (Bayard, 27 March and 9 November 1934); CE 4:4253–56 (Reymann, 9 November 1934).

19. Paul Allard, *L'Anarchie de la police* (Paris, 1934), 9–11.

20. AN MI 25376 (Comm. sp. Vidal to CGRJ, 3 February 1932, CGRJ to Comm. sp. Cannes, 18 February 1932, and note of CD Guillaume, 8 January 1934); ADP 1320W102

(Comm. Delgay report on Arlette Simon to CGRJ, 15 September 1934); ADP D2U8434 (Arlette Simon to Ordonneau, 24 December 1934); Bortchy-Melnikoff, *300.000 kilomètres avec Stavisky*, 52–67; Claude Stavisky, *Stavisky était mon père* (Paris, 1995), 34–35.

21. ADP D2U8431 (report of CD Orléans Fressard, 12 November 1931); CE 2:1890–96 (Génébrier, 9 May 1934). Génébrier seemed to think Aubin brought Stavisky along, which seems unlikely (cf. CE 2:2333, Turbat, 30 May 1934), as does his recollection that Stavisky was already talking of Bayonne (cf. CE 2:2163, Paul Maze, 23 May 1934).

22. CE 2:1890–96 (Génébrier, 9 May 1934).

23. AN BB18 6765, and ADP D2U8432 (report of Insp. gén. Rouvier, 19 January 1934); AN 334AP69 (Rouvier, 2 December 1935); ADP D2U8425 (accountant's report on the crédit municipal of Bayonne, 3 vols., submitted 19 July 1934, vol. 2: "Budget"); CE 2:1686ff. (Delamarche, 4 May 1934).

24. AN 334AP69 (Robert Mireur, 4 December 1935); CE 2:1713–15, Delamarche and Lafont, 4 May 1934); ADP D2U8432 (JI Ordonneau/Delamarche, 16 June 1934).

25. CE, 2:2334 (Turbat, 30 May 1934).

26. CE 2:1891, 1892, 1894 (Génébrier, 9 May 1934).

27. See chap. 4, 61–62; ADP D2U8438 (Demay/Puis, 23 March 1934); AN 334AP69 (Jean-Charles Legrand, 29 November 1935); CE 1:346–47 (Puis, 16 March 1934); CE 2:2341 (Turbat, 30 May 1934).

28. CE 2:2339 (Turbat, 30 May 1934); ADP D2U8431 (CD Fressard Orléans); *Le Jour*, 12 March 1934.

29. CE 2:2335 (Turbat, 30 May 1934); see chap. 4, 62.

30. AN MI 25376 (insp. gén. adjoint Sarraz-Bournet, 10 January 1934; the figure is given as twenty thousand francs); AN 334AP69 (Turbat, 29 November 1935); CE 1:421–22, 425 (Boyer, 21 March 1934).

31. AN 334AP69 (Turbat, 29 November 1935); CE 2:2336 (Turbat, 30 May 1934).

32. AN MI 25376 (Sarraz-Bournet, 10 January 1934); CE 2:2336 (Turbat, 30 May 1934); Bortchy-Melnikoff, *300.000 kilomètres avec Stavisky*, 31–32.

33. AN 334AP69 (Constantin, 3 December 1935); AN 334AP68 (Farault, 5 November 1935); ADP D2U8432 (JI Hude/Delamarche, 13 June 1934); CE 2:1741 (Constantin, 4 May 1934); photo of Constantin in *Le Populaire*, 5 May 1934; *Baedeker's Paris and Its Environs* (1924), 17, 20.

34. CE 2:2164–65 (Paul Maze, 23 May 1934); CE 2:2356–58 (Georges Bonnefous, 30 May 1934); CE 2:2349–50 (Oberkirch, 30 May 1934); CE 2:1758 (Constantin, 4 May 1934); CE 3:2411–13, 2415–18 (P.-E. Flandin, 4 June 1934); ADP D2U8432 (JI Hude/Delamarche, 19 June 1934); AN MI 25376 (Sarraz-Bournet, 10 January 1934).

35. CE 2:2418–19 (Flandin, 4 June 1934); AN BB18 6765 and ADP D2U8432 (Rouvier, 19 January 1934); ADP D2U8432 (JI Hude/Delamarche, 13 June 1934).

36. ADP D2U8417 (JI Demay/Maze, 18 January 1934); AN 334AP69 (Paul Maze, 6 December 1935); CE 2:2181, 2183 (Paul Maze, 23 May 1934); CE 2:2358 (Georges Bonnefous, 30 May 1934); CE 2:2349 (Oberkirch, 30 May 1934); CE 3:2409, 2414 (P.-E. Flandin, 4 June 1934).

37. AN MI 25376 (Sarraz-Bournet, 10 January 1934); ADP D2U8431 (CD Fressard Orléans, 12 November 1931); AN 334AP68 (Desbrosses, 5 November 1935); CE 2:1752 (Constantin, 4 May 1934).

38. CE 2:2165–66 (Paul Maze, 23 May 1934); CE 2:2418–19 (Flandin, 4 June 1934); ADP D2U8432 (JI Hude/Delamarche, 20 June 1934).

39. ADP D2U8417 (JI Demay/Maze, 18 January 1934); CE 2:2166–67 (Paul Maze, 23

May 1934); AN MI 25376 (Sarraz-Bournet, 10 January 1934); ADP D2U8 431 (Fressard Orléans, 12 November 1931); AN D2U8432 (JI Hude/Delamarche, 20 June 1934).

40. AN MI 25376 (Sarraz-Bournet, 10 January 1934); ADP D2U8431 (Fressard, 12 November 1931).

41. AN 334AP68 (Desbrosses, 5 November 1935); ADP D2U8418 (Desbrosses, 15 December 1934).

42. ADP D2U8418 (Desbrosses, 15 December 1934); ADP D2U8418 (de Chevert, 5 October 1934).

43. ADP D2U8418 (de Chevert, 5 October 1934); ADP D2U8418 (Desbrosses, 7 September 1934); AN 334AP69 (René Jacob, expert-comptable, 28 November 1935); ADP D2U8419 (report of René Jacob, 8 August 1934, vol. 2, chap. 5).

44. AN 334AP69 (Turbat, 29 November 1935); CE 2:2340 (Turbat, 30 May 1934).

45. ADP 1320W102 (Comm. Delgay to CGRJ, report on Arlette Simon, 15 September 1934); ADP D2U8433 (comm. sp., Biarritz, note of 24 February 1934; comm. sp., Saint-Jean-de-Luz, note of 22 February 1934; and Delgay to CGRJ, 11 September 1934); ADP D2U8428 (Edmond Londres, 16 January 1934); ADP D2U8434 (Arlette Stavisky to JI Ordonneau, 24 December 1934); ADP D2U8439 (Georges Détrimont, 6 March 1934); ADP D2U8440 (Colombani, 20 April 1934); ADP D2U8431 (Bortchy-Melnikoff, 6 February 1934); AN MI 25376 (note of CD Guillaume, 9 January 1934).

46. A small file on Mennevée at the prefecture of police reveals a number of investigations, apparently for defamation and blackmail (for example, in an article of 1928 entitled "Un avertissement"). His paper contains more information than other financial weeklies edited by known blackmailers, but his methods, such as spectacular open letters to the government, resemble theirs, as does the nature of his revelations. His sudden silence after all his revelations about Stavisky and the Foncière (see below, 91) is highly suspicious, and it is difficult not to discern in the congratulations of the president of the CE a heavy note of irony. I conclude, with some hesitation, that Mennevée operated on the borderline between blackmail and muckraking. CE 3:2776–92 (Mennevée, 18 June 1934); APP B/A 1972 (file Mennevée).

47. *Les Informations Politiques et Financières,* 7 October 1929 (from AN F7 16017/1); ADP (file Foncière, Hudelo, 17 November 1934); CE 2:1524 (Mouton, 1 May 1934); CE 3:2776–79, 2782, 2788 (Mennevée, 18 June 1934). For the creation of the Foncière. See chap. 4.

48. CE 2:1522 (Mouton, 1 May 1934), 1613–14 (Paul Reynaud, 2 May 1934), 1529–30 (Rateau, 1 May 1939).

49. CE 2:1564–66 (Pierre Laval, 2 May 1934); ADP (file Foncière, JI Baraveau/Verrier, 24 November 1934).

50. CE 2:1518–28 (Mouton, 1 May 1934); CE 2:1782–86 (Hudelo, 7 May 1934).

51. AN F7 13978 (Hanau affair, general information reports, 26 October, 28 and 30 November, 3 December 1928); AN BB18 6731 (Hanau affair); *Le Soir,* 14 March 1930; CE 2:1106–7 (Donat-Guigue, 18 April 1934) and 1529 (Rateau, 1529–30, 1 May 1934); CE, annexes (private report of René Besse), 135.

52. AN BB6 II 1153 (file Prince); *Le Petit Parisien,* 17 March 1934; CE 1:952 (Glard, 13 April 1934); CE 2:1045 (Fontaine, 17 April 1934); Gisèle Dessaux Prince, *Ils ont tué mon père. L'affaire Prince, 1934* (Paris, 1995), 19, 26.

53. JO (27 February, debate, esp. André Berthon; 28 February 1931, Anatole de Monzie of the financial section and reply by GdS).

54. CE 1:1026 (Fontaine, 17 April 1934); CE 4, 4379 (Geoffroy, 21 November 1934); CE

Notes to Pages 85–90

2:1785 (Hudelo, 7 May 1934); JO, 28 February 1931 (speech by Anatole de Monzie); JO, 18 January 1934 (Marcel Héraud on financial section); André Toulemon, in *La spéculation illicite* (Paris, 1931), claims La Santé held 135 bankers in 1931, but this appears to be a misprint (36).

55. CE 4:4381–83, 4384, 4391, 4401, 4805 (Geoffroy, 21 November 1934 and 8 January 1935); CE, annexes (individual reports, report of René Besse), 134–35.

56. CE 4:4392–93, 4398 (Geoffroy, 21 November 1934).

57. CE, annexes (individual reports, report of René Besse), 134–37; CE 5:4812 (Bruzin, 8 January 1935).

58. CE, annexes (individual reports, report of René Besse), 137; CE 1:841 (Pressard, 11 April 1934).

59. CE 1:1107–8 (Donat-Guigue, 18 April 1934); CE, annexes (individual reports, report of René Besse), 137–39; ADP (file Foncière, JI Baraveau/Séguela, 12 January 1935).

60. *Les Informations Politiques et Financières*, 16 December 1929, 10 February 1930 (from AN F7 16017/1); CE 3:2777–78, 2780–81 (Mennevée, 18 June 1934).

61. *Les Informations Politiques et Financières*, 17 February 1930; CE 3:2781, 2791 (Mennevée, 18 June 1934).

62. CE, annexes (individual reports, report of René Besse), 139–40; *Les Informations Politiques et Financières*, 31 March 1930; CE 1:841 (Pressard, 11 April 1934).

63. AN MI 25382 (Maurice-Moïse Zekri, 3 July 1934); ADP D2U8428 (Insp. Bonny/Hayotte, 6 January 1934, JI d'Uhalt/Hayotte, 31 January 1934, JI Ordonneau/Hayotte, 1 May 1934, and report of expert-comptable on Hayotte's finances, 16 April 1934); ADP D2U8439 (Roch Filippi, 15 March 1934); ADP D2U8431 (Eugène Bortchy-Melnikoff, 6 February 1934); Bortchy-Melnikoff, *300.000 kilomètres avec Stavisky*, 35, 157. Bortchy-Melnikoff was not alluding exclusively to the betting trips when he complained of the "dustbin"*(poubelle)*.

64. CE 1:963, 969, 975 (Cauwès, 13 April 1934); see chap. 3.

65. APP (Ministère public c/Benoist et Oustric, criminal court of the Seine, 26–29 May 1933, deposition of Emile Barthélémy); CE 2:1760–62 (André Benoist, 7 May 1934).

66. APP (Ministère public c/Benoist et Oustric, criminal court of the Seine, 26–29 May 1933); AN CAC (files Anquetil, 1a/332–940433/4 and 1/17361–940432/185, police note of 7 March 1922); AN BB18 6745 (file Oustric); ADP D2U8353 (Benoist/Oustric affair), esp. JI Brack/Joseph Petit, 23 June 1931; CE 2:2220ff. (Pécune, 25 May 1934); CE 3:3532 (Sevetre, 11 July 1934).

67. CE 3:3511–18 (Gripois, 11 July 1934); CE 2:1760–62 (André Benoist, 7 May 1934); CE 1:20, 22 (Pachot, 2 March 1934).

68. CE, annexes (individual reports, report of René Besse), 141–42.

69. AN 334AP69 (Edmond Pachot, 25 November 1935); CE 1:23 (Pachot, 2 March 1934); CE, annexes (individual reports, report of René Besse), 144.

70. Whether Prince ever gave or showed Pressard the Gripois report became a subject of dispute between the two in January and February 1934 (see below, chaps. 10 and 11). The evidence that he did not seems conclusive, and is summarized in the report of René Besse in CE, annexes (individual reports): he kept no record of having sent it to Pressard, even though he recorded sending other documents; since he attached little importance to it, by his own account, he would have seen no need to send it on; and no evidence survived anywhere in his papers of his having sent it, or of Pressard's having

asked for it. In *Ils ont tué mon père* Gisèle Dessaux Prince gives her father's belated recollection of Pressard taking the Gripois report and leaving it in his desk drawer for months, but passes over in silence all the other evidence to the contrary (49). It is entirely possible that, four years after the incident, which at the time was minor, Prince confused it in his memory with another exchange, perhaps the Cousin report; see below.

71. Observations on Pressard's character by Presiding Judge Lescouvé in CE 1:740 (10 April 1934); photos of Pressard in *Le Matin,* 11 November 1935, *Le Jour,* 25 February and 12 April 1934.

72. AN 334AP69 (Edmond Pachot, 25 November 1935).

73. AN 334AP70 (Georges Rateau, 12 December 1935); CE 2:1531–32, 1540–41 (Rateau, 1 May 1934); CE 2:1593–94 (Sergent, 2 May 1934), 1567 (Pierre Laval, 2 May 1934), 1586–87 (Raoul Peret, 2 May 1934), 1616, 1619–20 (Paul Reynaud, 2 May 1934).

74. AN 334AP70 (Georges Rateau, 12 December 1935); CE, annexes (individual reports, report of René Besse), 155–56.

75. *Les Informations Politiques et Financières,* 5 May 1930 (from AN F7 16017/1); CE 3:3615 (André Tardieu, 18 July 1934).

76. ADP (file Foncière), suit for swindle brought by J. Alexis Grand, 5 February 1934.

77. AN BB18 6745 (PR Seine to PG, 12 November 1930); AN BB18 6722 (file on Banque Industrielle de Chine).

78. AN 334AP70 (Georges Rateau, 12 December 1935).

79. Robert Charvin, *Justice et politique. Evolution de leurs rapports* (Paris, 1968), 25–29, 63–75, 104–19.

80. Ibid., 175–98; Martin, *The Shame of Marianne,* 191–96. The power of the minister of justice in matters of appointment and promotion was somewhat curtailed after 1906 by the adoption of competitive entry exams and by the *tableau d'avancement* (advancement list), which narrowed the choice of candidates eligible for promotion.

81. AN 334AP69 (Cousin and de Chevert, 25 November 1935); CE 2:3512 (Gripois, 11 July 1934); CE 2:3492, 3494 (Cousin, 11 July 1934); CE 1: 24 (Pachot, 2 March 1934).

82. The investigation of Benoist and Oustric, and the transcript of their trial, contain accounts of such procedures: ADP D2U8353 (Oustric affair), and APP (Ministère public c/Benoist and Oustric, 26–29 May 1933), 36ff.

83. Cousin report in ADP D2U8431, and summarized in CE, annexes (private reports, report of René Besse), 156–57.

84. AN MI 25376 (Chéron to Interior, 23 February 1934; Xavier-Guichard to Chéron, 21 February 1934; Pachot to *Contrôleur Général* [*sic*], 7 January 1934); AN 334AP69 (Cousin and comment by Maître Ribet, 25 November 1935); CE 1:24–25, 26 (Pachot, 1 March 1934); CE 3:3490–91, 3499 (Cousin, 11 July 1934); CE, annexes (private reports, report of René Besse, 157); ADP D2U8431 (Pachot to PR, 3 June 1931, and Pachot to financial section, 9 June 1931; Prince to PJ, 18 June 1931).

85. AN MI 25376 (Pachot to *Contrôleur Général* [*sic*], 7 January 1934); Xavier Guichard to Insp. gén. Mossé, 8 January 1934); CE 1:26, 28–29, 41 (Pachot, 11 December 1934); CE 1:664 (Xavier Guichard, 29 March 1934).

86. AN MI 25376 (Pachot to *Contrôleur Général* [*sic*], 7 January 1934); AN 334AP69 (Pachot, 26 November 1935); CE 1:44 (Pachot, 11 July 1934); APP (Ministère public c/Oustric et Benoist, criminal court of the Seine, 26–29 May 1933, deposition of Pachot; APP, B/A 1253, note, n.d., c. November 1910) regarding Clemenceau's testimony before the parliamentary commission of inquiry into Rochette.

87. AN MI 25376 (report of Armand Mossé, 21 January 1934) (Guichard thought he—

Guichard—had sent the report to Chiappe); photo of Guichard in *Le Populaire*, 23 January 1934.

88. APP (personnel dossiers of Edmond Pachot; letter from Pachot to Chiappe, 27 March 1928).

89. AN 334AP70 (André Bruzin, 12 December 1935, and Charles Fontaine, 13 December 1935); CE 1:1001–1003, and 5:4812 (Bruzin, 17 April 1934 and 8 January 1935); CE (individual reports, report of René Besse), 158.

90. AN 334AP69 (Cousin, 25 November 1935); ADP D2U8431 (Cousin, 17 and 30 September 1931; Pachot/de Chevert, 2 October 1931; Pachot to financial section, 3 October 1931).

91. De Chevert gave several accounts of this exchange with Stavisky: one during his interrogation in Fresnes, 19 March 1934, in ADP D2U8; another to the criminal court, 26 November 1935, in AN 334AP69; another to Pachot on 2 October 1931, in ADP D2U8431; and another to the CE (4:4130–31, 6 November 1934). I have used the first of these four, which is also consistent with the other versions.

92. AN 334AP70 (André Bruzin, 12 December 1935).

93. Ibid.; AN 334AP70 (Charles Fontaine, 13 December 1935); CE 1:1003–1004 and 5:4822–23 (Bruzin, 17 April and 8 January 1935).

94. ADP D2U8431 (report of CD Orléans Fressard, 12 November 1931; Fressard to PR Orléans 27 November 1931; Pachot to Bruzin, 7 December 1931; PR (financial section) to Pachot, 14 December 1931); AN 334AP70 (André Bruzin, 13 December 1935). The formal instructions from the prosecutor's office to Pachot had been drafted by him beforehand with Bruzin.

95. AN F7 13981 (police note on Guiboud-Ribaud, n.d. but January 1934); AN D2U8450 (JI Ordonneau/Guiboud-Ribaud, 17 August 1934, and aide-mémoire by Guiboud-Ribaud, n.d. but February 1934); ADP D2U8431 (JI comm. Barthelet/Lucienne Caillet, 17 January 1934, regarding Migeon); photos of Guiboud-Ribaud in *Le Populaire*, 14 March 1934 and *Le Petit Parisien,* 27 February 1934; description in *Le Petit Parisien,* 19 November 1935; CE 1:182–83 (Guiboud-Ribaud, 13 March 1934); CE 1:2225–26 (de Monzie, 25 May 1934).

96. CE 2:2227ff. (de Monzie, 25 May 1934).

97. Ibid.; ADP D2U8431 (Pachot to PR and Pachot to Cousin, 17 December 1931; Cousin to Pachot, 18 December 1931); AN 334AP70 (André Bruzin, 12 December 1935); CE 1:1006, 1021 (Bruzin, 17 April 1934).

98. CE (individual reports, report of Lescouvé, 171–74); CE 2:1440–41 (Fillaire, 26 April 1934); ADP 1320W132 (indictment by PR Seine of Dr. Vachet, n.d. but March 1936).

99. AN 334AP70 (André Bruzin, 12 December 1935); CE 1:1002, 1014–15 (Bruzin, 17 April 1934); CE 2:1447 (Fillaire, 26 April 1934); CE 1:858 (Pressard, 11 April 1934).

100. See chap. 3, 34–35; CE 1:944–49 (Glard, 13 April 1934); AN MI 25376 (police note of 23 November 1931); AN 334AP69 (Maître Legrand, 26 November 1935); Pressard claims that he ended up supporting Glard, which is conceivable since Glard continued his investigation, but is also compatible with the warning to "be careful" *(soyez prudent)*, which Pressard later could not deny. CE 1:874–75 (Pressard, 11 April 1934); CE 2:1241, 1246–47 (Pressard, 24 April 1934).

101. AN 334AP69 (Edmond Pachot, 25 November 1935); CE 1:951 (Glard, 13 April 1934); CE 4:4392 (Geoffroy, 21 November 1934).

102. *Paris-Midi,* 10 March 1934. The reporter, Léon Sazie, had himself been frequenting the hairdresser's for more than fifteen years.

CHAPTER 6. A BANK FOR BAYONNE

1. AN 334AP71 (Maître Noguères, 7 January 1936); ADP D2U8417 (JI d'Uhalt/Garat, February 1934); ADP D2U8425 (accountant's report on crédit municipal de Bayonne, 3 vols., 19 July 1934); CE 2:1857–58 (Garat, 8 May 1934).

2. ADP D2U8433 (note of Comm. de police, Bayonne, 30 June 1934); CE 2:1857 (Garat, 8 May 1934); AN 334AP69 (Marcel Ribeton, Emile Morinaud, and Maurice Salle, 9 December 1935); Bortchy-Melnikoff, *300.000 kilomètres avec Stavisky,* 127.

3. ADP D2U8433 (Comm. Delgay, 17 May 1934; Elise Garat Vve Bertrand, 17 November 1934; note of 6 July 1934, author unclear; note of comm. de police in Bayonne, 30 June 1934, and report of PJ, financial brigade, 6 July 1934).

4. ADP D2U8433 (reports of Delgay, 17 May 1934, PJ financial brigade, 6 July 1934; expert Paul Caujolle, 18 September 1934; Emile Alleaume, 15 November 1934; Gratiane Elizagaray Vve Luro, 16 November 1934; Elise Garat Vve Bertrand, 17 November 1934, letters from Garat to Elizagaray, 3 and 23 January 1931, and report of Comm. Bertrand, 15 November 1934); AN BB18 2632 (Garat to GdS, 15 May 1920, and PG Pau to GdS, 1 June 1920); ADP D2U8417 (JI d'Uhalt/Garat, 7 January 1934).

5. AN BB18 6089 (dossier Bolo, Mme Marcelle Bolo to Interior, 4 March 1915); AN 334AP69 (Ferdinand Irrigoyen, 6 December 1935); CE 2:1834 (Fié, 8 May 1934).

6. CE 2:1857–58 (Garat, 8 May 1934); ADP D2U8467 (Garat, 8 November 1935); ADP D2U8425 (accountant's report on Bayonne, 19 July 1934, vol. 3).

7. AN 334AP69 (Ferdinand Irrigoyen, mayor of Biarritz, 6 December 1935).

8. ADP D2U8432 (JI Hude/Delamarche, 21 June 1934); ADP D2U8425 (accountant's report on Bayonne, 19 July 1934, 1:7ff.).

9. ADP D2U8432 (JI Ordonneau/Mireur/Garat, 2 June 1934, and JI Hude/Delamarche, 21 June 1934); CE 2:1818–19 (Mireur, 8 May 1934), 1694–95 (Delamarche, 4 May 1934), and 1861 (Garat, 8 May 1934).

10. CE 2:1817, 1819–20 (Mireur, 8 May 1934).

11. ADP D2U8467 (Garat, 8 November 1935); ADP D2U8432 (JI Ordonneau/Dupouy, 20 April 1934); ADP D2U8425 (accountant's report [see n. 8], 1:7ff., and vol. 2, minutes of 13 February and 3 April 1931).

12. ADP D2U8428 (Comm. Peudepièce/Digoin, 20 January 1934, and Comm. Delgay/Derote and Kuven, 5 December 1934); ADP D2U8425 (accountant's report [see n. 8], vol. 1 [unpaid personnel]); ADP D2U8428 (JI Ordonneau/Capdevielle and Henri Cohen, 11 and 5 May 1934); AN MI 25382 (Comm. Delgay/Eliane Cohen, 5 July 1934); ADP D2U8429 (JI d'Uhalt/Capdevielle, 2 January 1934).

13. ADP D2U8428 (Bonny/Desbrosses, 15, 18 January 1934; Ordonneau/Desbrosses, 8 March 1934; Desbrosses to Ordonneau, 11 February 1934); AN 334AP68 (Desbrosses, 7 November 1935); ADP D2U8425 (accountant's report [see n. 8]); AN MI 25376 (Insp. gén. Sarraz-Bournet, 10 January 1934); ADP D2U8432 (Ordonneau/Garat, 20 April 1934 and Ordonneau/Mireur/Garat, 2 June 1934); CE 2:1818–20 (Mireur, 8 May 1934).

14. ADP D2U8433 (Comm. Bayonne to PR Bayonne, 21 July 1934, and JI Ordonneau/Tissier, 12 July 1934); *Le Jour,* 8 November 1935 (from AN F7 16019/2); AN 334AP68 (Tissier, 7 November 1935).

15. AN 334AP68 (Tissier, 7 November 1935); ADP D2U8433 (Tribunal de première instance report [Seine] on Tissier, 31 July 1934).

16. ADP D2U8428 (Bonny/Desbrosses, 18 January 1934; Desbrosses to JI, 11 February 1934; and Ordonneau/Desbrosses, 3 December 1934); AN 334AP68 (Desbrosses, 7 November 1935); ADP D2U8417 (Bonny/Desbrosses, 18 January 1934). AN MI 25379/87

(Comm. Delgay/Tranchandon, 11 July 1934; Tranchandon, who knew Tissier, thought he had actually worked at Le Touquet for the Etablissements Alex in the summer of 1929); ADP D2U8433 (Tissier, 4 December 1934); ADP D2U8417 (JI d'Uhalt/ Tissier, 28 December 1934); AN 334AP68 (Tissier, 7 November 1935); ADP D2U8433 (Comm. Bayonne to PR Bayonne, 21 July 1934); *Paris-Soir*, 2 January 1934; Bortchy-Melnikoff, *300.000 kilomètres avec Stavisky*, 119.

17. ADP D2U8428 (JI Peudepièce/Digoin, 20 January 1934); CE 2:1821 (Mireur, 8 May 1934).

18. ADP D2U8425 (accountant's report [see n. 8], vols. 2 [budget] and 4 [mechanism of the double swindle]); CE 2:1852–53 (Sadron, 8 May 1934).

19. Photo in *L'Oeuvre*, 1 January 1934.

20. ADP D2U8428 (Comm. Peudepièce/Digoin, 20 January 1934; JI Ordonneau/Hattot, 1 August 1934).

21. ADP D2U8467 (Garat 8 November 1935); ADP D2U8425 (accountant's report [see n. 8], vol. 3).

22. ADP D2U8428 (JI Ordonneau/Piet, 22 June 1934).

23. Ibid.; ADP D2U8417 (Lucien Piet, 5 January 1934); AN 334AP69 (Lucien Piet, 29 November 1935); CE 2:2270–76 (Piet, 28 May 1934).

24. ADP D2U8417 (JI d'Uhalt/Tissier, 8 February 1934); ADP D2U8425 (accountant's report [see n. 8]); AN 334AP68 (Tissier, 7 November 1935).

25. AN 334AP68 (Tissier, 7 November 1935).

26. ADP D2U8417 (Guébin to Garat, 31 March 1931).

27. ADP D2U8417 (JI d'Uhalt/Guébin, 25 January 1934); AN 334AP70 (Santi, Carteron, Semalaigne, and Rebyllet, 13 December 1935); AN F7 13981 (note on Paul Guébin, n.d. but January 1934); *Le Populaire*, 26 January 1934 (photo of Guébin); *Le Petit Parisien*, 24 and 26 January 1934. At the trial (AN 334AP70), Guébin's character witnesses, like Guébin himself, repudiated the police reports (AN F7 13981) that portrayed him as wildly extravagant, but did not deny some of the details.

28. ADP D2U8417 (d'Uhalt/Guébin, 25 January 1934); ADP D2U8425 (accountant's report on Bayonne canvassers, 2 vols. [1934], i, 5ff.); ADP D2U8448 (JI Demay/Guébin, 8 January 1934); AN 334AP68 (Guébin, 13 November 1935).

29. AN 334AP70 (Roger Suzanne and Etienne Isabelle, 10 December 1935); AN 334AP71 (Maître Ribet, 9 January 1936); ADP D2U8448 (Demay/Isabelle, 10 January 1934); ADP D2U8449 (Demay/Carteron, 11 January 1934); CE 2:2383 (Isabelle, 31 May 1934).

30. ADP D2U8467 (Garat, 9 November 1935, esp. comments by Maître Noguères); ADP D2U8417 (Guébin to Garat, 31 March 1931, and Garat to Guébin, 19 May 1931); ADP D2U8431 (d'Uhalt/Garat, 8 February 1934); AN 334AP68 (Guébin, 13 November 1935).

31. ADP D2U8448 (JI Demay/Isabelle, 10 January 1934); CE 2:2376 (Isabelle, 31 May 1934).

32. ADP D2U8448 (JI Demay/Victor Pougez, 9 January 1934, Insp. Bonny/Dubois, 4 January 1934); ADP D2U8425 (accountant's report [see n. 28]).

33. ADP D2U8448 (JI Demay/Victor Pougez, 9 January 1934, Insp. Bonny/Dubois, 4 January 1934); ADP D2U8425 (accountant's report [see n. 28]); ADP D2U8433 (report of expert-comptable Verlaguet on Bayonne bonds, January 1935); AN BB18 6765 (Department of Justice note of 9 January 1934); ADP D2U8417 (JI Demay/Guébin, 13 February 1934); ADP D2U8448 (JI Demay/Feindri, 12 January, 6 November 1934).

34. Guilleminault and Singer-Lecocq, *La France des Gogos*; John Kenneth Galbraith,

A Short History of Financial Euphoria, 2d ed. (New York, 1993); C. Kindleberger, *Manias, Panics and Crashes,* 2d ed. (New York, 1989).

35. See chap. 5; CE 2:1696 (Delamarche, 4 May 1934).

36. CE 2:1695, 1718, 1741–44, 1751–52 (Constantin and Delamarche, 4 May 1934); ADP D2U8467 (Garat, 8 November 1935); AN BB18 6772 (PR to PG Seine, 4 April 1935).

37. AN 334AP69 (Constantin, 3 December 1935); ADP D2U8452 (JI Demay/Proust, 30 March 1934); CE 1:385–87, 393, 397 (Proust, 20 March 1934).

38. *Dictionnaire des parlementaires;* ADP D2U8447 (Ordonneau/Gaulier, 25 April 1934); *L'Humanité,* 15 March 1934, *Paris-Midi,* 21 March 1934, *Le Populaire,* 7 April 1934.

39. CE 1:386, 390 (Proust, 20 March 1934).

40. CE 1:392 (Proust, 20 March 1934); ADP D2U8429 (Rollin to Garat, 30 May 1931).

41. ADP D2U8425 (accountant's report [see n. 8]); ADP D2U8467 (Garat 9 November 1935); ADP D2U8432 (Rouvier to Chautemps, 19 January 1934); ADP D2U8417 (JI Demay/Maze, 18 January 1934); AN 334AP68 (Tissier, 7 November 1935).

42. ADP D2U8431 (Comm. Barthelet/Bortchy-Melnikoff, 6 February 1934).

43. Bortchy-Melnikoff, *300.000 kilomètres avec Stavisky,* 148–49.

44. See chap. 5; CE 2:2263–69 (Gibert, 28 May 1934); CE 1:248 (Fressard, 14 March 1934); AN MI 25376 (Insp. gén. Sarraz-Bournet, 10 January 1934); *Le Petit Parisien,* 26 January 1934; *Le Populaire,* 14 March 1934.

45. CE 2:2263–69 (Gibert, 28 May 1934); CE 2:1858–59, 1867 (Garat, 8 May 1934); AN 334AP68 (Garat, 12 November 1935) ; AN 334AP69(Gibert, 5 December 1935); ADP D2U8417 (Gibert, 13 January 1934).

46. CE 2:2264–65 (Gibert, 28 May 1934); AN 334AP69 (Gibert, 5 December 1935); AN 334AP68 (Garat, 12 November 1935).

47. CE 2:2265 (Gibert, 28 May 1934).

48. Bortchy-Melnikoff, *300.000 kilomètres avec Stavisky,* 149–51 (account compressed here). This conversation, the date of which is not given, probably took place shortly after the Fressard episode in Bayonne.

CHAPTER 7. FREEDOMS OF THE PRESS

1. *D'Artagnan* 6 (26 September 1931): 257.

2. ADP D2U8429 (JI d'Uhalt/Henri Mercadier, 9 January 1934); ADP D2U8433 (report of comm. sp., Saint-Jean-de-Luz, 22 February 1934); ADP D2U8431 (JI Demay/Eugène Tribout, 6 February 1934); ADP 1320W132 (PR Seine to PG, 17 May 1934); ADP D2U8436 (JI Demay/Adrien Cerf, 13 March 1934, and report of PJ on Cerf, 9 April 1934; JI Ordonneau/Hayotte, 19 April 1934); ADP D2U8439 (JI Demay/Detrimont, 6 March 1934).

3. *D'Artagnan* 7 (26 March 1932): 283.

4. CE 2:2217–24 (Pécune, 25 May 1934); ADP D2U8421 (Louis Fabre, 8 September 1934); Pécune also had his contacts at the SG, see AN 334AP70 (Charles Brousse, 17 December 1935).

5. Transcript of Hanau-Anquetil trial (correctional court of the Seine, eleventh chamber, February 1930), in *Les Nouvelles Economiques et Financières,* 4 and 14 February 1930.

6. Alec Mellor, *Le chantage* (Paris, 1937), 75–79; see chap. 4, 58–60; AN BB18 6723 (PR Seine report on law of 24 July 1867, 22 May 1920, section 1); AN BB18 6775 (indictment of PR, April 1934; PG to PR 24 April 1934; and PR to PG 9 May 1934).

7. Mellor, *Le chantage,* 12–14.

8. Honoré de Balzac, *Illusions Perdues* (Paris, 1953), 362–65; C. Lafitte, *Scandale, Mis-*

ère et Cie (Nogent-le-Rotrou, 1896), 1:8–10, 91–97; Emile Fabre, *Les ventres dorés* (Paris, 1905), act 2; Jules Romains, *Le 6 octobre* (Paris, 1927).

9. Mellor, *Le chantage,* 66–75, 125–27; Pierre Albert, "La corruption du journalisme," *Pouvoirs* 31 (1984): 53–63; ADP D2U8437 (JI Ordonneau/Darius, 21 December 1934).

10. *Les Nouvelles Economiques et Financières,* 4 February 1930 (Hanau-Anquetil trial); C. Bellanger et al., *Histoire générale de la presse française* (Paris, 1972), 3:174, 310, 454–55; Jeanneney, *L'argent caché;* see comments of Chautemps in CE 3:3114–16 (22 June 1934) and Daladier in CE 1:1134 (13 April 1934): "I'm saying that a very large number of papers have been helped by all governments."

11. Jeanson, *70 ans d'adolescence,* 142.

12. ADP D2U8441 (Comm. Delgay/ A. Bornand [Saint-Jean de Luz], 25 June 1934); ADP D2U8428 (JI Ordonneau/Hayotte, 1 May 1934).

13. AN BB18 6767 (PR Grasse to PG Aix, 30 April 1934); AN MI 25376 (report of Insp. gén. Plytas, 19 January 1934); AN MI 25379/87 (Comm. Delgay/Zographos, 6 June 1934); CE 5:5406–24 (Zographos, 20 March 1935); CE 1:554ff. and 5:5433ff. (Montabré, 27 March and 20 March 1935). The incident was never cleared up.

14. CE 1:558–60, 569–71 (Montabré, 27 March 1934); CE, annexes (private reports, François Peissel), 76.

15. CE 1:554ff. and 5:5433ff. (Montabré, 27 March and 20 March 1935); AN MI 25382 (Police Mobile report, 10 January 1935).

16. AN BB18 6767 (PR Grasse to PG Aix, 30 April 1934); *D'Artagnan* 6 (26 March 1932): 283; the charges were dropped in the case on 18 May 1932.

17. *D'Artagnan* 7 (16 April 1932): 286; CE 1:275–76, 279–80 (Jullien, 15 March 1934); CE 2:2220–21 (Pécune, 25 May 1934).

18. CE 4:3996 (Dubarry, 30 October 1934); AN 334AP68 (Dubarry, 15 November 1935); *Paris-Soir,* 6 November 1935, 18 January 1936; *Le Matin,* 5, 16 November 1935; *Action Française,* 16 November 1935.

19. AN MI 25321 (police report of 11 October 1926); ADP D2U8444 (JI Ordonneau/Dubarry, 6 July 1934); CE 4:3997–98 (Dubarry, 30 October 1934); Garçon, *Histoire de la justice,* 2:287.

20. ADP D2U8446 (Insp. gén. of colonies, 18 May 1912; report to Ministry of Colonies, 14 January 1905; head of customs services to governor of French Guyana, 11 February 1908).

21. ADP D2U8444 (JI Ordonneau/Dubarry, 6 July 1934).

22. AN MI 25321 (police report of 11 October 1926).

23. AN MI 25321 (police reports of 11 April and 29 May 1918, 5 August 1921).

24. AN MI 25321 (police reports of 12 and 23 June 1922, 7 January 1924); AN CAC (dossier Anquetil, note of 8 March 1922).

25. AN MI 25321 (notes of 11 April and 29 May 1918); ADP D2U8444 (note of 31 May 1934); ADP D2U8445 (Insp. Raibaut of Cannes to CC Cannes, 28 March 1934).

26. AN MI 25321 (reports of 29 May 1918, 30 September 1922, 5 August 1921, 14 October 1926, 26 November 1926, 13, 19, and 28 March 1929).

27. AN 5AR404 (archives Havas, Dubarry to Havas, 13 September 1928, 13 January 1931).

28. AN MI 25321 (reports of 11 October 1926, 29 May 1918, 5 September 1922); ADP D2U8444 (Ordonneau/Dubarry, 6 July 1934, and PJ to Ordonneau, 9 April 1934); see chap. 2, 11, and chap. 3, 32ff.

29. CE 4:3996 (Dubarry, 30 October 1934); ADP D2U8428 (depositions of Café de Paris personnel, 16 January 1934).

30. CE 4:3997 (Dubarry, 30 October 1934); ADP D2U8445 (Comm. Delgay/Mme Dubois).

31. AN MI 25376 (report of Insp. gén. Plytas on SG, 19 January 1934, also summarized in CE, annexes, private report of M. François Peissel).

32. AN MI 25376 (report of Insp. gén. Plytas on Bayard, 24 January 1934); ADP D2U8454 (Ordonneau/Jullien, 26 October 1934); CE 1:269ff. (Jullien, 15 March 1934); CE 4:4003 (Dubarry, 30 October 1934).

33. AN MI 25376 (report of Insp. gén. Plytas on SG, 19 January 1934); CE 1:282ff. (Mahieu, 15 March 1934); CE 1:269ff. (Jullien, 15 March 1934); see n. 31.

34. CE 1:269ff. (Jullien, 15 March 1934).

35. ADP D2U8454 (JI Ordonneau/Jullien, 26 October 1934); CE 1:269ff. (Jullien, 15 March 1934); CE 1:527–28 (Thomé, 23 March 1934).

36. ADP D2U8445 (Ordonneau/Dubarry and Thomé, 8 May 1934); ADP D2U8454 (Ordonneau/Thomé, 26 October 1934); AN 334 AP 70 (Thomé, 20 December 1935); CE 1:516, 520 (Chautemps, 23 March 1934); CE 1:525–26 (Thomé, 23 March 1934); *Le Populaire*, 13 March 1934, and *Paris-Midi*, 7 March 1934.

37. AN MI 25376 (Chéron to Interior, 23 February 1934; reports of Insp. gén. Plytas, 19 January 1934 and Insp. gén. Mossé, 21 January 1934); Marcel Rougé, "La Sûreté Nationale" (doctoral thesis in law, Université de Dijon, 1935); JO, 6 May 1934; Jean-Marc Berlière, "Ordre et sécurité. Les nouveaux corps de police de la troisième république," *Vingtième siècle* 39 (July–September 1993): 23–37.

38. ADP D2U8454 (Ordonneau/Ducloux, 23 October 1934); AN MI 25376 (report of Insp. gén. Plytas, 19 January 1934); CE 1:149 (Ducloux, 9 March 1934).

39. ADP D2U8433 (JI Ordonneau/Garat, 13 November 1934); ADP D2U8444 (Ordonneau/Dubarry, 10 October 1934); ADP D2U8445 (JI d'Uhalt/Dubarry, 28 February 1934); CE 3:2769 (Pierre Strohl, 14 June 1934) and 4:4004 (Dubarry, 30 October 1934).

40. ADP D2U8417 (JI Ordonneau/Dubarry, 12 and 13 January 1934); ADP D2U8424 (Chaouat Myr, 20 June 1934); ADP D2U8445 (JI d'Uhalt/Dubarry, 28 February 1934); Bortchy-Melnikoff, *300.000 kilomètres avec Stavisky*, 133ff.; CE 4:4005 (Dubarry, 30 October 1934).

41. CE 4:4005 (Dubarry, 30 October 1934); ADP D2U8424 (René Machenaud, 29 June 1934); AN 3AR1 (*L'Oeuvre* archive, letter from Gustave Téry, 18 August 1929).

42. CE 4:4008 (Dubarry, 30 October 1934); ADP D2U8445 (JI Lapeyre/Dubarry, 6 January 1934).

43. ADP D2U8433 (JI Hude/Tissot, 2 November 1934).

44. ADP D2U8445 (JI Lapeyre/Dubarry, 7 January 1934); ADP D2U8444 (JI Ordonneau/Dubarry, 10 October 1934); ADP D2U8433 (Comm. Delgay, 11 September 1934); CE 2:1950 (Dalimier, 9 May 1934); Emile Buré on Dalimier in *L'Ordre*, 7 January 1934 (from AN F7 16019/1); *Dictionnaire des parlementaires*, s.v. "Dalimier"; photo in *Le Populaire*, 9 January 1934. In his CE testimony, Dalimier denied a close friendship with Dubarry but not contacts over the years (CE 1 466 [Dalimier, 22 March 1934]).

45. *Baedeker's Paris*, 298.

46. ADP D2U8445 (Lapeyre/Dubarry, 6 January 1934); CE 1:466 (Dalimier, 22 March 1934).

47. ADP D2U8443 (Hermant dossier); AN BB18 6722 (PR Seine to PG, 4 April 1935); CE 1:465–66 and 2:1953–55 (Dalimier, 22 March and 9 May 1934).

48. ADP D2U8445 (Lapeyre/Dubarry); CE 1:478–79 (Dalimier, 22 March 1934); Dubarry claimed that, at their meeting, Dalimier looked up the relevant legislation and then answered Dubarry in the affirmative, which Dalimier denied.

49. AN BB18 6722 (PR Seine to PG, 4 April 1935); ADP D2U8431 (Dalimier to Gds Chéron, 28 February 1934); CE 1:794–98 (Roussel, 11 April 1934), 804–5, 810–12 (Netter, 11 April 1934), 819 (Henry, 11 April 1934).

50. The caller's identity was never established, though Dubarry aroused strong suspicions when the scandal broke. Pierre Alype, Dalimier's chief of staff, may have made the call, but this seems unlikely. AN BB18 6722 (PR Seine to PG, 4 April 1935); ADP D2U8445 (JI Ordonneau/Dubarry, 6 July 1934, and minutes of 10 January 1907); AN 334 AP 70 (Paul Henry, 16 December 1935); CE 1:805–7, 810–13 (Netter, 11 April 1934), 819–22, 824–25, 828, 830–31 (Henry, 11 April 1934), 915–16, 922 (Ferdinand-Dreyfus, 13 April 1934).

51. AN BB186722 (PR Seine to PG, 4 April 1935); AN 334AP70 (Paul Henry, 16 December 1935); AN 334AP69 (Dalimier, 9 December 1935); CE 1:476–77 (Dalimier, 22 March 1934), 916 (Ferdinand-Dreyfus, 13 April 1934).

52. AN BB186722 (PR Seine to PG, 4 April 1935); ADP D2U8443 (note regarding bonds in circulation 31 December 1932, n.d.); ADP D2U8444 (JI Ordonneau/Dubarry, 10 October 1934); ADP D2U8417 (JI Demay/Yung, 18 January 1934); ADP D2U8420 (report of Caujolle on Hungarian bond venture, 28 September 1934).

53. ADP 1320W98 (PR Seine to PG, 29 April 1936); ADP D2U8444 (Boisgontier report on SAPIENS, 6 September 1934, JI Ordonneau/Dubarry 10 October 1934); CE 4:4004–8 (Dubarry, 30 October 1934).

54. AN 334AP70 (Jean Chiappe, 17 December 1935); ADP D2U8445 (JI Ordonneau/ Chiappe, 15 May 1934); ADP D2U8444 (Ordonneau/Dubarry 10 October 1934); CE 1:598 (Chiappe, 28 March 1934).

55. AN 334AP70 (Chautemps, 17 December 1935); ADP D2U8445 (Ordonneau/ Chautemps, Ordonneau/Thomé and Ordonneau/Dubarry-Thomé, 8 May 1934); ADP D2U8454 (Ordonneau/Thomé, 26 October 1934); CE 3:3135–39 (Chautemps, 22 June 1934).

56. Marc Martin, *Médias et journalistes de la République* (Paris, 1997), 161–62, 180–81.

57. ADP D2U8434 (Ordonneau/Arlette Stavisky, 12 March 1934).

58. ADP 1320W102 (Comm. Delgay to CGRJ, 15 September 1934); ADP D2U8429 (Insp. Bonny, 4 January 1934); ADP D2U8434 (JI Ordonneau/Arlette Stavisky, 4 December 1934); Joseph Kessel, *Stavisky. L'homme que j'ai connu* (Paris, 1974), 67; Stavisky, *Stavisky était mon père*, 51, 55; Bortchy-Melnikoff, *300.000 kilomètres avec Stavisky*, 59.

59. ADP D2U8428 (Insp. Bonny/Hayotte, 6 January 1934); ADP D2U8431 (Insp. Barthelet/Bortchy-Melnikoff, 6 February 1934); ADP D2U8441 (Insp. Borel/Barbou, 9 January 1934); AN MI 25376 (CD Guillaume to PJ, 9 January 1934); Stavisky, *Stavisky était mon père*, 52.

60. AN F7 13981 (SG note, 5 January 1934, Père Jean); ADP D2U8424 (PJ report, 27 June 1934, Drouant); Bortchy-Melnikoff, *300.000 kilomètres avec Stavisky*, 50, 53–55, 117–18.

61. AN BB18 6775 (indictment of PR, April 1936, PG to PR, 24 April 1934, and PR to PG, 9 May 1936); AN MI 25339 (notes of 12 and 23 June 1922); AN CAC (dossier Anquetil, 1a/332–940433/4, note of 20 March 1928); CE 2:2195–2206 (Albert Livet, 24 May 1934).

62. ADP D2U8428 (Hude/Joseph Kessel, 8 June 1934); Joseph Kessel, *Stavisky*, 11–14.

63. ADP D2U8428 (Hude/Georges Kessel, 15 June 1934); Kessel, *Stavisky,* 21–23.

64. Kessel, *Stavisky,* 25–28; ADP D2U8428 (JI Hude/Joseph Kessel, 8 June 1934 and Hude/Georges Kessel, 15 June 1934); ADP 1320W102 (Comm. Delgay to CGRJ, 8 September 1934); ADP D2U8453 (JI Ordonneau/Romagnino, 25 September 1934).

65. Kessel, *Stavisky,* 28–33; ADP D2U8428 (Hude/Joseph Kessel, 8 June 1934).

66. Kessel, *Stavisky,* 36–38, 39, 57–58.

67. Ibid., 43–44; ADP D2U8428 (Hude/Joseph Kessel, 8 June 1934); AN 334AP69 (Aymard, 22 November 1935).

68. ADP D2U8428 (Comm. Delgay to CGRJ, 8 February 1935); AN CAC, 26136/art. 284 (dossier Aymard); *Paris-Soir,* 13 January 1934 (Dubarry and Aymard).

69. Kessel, *Stavisky,* 45–46; AN 334AP69 (Aymard. 22 November 1935).

70. ADP D2U8428 (Ordonneau/Aymard, 10 January 1934); AN 334AP69 (Aymard, 22 November 1935). Aymard reprints his interrogations in his tendentious *La véritable affaire Stavisky. Lettres à mes jurés* (Paris, 1935).

71. See chap. 3, 40–42.

72. ADP D2U8451 (Comm. Delgay/Charles Kahn and Delgay/Fernand Hauser, 12 September 1934; Delgay to CGRJ, 29 January 1935; JI Ordonneau/Lévy, 30 May 1934); AN 334AP70 (Charles Kahn, 18 December 1935); CE 2:1391, 1403 (Lévy, 26 April 1934).

73. ADP D2U8429 (JI d'Uhalt/Mercadier, 9 January 1934); ADP D2U8445 (Mercadier, 25 May 1934); AN 334AP70 (Mercadier, 16 December 1935); *Détective,* 1 February 1934 (from APP E/A 144).

74. AN MI 25376 (Comm. Pujol to CGRJ, 21 April 1934); ADP D2U8445 (JI Ordonneau/Chaouat and Dubarry, 25 May 1934); CE 3:3973 (Myr Chaouat, 25 July 1934); CE 4:4028 (Dubarry, 30 October 1934); Dubarry later denied discussing the articles in *Aux Ecoutes* with Mercadier, but this is implausible (in light, for example, of the date of their meeting).

75. ADP D2U8417 (Paul Lévy, 18 January 1934); *Aux Ecoutes* 16, nos. 714, 715, 759 (23 and 30 January, 3 December 1932); CE 2:1385 (Paul Lévy, 26 April 1934).

76. AN F713981 (reports on Pierre Curral, n.d. but January 1934, and 15 January 1934); AN MI 25378 (dossier Curral); ADP D2U8451 (JI Hude/René Bellet, 24 January 1935); ADP 1320W98 (Bonny, 13 June 1933); ADP D2U8436 (JI Ordonneau/Pierre Curral, 2 March and 5 September 1934); ADP D2U8425 (accountant's report on Bayonne, outlays by Curral); CE 2:2031ff. (Curral, 17 May 1934).

77. CE 2:1389 (Paul Lévy, 26 April 1934); ADP D2U8451 (Comm. Delgay/Décis, 6 September 1934).

78. ADP D2U8437 (JI d'Uhalt/Darius, 21 February 1934 and PJ report, 5 July 1934); Guiboud-Ribaud called him a *hurluberlu* — "madman" — ADP D2U8441, 15 March 1934; AN 334AP71 (Freyssenge, 15 January 1936); AN MI 25377 (*La France Mutualiste* dossier, note on Darius); AN MI 25382 (SG report on Darius, 17 March 1933); *Le Journal,* 21 November 1935; *Paris-Soir,* 9 January and 17 February 1934, 22 November 1935; Pierre Darius, *L'amour au Maroc. Choses vues* (Paris, 1933).

79. ADP D2U8417 (d'Uhalt/Darius, 11 and 13 January 1934; and Ordonneau/Darius, 21 February 1934); AN MI 25382 (SG report, 17 March 1933); CE 2:1900–1901, 1908–9 (Darius, 9 May 1934).

80. ADP D2U8435 (JI Ordonneau/Darius, 1 June 1934; and JI Ordonneau/Chauchat, 25 July 1934); ADP D2U8417 (PR Seine to PG, 5 January 1934); ADP D2U8452 (JI Demay/Esperronnier, 19 April 1934).

81. *Bec et Ongles,* 15 October and 12 November 1932.

82. ADP D2U8432 (JI Lapeyre/Morinaud, 27 February 1934); ADP D2U8JI 417 (d'Uhalt/Garat, 10 January 1934).

83. ADP D2U8417 (JI d'Uhalt/Dubarry, 12 and 13 January 1934); ADP D2U8445 (JI Lapeyre/Dubarry, 6 January 1934; and d'Uhalt/Dubarry, 21 February 1934); CE 2:1901 (Darius, 9 May 1934).

84. ADP D2U8437 (JI Ordonneau/Darius, 8 January 1934, and JI d'Uhalt/Darius, 21 February 1934); ADP D2U8429 (PR Seine to PG, 5 January 1934); CE 2:1899 (Darius, 9 May 1934).

85. ADP D2U8429 (PR Seine to PG, 5 January 1934); ADP D2U8437 (JI Ordonneau/Darius, 8 January 1934); AN 334AP68 (Garat, 9 November 1935); AN 334AP69 (Darius, 20 November 1935).

86. AN 334AP68 (Maître Noguères, 12 November 1935), and AN 334AP69 (Maître Loewel, 20 November 1935).

87. See chap. 5, 81–87.

88. AN 334AP69 (Darius, 20 November 1935); CE 2:1899 (Darius, 9 May 1934); ADP D2U8417 (Darius, 11 and 13 January 1934).

89. *D'Artagnan* 8 (25 February 1933): 331, and 8 (4 March 1933): 332; ADP D2U8453 (JI Ordonneau/Romagnino, 3 May 1934); AN BB18 6772 (indictment of PR, n.d. but April 1936); CE 2:2217–18 (Pécune, 23 May 1934).

90. ADP D2U8437 (JI Ordonneau/Darius and Romagnino, 29 December 1934).

91. AN BB186772 (dossier "press and publicity," indictment of PR, n.d. but April 1936); CE 2:2195–2206 (Livet, 24 May 1934).

92. ADP D2U8436 (JI Demay/Anquetil, 16 March 1934); CE 2:2209–11 (Anquetil, 24 May 1934).

93. ADP D2U8453 (JI Ordonneau/Romagnino, 12 March 1934).

94. Ibid.; ADP D2U8436 (JI Hude/Chauchat, 25 July 1934); CE 2:2197 (Livet, 24 May 1934).

95. ADP D2U8417 (JI d'Uhalt/Bortchy-Melnikoff, 13 January 1934); ADP D2U8431 (Insp. Barthelet/Paul Barbou, 5 February 1934); ADP D2U8444 (JI Ordonneau/Dubarry, 10 October 1934); ADP D2U8445 (Comm. Delgay/Dubois); ADP D2U8450 (Ordonneau/Guiboud-Ribaud, 27 February 1934; and aide-mémoire, n.d. but February 1934).

96. ADP D2U8440 (Comm. Delgay/Hyacinthe Philouze, 9 May 1934).

CHAPTER 8. THE LIMITS OF PRETENSE

1. Kessel, *Stavisky,* 59, 60; ADP D2U8428 (JI Ordonneau/Joseph Kessel, 8 June 1934; and Ordonneau/Georges Kessel, 15 June 1934).

2. ADP D2U8424 (minutes of Paulette Luc, 26 September 1934, Salvatore Zelli, 4 April 1934, and Edmond Conquy alias Castel, 2 October 1934); ADP D2U8434 (Ordonneau/Poulner, 15 December 1934); see chap. 2.

3. Kessel, *Stavisky,* 61–64; see n. 1 above.

4. CE 2:2012 (Bonnaure, 16 May 1934); ADP D2U8420 (accountant's report on CADEGTI, 28 September 1934), 82.

5. ADP D2U8420 (accountant's report); CE 2:1981–83 (Bonnaure, 15 May 1934).

6. ADP D2U8417 (Insp. Bonny/Romagnino, 8 January 1934; and JI d'Uhalt/Bonnaure, 15 January 1934); ADP D2U8418 (PJ/de Chevert, 2 October 1931); ADP D2U8420 (accountant's report, 28 September 1934), 85; ADP D2U8431 (Comm. Pachot/de Chevert, 2 October 1931); ADP D2U8428 (Insp. Bonny/Niemen, 12 January 1934); ADP D2U8435 (Insp.

Barthelet/Bonnaure, 18 January 1934); ADP 1320w98 (PR to PG, 29 April 1936); ADP D2U8444 (Ameline/Vaissaire, 24 March 1934); *Le Quotidien,* 20 June 1934, and *L'Oeuvre,* 14 January 1934.

7. ADP D2U8435 (PJ report, 27 July 1934); *Dictionnaire des parlementaires;* AN CAC, 2/38186 94034/460 (notes of 30 August 1926, 5 October 1927, and 3 October 1929).

8. *Le Petit Parisien,* 15 February 1934; ADP 1320w98 (PR Seine to PG, 29 April 1936); AN CAC, 2/38186 940434/460 (dossier Bonnaur), notes of 22 and 29 April and 6 May 1932); Bortchy-Melnikoff, *300.000 kilomètres avec Stavisky,* 121–22.

9. Bortchy-Melnikoff, *300.000 kilomètres avec Stavisky,* 122–23; ADP D2U8431 (PJ/Alex Lafont and Georges Espagnol, head chasseurs, Fouquet, 3 March 1934).

10. ADP D2U8417 (Bonny/Arlette Stavisky, 12 January 1934); ADP D2U8431 (Barthelet/Bortchy-Melnikoff, 6 February 1934); ADP D2U8435 (Ordonneau/Bonnaure, 14 November, 5 December 1934).

11. ADP D2U8417 (Foreign Affairs to Justice, 25 January 1934); ADP D2U8420 (Foreign Affairs, note of 22 January 1934).

12. ADP D2U8435 (ambassador in Vienna to Foreign Affairs, 2 February 1934).

13. Ibid.; ADP D2U8431 (Insp. Barthelet/Bortchy-Melnikoff, 6 February 1934); Bortchy-Melnikoff, *300.000 kilomètres avec Stavisky,* 167–70.

14. ADP D2U8435 (ambassador in Vienna to Foreign Affairs, 2 February 1934).

15. See chap. 2, 10.

16. ADP D2U8432 (CGRJ report on Rita Georg, 27 March 1934); ADP D2U8435 (*Pester Lloyd,* 5 January 1935); ADP D2U8435 (JI Hude/Louis Brillat, 23 May 1934).

17. ADP D2U8428 (Hude report on Hayotte, 16 April 1934; Bonny/Hayotte, 6 January 1934; Peudepièce/Harry Baur, 10 January 1934; Insp. Antonini/Roger Cousin, 10 January 1934); ADP D2U8438 (Insp. Peudepièce to CGRJ, 30 March 1934); ADP D2U8432 (CGRJ to Ordonneau, 27 March 1934); AN MI 25382 (Chief Insp. Ravier/Audouard, 24 October 1934); *Paris-Soir,* 5 January 1934 (interview with Dranem).

18. Bortchy-Melnikoff, *300.000 kilomètres avec Stavisky,* 175, 180–81.

19. ADP D2U8428 (Hude report, 16 April 1934); ADP D2U8428 (Insp. Bonny/Desbrosses, 15 January 1934); ADP D2U8436 (Ordonneau/Curral, 2 March 1934).

20. Bortchy-Melnikoff, *300.000 kilomètres avec Stavisky,* 183–84; ADP D2U8432 (CGRJ to Ordonneau, 27 March 1934); ADP D2U8438 (Insp. Peudepièce to CGRJ, 30 March 1934, with report of Criminal Investigation Division, New Scotland Yard [CID], London, 28 March 1934).

21. ADP D2U8441 (Comm. Delgay/Georges Banyai, 30 March 1934); ADP D2U8428 (Delgay/Mme Sénevat, 6 December 1934); ADP D2U8431 (Barthelet/Bortchy-Melnikoff, February 1934).

22. ADP D2U8428 (Insp. Bonny/Hayotte, 6 January 1934; and report of Hude/accountant, 16 April 1934).

23. Ibid.

24. ADP D2U8420 (report of accountant Caujolle, on "Hungarian bond venture affair," 311 pp., 28 September 1934).

25. Ibid.

26. ADP D2U8421 (Vinson, 13 April 1934); CE 2:2461ff. (Vinson, 5 June 1934).

27. ADP D2U8420 (report of Caujolle, 28 September 1934).

28. ADP D2U8450 (JI Ordonneau/Guiboud-Ribaud, 27 February 1934); CE 1:186–87 (Guiboud-Ribaud, 13 March 1934).

29. ADP D2U8417 (Bonny/Arlette Stavisky, 12 January 1934); ADP D2U8428 (JI

Lapeyre/Arlette Stavisky, 16 January 1934); ADP D2U8435 (JI Ordonneau/Bonnaure, 16 May 1934).

30. ADP D2U8421 (Gaulier to Ordonneau, 25 April 1934); ADP D2U8453 (Ordonneau/Romagnino, 12 March 1934); ADP D2U8420 (report of Caujolle, 28 September 1934); ADP 1320w98 (Flandin to criminal court, 29 November 1935); ADP D2U8442 (Hude/Odin, 9, 10, 11 April 1934); CE 3:2407–8 (Flandin, 4 June 1934); CE 3:2548 (Bizot, 7 June 1934).

31. ADP D2U8420 (report of Caujolle, 28 September 1934); CE 3:2582 (Ambassador de Fontenay, 11 June 1934).

32. ADP D2U8440 (JI Demay/Suzanne Avril, née Ribardière, 11 April 1934); ADP D2U8432 (report of Insp. Le Gall, 10 March 1934); ADP D2U8440 (Demay/Avril, 5 and 7 May 1934; and Demay/Thomé, 8 May 1934); AN 334AP70 (Georges Thomé, 20 December 1935; and Suzanne Avril, 23 December 1935); Bortchy-Melnikoff, *300.000 kilomètres avec Stavisky*, 81–82.

33. ADP D2U8440 (JI Demay/Avril, 11 May 1934; Demay/Emile Schenaerts, 10 and 28 April 1934; Demay/Sperzagni and Josereau, barman and switchboard operator, respectively, at Carillon, 4 May 1934).

34. ADP D2U8440 (JI Demay/Avril, 11 April 1934; Demay/Hulin, 5 and 9 April 1934; Demay/Clegg, director of Talbot, 3 April 1934; Demay/Graux Talbot, 5 and 25 April 1934; Ordonneau/ Romagnino, 18 April 1934); AN BB18 6722 (PR to PG Seine, 7 May 1934); ADP D2U8431 (Barthelet/Bortchy-Melnikoff, 6 February 1934); Bortchy-Melnikoff, *300.000 kilomètres avec Stavisky*, 131.

35. ADP D2U8420 (report of Caujolle, 28 September 1934).

36. ADP D2U8444 (Ordonneau/Dubarry, 14 September 1934); ADP D2U8445 (Hude/Salomon, director of BCNI, 7 and 14 April 1934).

37. ADP D2U8425 (accountant's report on crédit municipal of Bayonne, 3 vols., 19 July 1934, vol. 3).

38. ADP D2U8433 (JI Demay/Alphonse Ravet, 4 and 8 October 1933; JI Hude/Tissot, 2, 13, 16 November 1934); AN 334AP70 (Charles Tissot, 18 December 1935).

39. ADP D2U8428 (JI Demay/Juillet, n.d. but 1934); CE 4:3881 (Juillet, 24 July 1934).

40. ADP D2U8428 (JI Demay/Juillet, n.d. but 1934); ADP D2U8428 (Demay/Juillet 18 April 1935).

41. ADP D2U8429 (JI d'Uhalt/Laffon, 2 January 1934); ADP D2U8432 (Hude/Delamarche, 22 June 1934); ADP D2U8431 (Barthelet/Bortchy-Melnikoff, 6 February 1934); ADP D2U8431 (d'Uhalt/Tissier, 1 February 1934); AN F7 13981 (note of 6 January 1934).

42. AN F7 13981 (note of 6 January 1934); ADP D2U8425 (accountant's report on crédit municipal of Bayonne, 3 vols., 19 July 1934, section 4).

43. ADP 1320w102 (Comm. Delgay to CGRJ, report on Arlette Simon, 15 September 1934).

44. ADP D2U8428 (JI Lapeyre/Arlette Stavisky, 16 January 1934).

45. ADP D2U8440 (Demay/Mme Avril, 11 April 1934); ADP D2U8444 (Ordonneau/Dubarry, 14 September 1933).

46. ADP D2U8444 (Ordonneau/Dubarry, 14 September 1934); CE 4:4034–35 (Dubarry, 30 October 1934).

47. AN F7 13981 (note of 10 January 1934); ADP D2U8428 (JI Ordonneau/Aymard, 10 January 1934).

48. ADP D2U8437 (Insp. Peudepièce/Boë, 6 January 1934; JI d'Uhalt/Boë, 21 February

1934; JI Ordonneau/Darius, 8 January 1934; d'Uhalt/Darius, 21 February 1934); CE 1:292 (Queuille, 15 March 1934); *Bec et Ongles,* 8 July 1933.

49. *Le Cri du Jour* 8 (1, 8, 15 and 29 July 1933); *D'Artagnan* 8 (24 June, 1, 15, 29 July 1933); *Bec et Ongles* 3 (24 June, 15 July 1933).

50. *La Bonne Guerre,* 24 April 1933 (from ADP D2U8435).

51. ADP D2U8471 (Stretti/Sartori affair, June and July 1926); CE 2:2067 (Sartori, 18 May 1934).

52. *La Bonne Guerre,* 19 March, 24 April, 8 and 24 May 1933 (from ADP D2U8435); AN 334AP68 (Romagnino, 19 November 1935).

53. ADP D2U8435 (JI Ordonneau/Bonnaure, 29 May 1934); ADP D2U8439 (Insp. Barthelet/Hainnaux, 18 April 1934); ADP D2U8441 (Comm. Delgay/F.-L. Raucoules, 14 September 1934); ADP D2U8444 (JI Hude/Delorme, 11 July 1934); CE 3:3095–96, 3109 (Chautemps, 22 June 1934).

54. ADP D2U8445 (JI Hude/Jean Contoux, editor-in-chief, *Le Pays,* 3 May 1934; Hude/Paul Merle, 5 May 1934; JI Ordonneau/Chiappe, 15 May 1934); ADP D2U8453 (Ordonneau/Romagnino, 12 May 1934); AN 334AP68 (Romagnino, 19 November 1935); CE 3:3433–37 (Paul Merle, 6 July 1934).

55. For Romagnino see n. 55 above; ADP 1320W132 (PR to PG Seine, 7 April 1934, Hainnaux); ADP D2U8439 (police note on Georges-Maurice Hainnaux, 4 April 1934); ADP D2U8428 (Insp. Bonny/Niemen, 12 January 1934).

56. AN MI 25376 (Insp. Bayard to Insp. gén. Plytas, 10 January 1934).

57. *Journal de la Bourse,* 29 July, 5 and 12 August 1933.

58. ADP D2U8441 (Comm. Delgay/Raucoules, 14 September 1934); *Commentaires,* 13 August, 17 September 1933; ADP D2U8432 (Hude/Delamarche, 22 June 1934); CE 5:4712 (Raucoules, 19 December 1934).

59. ADP D2U8437 (Comm. Delgay/Maxence Thomas, 30 October 1934); *Juvenal,* 4 and 18 August, 15 and 29 September 1933.

60. ADP D2U8451 (Delgay/Jean-Pierre Maxence, 3 July 1934); ADP D2U8451 (Hude/Hausser, 29 December 1934); AN 334AP69 (Paul Lévy, 21 November 1935).

61. AN 334AP66 (criminal court of the Seine, Bouilloux-Laffont affair, Colin [alias Lucco], Lubersac, Picherie, 20–29 March 1933). The research of Guillemette de Bure, currently (1998) in progress, should clarify these and other matters related to the Aéropostale scandal.

62. *Le Soir,* 14 March 1930 (from AN BB186731); AN MI 25335/43 (remarks of Raucoulles at Club du Faubourg, n.d. but April 1930).

63. ADP D2U8432 (Ordonneau/Mireur/Garat, 2 June 1934); AN 334AP69 (Joseph Anthelme, 29 November 1935; Robert Mireur, 5 December 1935; and Léon Béhotéguy, 6 December 1935); CE 2:1823 (Mireur, 8 May 1934) and 2150 (Anthelme, 23 May 1934). Garat could not have been unaware of Alexandre's identity at the time of his conversation with Mireur: the newspapers had already revealed it and it was widely known in the casinos the two had frequented.

64. See above, 157; Garat, of course, denied discovering the fraud at the time, but his panicky antics, including the doctoring of the minutes, leave little doubt.

65. ADP D2U8428 (JI d'Uhalt/Hayotte, 31 January 1934); ADP D2U8431 (d'Uhalt/Tissier, 1 February 1934); ADP D2U8438 (report of Criminal Investigation Division, New Scotland Yard, 28 March 1934); ADP 1320W98 (report of court-appointed jeweler Séror, 28 July 1934); ADP D2U8439 (Insp. Bonny/Samuel Maingourd, director of crédit municipal of Orléans, 9 March 1934); AN 334AP68 (Tissier, 7 November 1935).

66. *Paris-Soir,* 4 January 1934; ADP D2U8428 (Insp. Bonny/Hayotte, 6 January 1934; report on Hayotte's finances, 8 August 1934; Comm. Delgay/Boeri, 28 April 1934; JI Lapeyre/Arlette Stavisky, 16 January 1934); ADP D2U8438 (Insp. Peudepièce/Audouard, 13 March 1934).

67. Bortchy-Melnikoff, *300.000 kilomètres avec Stavisky,* 206-8.

68. ADP D2U8428 (JI Lapeyre/Arlette Stavisky, 16 January 1934).

69. ADP D2U8431 (reports of Insp. Cousin, 11 and 25 September 1933); ADP D2U8433 (Cousin to Mossé, 23 January 1934); AN MI 25376 (report of Xavier-Guichard, dir. of PJ, 21 February 1934, and of Insp. gén. Mossé, 21 January 1934).

70. APP (personnel dossiers of Edmond Pachot, esp. note of 2 February 1934, and Léon Ameline).

71. AN MI 25376 (report of Insp. gén. Mossé, 21 January 1934); CE 1:682ff. (Ameline, 29 March 1934); CE 3:3508 (Cousin, 11 July 1934).

72. CE 1:593, 600, 604, 610 (Chiappe, 28 March 1934); CE 3:4009, 4030 (Dubarry, 30 October 1934); AN MI 25376 (report of Insp. gén. Mossé, 21 January 1934; and Mossé to Chautemps, 24 January 1934); ADP D2U8444 (JI Ordonneau/Dubarry, 10 October 1934); ADP D2U8445 (Chiappe/Ordonneau, 15 May 1934); ADP D2U8431 (Insp. Barthelet/Barbou, 5 February 1934); CE 1 (Arlette Stavisky, 6 March 1934). Barbou, Stavisky's and Dubarry's driver on this occasion, confirmed the brevity of the meeting with Chiappe as well as the latter's warnings, which Dubarry, for evidently self-serving reasons, later attempted to deny.

73. ADP D2U8445 (JI Ordonneau/Chautemps, 8 May 1934); AN 334AP70 (Camille Chautemps, 17 December 1935); AN MI 25376 (report of Insp. gén. Plytas, 19 January 1934); CE 3:3519, 3523-24 (Insp. Lecerre, 11 July 1934).

74. CE 3:3519, 3523-24 (Insp. Lecerre, 11 July 1934); see chap. 5; AN MI 25376 (Interior to CE, 16 March 1934); ADP D2U8432 (JI Ordonneau/Mireur and Garat, 2 June 1934); ADP D2U8454 (Ordonneau/Thomé, 26 October 1934).

75. AN 334AP70 (John Hennet, 23 December 1935); AN MI 25376 (report of Insp. gén. Plytas, 19 January 1934); AN MI 25385 (report of Insp. gén. Gravereax on Hennet, 27 September 1934); for the Labbé affair see chaps. 3 and 5. Hennet denied discussing Bayonne with Comby, implausibly, in view of the timing and Comby's account to Insp. Simon. Hennet appears to have confused Bayonne with the fiscal stamp fraud.

76. AN F7 14599 (personnel dossier on John Hennet); CE 1:575ff. (Hennet, 28 March 1934); photos of Hennet in *Excelsior,* 20 November 1934, and *L'Oeuvre,* 23 January 1934.

77. AN F7 14599 (dossier on John Hennet).

78. Ibid.

79. Ibid.

80. CE 2:1817, 1831 (Mireur, 8 May 1934).

81. ADP D2U8432 (JI Hude/Delamarche, 22, 26, 29 June 1934); ADP D2U8432 (report of Insp. gén. Rouvier, 19 January 1934); AN MI 25376 (report of Insp. gén. Plytas, 19 January 1934); CE 2:1733-40 (Delamarche, 4 May 1934); CE 2:1816-41, passim (Mireur, 8 May 1934).

82. AN 334AP 69 (Béhotéguy, 6 December 1935); ADP D2U8431 (summary of report on SG in Bayonne, 11 January 1934); ADP D2U8429 (d'Uhalt/Cohen, 24 December 1933).

83. ADP D2U8432 (JI Hude/Delamarche, 29 June 1934).

84. ADP D2U8417 (JI Demay/Maze, 18 January 1934); CE 2:2179-80 (Maze, 23 May 1934).

85. CE 2:1842–44 (Sadron, 8 May 1934); ADP D2U8417 (JI d'Uhalt/Sadron, 28 December 1933).

86. For Thérèse Humbert, see press clippings in AN F7 12550; for Meg Steinheil, press clippings in AN F7 12551; for Banque Industrielle de Chine, see dossier AN BB18 6722.

87. CE 2:1843–44 (Sadron, 8 May 1934); AN 334AP69 (Sadron, 29 November 1935); ADP D2U8417 (JI d'Uhalt/Garat, 30 December 1933).

88. CE 2:1845 (Sadron, 8 May 1934); ADP D2U8429 (d'Uhalt/Anthelme and d'Uhalt/Sadron, 23 December 1933; d'Uhalt/Sangla, 26 December 1933); AN 334AP69 (Sadron, 29 November 1935.)

89. ADP D2U8434 (JI Ordonneau/Tissier, 17 April 1934, and CGRJ report, Biarritz, 6 April 1934).

90. ADP D2U8441 (Comm. Ameline/Décis, 28 March 1934, and JI Bordeaux/Lardy, 17 April 1934).

91. ADP D2U8428 (JI Hude/Joseph Kessel, 8 June 1934, and Hude/Georges Kessel, 15 June 1934); Kessel, *Stavisky*, 80–84; Colette, *Belles saisons* (Paris, 1955), 194–98.

92. ADP D2U8428 (JI Hude/Joseph Kessel, 8 June 1934); Kessel, *Stavisky*, 86–87.

93. Bortchy-Melnikoff, *300.000 kilomètres avec Stavisky*, 214.

CHAPTER 9. FAME

1. CE 1:211 (Guiboud-Ribaud, 13 March 1934), 683 (Léon Ameline, 29 March 1934); ADP D2U8435 (JI Ordonneau/Pigaglio, 26 June 1934); ADP D2U8450 (Ordonneau/Guiboud-Ribaud, 17 August 1934); AN F7 13981 (police note of 23 December 1933); AN MI 25376 (prefect of police to Interior, 1 February 1934). Pigaglio places the meeting on Rue Caumartin, while both Romagnino and Guiboud-Ribaud place it on Rue Marignan. So does Hayotte, though he appears to place it in the morning (ADP D2U8417, Hayotte, 11 and 30 January 1934). Pigaglio seems to have been mistaken. In testimony Romagnino confused 23 December with the 24th; see CE 4:4511 (Romagnino, 28 November 1934).

2. CE 1:218–19 (Guiboud-Ribaud, 13 March 1934).

3. ADP D2U8445 (Insp. Peudepièce/Pigaglio, 8 January 1934); ADP D2U8435 (JI Ordonneau/Pigaglio, 26 June 1934); AN F7 13981 (note on René Henri Pigaglio, n.d. but December 1933); Bortchy-Melnikoff, *300.000 kilomètres avec Stavisky*, 117–18.

4. CE 1:220 (Guiboud-Ribaud, 13 March 1934); ADP D2U8430 (note of d'Uhalt, 18 January 1934); ADP D2U8435 (Ordonneau/Pigaglio, 26 June 1934); ADP D2U8454 (Ordonneau/Romagnino, 29 October 1934); AN 334AP68 (Romagnino, 19 November 1935); AN BB18 6768 (PR Seine to PG, 11 June 1934).

5. APP B/A 1276 (dossier Syveton, 1899–1910).

6. Garçon, *Histoire de la justice*, 2:29; Mollier, *Le scandale de Panama*, 38, 45; Bouvier, *Les deux scandales de Panama*, 140ff.; *Le Matin*, 13, 14 and 15 March 1932, and *Le Temps*, 14 March 1932; see chap. 8 above, 170.

7. ADP D2U8453 (Ordonneau/Romagnino, 5 March and 3 May 1934); ADP D2U8454 (Ordonneau/Romagnino, 29 October 1934); AN 334AP69 (Romagnino, 19 November 1935); CE 4:4491, 4511, 4515 (Romagnino, 28 November 1934).

8. *Die Zeit*, 5 September 1903 (from Humbert dossier in AN F7 12550); APP BA 1253 (Rochette dossier, police notes of 26 March 1908).

9. ADP D2U8417 and 428 (Insp. Bonny/Arlette Stavisky, 12 January 1934, and JI Lapeyre/Arlette Stavisky, 16 January 1934); ADP D2U8429 (Bonny to CGRJ, 30 December 1933); ADP D2U8434 (Ordonneau/Arlette Stavisky, 2 March, 20 June, and 24 December

1934, and note of Insp. Arrarat, 6 February 1935); ADP D2U8445 (Insp. Peudepièce/Pigaglio, 8 January 1934); CE 3:2857 (Pigaglio, 19 June 1934). At one point, Pigaglio told Peudepièce that he had met Stavisky at the Gare d'Orsay, but Romagnino independently confirmed the meeting at the Porte de Champerret. Romagnino and Hayotte claimed also to have met Stavisky that night, but their accounts are inconsistent and Hayotte has the date wrong. They appear to be confusing it with other occasions: ADP D2U8428 (Bonny/Hayotte, 6 January 1934); and ADP D2U8454 (Ordonneau/Romagnino, 29 October 1934).

10. CE 3:2857 (Pigaglio, 18 June 1934); ADP D2U8445 (Insp. Peudepièce/Pigaglio, 8 January 1934).

11. ADP D2U8429 (PR Bayonne note, 23 December 1933; d'Uhalt/Tissier, 23 December 1933); cf. also *Le Temps*, 31 December 1933.

12. AMJ (personnel dossiers, d'Uhalt, Albert, Victor, Prosper, 1923–55); *Le Populaire*, 14 January 1934.

13. ADP D2U8429 (note of d'Uhalt, 23 December 1933); ADP D2U8429 (d'Uhalt/Cohen, 24 December 1933); see chap. 4, 46–47, and chap. 6, 103 and 106; chap. 8,168; AN BB18 6765 (PG Pau to Gds, 28 December 1933).

14. AN MI 25376 (D'Uhalt to SG, 26 December 1933).

15. ADP D2U8432 (JI Hude/Delamarche, 29 June 1934).

16. AN BB18 6765 (PG Pau to Gds, 28 and 30 December 1933, 4 January 1934); CE 1:151 (Ducloux, 9 March 1934).

17. *Paris-Soir*, 31 December 1933.

18. *Le Populaire*, 30 December 1933; *Le Temps*, 31 December 1933; *Agence Technique de la Presse*, 30 December 1933, and *Journal de la Bourse*, 30 December 1933, regarding Havas.

19. *Agence Technique de la Presse*, 27 December 1933; CE 2:2104ff. (Landau, 23 May 1934); AN CAC, 12/6698–940459/74 (dossier Landau); see chap. 2, 11; *Journal de la Bourse*, 30 December 1933.

20. AN 1AR 6 (minutes of the administration councils of *Matin*): profits for 1933 came to 1,677,091.461 francs, for 1934 555,871.47 francs. By 1937 *Le Matin* had losses of 1,703,485.87 francs. AN 1AR 25 (printing runs of *Le Matin*, as of December 1935); AN 5AR 404 (Havas to *Le Temps*, 30 October 1930); AN 5AR 402 (Havas to *L'Oeuvre*, 30 December 1930); cf. also chap. 7,125.

21. AN 3AR 1 (circular from Gustave Téry, 18 Aug 1929); AN 3AR 2 (letter from International Exposition to *L'Oeuvre*, 5 June 1934, and answer from *L'Oeuvre*, 7 June 1934).

22. AN 3AR 1 (*L'Oeuvre* to Jean Calmette, 19 December 1932; *L'Oeuvre* to Anrich, 16 October 1934; dossier Raoul); AN 3AR 2 (*L'Oeuvre;* dossier Letellier).

23. AN 5AR 337 (Havas-Bayonne correspondence); Havas telegram to Joinaud, 3 January 1934.

24. *Paris-Soir*, 1, 4, and 6 January 1934; *Le Figaro*, 1 January 1934; *L'Oeuvre*, 4 January 1934.

25. ADP D2U8454 (Ordonneau/Voix, 24 October 1934); ADP D2U8440 (Ordonneau/Voix, 8 May 1934).

26. ADP D2U8440 (Ordonneau/Voix, 8 May 1934); ADP D2U8440 (JI Demay/Schenaerts, 10 April 1934); ADP D2U8454 (Ordonneau/Voix, 26 September 1934, and PJ report on Voix, 15 March 1934). Who precisely asked Voix to go to Servoz is unclear. He maintained that an unidentified man asked him; the JI believed Guiboud-Ribaud had

sent him, but both Guiboud-Ribaud and Voix denied this. The matter was never cleared up.

27. See photo of Voix in *L'Oeuvre* (19 January 1934); ADP D2U8454 (Ordonneau/Voix, 24 October 1934).

28. CE 2:2804 (Voix, 18 June 1934), 2858, 2864, 2874 (Pigaglio, 19 June 1934).

29. CE 2:2863 (Pigaglio, 19 June 1934); ADP D2U8428 (Insp. Bonny/Niemen, 12 January 1934).

30. ADP D2U8440 (Ordonneau/Voix, 4 May 1934); ADP D2U8430 (Burgède/Bossoney, 10 January 1934; and police note of 9 January 1934, plan of Le Vieux Logis).

31. AN F7 11 (police note on Lucette Alméras, January 1934); CE 2:2820 (Voix, 18 June 1934, 2858 (Pigaglio, 19 June 1934); photo of Lucette in *L'Oeuvre*, 19 January 1934).

32. AN BB18 6767 (Burgède/Lucette Alméras, 9 January 1934); ADP D2U8430 (Lapeyre/Lucette Alméras, 18 January 1934); CE 3:2821 (Voix, 18 June 1934).

33. AN BB18 6767 (Burgède/Voix, 9 January 1934); ADP D2U8454 (Ordonneau/Voix, 24 October 1934).

34. ADP D2U8417 and 429 (d'Uhalt/Tissier, 28 December 1933).

35. *Paris-Soir,* 8 January 1934; ADP D2U8417 and 429 (d'Uhalt/Garat, 30 December 1933).

36. *Paris-Soir,* 8, 9 January 1934.

37. *Paris-Soir,* 9 January 1934; ADP D2U8417 and 429 (d'Uhalt/Garat, 7 January 1934); see chap. 7, 139–42.

38. Charlier and Montarron, *Stavisky;* CE 1:151 (Ducloux, 9 March 1934); CE 3:3012 (Hennet, 31 June 1934); ADP 1320WC32 (arraignment of Bonny, 8 July 1935); AN MI 25378 (report of Insp. gén. Plytas on Bonny, 24 January 1934); photo of Bonny in *Paris-Soir,* 6 January 1934; Jacques Bonny, *Mon père l'inspecteur Bonny* (Paris, 1975), 37, 41.

39. CE 1:134–35 (Bonny, 8 March 1934); according to Romagnino, Stavisky boasted of power over Bonny, but no evidence supports this—ADP D2U8428 (Ordonneau/Romagnino, 27 June 1934). More than a year after his arrest by Bonny during the Prince affair (see chap. 10), Gaëtan de Lussatz ("le baron") claimed that Bonny and Stavisky knew each other, but his testimony is hardly credible; see ADCdo UIX ch 9 (JI Rabut/de Lussatz, 13 June 1935).

40. ADP D2U8429 (Bonny notes of 30 December 1933 and 4 and 5 January 1934); CE 1:126–28 (Bonny, 8 March 1934); *Paris-Soir,* 7 January 1934.

41. ADP D2U8 (Insp. Delgay/M et Mme Delaire, 8 December 1934); CE 1:126–27 (Bonny, 8 March 1934) and 3:2914 (Bonny, 19 June 1934).

42. ADP D2U8428 (report of expert-comptable Curmond, delivered 8 August 1934); ADP D2U8432 (CGRJ Mondanel to Odonneau, 27 March 1934); ADP D2U8 (Ordonneau/Curral, 2 March 1934); *Paris-Soir,* 4 January 1934; *Le Populaire,* 4 January 1934.

43. ADP D2U8438 (Insp. Peudepièce/Angelo Boeri, 13 March 1934); ADP D2U8428 (report of accountant Curmond, 8 August 1934; Bonny/Hayotte, 6 January 1934; anonymous letter from neighbor, 7 January 1934); *Paris-Soir,* 7 January 1934.

44. *Paris-Soir,* 8 January 1934; ADP D2U8445 (JI Lapeyre/Dubarry, 6, 7, 9 January 1934).

45. ADP D2U8437 (Ordonneau/Darius, 8 January 1934); *Paris-Soir,* 9 January 1934; *Le Figaro,* 9 January 1934.

46. ADP D2U8432 (CD Guillaume/Zweifel, 20 April 1934); *Paris-Soir,* 8 January 1934; CE 1:87 (Thomé, 7 March 1934) and 3:2918 (Bonny, 19 June 1934).

47. *Paris-Soir,* 9 January 1934; *Le Figaro,* 9 January 1934.

48. ADP D2U8432 (Ordonneau/Delamarche, 29 June 1934).

49. AN F7 13981 (police notes of 29 December 1933).

50. CE 3:3120–21 (Camille Chautemps, 22 June 1934); see chaps. 7 and 8.

51. Ibid.; *Le Populaire*, 3 January 1934; *Le Figaro*, 3 January 1934; *Le Quotidien*, 8 June 1934ff.; CE 3:2870–71, 2885 (Pigaglio, 19 June 1934).

52. *Dictionnaire des parlementaires;* Jean-Pierre Maxence, *Histoire de dix ans* (Paris, 1939), 239.

53. *Action Française*, 3 January 1934; *Paris-Soir,* 5 January 1934 (*Paris-Soir* was an evening paper, dated the following day).

54. Jeanneney, *L'argent caché,* 168ff.; AN BB18 6722 (dossier on Banque Industrielle de Chine); Garçon, *Histoire de la justice,* 2:89–100.

55. *Paris-Soir,* 6 January 1934, *Le Figaro,* 6 and 9 January 1934, *Le Populaire,* 7 January 1934.

56. CE 1:99 (Thomé, 8 March 1934) and 152 (Ducloux, 9 March 1934).

57. ADP D2U8454 (Ordonneau/Marcel Charpentier, 27 October 1934, and Ordonneau/Ducloux, 23 October 1934); CE 1:152 (Ducloux, 9 March 1934); CE 3:2914, 2941 (Bonny, 29 June 1934); CE 4:3362–63 (Charpentier, 5 July 1934); Bonny's informer was Hainnaux, as both he and Ducloux acknowledged.

58. ADP D2U8454 (Ordonneau/Charpentier, 27 October 1934); AN BB18 6767 (minutes of the gendarme Brun, 9 January 1934); CE 3:3363–64 (Charpentier, 5 July 1934).

59. AN BB18 6767 (minutes of Brun, 9 January 1934; report of Chamonix gendarmerie, 17 January 1934; report of Lt. Robini, gendarmerie, Bonneville, 9 January 1934); CE 3:3363 (Charpentier, 5 July 1934); CE 3:2899–900 (Pigaglio, 19 June 1934); *Paris-Soir,* 8 January 1934; *Le Matin,* 8 January 1934.

60. AN BB18 6767 (Antoine Chatou, 9 January 1934); ADP D2U8430 (Burgède/Chatou, 16 January 1934); CE 3:3364 (Charpentier, 5 July 1934); CE 4:3918 (Chatou, 24 July 1934); *Le Figaro,* 9 January 1934.

61. CE 3:2873, 2886, 2893 (Pigaglio, 19 June 1934); CE 3:2969, 2977 (Bonnaure, 20 June 1934); CE 3:3082–83 (Ducloux, 22 June 1934).

62. ADP D2U8435 (Ordonneau/Pigaglio, 26 June 1934); CE3:2968ff. (Bonnaure, 20 June 1934); CE 3:2874–75, 2866, 2889, 2900–2901 (Pigaglio, 19 June 1934); CE 3:2902–3 (Marcombes, 19 June 1934); CE 3:3076–83 (Ducloux, 22 June 1934); CE 3:3084–85 (Thomé, 22 June 1934). Bonnaure made at least two, and possibly three, visits that day to the Ministry of the Interior. He denied betraying Stavisky's whereabouts, but contradicted himself several times during his CE testimony, while Marcombes and Thomé independently confirmed, and Pigaglio strongly suspected, his betrayal that day. Ducloux apparently mistook the time of Thomé's communication to him, as well as the identity of the visitor to the Interior—Bonnaure, rather than Pigaglio, who did turn up at the Sûreté later that day, after Bonnaure had already made his visits to Marcombes. The CE, in its conclusions, had no doubt that Bonnaure had "given up" Stavisky. See the general report "Conclusions individuelles," 319–20.

63. CE 1:152 (Ducloux, 9 March 1934); CE 3:3077 (Ducloux, 22 June 1934); CE 3:2969 (Bonnaure, 20 June 1934); AN BB18 6767 (PG Chambéry to Gds, 17 January, 25, 26 February 1934).

64. ADP D2U8454 (Ordonneau/Voix, 24 October 1934); CE 3:2804–5 (Voix, 18 June 1934), 2869–70, 2873–74 (Pigaglio, 19 June 1934).

65. ADP D2U8454 (Ordonneau/Voix, 24 October 1934).

66. Ibid.; AN BB18 6767 (JI Burgède/Henri Voix [twice] and Burgède/Lucette Alméras, 9 January 1934); ADP D2U8430 (Lapeyre/Alméras, 18 January 1934;

Burgède/Elise Vuarand, Célestin Moreau, and Jean Lèse, 16 January 1934); CE 3:2815–16 (Voix, 18 June 1934).

67. ADP D2U8454 (Ordonneau/Marcel Charpentier, 27 October 1934); AN BB18 6767 (minutes of 9 January 1934, Charpentier et al. before JI, Bonneville; and PG Chambéry to GDs, 10 January 1934); CE 3:3364 (Charpentier, 5 July 1934).

68. ADP D2U8454 (Ordonneau/Charpentier, 27 October 1934); CE 3:3918 (Chatou, 24 July 1934); CE 3:3364 (Charpentier, 5 July 1934); AN BB18 6767 (minutes of Charpentier et al. before JI Bonneville, 9 January 1934).

69. AN BB18 6767 (minutes of Charpentier et al. before JI Bonneville, 9 January 1934); ADP D2U8454 (Ordonneau/Ducloux, 23 October 1934); CE 1:158 (Ducloux, 9 March 1934). In his CE testimony, Ducloux recalled telling Charpentier to try the door with Chatou's keys; Charpentier recalls being told to break in.

70. CE 1:158 (Ducloux, 9 March 1934).

71. AN BB18 6767 (notes of transfer of victim, before JI Bonneville, 8 January 1934; and reports of Dr. Jamin, 9 January 1934; report of gendarme/sergeant Petit-Prestoud et al., 9 January 1934); ADP D2U8430 (reports of Petit-Prestaud, 12 January 1934, and Dr. Briffaz, 8 January 1934, and photos of Stavisky in suicide dossier). Inspector Le Gall initially declared that he removed the revolver from Staviksy's right hand, an account confirmed by others: AN BB18 6767 (PG Chambéry to GDs, 10 January 1934, and report of Dr. F. Briffaz, 9 January 1934); ADP D2U8454 (Ordonneau/Charpentier, 27 October 1934). But in his CE testimony Le Gall had doubts; he seemed to recall finding it in his left hand. CE 3:3318, 3324–25, 3331–32 (Le Gall, 5 July 1934); and CE 3:3395–3403 (confrontation between Le Gall and Charpentier, 5 July 1934). Since the bullet entered through the right temple, this would rule out suicide and suggest that someone preceding Le Gall into the room—Charpentier?—had placed the revolver in Stavisky's hands. Le Gall hypothesized that, as Stavisky's two hands lay close together on his stomach, the revolver might have passed from one to the other. The confusion fueled suspicions of foul play (see chap. 10), but Le Gall himself never doubted that suicide was the cause of death.

72. CE 3:3318 (Le Gall, 5 July 1934) and 3365 (Charpentier, 5 July 1934); ADP D2U8454 (Ordonneau/Charpentier, 27 October 1934); AN BB18 6767 (statement before JI Bonneville, 9 January 1934).

73. AN BB18 6767 (Voix/Burgède, 9 and 10 January 1934; and Burgède/Lucette Alméras, 9 January 1934); ADP D2U8430 (Elise Vuarrand, sommelier at La Potinière, 16 January 1934).

CHAPTER 10. THE AFFAIR

1. *Le Figaro,* 9 January 1934; AN F7 13981 (note of 9 January 1934 regarding Radical Party's executive committee).

2. AN F7 13981 (police note of 9 January regarding cabinet meeting of 8 January); *Le Figaro,* 9 January 1934; *Le Temps,* 10 January 1934. Like other such police notes, this one is based on accounts overheard in newsrooms that never surfaced in the politer accounts in print.

3. Auguste Soulier, *L'instabilité ministérielle sous la troisième République, 1871–1938* (Paris, 1939), 146–47, 232–34.

4. *Le Canard Enchaîné,* 10 January 1934.

5. *Le Populaire, Action Française, L'Humanité, L'Ordre,* 9 January 1934; *La République,* 12 and 13 January 1934; *L'Oeuvre,* 6 and 9 January 1934.

6. Cf., for example, Dubufe's portrait of Fouché in Jean Tulard, ed., *Dictionnaire Napoléon* (Paris, 1995); Jean Tulard, "Le mythe de Fouché," in *L'Etat et sa police en*

France 1789–1914, ed. Jacques Aubert (Geneva, 1979), 27–34; Pierre Guiral, "Police et sensibilité française," ibid., 161–75; "Notre interview de M. Lépine," *Lectures pour Tous,* May 1909; "Les Trente-six incarnations d'un policier," *Lectures pour Tous,* January 1905, 341–48; Maurice Descotes, *Enquête sur un policier au-dessus de tout soupçon: Javert* (Pau, 1987), 41–42; Victor Hugo, *Choses vues,* rev. ed. (Paris, 1997), 1:167–71; "Police," in *Grand Dictionnaire Larousse du XIXe siècle*; Jean-Baptiste Duroselle, *Clemenceau* (Paris, 1988), 95–96.

7. AN F7 13981 (note of 9 January 1934 regarding socialists; notes of 10 January 1934 regarding Adrien Marquet and Radical deputy from L'Eure); AN BB18 6774 (list of deputies' questions, 3 January 1934); *Le Figaro,* 9 January 1934; cf. also Edouard Bonnefous, *Histoire politique de la troisième politique,* 2d ed. (Paris, 1973), 5:193ff.

8. Bonnefous, *Histoire politique,* 193.

9. AN BB18 6746 (dossier Oustric, Chamber of Deputies, annex to the minutes of the session of 11 March 1931, report on the Snia Viscosa); Flandin, in JO, 12 March 1931; Bonnefous, *Histoire politique,* 48–49, 54–55, 69–71.

10. *Le Figaro,* 10 January 1934; *Paris-Soir,* 11 January 1934; AN BB18 6767 (PR Bonneville to PG Chambéry, 10 January 1934; PG Chambéry to Gds, 10 January 1934; autopsy of Dr. F. Briffaz, 9 January 1934).

11. *Le Figaro,* 10 January 1934.

12. AN BB18 6767 (note of search and seizure, investigating magistrate Bonneville, 9 January 1934).

13. ADP D2U8434: the dossier of 7 May 1934 contains three photos (life size) of Stavisky's letter to Arlette. Some garbled allusions to these letters appeared in the press, and Claude Stavisky, in his recently published memoir (*Stavisky était mon père,* 308–9), gives the sense of the letter to his mother but not the exact wording, and an extract from the letter to him. Since no copy was kept of the letter to him, I cannot verify its accuracy. Arguing that his father was murdered, he suggests that the letters were forged. He finds it suspicious that the word "suicide" was never used, only the word "disappear," and that the letters became known so quickly to the public. The first evidence is hardly conclusive, and the second can easily be explained by one of the many leaks by the police to the invasive, tenacious reporters around them. The details of the transmission of the letters to Arlette are given in AN BB18 6767 (note of search and seizure, investigating magistrate Bonneville, 9 January 1934).

14. ADP 1320W132 (PR to PG Seine, 22 October 1934, note regarding Hennet); ADP D2U8431 (JI Peyre/Bonny, 8 February 1934); CE 1:56–57, 64–65 (Arlette Stavisky, 6 March 1934); CE 1:129, 133–34, 140, 142; Jacques Bonny, *Mon père l'inspecteur Bonny,* 57, 61. (The shallowness of Bonny's left-wing convictions was later demonstrated during his sinister collaborationist wartime career.) Arlette maintained that she had simply made a "réflexion" about Chiappe, which she did not want taken down, Bonny that she had expressed fear of the prefect of police and for that reason asked that her reference to him be erased.

15. ADP D2U8417 (Bonny/ Romagnino, 8 January 1934); CE 1:130 and passim (Bonny, 8 March 1934).

16. ADP D2U8417 (Bonny/Depardon, 11 January 1934; Fernand Desbrosses, 18 January 1934; Pierre Curral, 10 January 1934); ADP D2U8428 (Bonny interrogations of Henri Hayotte, 10 January 1934; and Maurice-Léon Niemencynski, 12 January 1934); CE 1:128ff. (Bonny, 8 March 1934).

17. ADP D2U8417 (reports of Insp. Peudepièce, 12, 16, 17, 18 January 1934); CE 1:707–8 (Peudepièce, 30 March 1934).

18. ADP D2U8417 (confrontation Garat-Tissier, 10 January 1934); *Le Figaro,* 11 January 1934.

19. AMJ (dossier Ordonneau); *Le Populaire,* 9 January 1934.

20. ADP D2U8437 (Ordonneau/Darius, 8 January 1934); *Paris-Soir,* 12 January 1934; *Le Figaro,* 10 January 1934.

21. ADP D2U8445 (JI Lapeyre/Dubarry, 7, 9 January 1934); ADP D2U8428 (Ordonneau/Aymard, 10 January 1934); *Paris-Soir,* 12 January 1934; *Le Figaro, Le Populaire,* 12 January 1934.

22. See chap. 7; ADP D2U8417 (Lapeyre/Lévy, 18 January 1934).

23. Camille Aymard, *La véritable affaire Stavisky* (Paris, 1935), 11–63; AN BB18 2225 (Boulaine affair); *La Guerre Financière et Politique,* 6 December 1902. Ernest Judet, the editor of *L'Eclair,* was also tried for treason, and eventually acquitted in 1923. The journalists of *La Gazette des Ardennes,* which appeared under the German Occupation, were also tried, but here the matter of German funding was less in question than the nature and impact of their articles.

24. APP B/A 1253 (note of 22 November 1910); JO, 12 and 20 March 1912.

25. "Les conditions de l'immunité parlementaire," *Le Figaro,* 8 January 1934.

26. *Le Figaro,* 23 January 1934.

27. ADP D2U8417 (Insp. Bonny/Romagnino, 8 January 1934); *Le Figaro,* 11 and 12 January 1934; *Paris-Soir,* 12 January 1934.

28. ADP D2U8417 (d'Uhalt/Bonnaure, 15 January 1934); ADP D2U8435 (Ordonneau/Romagnino, 9 January 1934); *Le Figaro,* 16 January 1934; *Le Populaire,* 16 January 1934.

29. ADP D2U8417 and D2U8435 (d'Uhalt/Bonnaure, 29 January 1934); *L'Oeuvre,* 30 January 1934.

30. AN MI 25385 (note of Insp. gén. Plytas, 20 February 1934); *Le Figaro,* 7 January 1934.

31. AN MI 25376 (Insp. gén. Plytas to Chautemps, 19 January 1934; Insp. gén. Mossé to Chautemps, 21 January 1934); AN BB18 6765 (Insp. gén. Rouvier to Chautemps, 19 January 1934).

32. See chap. 5.

33. See n. 30 above; AN BB18 6765 (Justice to Commerce, 23 February 1934).

34. CE 2:1701 (Delamarche, 4 May 1934).

35. See chap. 9, 174; CE 1:130, 139–40 (Bonny, 8 March 1934); ADP 1320Wc32 (arraignment of Bonny, 8 July 1935); AN MI 25378 (24 January 1934, Insp. gén. Plytas to Chautemps regarding Bonny affair, 24 January 1934). It is not clear how or where the move to drop Bonny started, but it probably came from Chiappe, the prefect of police: Superintendent Oudard could not have suddenly denounced so prominent a figure without the prefect's knowledge, and only days earlier Bonny had carefully noted and kept Arlette's allegations about Chiappe's supposed friendship with Stavisky. The rightwing Chiappe and the Radical or *Cartelliste* Bonny had been on bad terms ever since 1927; see Bonny, *Mon père l'inspecteur Bonny,* 61.

36. CE 1:1090 (Dreyfus, 18 April 1934); ADCdo UIX ch 8 (Pierre Guerithault, 5 March 1934).

37. CE 1:1090ff. (Dreyfus, 18 April 1934); AMJ (personnel dossier of Eugène Dreyfus).

38. CE 1:1090ff. (Dreyfus, 18 April 1934); CE 1:843–44 (Pressard, 11 April 1934); ADCdo UIX ch 8 (Pierre Guérithault, 5 March 1934). According to Guérithault, Prince reported that night that Pressard had been *grossier* (crude) and had gone so far as to comment to

him: "I note, my dear friend, that you lack nerves," but Pressard denied this, and Dreyfus, who affirmed that Pressard had not been *grossier* in any way, could not recall the comment.

39. The account here is based on Pressard's handwritten notes prior to his appearance before the CE, which substantially followed them. I am grateful to Mme Chautemps-Samuels for allowing me to see these. The conversations with Prince were reported to Pressard by those involved.

40. CE 1:843ff. (Pressard, 11 April 1934); at one point, President Lescouvé, who took over Dreyfus's investigation, reported that Pressard had acknowledged hearing of the Cousin and Gripois reports from prince, but not of ever seeing them. Prince had no reason to keep them secret. CE 1:741 (Lescouvé, 10 April 1934).

41. Cf. comments of Maître Torrès during Penancier's appearance before CE (1:792, 10 April 1934).

42. Sarah Maza, "Le Tribunal de la nation: Les mémoires judiciaires et l'opinion publique à la fin de l'ancien régime," *Annales* ESC 1 (January–February 1987): 73–90; AN F7 12549 (report of Comm. sp. Le Creusot, 19 December 1887, and *Le Progrès* of Saône-et-Loire, 16 December 1887; report of Comm. sp., Albi, 14 October 1887); AN BB18 6089 (Caillaux affair); *Bulletin de la Ligue des Droits de l'Homme*, 15 June 1919. In *Port Tarascon*, Daudet shows his hero Tartarin saved in extremis from hostile magistrates from the north; in *La bête humaine* (1890), Zola shows a criminal procedure being turned against the weakest members of society; in *Bella*, Giraudoux (1926) shows Rebendart (pseudonym for Poincaré) trying to use the justice system to destroy Dubardeau (pseudonym for Berthelot).

43. ADCdo, UIX ch 8 (Deputy Max Buteau, 1 March 1934).

44. JO, 11 January 1934; *Paris-Soir*, 12 and 28 January 1934.

45. JO, session of 11 January 1934; *Le Figaro*, 12 January 1934; *Paris-Soir*, 13 January 1934.

46. Serge Berstein, *Histoire du parti radical* (Paris, 1980), 2:251ff.

47. *Paris-Soir*, 13 January 1934; *Le Figaro*, 12 January 1934; CE (6 February) 4: chap. 2.

48. *Paris-Soir*, 15 November and 7–8 December 1933.

49. Ibid., 30 December 1933; AN F7 13981 (Chautemps to Finances, 12 January 1934); AN MI 25382 (CC Perpignan to prefect of the Pyrénés Orientales, 10 January 1934).

50. Soulier, *L'instabilité ministérielle*, 375–76.

51. Ibid., 378–81; Daniel Halévy, *La République des Ducs* (Paris, 1937), 267; Schuker, *The End of French Predominance*.

52. *Le Figaro*, 6 and 18 January 1934; *L'Intransigeant, Le Quotidien*, 7 January 1934; *Le Matin*, 7 January 1934; *Action Française*, 7 January 1934; *Le Temps*, 14 January 1934; *L'Ordre*, 7 and 11 January 1934.

53. *L'Humanité*, 8, 9, 11, 14 January 1934; *Le Populaire*, 7, 12, 13 January (Paul Faure), and 14 January 1934; *Le Figaro*, 8 January 1934.

54. *L'Oeuvre*, 7 January 1934; *L'Ere Nouvelle*, 7 January 1934; *Notre Temps*, 7 January 1934.

55. *Paris-Soir*, 13 January 1934; JO, 12 January 1934; *Le Populaire*, 5 June 1934 (regarding Astruc); CE 2:2438ff. (Astruc, 4 June 1934); see chap. 4, 58–60.

56. JO, 12 January 1934; *Dictionnaire des parlementaires*, s.v. "Franklin-Bouillon."

57. JO, 12 January 1934; *L'Humanité*, 26 January 1934; *Paris-Soir*, 14 January 1934.

58. JO, 18 January 1934; *Le Petit Parisien*, 19 January 1934.

59. JO, 18 January 1934.

60. *Le Figaro*, 23 January 1934; CE (6 February) 4:ii, 28ff.

61. *L'Ordre*, 24 January 1934; *L'Oeuvre*, 24 January 1934; *Paris-Soir*, 21 January 1934.

62. *Le Figaro*, 15 and 24 January 1934; *Le Temps*, 15 January 1934.

63. JO, 18, 23 January; *L'Ordre*, 27 January 1934; *Le Quotidien*, 27 January 1934; *Paris-Soir*, 28 January 1934.

64. AN 334AP70 (Georges Thomé, 20 December 1934).

65. CE (6 February) 4:i, 65ff.; *Paris-Soir*, 29 January 1934.

66. AN 334 AP 70 (Georges Thomé, 20 December 1935).

67. CE (6 February) 4:i, 65ff. Daladier, most implausibly, denied that his attempt to move Chiappe was connected to the Stavisky affair.

68. See nn. 62 63.

69. CE (6 February) 4:ii (demonstrations) and 65ff.; *Paris-Soir*, 6 and 7 February 1934.

70. *Paris-Soir*, 7 February 1934; Blandine Kriegel, "La défaite de la justice," *Autrement*, 16 (1994): 135–41; the popular General Boulanger, who had intimated that the government had covered up the Wilson scandal, was replaced as suddenly in 1889 as Chiappe in 1934.

71. *Paris-Soir*, 8 February 1934; Kessel, *Stavisky*, 107–12; see above, chap. 8, 171.

CHAPTER 11. SACRIFICIAL MAGISTRACY

1. ADP 1320W132/155 (note of central services, Tribunal de première instance of the Seine, 19 May 1934, and note of general secretary of the public prosecutor's office of the Seine, 23 May 1934).

2. *Le Canard Enchaîné*, 10 January 1934.

3. See n. 1 above. Pressard was to be moved to the court of appeal while his own role in the affair was investigated.

4. ADCdo UIX ch 8 (JI Lapeyre/Lescouvé, 26 February 1934).

5. Ibid. (JI Lapeyre/Max Buteau, 1 March 1934); ADCdo UX5 (CD Guillaume/Mme Prince, 26 June 1934).

6. ADCdo UIX ch 8 (JI Lapeyre/Paul Caujolle, 2 March 1934; Lapeyre/Fontaine, 12 April 1934; Lapeyre/Ordonneau and Bruzin, 13 and 14 April 1934); ADCdo UIX ch 12 (Guillaume/Mme Simon, 29 June 1934; and PJ report on Pierre and Jeanne Lecomte, 7 July 1934) On Oustric and Peret, see chap. 5, 69, and chap. 10, 196–97, 215.

7. Pierre Chevalier, "Un document inédit sur la mort tragique du Conseiller Albert Prince, ancien procureur de la République à Troyes (1883–1934)," *Mémoires de la Société Académique d'Agriculture, des Sciences, Arts et Belles-lettres du Département de l'Aube (Troyes)* 109 (1978): 45–46. This is the published transcript of André Lapeyre, *L'Affaire Prince*, Bibliothèque Nationale, ms. nouv. acq. françaises no. 15767, which contains the final conclusions of Lapeyre, the investigating magistrate in Paris in charge of the Prince affair. Professional scruples prevented Lapeyre from publishing the memoir during his lifetime. Given to his friend Sacha Guitry, it was purchased from the latter's estate by the Bibliothèque Nationale in 1966. The author's professional identity and the soundness of his reasoning make it the best account of the Prince affair to date. The page references to "Lapeyre, *L'Affaire Prince*" that follow are to the published transcript identified above, which is entirely faithful to the manuscript.

8. ADCdo UIX ch 8 (Lapeyre/Caujolle, 2 March 1934).

9. ADCdo UIX ch 5 (JI Rabut/Madame Prince, 21 February 1934; and Lapeyre/Madame Prince, 7 March 1934); ADCdo UIX ch 3 (Sannié to Lapeyre, 10 March 1934); Lapeyre, *L'Affaire Prince*, 22–23.

10. ADCdo (report of Insp. Moreux, 12 July 1934).

11. *Le Figaro,* 22 February 1934; *Le Populaire,* 22 February 1934; *L'Humanité,* 22 February 1934; *La Liberté,* 23 February 1934; *Le Petit Parisien,* 24 February 1934.

12. *L'Ordre,* 23 February 1934; *Le Matin,* 24 February 1934.

13. ADCdo UIX ch 3 (reports of Dr. Charles Sannié, 5 and 10 March 1934); Lapeyre, *L'Affaire Prince,* 25–26, 50.

14. Lapeyre, *L'Affaire Prince,* 24; Charles Chenevier (honorary assistant director of the Sûreté Nationale), *De La Combe aux Fées à Lurs. Souvenirs et Révélations* (Paris, 1962), 22ff.; Jean Belin, *Trente ans de Sûreté Nationale* (Paris, 1950), 193ff.

15. Comments of Goron (former SG director) in *L'Intransigeant,* 8 December 1908; *Le Matin* and *L'Echo de Paris,* 26 and 27 November 1908; APP (personnel dossier of Edmond Pachot, note from him to prefect of police, 9 July 1927); Pierre Assouline, *Simenon* (Paris, 1992), 195–207; *Le Matin,* 26 February 1934, *L'Oeuvre,* 9 April 1934.

16. *Le Petit Parisien,* 27 February 1934; *Les Débats,* 23 February 1934; *Le Figaro,* 26 February 1934; *La Victoire,* 23 February 1934.

17. ADP 1320 W 132 (Ordonneau to PG, 9 January 1935; and note of PG, 19 January 1935); *Le Petit Parisien,* 14 January 1934.

18. *Le Petit Parisien,* 26 January 1934; ADP 1320W155 (PG to Gds, 24 March 1934 and 4 March 1934; PR to PG, 7 March 1934; Ordonneau to PR, 5 December 1934).

19. *Le Petit Parisien,* 26 January and 14 February 1934; *Paris-Soir,* 27 January 1934; *L'Oeuvre,* 27 January 1934.

20. *Le Petit Parisien,* 14 February 1934.

21. *Le Figaro,* 3 March 1934; ADP D2U8434 (Delgay/Camille Lefrançois, 19 December 1934).

22. ADP D2U8439 (Ordonneau/Depardon, 27 and 28 February 1934; Ordonneau/Farault, 10 March 1934; Borel/Niemen 10 March 1934); *Le Figaro,* 11 and 12 March 1934.

23. ADP 1320W155 (Ordonneau to PR, 5 December 1934); ADP D2U8439 (Comm. Delgay/Hainnaux, 1 March 1934; Ordonneau/Hubert, 5 April 1934; note on Georges-Maurice Hainnaux, 4 April 1934; Ordonneau/Hainnaux, 24 July 1934); ADP D2U8453 (Ordonneau/Romagnino, 5 March 1934); AN 334AP68 (Romagnino, 19 November 1935). Hainnaux concocted an implausible story of finding the check stubs in a bus on the Champs-Elysées, possibly, as argued by Romagnino's lawyer, to please the public and hide Bonny; AN 334AP68 (Me. Zevaes, 19 November 1935). Hainnaux recanted this version before the CE (4:4409, 21 November 1934). See also chap. 8, 160.

24. *Le Figaro,* 25 March 1934; ADP 1320W98 (report of expert jeweler Séror, 28 July 1934).

25. ADP 1320W155 (PR to PG, 12 May 1934 and 4 June 1934); *Le Figaro,* 21 March 1934; AMJ (personnel dossier of Albert d'Uhalt).

26. Lapeyre, *L'Affaire Prince,* 31, 33–34, 38, 55–56; ADP 1320W155 (Gds to PG, 3, 8, 24, 30 March, 9 May, 11 August 1934; PG to Gds, 30 May, 4 June 1934); AN BB18 6768 (Gds to PG, 17 September 1934); *Dictionnaire des parlementaires,* s.v. "Chéron"; *Le Populaire,* 27 August 1934.

27. ADP 1320W132 (Gds to PG, 20 July 1934; and PG note of 23 July 1934); AN BB18 6773 (Gds to president of CE, 24 July 1934); AN BB18 6774 (Etienne Riché, deputy of the Ardennes, to Gds, 24 March 1934).

28. CE (general report: history of commissions of inquiry), 13–33, 38–39; *Paris-Soir,* 11 January 1934; *L'Oeuvre,* 13 January 1934; Soulier, *L'instabilité ministérielle,* 220, 221.

29. AN BB18 6768 (Gds to PG, 7, 9, 15, 24, 26, 30 March 1934; PG to Gds, 22 January, 23 March 1935); BB18 6773 (Gds to Guernut, 28 March 1934); ADP D2U8451 (JI Hude/Mau-

rice Nau, 27 December 1934). The journalist Nau, who had connections on the CE, linked the actions against Lévy and Hesse.

30. AN CAC (dossiers of Jean Odin, René Renoult, Louis Proust, André Hesse, Gaston Hulin); AN BB18 6768 (PG to Gds, 22 June 1934; PR to PG, 15 September 1934 and 18 February 1936); ADP D2U8442 (Hude/Odin, 11 April 1934); ADP D2U8452 (PG note of 8 May 1934); *L'Echo de Paris*, 23 March 1934; *L'Oeuvre*, 28 January 1936. Of those indicted, Renoult was acquitted and subsequently readmitted to the Radical Party; Proust was eventually readmitted as well after charges against him were dropped.

31. ADP 1320W155 (Gds to PG, 30 March 1934; and prefect of police to PJ, 3 April 1934).

32. ADP D2U8432 (CGRJ to Ordonneau, 27 March 1934; and CGRJ to d'Uhalt, 10 February 1934); AN BB18 6775 (reports of 11 and 17 April 1934 regarding rumors of German espionage); ADP D2U8434 (Ordonneau/Arlette Stavisky, 2 March 1934); ADP D2U8428 (item in *Le Matin* of 28 July 1934; and Ordonneau/Schenaerts, 31 July 1934); ADP D2U8435 (JI Demay/Cerf, 13 March 1934); ADP D2U8454 (reports on items in *L'Intransigeant*, 4 March 1934, and *Le Populaire*, 10 March 1934); *La Liberté*, 19 September 1934 (from ADP D2U8447).

33. Lapeyre, *L'Affaire Prince*, 29; ADCdo UIX ch 8 (Bonny et Sûreté Générale).

34. Lapeyre, *L'Affaire Prince*, 32–34; see, for example, "press articles noted" in ADP 1320W155.

35. AN BB18 6773 (Gds to CE Guernut, 29 March, 30 August, 12 September 1934; Guernut to Gds, 17 November 1934).

36. ADCdo UIX ch 5 (report of Insp. Moreux, 12 July 1934); UIX ch 8 (report of Insp. Belin, 22 February 1934); UX ch 10 (JI Rabut/Jeanne Ruaux, 26 February 1934); AN MI 25363 (PR Dijon to PG, 7 April 1934); ADCdo UIX ch 9(PR to PG, 7 April 1934); AN BB18 6773 (Guernut to Gds, 9 January 1935; and PR Seine to PG, 15 January 1935); *L'Oeuvre*, 1 March 1934.

37. *Le Petit Parisien*, 4 March 1934.

38. The affair provoked hundreds of anonymous letters: see ADCdo UIX ch 4. Of the various sightings of Prince and others reported, none proved verifiable, and most had clearly been invented: ADCdo UIX ch 8 (Belin to CGRJ, 23 February 1934). Most of the logical (as distinct from circumstantial) arguments against the hypothesis of murder can be found in the analysis of Maître Philippe Lamour, *L'Oeuvre*, 7 October 1934, and in Lapeyre, *L'Affaire Prince*, 39–42.

39. Léon Daudet in *L'Action Française*, 11 November 1934; Jean Piot in *L'Oeuvre*, 9, 20, 30 April and 24 August 1934.

40. *Le Matin*, 5 March 1934; *Le Petit Journal*, 24 February 1934; CE 1:741 (Lescouvé, 10 April 1934).

41. APP (dossier of Marcel Guillaume); CE 4:4061–63 (Guillaume, 31 October 1934). The best argument based on circumstantial (as distinct from logical) grounds is found in Lapeyre and in Marcel Guillaume, "La Mort du Conseiller Prince," *Paris-Soir*, 16 April 1937, and "Pourquoi j'ai conclu au suicide du Conseiller Prince," *Paris-Soir*, 17 April 1937, in which the superintendent, almost three years after his investigation and once the public prosecutor's office had abandoned its own case, describes his conclusions. Later, two of his colleagues published their own accounts of how they reached the same conclusions: Chenevier, *De La Combe aux Fées à Lurs*, and idem, *La grande maison* (Paris, 1976), 28–46; and Belin, *Trente ans de Sûreté Nationale*, 193ff.

42. ADCdo UIX ch 3 (legal medical reports of 2 and 5 March and 6 June 1934); Lapeyre, *L'Affaire Prince*, 26, 35–37, 48–52.

43. CE (private reports, Guillaume report), 229; Chenevier, *La grande maison,* 40. Chenevier's memoirs contradict Guillaume's version in his report. According to Guillaume, the waiter at Lutétia could not remember the day he had seen Prince, and placed the time at about twelve thirty—a clear impossibility, since by then Prince was on the train for Dijon. But Inspector Chenevier placed Prince's observed appearance earlier— at about the time of the call and on the day of his death. I have not found his original reports in the archival records.

44. ADCdo UX ch 10 (Guillaume interrogations of 23, 25, 27 April; anonymous letter to Guillaume of May 1934, and investigation of it, 23 August, 20 September, 11 October 1934). The testimonies of Mme Nolin and of one Hugues de Bernardi about adulterous affairs with Prince proved spurious: Guillaume to Ordonneau, 24 May 1934, and declarations of de Bernardi, 19 April 1934. Lapeyre speculated that Prince's acute sense of honor lay behind his act: he did not wish his negligence (however minor) in the affair, or his suicide, to embarrass his family, and therefore disguised his death as a murder. It is perhaps significant that the professionals who believed at the time in his suicide later wrote of their conclusions, while those who believed in his murder later withdrew into silence. The exception was Inspector Bonny: according to his son, he confessed before his execution for collaboration in December 1944 to having organized the assassination of Prince. The claim, if made, was demonstrably false, and the son's account of check stubs entering into the possession of Prince and mysterious orders reaching Bonny from the inevitably unnamed "highly placed personage" is equally preposterous, for reasons set forth by Pierre Chevalier in his introduction to Lapeyre's account. In *Ils ont tué mon père* (322ff.), Gisèle Dessaux Prince, seeking to provide a motive for the supposed assassination of her father, is unfortunately obliged to pile speculation on speculation.

45. AN BB18 6722 (PR Seine to PG, 18 October 1934); AN MI 25385 (Ordonneau to director of personnel, AMJ, 10 September 1934); *Le Matin,* 23 August 1934; *L'Oeuvre,* 25 August 1934; *Action Française,* 24 August 1934; *L'Echo de Paris,* 24 August 1934; *Le Jour,* 24 August 1934; *Le Quotidien,* 24 August 1934. The person responsible for the leak was never identified. Guillaume denied that it came from him and his colleagues: *Paris-Soir,* 16 April 1937.

46. Remarks attributed to Mandel in *Le Peuple,* 26 August 1934; the confusion of powers implied by the commission's actions is noted in *Le Temps,* 15. November 1934.

47. *L'Oeuvre,* 10 September 1934; *Dictionnaire des parlementaires,* s.v. "Chéron."

48. AN BB18 6768 (min. of justice to Guernut, 29 January 1935); ADP D2U8465 (rulings of Ordonneau, n.d. but February 1935).

49. Ibid.; ADP D2U8463 (final arraignment by PR, 6 March 1935); ADP D2U8465 (ruling of Chamber of Indictments, 14 May 1935); ADP D2U8466 (court of appeal of the Seine, 6 June 1935); AN 334AP70 (summation by PG Fernand-Roux, 28 December 1935).

50. AN BB18 6768 (Guernut to Justice, 31 January 1935); CE (general conclusions), 476–99.

51. CE 1:751 (Guernut, 10 April 1934); CE 2:1356 (Mandel, 25 April 1934).

52. CE 2:1715 (Lafont, 4 May 1934); CE 1:569 (Mandel, 27 March 1934); CE 2:2177 (Guernut, 23 May 1934).

53. CE 2:1446 (Guastavino, 26 April 1934); CE 2:1550 (Martin, 1 May 1934); CE 3:2786–87 (Mennevée, 18 June 1934).

54. CE 3:2443 (Astruc and Guernut, 4 June 1934).

55. *Le Figaro,* 30, 31 December 1934; *Le Populaire,* 30 December 1934; AN CAC (dossier Poulner, carton 940469/376, dossier 16/32401); AN MI 25376 (note of 21 December 1934;

The report about *Paris-Soir* and Bonny came to the police from an informer and from Bunau-Varilla of *Le Matin*); ADP D2U8434 (UPI London to Mme Stavisky, 28 August 1934).

56. AN (personnel dossier of Henri Camille Hurlaux); *Le Populaire*, 7 March 1934; *Le Figaro*, 6 March 1934.

57. See chap. 9, 174; chap. 11, 228; AN MI 25379 (Havas dispatch of 9 March); *Paris-Midi*, 9 March 1934 (Hurlaux is confused with Hubert); *Le Jour*, 13 March; AN D2U8 439 (Ordonneau/Hubert, 5 April 1934).

58. See chap. 4; ADP D2U8439 (Insp. gén. of Agriculture to minister of agriculture, 22 January 1934; police notes of 16, 17, 19 March 1934).

CHAPTER 12. A LIGHT IN THE COURTROOM

1. AN 334AP68 (Barnaud, 5 November 1935); *Le Populaire*, 6 November 1935; *Le Petit Parisien*, 6 November 1935.

2. AN 334AP68 (Desbrosses, 5 November 1935); *Le Matin*, 6 November 1935; *Le Populaire*, 6 November 1935; *Le Journal*, 6 November 1935; *Le Petit Parisien*, 6 November 1935; *Paris-Soir*, 7 November 1935; AN F7 12926 (affair of Sister Candide); AN F7 12550 (Humbert affair).

3. AN 334AP68 (Hayotte, 6 November 1935); *Paris-Soir*, 8 November 1935; *Le Matin*, 7 November 1935.

4. AN 334AP68 (Hayotte, de Poorter, and Legrand, 6 November 1935); *Paris-Jour*, 5 February 1965 (from APP E/A 144, regarding Legrand), obituary of Legrand in *Le Monde*, 3 December 1982; Joseph Barthélémy, *Ministre de la justice: Vichy, 1941–43: Mémoires* (Paris, 1989), 54–55 and 58n.

5. AN 334AP68 (Tissier, Legrand, Lamour, 7 November 1935); *Le Petit Parisien*, 8 November 1935; *Le Jour*, 8 November 1935; *Le Matin*, 8 November 1935; *Paris-Soir*, 9 November 1935.

6. AN 334AP68 (Romagnino, 19 November 1935); *Le Petit Parisien*, 20 November 1935; *Action Française*, 20 November 1935; *Paris-Soir*, 21 November 1935.

7. AN 334AP68 (Farault, 5 November 1935); *Le Matin*, 6 November 1935; *Le Petit Parisien*, 6 November 1935; *Paris-Soir*, 7 November 1935.

8. AN 334AP70 (summation of Maître Jacques-Cartier, 3 January 1936).

9. Antoine de Baecque, "Le discours anti-noble, 1787–1792. Aux origines d'un slogan 'le peuple et les gros,' " *Revue d'Histoire Moderne et Contemporaine* 36 (January–March 1989): 3–28; Raoul Girardet, *Mythes et mythologies politiques* (Paris, 1986).

10. AN 334AP68 (Cohen, 7 November 1934); *Paris-Soir*, 9 November 1935.

11. AN 334AP68 (Digoin, 8 November 1935); *Action Française*, 8 November 1935; *Le Journal*, 9 November 1935.

12. AN 334AP69 (Depardon, 20 November 1935); *Le Matin*, 21 November 1935.

13. AN 334AP68 (Hattot, 6 November 1935); *Le Petit Parisien*, 7 November 1935.

14. AN 334AP68 (Guébin, 12 November 1935); *Le Journal*, 14 November 1935; *Action Française*, 14 November 1935; *Paris-Soir*, 15 November 1935; *Le Matin*, 15 November 1935.

15. AN 334AP69 (Arlette Stavisky, 22 November 1935); *Action Française*, 23 November 1935; *Le Journal*, 23 November 1935; *Le Petit Parisien*, 23 November 1935; *Le Matin*, 23 November 1935.

16. *Le Journal*, 19 November 1935; *Le Petit Journal*, 19 November 1935 (transcriptions

missing from trial dossiers in AN); ADP D2U8450 (report of accountant Boisgontier, 18 July 1934); ADP D2U8447 (Ordonneau/Gaulier, 16 August 1934).

17. *Paris-Soir,* 7 November, 29 December 1935; *Le Petit Parisien,* 6 November 1935.

18. AN 334AP68 (Dubarry, 15 November 1935); *Le Journal,* 16 November 1935; *Le Matin,* 16 November 1935; *Le Petit Parisien,* 16 November 1935; *Action Française,* 16 November 1935; *Paris-Soir,* 7, 17 November, 29 December 1935.

19. AN 334AP69 (Lévy, 21 November 1935); *Le Petit Parisien,* 22 November 1935; *Le Journal,* 22 November 1935; *Action Française,* 22 November 1935; *Le Matin,* 22 November 1935; *Paris-Soir,* 23 November 1935.

20. AN 334AP69 (Aymard, 22 November 1935).

21. See chap. 4, 56–57; AN BB18 6730/6738 (dossier 86BL, Société foncière, 1934–36, judgment of the first chamber of the court of appeal, 15 May 1935).

22. AN 334AP68 (Bardi de Fourtou, Ribet, Loewel, Dominique, 6 November 1935); Bibliothèque de l'Ordre des Avocats, "Eloge de Maurice Ribet" by Me Jean-René Farthouat, Paris court of appeal, 1 December 1962; speech of *bâtonnier* René-William Thorp to conférence des Avocats, 26 November 1955; *Le Petit Parisien,* 13 November 1935.

23. AN 334AP68 (Robert Cousin, 25 November 1935; and Edmond Pachot, 26 November 1935); *Le Jour,* 26 November 1935; *Le Matin,* 26 November 1935.

24. AN 334AP70 (Georges Thomé, 20 December 1935); *Le Populaire,* 20 December 1935.

25. AN 334AP70 (Pierre Bonny, John Hennett, Louis Simon, 23 December 1935; and Robert Bayard, 20 December 1935); *Le Matin,* 24 December 1935; *Paris-Soir,* 24 December 1935.

26. AN 334AP68 (Garat, 8–12 November 1935); *Le Petit Parisien,* 9, 10, 13 November 1935; *Le Journal,* 9, 13 November 1935; *Action Française,* 8, 14 November 1935; *Paris-Soir,* 9, 10, 11 November 1935; *Le Matin,* 9, 10, 13 November 1935.

27. AN 334AP68 (Garat, 12 November 1934); *Le Matin,* 13 November 1935.

28. Alexis de Tocqueville, *L'Ancien Régime et la Révolution* (Paris, 1856), bk. 2; François Furet, "L'Idée de République et l'histoire de France au XIXᵉ siècle," in *Le siècle de l'avènement républicain,* ed. François Furet and Mona Ozouf (Paris, 1993), 287–312.

29. AN 334AP69 (Delamarche, 2 December 1935, and Constantin, 3 December 1935).

30. AN 334AP68 (Romagnino, 19 November 1935); *Le Petit Parisien,* 20 November 1935; *Action Française,* 20 November 1935; *Paris-Soir,* 21 November 1935; Robert de Jouvenel, *La République des camarades* (Paris, 1914; new ed., Paris, 1979), 6.

31. AN 334AP69 (Albert Dalimier, 9 December 1935); *Le Journal,* 10 December 1935; *Paris-Soir,* 10 December 1935; AMJ, dossier of Charles Barnaud (Doumergue wrote on his behalf in 1906 and again in 1907, when minister of commerce and industry).

32. AN 334AP70 (Appleton, 26 December 1935); *Le Journal,* 27 December 1935; AN 334AP69 (Darius, 20 November 1935); *Le Matin,* 21 November 1935; *Le Petit Parisien,* 21 November 1935; *Le Journal,* 21 November 1935; *Paris-Soir,* 22 November 1935.

33. AN 334AP68 (Bonnaure, 16 November 1935); *Le Petit Parisien,* 17 November 1935; *Action Française,* 17 November 1935; *Le Journal,* 17 November 1935.

34. AN 334AP70 (Camille Chautemps, 17 December 1934); *Paris-Soir,* 19 December 1935; *Le Matin,* 18 December 1935; *Le Petit Parisien,* 18 December 1935.

35. AN 334AP70 (Jean-François Chiappe, 17 December 1935, and Joseph Caillaux, 19 December 1935); *Le Petit Parisien,* 20 December 1935; *Paris-Soir,* 19 December 1935; *Le Matin,* 18 December 1935.

36. *Le Petit Parisien,* 4 December 1935; *La Liberté,* 4 January 1936; *Paris-Soir,* 13, 17, 22 November 1935.

37. *Le Populaire*, 29 November 1934.

38. *Le Petit Parisien*, 15, 19, 23 November 1935; *Le Matin*, 13 December 1935; *Paris-Soir*, 13 December 1935; *Le Journal*, 17 December 1935.

39. AN 334AP71 (summation of Maître Jean-Charles Legrand, 6 January 1935); *Le Matin*, 7 January 1936.

40. AN 334AP69 (Saunois-de Chevert, 26 November 1935); *Le Matin*, 27 November 1935; *Le Journal*, 27 November 1935; *Le Petit Parisien*, 27 November 1935; *Paris-Soir*, 28 November 1935; see chap. 4, 49–50, 52; chap. 5, 93.

41. Jeannine Verdès-Leroux, *Scandale financier et antisémitisme catholique. Le krach de l'Union générale* (Paris, 1969); Jean-Yves Mollier, *Le Scandale de Panama* (Paris, 1991), 187, 194–95; Georges Clarétie, "L'Affaire Lemoine," *Drames et comédies judiciaires. Chronique du Palais, 1909* (Paris, 1910).

42. AN 334AP69 (Paul Maze, 6 December 1935).

43. *Le Populaire*, 6 November 1935.

44. AN 334AP71 (summation of Me Zévaès, 14 January 1936).

45. *Le Matin*, 23 November 1935; see chap. 10, 211.

46. *La Petite Illustration*, 698, 10 November 1934.

47. AN 334AP70 (summation of Fernand-Roux, 28 and 30 December 1935); *Le Petit Parisien*, 15 January 1936; *Le Petit Journal*, 15 January 1936.

48. Jean-Marie Goulemot, "Du républicanisme et de l'idée républicaine au XVIIIᵉ siècle," in *Le siècle de l'avènement républicain*, 25–56.

49. *Le Matin*, 7 January 1935; *Paris-Soir*, 14 January 1935.

50. Georges Claretie, "De l'Amour, de la boue, et du sang," *Drames et comédies judiciaires*.

51. AN 334AP71 (judgments of the criminal court, 17 January 1936, and of the Cour de Cassation, 1, 2 April and 3 August 1936: the court had dropped the prosecution of Aymard, Lévy, and Depardon); AN 334AP70 (Me Moro-Giafferi, 15 January 1936); *Le Matin*, 16, 17, 18, 24 January 1936; *Paris Soir*, 16, 17, 18, 19 January 1936; *Le Petit Parisien*, 16, 17, 18 January 1936; William Shakespeare, *King Lear*, act 4, scene 6.

EPILOGUE

1. See, for example, Régis Debray, *Que vive la République* (Paris, 1998); "Républicains, n'ayons plus peur!" *Le Monde*, 4 September 1998; Hugues Jallon and Pierre Mounier, *Les enragés de la République* (Paris, 1999).

2. *Le Monde*, 29 January 1992.

BIBLIOGRAPHY

Primary Sources

ARCHIVES

ARCHIVES NATIONALES

334AP68: Ministère public c/René Renoult, criminal court of the Seine, 5 and 6 June 1935 (trial transcripts).

334AP68 to 71: Ministère public c/Arlette Stavisky et al., criminal court of the Seine, 5 November 1935–18 January 1936 (trial transcripts).

334AP66: Ministère public c/Bouilloux-Laffont, Colin [alias Lucco], Lubersac, Picherie, criminal court of the Seine, 20–29 March 1933 (trial transcripts).

BB18: Correspondence of the criminal division of the Ministry of Justice: 2213, 2225, 2434, 2632, 6089, 6722, 6723, 6730, 6738, 6731, 6732, 6733, 6745, 6746, 6765, 6767, 6768, 6772, 6773, 6774, 6775, 2340 (1), 2536, 2632.

MI: Ministry of the Interior, Fonds Panthéon since reclassified in the F7 series: 25321, 25326/34, 25335/43, 25339, 25347, 25372/80, 25376, (25377), 25377/85, 25378, 25379/87, 25381, 25382, 25385, 25303/11.

F7: Ministry of the Interior: Police générale and Renseignements Généraux: 12549, 12926, 14599, 16010/1, 12550, 12551, 13978, 13981.

CAC: Centre d'Archives Contemporaines (Fontainebleau), dossiers of the Sûreté Générale returned to France from Moscow: dossiers of Anquetil, Astruc, Aymard, Bonnaure, Brouilhet, Hesse, Hulin, Odin, Poulner, Proust, Renoult, Wurtz.

5AR 402, 404: Correspondence of the Havas agency.

3AR 1, 2: Correspondence of L'Oeuvre.

1AR 6, 25: Minutes of the board of directors of Le Matin.

ARCHIVES DE PARIS

1320W98, 1320W102, 1320W132, 1320W155, 1320W32: Archives of the prosecutor's office.

D2U8417 to 462: Ministère public c/Gustave Tissier et al., 5 November 1935–17 January 1936 (pretrial investigations relating to Ministère public c/Arlette Stavisky et al. above).

D2U8463 to 466: Rulings and arraignments from Ministère public c/Arlette Stavisky et al. above.

D2U8467 to 470: Excerpts from transcripts of Ministère public c/Arlette Stavisky et al. above.

Bibliography

D2U8470 and 471: Tribunal civil de première instance (Seine), twelfth and eighth chambers, court of appeal of Paris (cases involving Stavisky before 1935).

D3U6179: Correctional court cases in which charges were dropped. Dossier of the Société Foncière (no classification number).

D2U8353: Ministère public c/Oustric et Benoist, criminal court of the Seine, 26–29 May 1933 (pretrial investigations).

ARCHIVES DE LA PRÉFECTURE DE POLICE
B/A 1276 (Syveton dossier, 1889–1910).

B/A 1590 (Cadet-Roussel dossier).

B/A 1253 et 1254 (Rochette affairs).

B/A 1972 (Mennevée dossier).

Ministère public c/Oustric et Benoist, 26–29 May 1933, criminal court of the Seine (trial transcripts).

Personnel dossiers: Edmond Pachot, Léon Ameline, Marcel Guillaume.

E/A 134 Press clippings on Stavisky.

ARCHIVES OF THE MINISTRY OF JUSTICE
Personnel dossiers: Victor d'Uhalt, Eugène Dreyfus, Henri Hurlaux, André Bruzin, Charles Barnaud, Cassagnau.

ARCHIVES DÉPARTEMENTALES DE LA CÔTE D'OR
Investigation into the death of Judge Prince: UIX: ch 3, 4, 5, 8, 12; UX5; UX ch 10

BIBLIOTHÈQUE NATIONALE
André Lapeyre, L'Affaire Prince, Bibliothèque Nationale, ms. nouv. acq. françaises no. 15767.

Ars. Ro. 15844 (Jeanne Bloch dossier).

Ars. Ro. 15736 (Fonds Rondel, Marigny theater dossier).

UNITED STATES NATIONAL ARCHIVES
M1442/12: Correspondence between the Consulate of the United States in Paris and the State Department.

PUBLISHED PRIMARY SOURCES

Baedeker's Paris and Its Environs. Leipzig, 1924.

Commission d'enquête chargée de rechercher toutes les responsabilités politiques ou administratives encourues depuis l'origine des affaires Stavisky. 6 vols. Journal Officiel, 1935.

Commission d'enquête sur les origines des évènements survenus le six février 1934. 4 vols. Journal Officiel, 1934.

Dictionnaire des parlementaires. Edited by Jean Jolly. 8 vols. Paris, 1960–77.

Dictionnaire des préfets. Paris, 1994.

Larousse, Pierre. *Grand Dictionnaire universel du XIXe siècle*. 15 vols. and 2 supp. Paris, 1866–90.

PRESS

Action Française
L'Autorité (1908 and 1909)
Aux Ecoutes
Bec et Ongles
La Bonne Guerre
Bulletin de la Ligue des Droits de L'Homme
Le Canard Enchaîné
Commentaires
Le Cri du Jour
D'Artagnan
Les Débats
L'Echo de Paris (1908)
Excelsior
Le Figaro
La Guerre Financière et Politique (1902)
La Guerre Sociale (1908)
L'Humanité
Les Informations Politiques et Financières
L'Intransigeant
Le Jour
Le Journal
Le Journal de la Bourse
Juvenal
Lectures pour tous (1900, 1901, 1904, 1906, 1909)
La Liberté
Le Matin
Les Nouvelles (1909)
Le Nouvelliste de Bordeaux (1902)
L'Oeuvre
Le Parisien
Paris-Journal (1908)
Paris-Midi
Paris-Soir
Le Pays
Le Petit Parisien
La Petite Illustration
Le Populaire
Le Soir
Le Temps

Bibliography

Secondary Sources

Alain [Emile Chartier, pseud.]. *Eléments d'une doctrine radicale.* Paris, 1925.
——. *Propos.* 2 vols. Paris, 1956–70.
Albert, Pierre. "La corruption du journalisme." *Pouvoirs* 31 (1984): 53–63.
Allard, Paul. *L'Anarchie de la police.* Paris, 1934.
Ameline, Léon. *Ce qu'il faut connaître de la police et ses mystères.* Paris, 1926.
Appleton, Jean. *Traité de la profession d'avocat.* Paris, 1928.
Assouline, Pierre. *Simenon.* Paris, 1992.
Aymard, Camille. *La véritable affaire Stavisky. Lettres à mes jurés.* Paris, 1935.
Baecque, Antoine de. "Le discours anti-noble, 1787–1792. Aux origines d'un slogan 'le peuple et les gros.'" *Revue d'Histoire Moderne et Contemporaine* 36 (January–March 1989): 3–28.
Balzac, Honoré de. *Illusions Perdues.* Rev. ed. Paris, 1953.
Barrès, Maurice. *Leurs figures.* Paris, 1902. Rev. ed. Paris, 1932.
Barrot, Olivier, and Pascal Ory, eds. *Entre deux guerres. La création française, 1919–1939.* Paris, 1990.
Barthélémy, Joseph. *Ministre de la justice: Vichy, 1941–43: Mémoires.* Paris, 1989.
Baruch, Marc-Olivier. *Servir l'état français. L'administration en France de 1940 à 1944.* Paris, 1997.
Bataille, Henry. *Le scandale, pièce en quatre actes.* Paris, 1909.
Belin, Jean. *Trente ans de Sûreté Nationale.* Paris, 1950.
Bellanger, C., et al. *Histoire générale de la presse française.* Vol. 3. Paris, 1972.
Bénazet, Henry. *Dix ans chez les avocats.* Paris, 1929.
Benjamin, René. *Le Palais et ses gens de justice.* Paris, 1919.
Berl, Emmanuel. *Mort de la pensée bourgeoise.* Paris, 1929.
Berlière, Jean-Marc. "Ordre et sécurité. Les nouveaux corps de police de la troisième république." *Vingtième Siècle* 39 (July–September 1993): 23–37.
Bernanos, Georges. *Journal d'un curé de campagne.* Paris, 1936. Rev. ed. Paris, 1974.
Berstein, Serge. *Histoire du parti radical.* 2 vols. Paris, 1980.
——. *Le 6 février 1934.* Paris, 1975.
Berton, E. *Les coulisses du notariat.* Paris, 1904.
Birnbaum, Pierre. *Le Peuple et les gros. Histoire d'un myth.* 3d ed. Paris, 1995.
Bonnefous, Edouard. *Histoire politique de la troisième politique.* Vol. 5. Rev. ed. Paris, 1973.
Bonny, Jacques. *Mon père l'inspecteur Bonny.* Paris, 1975.
Bortchy-Melnikoff, Eugène. *300.000 kilomètres avec Stavisky.* Paris, 1934.
Bourdon, Georges, et al. *Le journalisme d'aujourd'hui.* Paris, 1931.
Bourgeois, Charles. "De la corruption des fonctionnaires publics." Doctoral thesis, Faculté de Droit, Université de Paris, 1902.
Bouvier, Jean. *Les deux scandales de Panama.* Paris, 1964.
Brasillach, Robert. *Notre avant-guerre.* Paris, 1941.
Bruguière, Michel, et al. *Administration et parlement depuis 1815.* Geneva, 1982.
Cendrars, Blaise. *Rhum.* Paris, 1930.

Charlier, Jean-Michel, and Marcel Montarron. *Stavisky. Les secrets du scandale.* Paris, 1974.

Charlot, Jacques. "A la découverte des symboles dans le palais de justice de Paris." *Histoire de la Justice* 8–9 (1995–96): 149–74.

Charvin, Robert. *Justice et politique. Evolution de leurs rapports.* Paris, 1968.

Chavardès, Maurice. *Une campagne de presse. La droite française et le 6 février 1934.* Paris, 1970.

Chenevier, Charles. *De La Combe aux Fées à Lurs. Souvenirs et Révélations.* Paris, 1962.

———. *La grande maison.* Paris, 1976.

Chevalier, Pierre. "Un document inédit sur la mort tragique du conseiller Albert Prince, ancien procureur de la République à Troyes (1883–1934)." *Mémoires de la Société Académique d'Agriculture, des Sciences, Arts et Belles-Lettres du Département de l'Aube* 109 (1978): 5–61.

Clarétie, Georges. *Drames et comédies judiciaires. Chronique du Palais, 1909.* Paris, 1910.

Colette [Sidonie Gabrielle, pseud.]. *Belles saisons.* Paris, 1955.

Dabit, Eugène. *Journal intime, 1928–1934.* Paris, 1939.

Darius, Pierre. *L'amour au Maroc. Choses vues.* Paris, 1933.

Daudet, Alphonse. *Port Tarascon.* Paris, 1890.

Debray, Régis. *Que vive la République.* Paris, 1998.

Delcourt, Pierre. *Le vol à Paris.* Paris, 1888.

Deneux, Henri. "La responsabilité civile des notaires comme conseils de leurs clients." Doctoral thesis, Faculté de Droit, Université de Paris, Beauvais, 1932.

Descotes, Maurice. *Enquête sur un policier au-dessus de tout soupçon: Javert.* Pau, 1987.

Duroselle, Jean-Baptiste. *Clemenceau.* Paris, 1988.

Duval, René. "Ondes. Radio-Paris." In *Entre deux guerres. La création française, 1919–1939,* edited by Olivier Barrot and Pascal Ory. Paris, 1990.

Fabre, Emile. *Les ventres dorés.* Paris, 1905.

Farnier, Charles, et al. *Les problèmes actuels du crédit.* Paris, 1930.

Furet, François. "L'Idée de République et l'histoire de France au XIXe siècle." In *Le siècle de l'avènement républicain,* edited by François Furet and Mona Ozouf. Paris, 1993, 287–312.

Galbraith, John Kenneth. *A Short History of Financial Euphoria.* 2d ed. New York, 1993.

Garçon, Maurice. *Histoire de la justice sous la Troisième République.* 3 vols. Paris, 1957.

Gardenat, Louis. *Traité pratique des fraudes.* Paris, 1923.

Gebelin, François. *La Sainte-Chapelle et la Conciergerie.* Paris, 1931.

Girardet, Raoul. *Mythes et mythologies politiques.* Paris, 1986.

Giraudoux, Jean. *Bella.* Paris, 1926.

Goulemot, Jean-Marie. "Du républicanisme et de l'idée républicaine au XVIIIe siècle." In *Le siècle de l'avènement républicain,* edited by François Furet and Mona Ozouf. Paris, 1993, 25–56.

Guilleminault, Gilbert, and Yvonne Singer-Lecocq. *La France des gogos. Trois siècles de scandales financiers.* Paris, 1975.

Guiral, Pierre. "Police et sensibilité française." In *L'Etat et sa police en France 1789–1914*, edited by Jacque Aubert. Geneva, 1979, 161–75.

Guitry, Sacha. *Mémoires d'un tricheur.* Paris, 1935.

Halévy, Daniel. *La République des ducs.* Paris, 1937.

Henri-Robert. *L'avocat.* Paris, 1923.

Herment, Raymond. *Sous la poussière des panonceaux.* Nice, 1955.

Hugo, Victor. *Choses vues.* Vol. 1. Rev. ed. Paris, 1997.

Huysmans, Joris Karl. *A Rebours.* Paris, 1884.

Hyman, Paula. *The Jews of Modern France.* Berkeley, 1998.

Jallon, Hugues, and Pierre Mounier. *Les enragés de la République.* Paris, 1999.

Jeanneney, Jean-Noël. *L'argent caché. Milieux d'affaires et pouvoirs politiques dans la France du XXᵉ siècle.* Paris, 1982.

Jeanson, Henri. *70 ans d'adolescence.* Paris, 1971.

Jouvenel, Robert de. *La République des camarades.* Paris, 1914. Rev. ed. Paris, 1979.

Kessel, Joseph. *Stavisky. L'homme que j'ai connu.* Paris, 1974.

Kindleberger, Charles. *Manias, Panics and Crashes.* New York, 1989.

Kriegel, Blandine. "La défaite de la justice." *Autrement* 16 (1994): 135–41.

Lafitte, C. *Scandale, misère et cie.* Nogent-le-Rotrou, 1896.

Lenglois, Paul. *Vie et mort de Stavisky.* Paris, 1934.

Martin, Benjamin. *The Shame of Marianne: Criminal Justice under the Third Republic.* Baton Rouge, 1990.

Martin, Marc. *Médias et journalistes de la République.* Paris, 1997.

Martin du Gard, Roger. *Journal.* 3 vols. Paris, 1992–93.

Maxence, Jean-Pierre. *Histoire de dix ans, 1927–37.* Paris, 1939.

Maza, Sara. "Le Tribunal de la nation: Les mémoires judiciaires et l'opinion publique à la fin de l'ancien régime." *Annales ESC* 1 (January–February 1987): 73–90.

Mellor, Alec. *Le Chantage.* Paris, 1937.

Meyer, Arthur. *Ce que mes yeux ont vu.* Paris, 1911.

Mirbeau, Octave. *Le Jardin des supplices.* Paris, 1898.

Mollier, Jean-Yves. *Le Scandale de Panama.* Paris, 1991.

Mouthon, François-Ignace. *Du bluff au chantage. Les grandes campagnes du "Matin."* N.d., c. 1910.

Nathan, Michel. *Anthologie du roman populaire, 1836–1918.* Paris, 1985.

Nora, Pierre. "La République." In *Dictionnaire critique de la Révolution française*, edited by François Furet. Paris, 1989.

Petit, Georges. *De l'organisation du marché des valeurs mobilières. Bourses de valeurs et agents de change.* Paris, 1955.

Prince, Gisèle Dessaux. *Ils ont tué mon père. L'affaire Prince, 1934.* Paris, 1995.

Proust, Marcel. *A la recherche du temps perdu.* Vol. 1. Rev. ed. Paris, 1954.

Rogers, James Harvey. *The Process of Inflation in France.* New York, 1929.

Romains, Jules. *Le 6 octobre.* Paris, 1927.

Roubaud, Louis. *La Bourse. Foire aux entreprises. Criéé des valeurs. Maison de jeu.* Paris, 1929.

Rougé, Marcel. "La Sûreté nationale." Doctoral thesis in law, Université de Dijon, 1935.

Rousselet, Marcel. *Histoire de la magistrature.* Paris, 1957.

Rudelle, Odile. *La République absolue, 1870–1899.* Paris, 1986.

Schor, Ralph. *L'Antisémitisme en France pendant les années trente: Prélude à Vichy.* Bruxelles, 1992.

Schuker, Stephen. *The End of French Predominance in Europe.* Chapel Hill, N.C., 1976.

Soulier, Auguste. *L'instabilité ministérielle sous la troisième République, 1871–1938.* Paris, 1939.

Stavisky, Claude. *Stavisky était mon père.* Paris, 1995.

Stein, Henri. *Le Palais de justice et la Sainte-Chapelle.* Paris, 1912.

Taylor, Katherine Fischer. *In the Theater of Criminal Justice: The Palais de Justice in Second Empire Paris.* Princeton, 1993.

——. "The Palais de Justice of Paris: Modernization, Historical Self-Consciousness, and Their Prehistory in French Institutional Architecture (1835–1869)." 7 vols. Ph.D. diss., Harvard University, 1989.

Tocqueville, Alexis de. *L'Ancien Régime et la Révolution.* Paris, 1856.

Tonnet-Lacroix, Eliane. *La littérature française de l'entre-deux-guerres.* Paris, 1993.

Toulemon, André. *La spéculation illicite.* Paris, 1931.

Tulard, Jean. "Le Mythe de Fouché." In *L'Etat et sa police en France 1789–1914,* edited by Jacques Aubert. Geneva, 1979, 27–34.

——, ed. *Dictionnaire Napoléon.* Paris, 1995.

Verdès-Leroux, Jeannine. *Scandale financier et antisémitisme catholique. Le krach de l'Union générale.* Paris, 1969.

Werth, Léon. *Cour d'assises.* Paris, 1932.

Zola, Emile. *L'argent.* Paris, 1891.

——. *La bête humaine.* Paris, 1890.

INDEX

Index

Index

Index

DATE DUE

GAYLORD

PRINTED IN U.S.A.